Religion and State in Iran 1785-1906

Published under the Auspices of the Near Eastern Center

University of California, Los Angeles

Religion and State in Iran 1785-1906

The Role of the Ulama in the Qajar Period

by
HAMID ALGAR

UNIVERSITY OF CALIFORNIA PRESS
BERKELEY, LOS ANGELES, LONDON

University of California Press
Berkeley and Los Angeles, California
University of California Press, Ltd.
London, England

California Library Reprint Series Edition, 1980
ISBN 0-520-04100-3
Library of Congress Catalog Card Number: 72-79959
Designed by W. H. Snyder
Printed in the United States of America

1 2 3 4 5 6 7 8 9

Preface

The history of Islamic Iran is a field in which detailed and systematic studies of single periods are rare, and an adequate general survey is nonexistent. While there are many excellent studies of isolated topics, a broad synthesis of the history of Islamic Iran has yet to be undertaken. Several reasons for this may be suggested, among them the traditional preoccupation of Persian-reading orientalists with literary and philological subjects, the lack of critical editions of many important texts, and the deficient cultivation of historiographical technique in Iran itself. Recently, however, there have been signs of increasing concern with the history of Iran in the Islamic era, and, as critical studies of various periods emerge, the time when an adequate general history may be written comes nearer. This book—a survey of the political role of the ulama, the men of religion, in nineteenth-century Iran—is intended as a contribution toward that aim.

The topic suggests itself for several reasons. First, it embraces most of the events of the period: the comprehensive nature of the ulama's interests occasions a study of the happenings they influenced or to which they reacted. Some episodes discussed in the work, such as the murder of the Russian envoy Griboyedov in 1829 (chap. v) and the agitation leading to the repeal of the tobacco concession granted to a British company (chap. xii), contain details that are still subject to controversy. It has nonetheless proved possible to deduce that the ulama played a fairly consistent role throughout the nineteenth century, and it is hoped that questions raised but not fully answered here will offer suggestions for more conclusive study of certain points.

Second, this study affords the opportunity to examine in theory and, in greater detail, in practice, the relations between religious and secular authority in a Shi'i context. In its nineteenth-century history, as in general, Shi'i Islam has received considerably less attention than Sunni Islam. Analysis of relations between ulama and state in Qajar Iran could supply a basis for fruitful comparison with those obtaining in the Ottoman Empire in the same period. Although Qajar rule did not come to an end in Iran until 1926, this study, which begins with the year 1785, concludes with the decree of July, 1906, that called for the establishment of a consultative assembly. Thereafter, the role of the ulama as leaders and spokesmen of popular or sectional discontent was progressively reduced by the emergence of at least the semblance of a type of Western political life. The position of the monarch was modified not only by this factor, but also by the intensification of foreign pressure on Iran, which eventually took the form of military intervention and occupation. By contrast, before 1906 we see the ulama as the chief if not sole opponents of a state that is increasingly associated with foreign encroachers but not yet under their absolute dominance.

Third, in the course of nineteenth-century history of Iran, various aspects of Muslim reaction to the Western impact—military, economic, and finally ideological—became apparent. This reaction, until the latter part of the period, was formulated primarily by the ulama, and an analysis of it offers another basis for comparison with related developments elsewhere in the Muslim world.

From a reading of chapter 1, in which the function of the ulama in Ithnā'asharī Shi'ism is discussed, it will become apparent that the ulama are not a priesthood. The ulama are essentially those who have acquired prominence in religious learning, transmitted by former generations, and who can lay no claim to ultimate doctrinal authority. Furthermore, the implications of sacrament and hierarchy contained in the word "priesthood" are entirely foreign, indeed repugnant, to Islam. For the sake of convenience, the adjective "clerical" has been freely used in this work. Partial justification for use of the word is provided by its connotations of scholastic learning, a learning akin to that which held so important a place in the training and functions of the ulama.

A glossary with summary definitions of technical terms occurring more than once in the text is included at the end of the book. The aim of its compilation was not exhaustiveness, but the furnishing of an approximate and convenient guide to the reader.

The system of transcription used in this work suffers, like all others, from imperfections and inconsistencies. In general, I have employed a fairly narrow transliteration, with little attempt to convey accurate phonetic information. Thus, different letters of the Arabic alphabet which have acquired an identical sound in Persian have been transliterated according to their Arabic value in order to preserve awareness of orthography. There seemed, on the other hand, to be no reason not to render consonantal *vāv* as 'v' rather than 'w.' The vowel of the Arabic definite article, when it occurs in the titles of Persian books and in Persian personal names and titles, has been given the value 'u' which it commonly receives in Persian speech; but in the case of Arabic book titles, it has been transliterated as 'a.' Well-known place names and commonly used words of Arabic and Persian origin listed in *Webster's International Dictionary* (3d ed.) are printed in the text without diacritics.

All years mentioned separately in the text relate to the Christian era. Where two dates are given together and are separated by a diagonal stroke, the first relates to the lunar Islamic calendar and the second to the Christian calendar. Years reckoned according to the lunar and solar Islamic calendars are distinguished in the notes and the bibliography by use of the symbols "Q" and "Sh," respectively. Solar Islamic dates do not occur in the text.

This book is substantially the revised version of a doctoral dissertation, submitted at Cambridge in 1965. For a number of useful criticisms and suggestions, received in the course of revision, I am indebted to Nikki Keddie and Joseph Eliash of the University of California, Los Angeles. Thanks are also owed to Peter Avery of King's College, Cambridge, and to a number of Iranian friends for bibliographical suggestions, and to Mrs. Teresa Joseph for seeing the manuscript through the Press.

HAMID ALGAR

Contents

A Note on the Sources

Despite its relative proximity in time and the abundance of historical material available, the Qajar period has received little detailed scholarly attention. An adequate general history of nineteenth-century Iran has yet to be published: 'Alī Aṣghar Shamīm's *Īrān dar Daura-yi Salṭanat-i Qājār* (2d ed.; Tehran, 1342 Sh/1963) is informative but poorly organized and uncritical; the relevant chapters in M. S. Ivanov's *Ocherk Istorii Irana* (Moscow, 1952), and in P. W. Avery's *Modern Iran* (London, 1965) offer little more than brief summaries, and both require, for different reasons, to be used with much caution. It is to be expected that Professor A. K. S. Lambton's forthcoming work on Qajar Iran will fill this lacuna.

The primary Persian source for most of the Qajar period consists of the various chronicles produced, with or without royal patronage, throughout the entire nineteenth century. Many of these remain in manuscript (for a partial list see Sa'īd Nafīsī, *Tārīkh-i Ijtimā'ī va Siyāsī-yi Īrān dar Daura-yi Mu'āṣir* [Tehran, 1340 Sh/1961], I, 12) but the most important were published in lithographed editions in the last century, and some have recently reappeared in fixed type. Although none of these chronicles satisfy the critical criteria of the historian, they represent a valuable source of information, usually detailed and precise. They also provide good examples of the evolution in Persian prose toward a simpler, less adorned, and more utilitarian style that was initiated by Mīrzā Abū-l-Qāsim Qā'im Maqām in his correspondence.[1] That this literary development went together with other aspects of modernization is clearly seen with the printing, in 1242/1826, of one of the earliest Qajar chronicles, the *Ma'āthir-i Sulṭānīya* of 'Abd ur-Razzāq Dunbulī, on the press newly established by 'Abbās Mīrzā in Tabriz.[2] Among works commissioned by Nāṣir ud-Dīn Shāh, three chronicles deserve special mention. The first is the *Nāsikh ut-Tavārīkh* (Tehran, n.d.) of Mīrzā Muḥammad Taqī Sipihr Lisān ul-Mulk, a general history composed on traditional lines and of interest only because of the sections concerning the Qajar period. Here, however, it is of considerable value, supplying a detailed, if dry, chronological account of military and political events. The second, Riḍā Qulī Khān Hidāyat's *Rauḍat us-Ṣafā-yi Nāṣirī* (10 vols.; Tehran, 1339 Sh/1960) is a supplement to Mirkhvānd's *Rauḍat uṣ-Ṣafā,* and deals with the history of the Safavid, Afsharid, Zand, and Qajar periods. Of all the Qajar chronicles, this is probably the best; although it was written in evident haste, its style has the merits of simplicity and clarity, for Riḍā Qulī Khān, unlike other chroniclers, was a writer and poet of genuine ability.[3] Even though his attachments to the court inhibited the free assessment of events, his ordering of the material reveals a critical and selective sense, and at times he offers independent comment, a rare phenomenon in Persian historical writing of the period. Finally, the *Tārīkh-i Muntaẓam-i Nāṣirī* of Mīrzā Muḥammad Ḥasan Khān I'timād us-Salṭana (3 vols.; Tehran, 1300 Q/1883), like the other works ascribed to the author and listed in the bibliography, is of limited usefulness because of its bombastic style and incoherent arrangement of content.[4]

1 See E. G. Browne, *A Literary History of Persia* (Cambridge, 1924), IV, 311–316; and Bozorg Alavi, *Geschichte und Entwicklung der modernen persischen Literatur* (Berlin, 1964), p. 18.

2 For a biographical sketch of 'Abd ur-Razzāq Dunbulī, see Ḥājj Ḥusayn Nakhchivānī, *Chihil Maqāla* (Tabriz, 1343 Sh/1964), pp. 221–232.

3 For an assessment of this work, see Muḥammad Taqī Bahār (Malik ush-Shu'arā), *Sabkshināsī* (Tehran, 1337 Sh/1958), III, 368.

4 On I'timād us-Salṭana's methods of work, see Browne, *op. cit.*, IV, 453–457, and the same author's *The Press and Poetry of Modern Persia* (Cambridge, 1914), pp. 156, 164–166.

Other nineteenth-century Persian prose works were of marginal usefulness in the preparation of this work but are of general interest to students of the history of Qajar Iran. The account of the history and geography of Tabriz by the Qajar prince, Nādir Mīrzā, entitled *Tārīkh va Jughrāfī-yi Dār us-Salṭana-yi Tabrīz* (Tehran, 1323 Q/1905) is a carefully composed and executed treatment of its theme and deserves a modern reprint.[5] Similarly, the work on the monuments and history of the province of Fars, *Āthār-i 'Ajam* by Furṣat Shīrāzī (Tehran, 1314 Q/1896–1897), while considerably out of date in its archaeological sections, is still valuable for its account of the local history and physical appearance of the province in the nineteenth century.

A source heavily relied upon, especially for the early part of the period, consisted of the biographical dictionaries of the ulama, in particular the *Qiṣaṣ ul-'Ulamā* of Muḥammad b. Sulaymān Tunukābunī (Tehran, 1304 Q/1887) and the *Rauḍāt al-Jannāt fi Aḥwāl al-'Ulamā' wa-s-Sādāt* (in Arabic) of Muḥammad Bāqir Khvānsārī (Tehran, 1304 Q/1887). After a brief mention of the ancestry, studies, and works of the subject of the biography, illuminating anecdotes about his life are often related, which, even if partly fictitious or adorned to taste by the teller, nonetheless give a vivid picture of the quality of life of the ulama concerned. Particularly interesting are the anecdotes illustrating clerical attitudes to royal power (see chap. iii).

Autobiographies were of considerable relevance to the topic dealt with here, those of 'Abdullāh Mustaufī (*Tārīkh-i Idārī va Ijtimā'ī-yi Daura-yi Qājārīya yā Sharḥ-i Zindagānī-yi Man* [2 vols.; Tehran, 1321 Sh/1942]), 'Abbās Mīrzā Mulkārā (*Sharḥ-i Ḥāl*, ed. 'Abd ul-Ḥusayn Navā'ī [Tehran, 1325 Sh/1946–1947]), Yaḥyā Daulatābādī (*Tārīkh-i Mu'āṣir yā Ḥayāt-i Yaḥyā* [4 vols.; Tehran, n.d.]), and Mīrzā 'Alī Khān Amīn ud-Daula (*Khāṭirāt-i Siyāsī*, ed. Ḥāfiẓ Farmānfarmā'īān [Tehran, 1341 Sh/1962]) in particular. The complete edition of the diaries of I'timād us-Salṭana (*Rūznāma-yi Khāṭirāt-i I'timād us-Salṭana*, ed. Īraj Afshār [Tehran, 1345 Sh/1967]) unfortunately appeared too late for use in the preparation of this book. A caveat with respect to autobiographies is necessary: they frequently reflect personal rivalries and ambitions, particularly when discussing the events of the Constitutional Revolution.

5 Bahār (*op. cit.*, III, 396–397) praises its style, comparing it to the celebrated *Tārīkh-i Bayhaqī*.

Memoirs of travel, an important genre in nineteenth-century Persian prose, were of little relevance to the concern of this work, but they are recommended as evidence of the nature of the Iranian reaction to Europe and European culture. Thanks to the industry of Ḥāfiẓ Farmānfarmā'īān, a number of such memoirs have already been published, including Mīrzā Ḥusayn Farāhānī's *Safarnāma* (Tehran, 1342 Sh/1963) and Ḥājjī Pīrzāda's *Safarnāma* (2 vols.; Tehran, 1342–1343 Sh/1963–1964), and it is hoped that he will continue to make available this important source to students of nineteenth-century Iran.

The products of modern Iranian historiography vary widely in quality and usefulness. Too often one notes a lack of critical assessment of material and a failure to refer to sources of information. Possibly the earliest example of modern Iranian historiography is Nāẓim ul-Islām Kirmānī's *Tārīkh-i Bīdārī-yi Īrānīān* (new ed.; Tehran, 1332 Sh/1953), a source of primary importance for the constitutional period that reproduces *in extenso* a wide selection of contemporary documents. A good account of the constitutional period is also given by Aḥmad Kasravī in his *Tārīkh-i Mashrūṭa-yi Īrān* (5th imp.; Tehran, 1340 Sh/1961), whereas the work of Mihdī Malikzāda (*Tārīkh-i Inqilāb-i Mashrūṭīyat-i Īrān* [6 vols.; Tehran, 1327 Sh/1948]) suffers from diffuseness and imprecision.

Works found useful on earlier parts of Qajar history include the biographies of Amīr Kabīr by 'Abbās Iqbāl (*Mīrzā Taqī Khān Amīr Kabīr* [Tehran, 1840 Sh/1961]) and Firīdūn Ādamīyat (*Amīr Kabīr va Īrān* [Tehran, 1334 Sh/1955]), and the work of the latter writer on the development of thought in the late nineteenth century (*Fikr-i Āzādī va Muqaddima-yi Nihḍat-i Mashrūṭīyat-i Īrān* [Tehran, 1340 Sh/1961]), which is recommended for its lucid and scholarly style. The two works by Ibrāhīm Taymūrī on foreign concessions in Iran, *Taḥrīm-i Tanbākū yā Avvalīn Muqāvamat-i Manfī dar Īrān* (Tehran, 1328 Sh/1949) and *'Aṣr-i Bīkhabarī yā Tārīkh-i Imtiyāzāt dar Īrān* (Tehran, 1336 Sh/1957), are informative; unfortunately in the former, that dealing with the tobacco concession, the author neglected to indicate his sources of information.

Various articles were found useful in illuminating minor points. A reliable guide to Persian periodical literature is Īraj Afshār's *Fihrist-i Maqālāt-i Fārsī* (Tehran, 1341 Sh/1962).

European published sources for the history of nineteenth-century Iran are numerous, but they require careful sifting for critical historical use. The history of Iran by Sir Percy Sykes (*History of Persia* [2 vols.; 3d ed.; London, 1930]) may fairly be called useless for an understanding of the Qajar period. Sir John Malcolm's *A History of Persia* (2 vols.; London, 1815) is valuable for its account of Āghā Muḥammad Khān and Fatḥ 'Alī Shāh, and R. G. Watson in his *A History of Persia from the Beginning of the Nineteenth Century to the Year 1858* (London, 1866) offers an adequate if prosaic supplement. E. G. Browne's *The Persian Revolution* (Cambridge, 1910) is still serviceable, although outdated in some parts.

Among European sources travel books contain much useful material for the student of nineteenth-century Iran. These are usually not helpful in religious matters; because of bigotry, ignorance, or mere lack of interest, the information they supply on the activities of the ulama is much sparser than that, for example, on topography, trade, or military organization. Among travelers to Iran in the first half of the nineteenth century, J. B. Fraser and J. Morier are remarkable for the high literary value of their works (see bibliography), but their accuracy of observation and freedom from malice are not always above question. The Russian traveler, C. A. de Bode's *Travels in Luristan and Arabistan* (2 vols.; London, 1845) gives a greater impression of impartiality. G. Curzon's monumental *Persia and the Persian Question* (2 vols.; London, 1892) contains a vast amount of carefully observed information, although many of his preoccupations are of little interest today. Probably the best of all works written by Europeans in the nineteenth century about Iran are Jakob Polak's *Persien: das Land und seine Bewohner* (2 vols.; Leipzig, 1865) and Jean-Baptiste Feuvrier's *Trois Ans à la cour de Perse* (Paris, 1899), both written by private physicians to Nāṣir ud-Dīn Shāh. The former, in particular, is full of valuable material about most aspects of life in nineteenth-century Iran.

In the preparation of this work, regrettably little use was made of unpublished sources, either Persian or European. In the absence of properly constituted archives in Iran, one can hope at best to obtain access to private papers preserved by the descendants of historical figures. Unfortunately this was not possible during recent brief visits to Tehran. Selective use was made of British diplomatic and consular records kept in the Public Records Office, London, and these represent a valuable source for much of the history of Iran, not only of its foreign relations, but also of its internal developments. Diplomatic records of other countries, notably France and Russia, deserve investigation, and the Ottoman archives in Ankara and Istanbul need too to be searched for reports from Tehran.

Abbreviations

AKM	*Abhandlungen für die Kunde des Morgenlandes*
BSOAS	*Bulletin of the School of Oriental and African Studies*
HAN	Mīrzā Ja'far Khān Ḥaqā'iqnagār. *Ḥaqā'iq-i Akhbār-i Nāṣirī*. Tehran, 1284 Q/1867–1868.
HY	Yaḥyā Daulatābādī. *Tārīkh-i Mu'āṣir yā Ḥayāt-i Yaḥyā*. Tehran, n.d. 4 vols.
JRAS	*Journal of the Royal Asiatic Society*
JRCAS	*Journal of the Royal Central Asian Society*
KSIV	*Kratkiye Soobshcheniya Instituta Vostokovedeniya*
KhS	Mīrzā 'Alī Khān Amīn ud-Daula. *Khāṭirāt-i Siyāsī*. Ed. Ḥāfiẓ Farmānfarmā'īān. Tehran, 1341 Sh/1962.
MM	*Majalla-yi Mardumshināsī*
MN	Mīrzā Muḥammad Ḥasan Khān I'timād us-Salṭana. *Tārīkh-i Muntaẓam-i Nāṣirī*. Tehran, 1300 Q/1883. 3 vols.
NT	Mīrzā Muḥammad Taqī Sipihr Lisān ul-Mulk. *Nāsikh ut-Tavārīkh*. Tehran, n.d.
Q	*Qamarī*. This symbol is used in the notes and bibliography to indicate a date in the lunar Islamic calendar.

Q'U Muḥammad b. Sulaymān Tunukābunī. *Qiṣaṣ ul-'Ulamā'*. Tehran, 1304 Q/1887.

RJ Muḥammad Bāqir Khvānsārī. *Rauḍāt al-Jannāt fī Aḥwāl al-'Ulamā' wa-s-Sādāt*. Tehran, 1304 Q/1887.

RMM *Revue du Monde Musulman*

RSN Riḍā Qulī Khān Hidāyat. *Rauḍat us-Ṣafā-yi Nāṣirī*. Tehran 1339 Sh/1960–1961. 10 vols.

RSO *Rivista degli Studi Orientali*

SI *Studia Islamica*

Sh *Shamsī*. This symbol is used in the notes and bibliography to indicate a date in the solar Islamic calendar current in Iran.

TB Nāẓim ul-Islām Kirmānī. *Tārīkh-i Bīdārī-yi Irānīān*. New ed. Tehran, 1332 Sh/1953.

TM Aḥmad Kasravī. *Tārīkh-i Mashrūṭa-yi Īrān*. 5th imp. Tehran, 1340 Sh/1961.

TRS Maḥmūd Maḥmūd, *Tārīkh-i Ravābiṭ-i Siyāsī-yi Īrān va Inglīs dar Qarn-i Nūzdahum-i Mīlādī*. Tehran, 1328 Sh/1949–1950. 8 vols.

ZDMG *Zeitschrift der deutschen morgenländischen Gesellschaft*

I

The Foundations of Clerical Influence

THE DOCTRINAL BASIS OF THE POSITION OF *Mujtahid*

Discussion of relations between the ulama and the state in nineteenth-century Iran presupposes some consideration of the concept of authority in Ithnā'asharī Shi'ism in order to discover whether there existed any theological basis for the conflict between the secular and religious bodies related in this work. An adequate investigation of the theme would require an examination of the entire history of Shi'ism and, in particular, of the antecedents of Ithnā'asharī Shi'ism, the only form that concerns us here. The present incomplete state of knowledge about the development of this and other heterodox movements in Islam does not permit this to be achieved here in summary fashion. Moreover, much of early Shi'i history is irrelevant to the course of events in nineteenth-century Iran. For the purposes of this study, Shi'i history begins to claim our attention with the establishment of Shi'ism as state religion of Iran by the Safavids in the early sixteenth century, an act that marks a turning point in the nature and tenor of much of Shi'i thought and jurisprudence. Certain features of the antecedents of Safavid Shi'ism are, however, isolated and presented as indicative of characteristic attitudes to worldly and spiritual authority which helped to determine the role of the ulama in nineteenth-century Iran.

The dominant theme of Shi'i Islam is clearly and indisputably the Imamate, an institution of a succession of charismatic figures who dispense true guidance in comprehending the esoteric sense of prophetic revelation. Concepts of the Imamate have varied widely, not only with regard to the identity and number of the Imams, but also with respect to the modus operandi and extent of their guidance of the community. Recent research has established that the Twelve Imams now recognized by the branch of Shi'ism dominant in Iran and represented elsewhere by minority groups were not all in their lifetimes the leaders of a sharply defined following that stood aside from the main body of the Muslim community.[1] The messianic hopes attached to charismatic leaders in both Umayyad and Abbasid times did not rest solely on the descendants of the Prophet through his daughter Fāṭima and his cousin 'Alī: uprisings took place in the name of, among others, Muḥammad b. al-Ḥanafīya, a son of 'Alī by another wife.[2] Moreover, both activist and quietist attitudes to prevailing authority could be deduced from the Imami belief, but it is clear that the latter came gradually to dominate the mainstream of Shi'ism, leaving its trace also on the Safavid and post-Safavid Shi'ism of Iran. Insofar as any attitude to the state and existing authority can be deduced from the teachings of the Imams, it is one that combines a denial of legitimacy with a quietistic patience and abstention from action. The Imam Ja'far aṣ-Ṣādiq, sixth in the succession and from whom originates so much of Imami hadith (traditions concerning the sayings and deeds of the Prophet and the Imams), recommended to his followers total abstention from even so much as verbal dispute with their opponents.[3]

In Abbasid times, too, Imami Shi'ism failed to detach itself from this ambivalent attitude to de facto authority. It is well known

1 W. Montgomery Watt, "The Reappraisal of 'Abbāsid Shi'ism," in *Arabic and Islamic Studies in Honour of Hamilton A. R. Gibb* (Leiden, 1966), pp. 638–639.

2 Watt, "Shi'ism under the Umayyads," *JRAS*, n.v. (1960), 161 ff.

3 Relevant hadith given by Muḥammad b. Ḥasan al-Ḥurr al-'Āmulī, *Wasā'il ash-Shī'a ilā Taḥṣīl Masā'il ash-Sharī'a* (Tehran, 1372–1378 Q/1952–1958), VI, chap. xxii.

that the Abbasids heavily invoked Imami themes in their movement to overthrow the Umayyads, and many of the later Abbasids also harbored a certain sympathy toward Imami Shi'ism. Moreover, Imami Shi'is were found in all levels of society, including the highest: the Iranian family of the Naubakhtīs is the most important example; from among their ranks emerged both *vazīr*'s (ministers) and exponents of Imami doctrine.

It was one of the Naubakhtīs, Abū Sahl 'Alī b. Ismā'īl, who took a prominent part in formulating the doctrine of *ghaybat,* the occultation of the Imam.[4] The cycle of the Twelve Imams came to an end in 874, when the infant son of the eleventh Imam, Ḥasan al-'Askarī, disappeared from view.[5] This date inaugurated the "Lesser Occultation," a period of some seventy years during which the Hidden Imam was visible only to a succession of four agents (*vakīl*'s). The death of the last vakīl, 'Alī b. Muḥammad as-Samarrī, in 940, put an end to this limited communication with the Hidden Imam, and the community was led into the "Greater Occultation," the *ghaybat-i kubrā,* that period characterized by the absence of a human intermediary, which shall continue until the Imam's return to earth as the Mahdi.

The occultation of the Imam has given a distinctive character to Ithnā'asharī Shi'ism, and elaboration of the concept has been a constant preoccupation of Shi'i philosophers, particularly in Safavid and post-Safavid Iran. In combination with the equally important and related concept of *taqīya* (prudential dissimulation of belief, particularly in time of danger), it intensified the essentially quietist position of Imami Shi'ism with respect to worldly authority. Already in Umayyad times, the theme of occultation had made its appearance, applied to Muḥammad b. al-Ḥanafīya, and the remarks on its political implications made by W. Montgomery Watt are worth quoting for their relevance to the political attitudes of Ithnā'asharī Shi'ism as a whole: "In their historical context, however, they [the doctrines of ghaybat] can be regarded as justifying a de facto acceptance of the existing regime. Those who believe in the 'hidden Imam' are not required to do anything in the immediate future, not even to work for any particular reform.

4 On the Naubakhtī family, see 'Abbās Iqbāl, *Khāndān-i Naubakhtī* (Tehran, 1312 Sh/1933); 'Abdullāh Ni'ma, *Falāsifat ash-Shī'a* (Beirut, n.d.), pp. 152–181; and Louis Massignon, *La Passion d'Al-Ḥosayn ibn Manṣour* (Paris, 1922), I, 142 ff.

5 Massignon, *op. cit.*, I, 144 n. 3.

At the same time it is implied that the regime is not perfect, and the way is left open for action at some future date. Such an attitude might often be politically harmless, but there lurked in it a potential danger. A change of circumstances might suggest to the adherents of the movement that the time for action had come."[6]

After the occultation of the Twelfth Imam, Shi'ism became even more quietist in its attitude to worldly power. This passivism, although combined with a denial of legitimacy and not excluding repeated clashes with regimes and dynasties, prohibited the advocacy of a total overthrow of the existing order in the name of a legitimate alternative. While the Imam remained in occultation, a shadow of illegitimacy was bound to cover all worldly strivings and activities, above all those related to government. There was no true authority nor the possibility thereof: only power.

This attitude of Shi'ism was clearly illustrated soon after the beginning of the Greater Occultation when the Buwayhids, a dynasty with Shi'i loyalties, gained control of the center of the Abbasid caliphate. The fact that the Buwayhids did not replace it with an Imami caliphate has given rise to much discussion. The historian Ibn al-Athīr (d. 1234) felt it necessary to explain their action in terms suggested by the later evolution of Shi'ism toward separation from the main body of the community, while more recently it has been suggested that the Buwayhids were obliged to compromise with the status quo.[7] The problem appears to be misconceived. The Buwayhids, no less than the Sunni dynasties of eastern Iran, derived their legitimacy from formal appointment by the Abbasid caliphs. Moreover, the newly developing Shi'i *fiqh* (jurisprudence) made no provision for the establishment of a legitimate state after the occultation of the Imam: its political theory was merely a part of its overall definition of the Imamate. Like the Buwayhids, the Ḥamdānids, another dynasty of Shi'i affiliation, gave formal allegiance to the Abbasid caliphate, and the political philosophy of al-Fārābī, himself a Shi'i who was patronized by the Ḥamdānid court in Aleppo, seems to have paid little attention to specifically Shi'i themes: the "Second Chief" of

[6] Watt, *op. cit.*, p. 167.

[7] H. A. R. Gibb discusses the former explanation in his "Government and Islam under the Early 'Abbāsids: The Political Collapse of Islam," in *L'Elaboration de l'Islam* (Paris, 1961), pp. 116 ff.; and the latter is put forward by Leonard Binder in his *Iran: Political Development in a Changing Society* (Berkeley and Los Angeles, 1964), p. 73.

the *Fuṣūl al-Madanī*, for example, is a concept of Platonic origin.[8]

The elevation of Shi'ism to the status of national religion in Iran by the Safavids in the early sixteenth century brought a turning point in its history: it became finally and inalienably associated with Iran as its homeland and stronghold. It is also from the Safavid period onward that one may meaningfully talk about the existence of a body of Shi'i ulama. Yet one essential element of pre-Safavid Shi'ism survived to be passed on, after temporary obscurity, to the Qajar period and beyond: the necessary and inescapable illegitimacy of the state. One might maintain that a Shi'i state itself is a contradiction in terms, since the essence of Shi'ism demands a minority status for its adherents, who are in opposition, often quiescent but unyielding, to de facto authority. The real triumph of Shi'ism is possible only through the return and manifestation of the Hidden Imam, when legitimacy will return to the world and be fulfilled.

Henri Corbin, the eminent scholar of Shi'ism, has indicated the significant consequences of the establishment of Shi'ism as state religion by the Safavids. Their Shi'ism gave birth "to something like an official clergy, exclusively concerned with legality and jurisprudence, to such a point that original Shi'ism, in its essence gnostic and theosophic, has, so to speak, to hide itself."[9] The body of ulama that emerged in Safavid times came in effect to partake of the charisma and authority of the Imams, but as Shi'ism denies legitimate authority to worldly power, so, too, no authority in the strict sense of the term resided in the ulama. Rather, they fulfilled a practical function of considerable importance to the community, as a result of which de facto authority came increasingly to adhere to them. The function arose from the need to provide some kind of living and continuous direction to the community and was based on the imitation of exemplary models, the *mujtahid*'s, the highest ranking of the ulama. A comparison may be drawn between the relation of the ulama to the Hidden Imam and that of the Imams to God.[10] The ulama were, in a limited sense, intermediaries between the community and the Imams, with some of the authority of the latter reflected upon them: they were the "proofs" (*ḥujaj*) of the Imams. Similarly, the Imams were intermediaries between the

8 D. M. Dunlop, *Fuṣūl al-Madanī* (Cambridge, 1961), p. 14.

9 "Pour une Morphologie de la Spiritualité Shî'ite," *Eranos-Jahrbuch* (Zurich), XXIX (1960), 69.

10 The comparison is made by Mahmood Shehabi ("Shi'a," in *Islam: The Straight Path*, ed. K. W. Morgan [New York, 1958], p. 202).

source of divine guidance and the community. It would be wrong, however, to conclude from this comparison that the ulama possessed any authority similar to that of the Imams, or that they could legitimately lay claim to infallibility. The resemblance of the ulama to the Imams lies rather in their supplying a living source of reference and leadership for the Shi'i community. The lavish devotion accorded to some of the great mujtahids should be attributed to this resemblance rather than to any overestimation of their function and authority. The mujtahids came to personify the leadership of the community, and this was one of the chief sources of their political and social influence in Qajar Iran.

In Shi'ism, the primary duty of the believer, after belief in God and the Prophet, is *vilāyat,* total loyalty and obedience to the Hidden Imam. "He who dies without recognizing the Imam dies an unbeliever."[11] Since the withdrawal of the Imam from the control and guidance of the community is only apparent, and not actual, this primary duty remains intact. At the same time, the mujtahid is needed to provide immediate guidance in matters of practice. "The belief of a Muslim in the principles (*uṣūl*) of the faith must be based on a logical proof (*dalīl*), and he may not accept anyone's pronouncement without a proof. Concerning, however, the ordinances (*aḥkām*) of religion, he must either be a mujtahid and able to deduce the ordinances according to logical proof, or imitate a mujtahid, that is to say, act according to his instructions."[12] Thus the faithful, who in a certain sense are all bound to follow the guidance of the Imam, are at the same time divided into those who may act according to their own judgment (mujtahid), and those who must accept the judgment of others (*muqallid*).

Those whose judgments are to be thus accepted are the mujtahids, the most important of the Shi'i ulama. Their eminence depends essentially on the acquisition of the rank of *ijtihād.* The mujtahid is literally one who exercises ijtihād, that is, "the searching for a correct opinion (*ra'y-i ṣavāb*)," particularly in "the deducing of the specific provisions of religious law (*furū'*) from its principles (*uṣūl*) and ordinances (*aḥkām*)."[13] The principles forming the material upon which ijtihād may be exercised are the Quran, the *sunnat* (practice) of the Prophet, the traditions of the

[11] Muḥammad b. Ya'qūb al-Kulaynī, *al-Kāfī fī 'Ilm ad-Dīn* (Tehran, 1379 Q/1959–1960), VIII, 146.

[12] Ḥusayn Ṭabāṭabā'ī Burūjirdī, *Tauḍiḥ ul-Masā'il* (Tehran, n.d.), pp. 2–3.

[13] Ḥujjat ul-Islām Muḥammad Sanglajī, *Qaḍā dar Islām* (Tehran, 1338 Sh/1959–1960), p. 14.

Imams, and the consensus (*ijmā'*) of the learned since the beginning of the Greater Occultation.[14] *Qiyās* (the use of analogical reasoning) is an acceptable method for the exercise of ijtihād, and because of its obvious fallibility and limitations, the result it produces can never be more than *ẓann,* a contestable expression of personal opinion. Even after the beginning of the Greater Occultation certain possibilities for communication with the Hidden Imam remain, but these may be vouchsafed to any believer, and such communication is not continuous.[15] Thus to accept the pronouncements of any one mujtahid is not, per se, obligatory, for the mujtahid may claim no infallibility and mujtahids will vary in their opinion and rulings. What is obligatory is the principle of following the direction of a certain mujtahid in order to ensure some continuity of authority.

The tensions inherent in this distinction have expressed themselves in various sectarian disputes whose historical aspects are discussed below. Here, only their doctrinal implications are briefly noted. These concern the function of the mujtahid as guide of the community. The Akhbārīs, who dominated the shrines of Arab Iraq in the period between the fall of the Safavid dynasty and the establishment of Qajar rule, rejected his function as incompatible with the authority of the Imams. Even his limited use of ijtihād seemed as reprehensible as it would have been before the Greater Occultation. The division of the comunity into muqallid and mujtahid was rejected in favor of the earlier concept of the whole community as muqallid to the Imams.[16]

For the Shaykhīs, on the other hand, the mujtahid was not an adequate intermediary between the community and the Hidden Imam; a more authoritative incarnation of divine guidance was necessary. Such was to be the "Perfect Shi'a" (*shī'a-yi kāmil*), later termed the "Fourth Pillar" (*rukn-i rābi'*).[17] The authority of this

14 'Alī Akbar Dihkhudā, *Lughatnāma,* Fasc. IV (Tehran, 1326 Sh/1947), p. 1033, article on *ijtihād.*

15 Thus the Imam may be glimpsed in a dream; and messages written on paper and then cast into running water are thought to reach his presence (D. M. Donaldson, *The Shi'ite Religion* [London, 1933], p. 235).

16 G. Scarcia, "Intorno alle Controversie tra Aḫbārī e Uṣūlī," *RSO,* XXXIII (1958), 244–245.

17 *RJ,* p. 246. Shaykh Aḥmad Aḥsā'ī, founder of the sect, considered his pronouncements to be literally—not merely in form or content—those of the Imams (see Muḥammad Hāshim Kirmānī, "Ṭā'ifa-yi Shaykhīya," *MM,* II [1337 Sh/1958], 240).

guide of the community, laying claim to direct contact with the Hidden Imam, would have put an end to the function of the mujtahid no less decisively than universal acceptance of the Akhbārī position.

That these questionings of the permissibility and adequacy of ijtihād were unable to disturb the position of mujtahid is attributable to many reasons. Comprehension of the nature of the Imamate was ultimately beyond human capacity, and hence too of the exact manner of the occultation and the way in which the unseen control of the Imam over the community was exercised. The institution of the mujtahid had, moreover, the practical merit of ensuring a continuous leadership of the community and of providing a source of immediate authority that was neither too great to offend the claims of vilāyat, nor too restricted to be without practical effect. The tension between the unseen, superior authority of the Imam, and the immediate, incorporate one personified by the ulama, was largely offset by the existence of parallel religious practices: respect and obedience were granted to the mujtahids as expounders and enforcers of the law, while the emotional need for communication with the Hidden Imam was at least partly met by pilgrimages to shrines and the devotional practices connected with them.

The practical nature of the mujtahid's function of leadership and guidance is emphasized by the conditions laid down for the position of *marja'-i taqlīd*, that is, the mujtahid whose example in matters of practice is, above all others, binding. Six of these conditions are accepted unanimously by Shi'i theologians, namely maturity (*bulūgh*),[18] intelligence (*'aql*), being of the male sex (*dhukūrat*),[19] faith (*īmān*), justice (*'adālat*), and legitimate birth (*ṭahārat-i maulad*).[20] The concept of 'adālat in this context implies one "who performs that which is obligatory upon him (*vājib*), and abandons that which is forbidden to him (*ḥarām*)";[21] or one "who possesses a quality impelling him to piety and abstemiousness."[22]

18 Minors might, however, reach the degree (*martaba*) of ijtihād without being considered mujtahid (see, e.g., note on Mīrzā Muḥammad Mihdī Shahristānī in *Q'U*, p. 145).

19 Women might nonetheless attain a certain general respect based on religious learning, if not the position of marja'-i taqlīd (see *ibid.*, p. 137).

20 Burūjirdī, *op. cit.*, p. 4; Sanglajī, *op. cit.*, pp. 46–47.

21 Burūjirdī, *op. cit.*, p. 4.

22 Sanglajī, *op. cit.*, p. 58.

Other conditions sometimes adduced as necessary are literacy, possession of both sight and hearing, and freedom of one's own person, that is, not being a slave.[23]

The nonfulfillment of some or all of these conditions may disqualify the aspirant to the position of mujtahid. Their fulfillment is merely a preliminary to assessment by a further set of criteria, pertaining to the learning of the aspirant. Sayyid Muḥammad Mihdī Shahīd-i Thānī enumerated six preconditions of learning for the attainment of the rank of ijtihād: knowledge of theology (*kalām*); of the principles of the faith (*uṣūl-i dīn*); of grammar (*ṣarf-au-naḥv*); of the Arabic language; of logic (*manṭiq*); and of the principles of jurisprudence (*uṣūl-i fiqh*).[24] Clearly, the acquisition of such comprehensive knowledge is not in the power of all the believers. The Prophet promised that "whosoever of my community memorizes forty hadith necessary to him for his faith, God wil resurrect on the Day of Judgement as an *'ālim* (scholar) and *faqīh* (jurisprudent)."[25] For the direction of the Shi'i community after the beginning of the Greater Occultation, it is nonetheless necessary for a number of men to devote themselves fully to the acquisition of religious knowledge. This they do on behalf of the community, and they are obliged to impart their acquired knowledge.[26] At the same time, this knowledge bestows a certain authority and privilege, for it implies a greater acquaintance with the religious law. Whereas one of the principles of jurisprudence in Sunni Islam is a consensus of the entire living community, in Shi'ism the consensus is restricted to the ulama, both the living and the dead. Similarly, to engage in religious disputation is forbidden to those without the learning possessed by the ulama.[27] Since, moreover, greater knowledge is more likely to ensure a correct pronouncement on the part of the mujtahid, the degree of knowledge must be taken into consideration in the choice of a marja'-i taqlīd.

The ways of recognizing a mujtahid as *a'lam* (most learned), and hence worthy of *taqlīd* (adherence to the exemplary model), are either through personal ability to ascertain degrees of learning, or

23 *Ibid.*, p. 47.

24 Quoted in *ibid.*, p. 45.

25 Muḥammad Bāqir Majlisī, *Biḥār al-Anwār* (Tehran, 1327 Sh—/1948—), II, 153.

26 *Ibid.*, pp. 64–66.

27 Shaykh Ṣaddūq b. Bābūya Qummī, *Risālat al-I'tiqādāt*, trans. A. A. A. Fyzee as *A Shi'ite Creed* (Oxford, 1942), p. 43; and Majlisī, *op. cit.*, II, 111.

by accepting the testimony of two pious and learned persons, not conflicting with that of two similarly qualified persons; or by following the judgment of a group of people who accept as a'lam a certain mujtahid.[28] If the muqallid is still unable to decide whether the mujtahid is a'lam, but on the other hand knows of none more learned than him, he may then consider him worthy of taqlīd.[29] It is clear that these criteria represent only general principles for the choice of a marja'-i taqlīd, and, in fact, no specific process was ever established. Methods whereby mujtahids attained prominence in the Qajar period are discussed below.

The concept and practice of taqlīd, then, provide the ultimate basis for the place of the mujtahid in the Shi'i community. In order to ensure the vitality of the direction that taqlīd provides, following the ruling of a deceased mujtahid is prohibited. If recourse to a living mujtahid is not to be had, it is permissible to follow the practice of a deceased marja'-i taqlīd as contained in his writings.[30] Even indirect access to a living mujtahid is preferable, and taqlīd may follow hearing the pronouncement of a mujtahid from a trustworthy person or reading it.[31] If the comprehension of a book or treatise written by a marja'-i taqlīd proves beyond the capacity of the muqallid, he may request help from one capable of understanding it.[32] The muqallid must conform not only to the practice of a living mujtahid but also to any changes in the rulings and pronouncements of the marja'-i taqlīd he has chosen.[33]

On the basis of these provisions, the link between believer and mujtahid has remained a living one, constantly renewed. In this sense, the "gate of ijtihād" was never shut in Shi'ism as it was imagined to be in Sunni Islam after the death of the founders of the four great *madhhab*'s (schools of law). Theoretically, at least, a select few might benefit their followers with the results of their reasoning and prevent taqlīd from becoming a mere static acceptance of unexamined, even unassimilated, teaching. In fact, ijtihād in this sense was little used, if at all; and the consequences of it were more political and social than doctrinal. The guidance given

28 Burūjirdī, *op. cit.*, p. 3.

29 *Ibid.*

30 Muḥammad Bāqir Majlisī, *Kitāb-i Su'āl va Javāb* (Isfahan, 1274 Q/1831–1832), p. 3.

31 Burūjirdī, *op. cit.*, p. 4.

32 Majlisī, *op. cit.*, p. 3.

33 Burūjirdī, *op. cit.*, p. 5.

to the community was less toward understanding of the faith than toward political self-assertion.

PRACTICAL FUNCTIONS OF THE *Mujtahid*

Although the mujtahid is, strictly speaking, one who exercises ijtihād, and although it is possible to make a distinction between mujtahid, faqīh, and *muftī* (one whose opinion is sought on a point of religious law),[34] in practice the various functions implied in these three titles are often united in one person. Moreover, certain duties fulfilled by the Sunni ulama, and hence bearing no special relationship to the Shi'i concept of ijtihād, also fall to the mujtahid. Thus, while taqlīd provides the ultimate basis for the authority of the mujtahid, this authority finds expression in a variety of functions.

Some of these are summarized in a saying attributed to the Prophet: "The ulama are guardians of those who are without protector; and in their hands is the enforcement of divine ordinance concerning what has been permitted or prohibited."[35] Thus, as persons thought worthy of confidence, ulama might be entrusted with deposits, the estates of minors, and the guardianship of orphans.[36] They might further be entrusted with the administration of private *vaqf*'s (inalienable endowments), that is, those established not for charitable purposes but as a means of guaranteeing security of tenure. If the administrator (*mutavallī*) of such an endowment were dismissed from his appointment, the ulama frequently acted as trustees.[37] Similarly, the ulama were given the task of certifying the legality of title deeds and other documents by affixing their seal.[38]

The collection and distribution of various kinds of alms and money intended for pious and charitable purposes (*zakāt, khums,* and so forth) were also the responsibility of the ulama.[39] The

[34] Sanglajī, *op. cit.*, p. 14.

[35] *Ibid.*, p. 13.

[36] C. Frank, "Über den schiitischen Mudschtahid," *Islamica,* II (1926), 182.

[37] A. K. S. Lambton, *Landlord and Peasant in Persia* (London, 1953), p. 230. This was particularly the case in the first quarter of the nineteenth century (see M. S. Ivanov, *Babidskiye Vosstaniya v Irane* [Moscow and Leningrad, 1939], p. 33).

[38] See below, p. 179.

[39] Atrpyet (pseudonym), *Imamat': Strana Poklonnikov Imamov* (Alexandropol, 1909), p. 35.

prominence of the mujtahids might well be reflected in the sums that passed through their hands: to give a donation represented an act of association with the piety embodied in their persons. At the same time, it is worth remarking that no system of enforcement existed for the collection of zakāt, a tax obligatory on every male Muslim; on occasion, prominent mujtahids did not hesitate to use coercion.[40]

More important than all of these, however, was the ulama's share in the administration of justice. In the judicial realm as in others, they became in effect the successors of the Imams through practical necessity. A hadith recounted by al-Kulaynī restricts the competence to sit in judgment to the Prophet, to the Imam, or to one designated by God and the Prophet to act on behalf of the Prophet (*vaṣī*).[41] It is clear that after the occultation of the Imam some kind of juridical authority is nonetheless necessary; a commentator's marginal note on the same hadith interprets it in such a way as to make the exercise of judgment by someone other than the Prophet, the Imam, and the vaṣī permissible.[42] In the Qajar period administration of the religious law by the ulama had to compete with the judicial administration of the state.

This duality of the judicial system was inherited from the Safavids and was not amended until the introduction of the first Civil Code in 1911.[43] The courts presided over by the ulama were known as *shar'* courts, with the law dispensed being that evolved by Shi'i Islam; the system of law controlled by the state was called *'urf*. 'Urf has been called common law or law of precedent, but since no records of proceedings were kept, and since the verdicts delivered were not necessarily committed to writing, it is difficult to see what basis of precedent could have been referred to. 'Urf jurisdiction was dispensed by the state without reference to established principles, according to the needs of the state at a given time, through the medium of governors of towns. It seems therefore more appropriate to call it arbitrary law, despite the apparent contradiction inherent in this description.

Although there was no precise demarcation of the respective

40 E.g., Shaykh Ja'far Najafī (see *Q'U*, p. 143).

41 al-Kulaynī, *op. cit.*, VII, 406.

42 *Ibid.*, n. 1 by 'Alī Akbar Ghaffārī.

43 J. Greenfield, "Die geistlichen Schariagerichte in Persien," *Zeitschrift für vergleichende Rechtswissenschaft*, XLVIII (1934), 157–158.

jurisdictions of 'urf and shar', it is possible to ascertain a certain division: the former dealt primarily with offenses directed against the state or public security, such as rebellion, embezzlement, forgery of coins, spreading false rumor, theft, banditry, and drunkenness; the shar' courts were concerned more with disputes and litigations of a personal or commercial nature. Theft and drunkenness might, however, come within the jurisdiction of a shar' court.[44]

Thus the jurisdictions of shar' and 'urf frequently overlapped, and in general the system was conducive to a certain interaction, not to say conflict, between its two parts. Shar' courts were powerless in that they lacked the ability, for the most part, to enforce their decisions: the execution of verdicts was in the hands of the *dārūgha* or *kadkhudā* (the town or village headman), an appeal to whom by bribery might nullify any decision.[45] Similarly, the workings of 'urf were not free from the intervention of shar'. The shar' court might serve as a court of appeal in which a decision reached by 'urf could be reversed.[46] A governor in judging a case brought before him might request a *fatvā* (expression of opinion on a point of religious law) from a mujtahid, as might either of the parties to the dispute; such a fatvā, once issued, was normally acted upon.[47] The fatvā of a mujtahid might also be used to settle a case out of court; since litigation was generally a costly and unprofitable business, recourse was had to it only in case of absolute necessity.[48]

Throughout the nineteenth century, this interaction of the two types of court, combined with the lack of any formal demarcation of their jurisdictions, was a major source of conflict between the state and the ulama. The state's attempts to assert its judicial power inevitably meant a lessening of the prerogatives of the ulama, who for their part could not accept the validity of 'urf jurisdiction. Although a certain community of interest arose between wealthy landowning ulama and provincial governors in the latter part of the century, which tended to reduce the independence of shar' jurisdiction,[49] this was a minor theme in the history

44 J. E. Polak, *Persien: das Land und seine Bewohner* (Leipzig, 1865), I, 328; and G. Curzon, *Persia and the Persian Question* (London, 1892), I, 462.

45 C. J. Wills, *Persia as It Is* (London, 1886), p. 47.

46 Sir Harford Jones Brydges, *Account of the Transactions of His Majesty's Mission to the Court of Persia in the Years 1807–1811* (London, 1834), p. 407.

47 Wills, *op. cit.*, p. 48.

48 *Ibid.*, p. 44.

49 For a case in point, see 'Abbās Mīrzā Mulkārā, *Sharḥ-i Ḥāl*, ed. 'Abd ul-Ḥusayn Navā'ī (Tehran 1325 Sh/1946–1947), p. 124.

of the period, less important than the attempts to expand the jurisdiction of 'urf at the expense of shar' and to submit the latter to some kind of supervision by the state.

Such then were the specific functions of the ulama in Qajar Iran. Before considering the general role in society which these functions and other factors secured for them, we will examine the material basis for their existence.

SOURCES OF INCOME OF THE ULAMA

The primary sources of income for the ulama were the endowments (*auqāf*) attached to shrines and mosques and the various grants of an individual and voluntary nature which were given to them. The exercise of the functions outlined above was not necessarily and directly accompanied by any financial reward.

In Safavid times, Isfahan, the capital city, had extensive auqāf lands attached to its mosques and madrasas, but these were largely usurped by local landowners during the interregnum between the Safavids and the Qajars.[50] The lands attached to the shrine of the Imam Riḍā in Mashhad, situated mostly in the province of Khurasan, constituted probably the largest single source of clerical income during the Qajar period. Curzon estimated the annual income derived from them at the time of his visit to Iran in 1890 at 60,000 tomans, and the total retinue connected with the buildings of the shrine at 2,000.[51] Money from these auqāf also served to support a number of ulama in the capital: disturbances in Khurasan which interrupted the operation of auqāf lands would immediately arouse their concern as a threat to their material existence.[52] Endowments were attached to other shrines, mosques, and madrasas throughout the country. The importance of the auqāf to the ulama as a means of securing prominence is seen in the various struggles among the ulama to gain control of their administration. It is remarkable, however, that the auqāf in general did not constitute a subject for dispute between the ulama and the state, for here too was a point of contact and possible friction between clerical and secular power. Since the foundation of the auqāf of Mashhad in 1015–1016/1606–1608 by Shah 'Abbās, their administration, up

50 Lambton, *op. cit.*, pp. 129–130.
51 Curzon, *op. cit.*, I, 163.
52 *KhS*, p. 243.

to the present day, has been formally vested in the reigning monarch, who in practice has delegated his responsibilities to the *mutavallībāshī* (chief administrator).[53] In Qajar times, the mutavallībāshī, who was initially selected from the ranks of the ulama, came to be the most important figure in the province of Khurasan, second only to the governor. It was possibly out of fear that his power might become an instrument of clerical opposition to the state that Nāṣir ud-Dīn Shāh united the post with that of governor in the person of Rukn ud-Daula in 1889.[54] Thereafter, the two posts appear to have remained combined.[55] On the whole, the situation of religious endowments was fairly constant throughout the nineteenth century: the state was apparently not interested in disturbing it, and the acquisitive instincts of certain ulama were able to find expression elsewhere.

First, fees could be charged for the fulfillment of certain functions. Thus a part of zakāt could legitimately be given to those engaged in collecting and distributing it.[56] If the mujtahid acted as administrator of a private vaqf, he could claim either 10 percent of the produce, or, if the amount was not specified in the letter of endowment, a sum commensurate with the work involved.[57] The extent to which the judicial activities of the ulama were accompanied by financial reward is difficult to determine. Theoretically, no fee might be claimed for issuing a fatvā, for the implication of bribery contained in the payment of such a fee cast doubt on the honesty of the judge.[58] Opinion varied on whether charging a fee for writing out a fatvā was permissible: Muḥammad Taqī Burghānī claimed that he might do so because writing was not an essential part of his duties,[59] whereas others held that writing out a fatvā was an inseparable part of the process of delivering it.[60]

Certain ulama, particularly those of less exalted rank, seem to

53 Lambton, *op. cit.*, p. 231. The appointment of other officials at the shrine has also depended on royal authority (see Mihdī Valā'ī, "Sharḥ-i Ḥāl Navvāb-i Tauliat-i 'Uẓmā-yi Āstān-i Quds-i Raḍavī," *Nāma-yi Āstān-i Quds*, V [1344 Sh/1965–1966], 86–95).

54 Curzon, *op. cit.*, I, 164.

55 'Abdullāh Mustaufī, *Tārīkh-i Idārī va Ijtimā'ī-yi Daura-yi Qājārīya yā Sharḥ-i Zindagānī-yi Man* (Tehran, 1321 Sh/1942–1943), II, 58.

56 Burūjirdī, *op. cit.*, pp. 203–204.

57 Lambton, *op. cit.*, p. 230.

58 Sanglajī, *op. cit.*, p. 92.

59 Muḥammad 'Alī Kashmīrī, *Nujūm us-Samā* (Lucknow, 1303 Q/1885–1886), p. 410.

60 Sanglajī, *op. cit.*, p. 185.

have engaged in trade on their own account. Some are reputed to have practiced moneylending at interest rates of 40 to 50 percent despite the clear prohibition of usury in the Quran.[61] Mujtahids are similarly reported to have speculated in land and urban property, usually through intermediaries.[62] There is a record of a mujtahid as prominent as Āqā Najafī planning the establishment of a bank charging 18 percent interest on loans and paying a dividend of 12 percent per annum.[63] In the second half of the nineteenth century, the hoarding of grain by such ulama as Ḥājjī Mullā 'Alī Kanī and Mīrzā Āqā Javād further illustrates that on occasion venality overcame religion.[64]

Even though the extent of this venality cannot be measured with any certainty, it is clear that in many respects the financial basis of the ulama's existence was unsatisfactory. Control of much vaqf property was in the hands of the state, and the yearly grants made to the ulama, from the reign of Fatḥ 'Alī Shāh (1797–1834) onward, could on occasion be intended as "silence money" (*ḥaqq us-sukūt*).[65] On the other hand, voluntary contributions from individuals tended to make the ulama subservient to the pressures of public opinion.[66] The growing tradition of inheriting clerical prominence caused a general increase in the wealth of the ulama, acquired over generations, thus increasing the temptations of venality. These serious weaknesses in the financial basis of the ulama's power were, however, unable to affect substantially the role of the ulama as a dominating, directive force in society.

OTHER FACTORS DETERMINING THE ROLE OF THE ULAMA IN SOCIETY

Although the position of marja'-i taqlīd is the doctrinal foundation of clerical power, and certain indications are given for the choice of the most suitable candidate to occupy it, no adequate

61 A. Sepsis, "Quelques Mots sur l'Etat Religieux Actuel de la Perse," *Revue de l'Orient*, III (1844), 101. Usury is prohibited in chap. ii, v. 275 of the Quran.

62 Sepsis, *op. cit.*

63 F.O. 60/557, report of Reece, British consul in Isfahan, Jan. 21, 1894.

64 See below, pp. 173, 220.

65 The phrase is used in a related context by Aḥmad Kasravī (*Zindagānī-yi Man* [Tehran, 1323 Sh/1944], p. 15).

66 *KhS*, p. 124.

process of selection has been established.[67] It is thus appropriate to examine by what means a mujtahid attained power and influence, and also to investigate the nature of that influence.

Piety and learning were the two chief characteristics by which to recognize one worthy of taqlīd. Piety, however, can be discerned by most of the faithful only indirectly and from a distance, particularly if the residence of the mujtahid in question is remote from that of the muqallid. His piety must be made known by reputation, and his reputation be spread by followers as numerous as possible. Learning might be established by the production of erudite treatises, huge numbers of which are attributed to some Shi'i ulama, but, again, personal assessment of erudition was impossible for most of the faithful, and the need arose for an intermediary who could bear witness to the learning of the mujtahid. Just as the mujtahids themselves acted as intermediaries between the Imams and the community, so, too, on a lesser scale, did others mediate between the marāji'-i taqlīd and the believers. The absence of hierarchic stratification in Shi'ism emphasizes the subtlety of this chain of authority.

The need for an intermediary was fulfilled to a certain extent by some of the mujtahids themselves. An aspirant to ijtihād would solicit an *ijāza,* a certificate testifying to his piety and knowledge, from a prominent mujtahid, hoping to gain for himself a share of the respect accorded to the mujtahid, but at the same time helping to increase the extent of that respect.[68] On occasion, ijāza's were sought from a number of mujtahids, primarily because none before Shaykh Murtaḍā Anṣārī (1216–1281/1801–1864) was able to establish himself as sole marja'-i taqlīd.[69] But it was above all the *mullā*'s (alternatively called *ākhūnd*'s) who acted as intermediaries between the prominent mujtahids and the mass of believers.

67 The subject has been reconsidered recently by a number of Shi'i thinkers in a collective work entitled *Baḥthī dar bāra-yi Marja'īyat* (Tehran, 1341 Sh/1962) and discussed by Lambton in her article "A Reconsideration of the Position of the *Marja' Al-Taqlīd* and the Religious Institution" (*SI*, XX (1964), 115–135). One of the group, Āyatullāh Sayyid Maḥmūd Ṭāliqānī, has proposed the creation of a collective marja'-i taqlīd as being a more realistic and effective institution than an individual source of exemplary guidance (see his "Tamarkuz va 'Adam-i Tamarkuz-i Marja'īyat," in *Jihād va Shihādat* [Tehran, 1385 Q/1965], pp. 82–92).

68 For an example of an *ijāza,* see *Q'U,* p. 155.

69 See below, p. 163.

The connotations of the word mullā are many and interesting. Although signifying primarily one distinguished by his dress and pretensions to knowledge as a member of the religious classes who had not attained the rank of ijtihād, it also is used to designate anyone learned or even literate.[70] This extension of its meaning is accounted for probably by the fact that the mullā often taught in the local *maktab* (elementary school) or was employed as tutor in private, especially well-to-do, homes.[71] The mullā was the most knowledgeable person in his immediate vicinity in matters of religion, and he therefore exercised a general authority over his neighbors. Thus, when the Dār ul-Funūn printed books on the prevention of disease and on the advantages of inoculation, it was decided to distribute them among the mullās so that they might impress the importance of the contents on the people.[72] The derivation of the word from the Arabic *maulā* (master, lord) confirms the concept of authority. The learning and authority of the mullā extended to everyday religious functions, such as leading prayer in the smaller mosques, pronouncing the Friday sermon, and performing betrothal and marriage ceremonies. His religious learning was inferior to that of the mujtahid, and hence, like other believers, he was compelled to be muqallid to a mujtahid of his choice.[73] In his choice, he would be followed by his neighbors, and thus he came to occupy a position intermediate between the mass of believers and the marja'-i taqlīd.

The link between the mujtahid and the mullā had other, more specific consequences. In certain circumstances, the mullā might act as a deputy (*nā'ib*) of the mujtahid. Thus he would confirm the validity of documents on his behalf, and the seal he affixed would be that of the mujtahid.[74] He would collect zakāt and other sums of money to be placed at the disposal of the mujtahid, receiving himself some recompense in return.[75] Another source of income for the mullās which bound them to the mujtahids were the auqāf:

[70] Definitions in *Burhān-i Qāṭi'*, ed. Muḥammad Mu'īn (Tehran, 1330 Sh/1952), IV, 2030, and Dihkhudā, *Lughatnāma*, Fasc. I (Tehran, 1325 Sh/1946).

[71] An example furnished by Kasravī, *op. cit.*, pp. 13 ff.

[72] Firīdūn Ādamīyat, *Fikr-i Āzādī va Muqaddima-yi Nihḍat-i Mashrūṭīyat-i Īrān* (Tehran, 1340 Sh/1961), p. 49.

[73] It is worth noting, however, that many of the ulama who attained the rank of ijtihād kept the title of "mullā" as part of their popular appellation, e.g., Mullā Āqā Darbandī and Mullā 'Alī Kanī.

[74] Atrpyet, *op. cit.*, p. 36.

[75] *Ibid.*, p. 37.

a recommendation to the administrator from a mujtahid would permit the mullā to benefit from them.[76] The share thus attained was frequently inadequate as a source of livelihood, and particularly in more remote areas the mullā supplemented it by petty trade or farming.

In still another sense the mullās added support to the authority of the mujtahids. Their numbers acted as a physical expression of the power of the mujtahid to whom they were attached, and on occasion they helped in the execution of that power. They were not alone in this. Throughout most of the Qajar period, we encounter cases of mujtahids, particularly in Isfahan and Tabriz, surrounded by what can only be called private armies. Initially they consisted more of straightforward brigands (*lūṭī*'s) than of mullās. The lūṭīs, who originally formed chivalrous brotherhoods similar to those of their counterparts, the *fatī*'s in Anatolia and the Arab lands, acted to support clerical power by defying the state and by enforcing fatvās. In return they were permitted to engage in plunder and robbery, taking sanctuary, when threatened with pursuit, in the refuge known as *bast* which mosques and residences of the ulama provided. Later in the nineteenth century, the lūṭīs seem to have been replaced largely by the *ṭullāb*, the students of the madrasas, whose numbers and strength represented a formidable branch of clerical power. Hence the control of a madrasa was doubly desirable—it offered the financial power of the auqāf and the physical strength of the ṭullāb. Furthermore, masses of *sayyid*'s (claimants to descent from the Prophet), genuine or false, enforced their claims on the charity of believers with the support of the ulama, and in return agreed to help in the enforcement of clerical authority in time of need.[77]

A further coercive element of clerical power was provided by takfīr, declaring an opponent or enemy to be an infidel. This weapon was used in the controversies of the main body of the ulama against the Akhbārīs and the Shaykhīs, and was used again later in the nineteenth century against reformers and innovators such as Fatḥ 'Alī Ākhūndzāda and Mīrzā Ḥasan Rushdīya. It is not clear to what extent takfīr was effective: the consent of the state seems to have been essential for the victim to be placed in serious dan-

76 Frank, *op. cit.*, p. 190.

77 A fact fictionally recorded by Zayn ul-'Ābidīn Marāgha'ī in his *Siyāḥatnāma-yi Ibrāhīm Bīg* (Calcutta, 1910), p. 164.

ger. It represented, however, a powerful weapon resulting in at least social ostracism and a device to be used against enemies of clerical influence.[78]

Since the power of the mujtahids was exercised in part on a basis of force and coercion, it is legitimate to ask to what extent abstract and theoretical considerations of taqlīd determined the influence of the mujtahids on the mass of believers. It must be remembered initially that there seems to have been no widely held belief that a contradiction existed between the material and physical power of the ulama and the religious justification on which they sought to base it. Rather, the former was seen as an expression and consequence of the latter. The ulama were deemed the leaders of the nation, and it was natural for leadership to enforce its directives.

As suggested above, the direction given by the ulama was primarily political. A brief comparison of the religious life and thought of the ulama and those of the mass of Shiʿis supports this contention. The ulama were concerned with a scholastic learning which, though not denied to anyone, was in practice inaccessible to those whose occupations or talents did not permit them to acquire it. Moreover, positions of religious eminence became increasingly hereditary throughout the period. The popular religiosity of the masses, by contrast, took on many forms, not all of which were regarded with favor by the ulama. In particular, *taʿzīya* and *rauḍakhvānī* (dramatic performances and recitations commemorating the martyrdom of the Imam Ḥusayn), both of which grew in popularity throughout the Qajar period, were considered reprehensible by many ulama. The *rauḍakhvān*'s (reciters) were, to a certain extent, their rivals in the control of religious loyalties, and the emotionalism of the taʿzīya ran counter to the scholastic spirit of their learning.[79] It is true that certain ulama engaged in superstitious practices and, no less than Sufis, laid claim to *karāmāt* (miraculous deeds), but on the whole the distinction between the religious approaches of the ulama and the mass of the community is valid.

Here again, the mullās seem to have occupied an intermediate position. They at least made pretensions to religious learning,

78 There also existed a lesser degree of condemnation, *tafsīq*, declaring someone *fāsiq* or immoral. Its consequences are not clear (see *QʿU*, p. 107).

79 At the same time, mujtahids encouraged rauḍakhvāns to mention their names favorably in the course of their recitations, in order to increase their fame and repute (see *HY*, I, 129).

though not to the same extent as the mujtahids; on the other hand, they were in more immediate contact with the people, and even to an extent financially dependent upon them.[80] *Mullābāzī* (mullā's tricks) or *ākhūndbāzī* (ākhūnd's tricks) became pejorative terms for various types of suspect activity engaged in by the mullās partly as a result of this financial weakness.[81]

We return, then, to the function of mujtahid as leader, deriving from the practical necessity of taqlīd and its acceptance by the community. If taqlīd was not comprehended in all its aspects, its necessity was instinctively understood. The adulation accorded the ulama is proof. At the same time, the difference in mentality between the ulama and the mass of believers caused the nature of this leadership to be largely external, political, and social. In this sense, taqlīd took on a real and immediate significance, and through it the ulama in the Qajar period were "the still fresh national voice of Persian Islam."[82]

GENERAL FACTORS DETERMINING THE ATTITUDE OF THE ULAMA TO THE STATE

It has been seen that Shi'i Islam denied legitimacy to secular power, and the occultation of the Imam removed all real authority from the sphere of this world. With the establishment of the Safavid state in 1501, the denial of legitimacy became partially obscured by the claim of the monarch to descent from the Imams and by the introduction of Sufi motives into the concept of rulership. At the same time, a body of Shi'i ulama emerged who, although equally deprived of ultimate authority, gradually acquired, through the exercise of a practical function, a de facto authority within the community. This development in their position was furthered by the fall of the Safavids and their replacement, after an interregnum, by the Qajars in the last quarter of the eighteenth century.

By the end of the interregnum, relations between the state and

80 Several European travelers perceived the difference in knowledge and way of life between the higher ulama and the mullās (see, e.g., Jane Dieulafoy, *La Perse, la Chaldée et la Susiane* [Paris, 1887], p. 56).

81 Dihkhudā (*op. cit.*, Fasc. I, p. 49) defines *ākhūndbāzī* as *tavassul ba ḥiyal-i shar'ī*, recourse to means permitted by the letter of the law, but not by its spirit.

82 G. Scarcia, "Kerman 1905: La Guerra tra Šeiḫī e Bālāsarī," *Annali del Istituto Universitario Orientale di Napoli*, XIII (1963), 198.

the ulama had been changed by two new factors. First, there took place an evolution in Shi'i fiqh which asserted the role of the mujtahid in directing the community and even in ruling it. One of the ulama, Shaykh Aḥmad Ardabīlī, indeed reminded his monarch, Shah 'Abbās, that he was ruling over a "borrowed kingdom" (*mulk-i 'āriya*), but the ulama in the Safavid period did not openly contest the legitimacy of the state.[83] Second, the establishment of Qajar rule presented the ulama with the spectacle of a state that made many of the same assumptions concerning the nature of royal power as had the Safavids but was itself deprived of the semilegitimacy provided by alleged descent from the Imams. The Qajars called themselves "Shadow of God," but the claim to divine appointment was only formal. Thus it might have been thought that some attempt would be made to justify, in religious terms, the claims of the state to the allegiance of its subjects.

In the new situation, however, a political theory to accommodate the state within the system of belief was still not developed. Such a theory was probably impossible: the ulama, having established their position as de facto regents of the Imams, could not then have allotted the monarchy a similar position. Without such a position the monarchy was bound to be regarded as illegitimate. The contradiction was seldom stated explicitly but was nonetheless the ultimate cause of most of the friction between the secular and religious powers throughout the nineteenth century.

Whereas the ulama could not reasonably demand of the state that it abdicate its power, they expected at least some kind of submission from it, however formal. Mīrzā Ḥasan Shīrāzī, who gained prominence in the agitation against the tobacco concession, was fond of quoting the hadith: "If you see the ulama at the gates of the kings, say, they are bad ulama and bad kings. If you see the kings at the gates of the ulama, say, they are good ulama and good kings."[84] During the Qajar period, both kinds of relationship existed, but without solving the fundamental contradiction. A policy of token submission by the state, such as that followed by Fatḥ 'Alī Shāh, could have only temporary success. When no such policy was followed, contradiction passed into conflict and was intensified under the pressure of events.

Even if the state had not been fundamentally illegitimate, it

83 *Q'U*, pp. 99–100.

84 Muḥammad Ḥusayn Ādamīyat, *Dānishmandān va Sukhansarāyān-i Fārs* (Tehran, 1338 Sh/1959), IV, 324.

would in any event have been condemned to virtual powerlessness. The ruler, like every other believer who had not attained the rank of ijtihād, was obliged to be muqallid to a certain mujtahid and to execute his rulings and pronouncements. The state could ultimately have been no more than the executive branch of clerical power. In the actual tyranny of the period, such considerations counted for little, and the monarch, by not submitting to clerical direction, effectively alienated himself from the nation. This is seen clearly in a number of episodes, above all in the agitation against the tobacco concession (chap. xii).

As a result, association with the state was largely shunned by the ulama. Since the state per se represented tyranny, any close relationship with it came to be regarded as disqualification for the position of marja'-i taqlīd. This is seen in the first decade of the present century, when Shaykh Faḍlullāh Nūrī, though generally admitted to be the most learned of the ulama of Tehran, was unable to attain the authority of such men as 'Abdullāh Bihbihānī and Muḥammad Ṭabāṭabā'ī, who opposed rather than supported the state.[85] Toward the end of the nineteenth century, there arose a semblance of mutual cooperation between certain ulama and the state; but those cooperating with the organ of tyranny were widely regarded as having forfeited their allegiance to the faith.[86] In general, government officials were regarded with abhorrence; Mustaufi remarks, even before the coming of the Belgian officials, that the customs in particular were considered contrary to religious law.[87] The state had no legitimate property; the property it had was thought by many of the stricter ulama to be ritually unclean.

There were nevertheless certain points of association between the ulama and the state. To the state belonged the traditional duty of appointing *shaykh ul-Islām*'s to supervise the shar' courts in each town, and *imām jum'a*'s to lead congregational prayer and pronounce the Friday sermon.[88] In making these appointments, the

85 See below, p. 248.

86 *HY*, I, 50. Similar attitudes toward association with organs of government persist in present-day Iran (see Leonard Binder, "The Proofs of Islam: Religion and Politics in Iran," in *Arabic and Islamic Studies in Honour of Hamilton A. R. Gibb* [Leiden, 1966], pp. 135, 137).

87 Mustaufī, *op. cit.*, I, 138 n. 1.

88 Ṭahmāsp I became the first Safavid ruler to appoint an imām jum'a after Shaykh Nūr ud-Dīn 'Alī Karkhī assured him of the obligatory nature of congregational prayer on Fridays during the Greater Concealment (see Muḥammad 'Alī Mu'allim Bīdābādī, *Makārim ul-Āthār dar Aḥvāl-i Rijāl-i Daura-yi Qājār* [Isfahan, 1337 Sh/1958], I, 80).

monarch did not act against popular wishes, and the imam jum'as, until the latter part of the nineteenth century, generally behaved impartially and independently. Acceptance of such posts did not bring forfeiture of popular respect or absorption into the administrative apparatus of the state.

There was a further contrast between the authority of the state and that of the ulama, proceeding from the total illegitimacy of the former: that between instability and stability. Power emanating from the government usually depended upon the favor of a few courtiers and ministers and might be given and removed with equal ease. That of the ulama on the other hand was based on a definite function and concept of authority; however limited, it was largely inaccessible to external influences. This difference was clearly recognized by the ulama. Mullā Muḥammad Ṣāliḥ Burghānī once told the governor of Qazvin: "Rule and rank last as long as your apointment by the king; after your dismissal, the pleasures you enjoyed are exposed to loss. But the ulama are constantly in the presence of the Creator. As soon as you and your like see us, you act with humility and submission to us, treating us with respect. . . . This then is a divine power, and superior to all other pleasures."[89]

The continuity of the power of the ulama made for a close link with the community, to whom the state, by contrast, appeared (particularly in the provinces) as alien and external, descending intermittently to extort taxes and to conscript soldiers. Bast was, despite its abuses, a symbol of the function fulfilled by the ulama between state and people: refuge from the illegitimate tyranny of the state was sought with representatives of the only legitimate authority.

Their common alienation from the state served to bring the nation and the ulama more closely together. The ulama acted not merely as communal but also as national leaders. National consciousness did not exist as a motive force until considerably later than the Qajar period: the prime sense of loyalty was to Islam rather than to Iran.[90] Throughout the century, objections, not only to the state but also to foreign aggression and encroachment, were voiced in Islamic rather than in nationalistic terms. Despite this

[89] *Q'U*, p. 64.

[90] An observation made by an English missionary in Yazd (N. Malcolm, *Five Years in a Persian Town* [London, 1905], pp. 38–39), among others.

lack of explicit national feeling, the peculiar position of Islam in Iran makes it possible to see in the ulama national leaders. The community was neither purely religious nor purely national, but what may best be termed religio-national. Shi'ism effectively isolated Iran from the rest of the Muslim world, both in feeling and in action. At the turn of the century, Pan-Islamism had a short and largely ineffective life in Iran, and the decline of hostility to Sunni Islam was to be as much the result of religious indifference as of incipient return to the original unity of the Islamic community. Shi'ism was regarded as the mainstream of Islam, but at the same time it was a fact that only in Iran was it the madhhab followed by the overwhelming majority. Traditions of Iranian cultural individualism increased the sense of separateness. Thus it was that Iran for some time did not suffer from the conflict between Islam and nationalism that occurred elsewhere in the Muslim world, and, to quote the Italian scholar G. Scarcia, there took place "a confluence between Shi'ism and the popular spirit, taking on the form of national consciousness."[91] The ulama embodied this consciousness.

91 Scarcia, *op. cit.*, p. 198.

II

The Eve of Qajar Rule

The 120 years from the rise of the Qajar dynasty in 1785 to the Constitutional Revolution in 1905 were years in which the ulama played a leading role in Iranian affairs. Religious activity and controversy were perhaps as vigorous as at any other time in the history of Iran. These characteristics of the period were apparent from the beginning. Almost contemporary with the establishment of Qajar rule there took place a renewal of religious studies, marked by the emergence of prominent theologians, notably in the *'atabāt* ("thresholds": the Shi'i holy places at Karbala, Kāẓimayn, Najaf, and Samarra in Iraq), and their achievements were preserved and expanded throughout the nineteenth century. It was in the Qajar period that the tensions inherent in a Shi'i monarchy took on an acute form, and these tensions, together with other factors that intruded on Iran from the outside world, combined to produce a continual struggle between ulama and state.

The Eve of Qajar Rule

THE HISTORICAL BACKGROUND

The Safavids (907/1501–1135/1722)

The establishment of the Safavid dynasty, the first Shi'i house after centuries of predominantly Sunni rule to control the whole extent of Iran, was accompanied by a vigorous assertion of Shi'ism. But this assertion was initially more external than doctrinal, involving the suppression of Sunnism. This fact, combined with the paucity of Shi'i ulama in Iran, reduced the role of the ulama in relation to that of the state. The absolute power of the ruler, having a religious sanction of both Sufi and Shi'i origin, tended in any event to exclude any influence of the ulama on the administration of affairs. Shah Ismā'īl, the first Safavid ruler (907/1501–930/1524) commanded obedience both as *quṭb* (or "pole," in Sufi terminology) and as descendant of Mūsā al-Kāẓim, the seventh Imam, while his poetry shows that he regarded his rank as even more exalted.[1] Under the Safavids, the ruler was assumed to be the representative of the Hidden Imam, and even attributes of the Imams tended to be transferred to him.[2] Even though with the development of the Safavid state its theocratic nature and its Sufi aspect diminished, the close relationship between the state and its established religion implied a domination of the ulama by the kingly power. When the relationship was loosened under the Qajars, the immediate power of the ulama increased vastly. The ascendancy of the political function of the Safavid state over its religious one was typified in the position of the *ṣadr,* the official who controlled religious affairs and institutions on behalf of the state and appointed the shaykh ul-Islām, the chief dignitary of the religious classes.[3] Shar' courts and their judges were subordinate to 'urf and to the *dīvānbīgī* (the supreme official in secular jurisdiction), and the ṣadr and his nominee, the shaykh ul-Islām, were instrumental in bringing about this subordination.[4] The dominance of the state over the ulama did not, however, prevent it from granting the religious classes,

[1] See Tourkhan Gandjei, *Il Canzioniere di Šāh Ismā'īl Haṭā'ī* (Naples, 1959), poems nos. 16, 20, 198, 207.

[2] A. K. S. Lambton, "Quis Custodiet Custodes: Some Reflections on the Persian Theory of Government," *SI,* VI (1956), 129.

[3] *Ibid.,* p. 138; R. M. Savory, "The Principal Offices of the Safavid State during the Reign of Ismā'īl I," *BSOAS,* XXIII (1960), 104.

[4] *Tadhkirat al-Mulūk,* ed. V. Minorsky (London, 1943), pp. 110, 119.

and especially the sayyids, certain privileges and marks of respect;[5] nor was it an obstacle to the personal reverence of the ruler for certain of the ulama, such as that held by Shah 'Abbās (989/1581–1038/1629) for Shaykh Aḥmad Ardabīlī (d. 993/1585).[6] The encouragement of theological studies and the endowment of shrines and madrasas in fact laid the foundation for the later expansion of the political and social role of the ulama, in the same way as the great mujtahids of the late twelfth and early thirteenth Hijri centuries were both physically and spiritually descendants of the prominent Safavid theologians.[7]

That careful observer, the French traveler Jean Chardin, records that some of the ulama raised the claim that the place of the Hidden Imam should ideally be taken by a mujtahid divinely protected from sin; and that the shah's duty toward the faith was only external and protective, to be executed under the direction of a mujtahid.[8] Nonetheless, the authority of the mujtahids was based strictly on their exercise of ijtihād in a limited, legalistic field. It remains true, moreover, that the preoccupation of theologians in the Safavid period was the exposition of Shi'i doctrine and the suppression first of Sunnism and then also of Sufism. Little attention was paid to relations with the state. If, as suggested,[9] the real moment of crisis for Shi'ism in Iran was the transition from a purely religious community to a national state, rather than that to an outwardly constitutional form of government, the implications of this transition were not realized or at least not treated doctrinally in the Safavid period. Possibly, this lack of interest of Shi'i theology in defining the role of the state arose partly from the expectation of the Mahdi, which threw into doubt all worldly authority;[10] but the chief reason appears to have been the absorption of the ulama in the exposition of basic Shi'i doctrine.

5 Thus grants known as *suyūrghāl* were made to some eminent families (see J. Chardin, *Voyages en Perse* [Paris, 1811], VI, 65); and other families of sayyids were granted exemption from taxation (see A. K. S. Lambton, *Landlord and Peasant in Persia* [London, 1953], p. 105).

6 *Q'U*, p. 245.

7 For instance, Muḥammad Bāqir Bihbihānī, entitled the *mujaddid* (renewer) and *muravvij* (propagator), who was among the descendants of Muḥammad Taqī Majlisī (*Q'U*, p. 147; and Muḥammad 'Alī Mu'allim Bīdābādī, *Makārim ul-Āthar dar Aḥvāl-i Rijāl-i Daura-yi Qājār* (Isfahan, 1337 Sh/1958), I, 80).

8 Chardin, *op. cit.*, V, 208 ff.

9 G. Scarcia, "Intorno alle Controversie tra Aḫbārī e Uṣūlī presso gli Imamiti di Persia," *RSO*, XXXIII (1958), 212, n. 1.

10 The extent to which the fact of the occultation of the Imam influenced

Negatively, to expound Shi'i doctrine meant controversy against and persecution of Sufism and Sunnism. These aspects of the ulama's activity dominated the last thirty years of the Safavid era and, ironically, contributed to the fall of the Shi'i-Iranian state in 1722. The ascendancy of the ulama over Shah Sulṭān Ḥusayn (1105/1694–1135/1722), last of the ruling Safavid monarchs, represented a reversal of the usual roles of ulama and state. The post of *mullābāshī* (chief mullā) created by Shah Sulṭān Ḥusayn superseded in importance that of ṣadr;[11] its occupation by Muḥammad Bāqir Majlisī (d. 1111/1700) and his grandson Mīr Muḥammad Ḥusayn Majlisī successively, marked a revival of the militancy of the earlier Safavid period.[12] This revival followed rigid, formalistic lines, such as might be expected to characterize an assertion of scholastic orthodoxy. The convent of the Sufi Mullā Muḥsin Fayḍ Kāshānī was destroyed, and the dervishes inhabiting it were massacred.[13] This act might almost be held to be a symbolic destruction of one of the foundations of the Safavid dynasty: the first elder of the order had been Shaykh Safī (d. 735/1334), and when later the Safavid prince Ṭahmāsp Mīrzā was attempting to regain the throne, the Shahsävän tribes refused him their assistance precisely because of their continuing attachment to Sufism.[14] If the other target of the reawakened militancy, Sunnism, had previously been an external one, embodied in the Ottoman Empire, now peace between Iran and that power released the full weight of the attack on the Sunni Afghans living within the boundaries of the Safavid state. This provocation of the Afghans by the ulama, followed by their mismanagement of the defenses of Isfahan,[15] closely identifies them with the fall of the Safavid dynasty. Afghan resentment led to an uprising and the invasion of Iran in 1722. The invaders, before leaving Qandahar, massacred all the Shi'i inhabitants of the city, and thus clearly proclaimed the nature of their uprising.[16]

The effective end of the Safavid dynasty at the hands of the

Shi'i thinking can be seen in the discussion as to whether congregational prayer was permissible in his absence (see Bīdābādī, *op. cit.*, I, 80).

11 Lambton, "Quis Custodiet Custodes," p. 142.

12 L. Lockhart, *The Fall of the Safavi Dynasty and the Afghan Occupation of Persia* (Cambridge, 1958), p. 70.

13 Muḥammad Mihdī Iṣfahānī, *Niṣf-i Jahān fī Ta'rīf ul-Iṣfahān* (Tehran, 1340 Sh/1961), p. 183.

14 *Ibid.*, p. 200.

15 Lockhart, *op. cit.*, p. 155.

16 Iṣfahānī, *op. cit.*, p. 186.

Afghans marked the beginning of a period of danger for Shi'ism in Iran, during which its learning declined, its shrines were treated with disrespect, its ulama neglected and oppressed, and it was itself almost reduced from that position of preeminence in Islam it regards as its own, to the status of a mere equal of the four Sunni schools. Ultimately, however, Shi'ism was to emerge from the interregnum between Safavid and Qajar rule with increased strength, and with the role of its guardians, the ulama, more clearly and consciously defined. Bearing this in mind, the Safavid period, despite its length and theological fecundity, can be regarded as no more than that of the introduction of Shi'ism to Iran, and the earliest stage of its formulation as the national religion.

Nādir Shāh (1148/1736–1160/1747)

The devastation wrought by the Afghan invaders totally disrupted the cultural and religious life of Iran. In particular Isfahan, not only the Safavid capital but also the chief center of religious learning, suffered heavily from the Afghans, and not until the time of Ḥājjī Muḥammad Ḥusayn Khān Niẓām ud-Daula, the first governor of Isfahan under Fatḥ 'Alī Shāh, the second Qajar ruler, were any serious attempts at reconstruction undertaken.[17] Leaving the chaos behind them, many residents emigrated to India or to the shrines of Arab Iraq.[18] Although others also sought the safety of the 'atabāt, it was chiefly the ulama who went there, and the few ulama whose names attained any prominence resided there.[19] The movement of renewal was also to start at the 'atabāt, and many of its accompanying controversies were fought out there.

When the political unity of Iran was temporarily reestablished by Nādir Shāh in 1736, it was no longer on the basis of Shi'ism. The true nature of his religious beliefs and of his ultimate ambitions is unknown:[20] whether his attempts to displace Shi'ism in Iran sprang from the Sunnism of his tribe, the Afshārs,[21] or from a desire effectively to unify the Islamic world under his own rule. Possibly he considered the religion of Shah Ismā'īl to be *bid'at* (reprehensible innovation), and himself called upon to remove it. His actions

17 *Ibid.*, p. 281.

18 Sir Harford Jones Brydges, *The Dynasty of the Kajars* (London, 1833), pp. 149–150.

19 E.g., Sayyid 'Abdullāh Shūshtarī (see *RJ*, p. 383).

20 L. Lockhart, *Nadir Shah* (London, 1938), p. 100.

21 Iṣfahānī, *op. cit.*, p. 139.

against the ulama are well known: the confiscation of vaqf property, the abolition of the post of ṣadr, the restriction of all jurisdiction to 'urf courts, and the strangling of the shaykh ul-Islām of Isfahan.[22] The resistance of the ulama to Nādir's kingship, even after his proclamation as king at Mughān, was probably motivated by a desire to see rule restored to the "legitimate" dynasty, the Safavids, either to Ṭahmāsp Mīrzā or to his son, 'Abbās Mīrzā.[23] Giving expression to this desire was the immediate cause for the death of Mīrzā 'Abd ul-Ḥusayn Mullābāshī.[24]

Sir John Malcolm suggests that popular indignation at the ulama surrounding Shah Sulṭān Ḥusayn enabled Nādir Shāh to plunder the vaqfs without fear.[25] That the catastrophies of the Afghan invasion were widely attributed to the ulama seems unlikely. The ulama went round Isafahan calling on the people to repent, for it was their sinfulness that had caused the disaster of which signs were already apparent; probably, then, it was regarded as beyond control.[26] The weakness of Iranian resistance to the Afghan invaders tends to support this view.

In any event, the ultimate failure of Nādir Shāh's attempts to incorporate an adapted Shi'ism into the main body of Islam indicates that Shi'ism had taken a permanent hold on Iran. These attempts were based on an artificial compromise: Shi'ism, which regarded itself as the sole recipient and guardian of esoteric doctrine and true belief through the medium of the Imams, was to be renamed as the Ja'farī school (after Ja'far aṣ-Ṣādiq [d. 148/765], the sixth Imam), and its relation to the four Sunni schools was to be that which they already held to one another. The Imam Ja'far was to be regarded as founder of the school, with no more divine sanction for his authority than Abū Ḥanīfa or ash-Shāfi'ī had for theirs.[27] The Ottoman government refused to support the project.[28] Nādir Shāh's attack on the position of Shi'ism was an inter-

22 Lambton, *Landlord and Peasant*, p. 131; Sir J. Malcolm, *History of Persia* (London, 1815), II, 440; G. A. Olivier, *Voyage dans l'Empire Othoman, l'Egypte et la Perse* (Paris, 1802), III, 219.

23 Lockhart, *op. cit.*, p. 99.

24 George Forster, *A Journey from Bengal to England* (London, 1798), II, 238.

25 Malcolm, *op. cit.*, II, 105.

26 An earthquake had occurred in Tabriz, the air of Isfahan was filled with a mysterious red dust, and catastrophe was predicted by the astrologers (see Iṣfahānī, *op. cit.*, p. 142).

27 Lockhart, *op. cit.*, p. 140.

28 On October 10, 1743, Sunni ulama from Balkh, Qandahar, and other parts of Iran deposited in the treasury of the shrine at Najaf a document to the effect that the Iranian nation had renounced Shi'ism on the accession of Nādir

lude of no lasting significance.[29] Whether or not it caused a further reaction, this time in favor of the ulama, they survived as the religious class of the nation, however depleted and impoverished.

The Zands and tribal conflict (1163/1750–1211/1795)

Between the death of Nādir Shāh and the establishment of the Qajar dynasty, only the brief reigns of Karīm Khān Zand (1163/1750–1193/1779) and his immediate successors present any element of order. Their administration, centered in Shiraz, provided again for a limited functioning of the ulama in public life. The shaykh ul-Islām of Shiraz, appointed directly by the ruler, again controlled shar' jurisdiction, though this was apparently more restricted in its scope than 'urf.[30] Personal judgment exercised by the ruler was in any case common. But the Shi'i nature of Zand rule was marked. Each of the twelve districts of Shiraz was held to be presided over by one of the Twelve Imams, who was formally commemorated every Thursday evening.[31] Karīm Khān built the Imāmzāda of Mīr Ḥamza[32] and repaired that of Shāh Chirāgh, a much venerated place of pilgrimage.[33] He built and endowed the madrasa named after him, the Madrasa-yi Khān, and was building another when he died.[34] Thus he established himself as a pious believer and anticipated the gifts made to shrines by the Qajars as an outward sign of religiosity. Yet the Zands had no ultimate religious sanction and sought none, their power being based on a coalition of tribes of Fars and the Zagros.

Indeed, the struggles among Afshars, Zands, and Qajars, lasting

---

Shāh, and that the Ottoman government had been informed of this but had rejected the proposal for a fifth orthodox school (see Olivier, *op. cit.*, III, 244).

29 On his death, his army immediately divided itself into Sunni and Shi'i, and the Sunnis, seeing themselves outnumbered, withdrew to Qandahar (see report of Guillaume, French consul in Baghdad, in A. Guillou, "Les Dynasties Musulmanes de la Perse," in *Revista del Instituto de Estudios Islámicos en Madrid* [Madrid, 1959–1960], p. 142).

30 William Francklin, *Observations Made on a Tour from Bengal to Persia in the Years 1786–1787* (London, 1790), pp. 131, 183.

31 *Ibid.*, p. 199. Evidently this custom was continued at least into early Qajar times (see E. Scott Waring, *A Tour to Sheeraz, by the Route of Kazroon and Feerozabad* [London, 1807], p. 64).

32 J. B. Fraser, *An Historical and Descriptive Account of Persia from the Earliest Ages to the Present Time* (Edinburgh, 1834), p. 265.

33 Francklin, *op. cit.*, p. 77; Furṣat Shīrāzī, *Āthār-i 'Ajam* (Tehran, 1314 Q/1896–1897), p. 448.

34 Francklin, *op. cit.*, pp. 63, 66. Karīm Khān's campaign in Arab Iraq was probably motivated by religious considerations—a desire to bring the shrines (*'atabāt*) under Shi'i rule (see Olivier, *op. cit.*, III, 335).

from the death of Karīm Khān until the establishment by Āghā Muḥammad Khān of Qajar supremacy in 1779, were chiefly a contest among tribal factions and alliances. As Ḥājjī Ibrāhīm Khān, who showed his own indifference by transferring his loyalties from the Zand, Luṭf ʻAlī Khān, to Āghā Muḥammad Khān Qājār, remarked to Malcolm: "None . . . except some plundering soldiers cared whether a Zund or a Kujur was upon the throne."[35] This elevation of the tribal element to the position of arbitrator between contestants for the throne, necessarily excluded any urban participation, and the ulama were essentially urban in position and influence; instances of contact between them and the tribes are extremely rare. Although certain happenings in the struggle among the Zands, the Afshars, and the Qajars were of a nature to arouse a reaction on the part of the ulama, they did not represent a constant attitude of any of the contestants. Shāhrukh the Afshar (1748–1795) had aroused the opposition of the ulama of Mashhad, one of whom, Sayyid Muḥammad Mujtahid, himself of Safavid descent, had ruled for forty days as Sulaymān II.[36] The sons of Shāhrukh, Naṣrullāh Mīrzā and Nādir Mīrzā, despoiled the shrine in Mashhad of its treasury and melted down the golden railings enclosing the tomb of the Imam to pay their soldiery.[37] One of the Zands, Zakī Khān, was responsible for the murder of an aged and venerable sayyid in Yazdikhvāst.[38]

The struggles that took place did so without any profession of religious motivation and without any participation by the religious classes. Although during this period the ulama were not influencing the course of events in Iran, they were engaged, chiefly at the shrines in Arab Iraq, in developments of a different nature.

DOCTRINAL REASSERTION

Controversy against Akhbārism

The fall of the Safavid dynasty had led to an emigration of ulama to the ʻatabāt.[39] Their concentration there failed to produce any immediate prospering of theology or of jurisprudence. Of the mujtahids most prominent in the interregnum—Mullā Ismāʻīl

35 Malcolm, *op. cit.*, II, 183.

36 Emineh Pakravan, *Agha Mohammad Ghadjar* (Tehran, 1953), p. 192; Olivier, *op. cit.*, III, 268.

37 Malcolm, *op. cit.*, II, 217; Forster, *op. cit.*, II, 152–153.

38 Francklin, *op. cit.*, p. 319.

39 In some cases, the ulama after leaving Isfahan stayed in Hamadan, Kir-

Khājū'ī Iṣfahānī (d.1173/1758), Muḥammad Rafī' Gīlānī (*fl.* late eighteenth century), Āqā Muḥammad Bīdābādī (d. 1197/1783),[40] and Shaykh Yūsuf Baḥrānī (d. 1186/1772)—only the last produced a work that attained any fame: the *Kashkūl*.[41] Until the advent of Āqā Muḥammad Bāqir Bihbihānī (1117/1705–1208/1803),[42] the Akhbārī school, one denying the very function of the mujtahid, dominated the 'atabāt. The whole basis of Shi'i jurisprudence stood under discussion.

It was Bihbihānī who put an end to the supremacy of the Akhbārīs, and in so doing introduced a renewal of Shi'i religious thought and defined with greater clarity the functions and duty of the mujtahid. He established the Uṣūlī position, which asserted the legitimacy of the functions of mujtahid, as the dominant one in Shi'i Islam, attempted to repress Sufism,[43] taught and inspired a large number of mujtahids who attained great influence in Iran in the reign of Fatḥ 'Alī Shāh (1797–1834), and in his own person vigorously asserted the functions of mujtahid, claiming "enjoining good and prohibiting evil" to be his peculiar duty.[44] The principles of fiqh he established were, with later modifications made by Shaykh Murtaḍā Anṣārī 1216/1801), those in application throughout the Qajar period.[45] Thus he amply deserved the title of *mujaddid*, "renewer," bestowed on him in accordance with the belief that each century of the Islamic era is heralded by the appearance of an exponent who strengthens the faith and supplies instruction and inspiration for the new century.[46]

Born in Isfahan in 1117/1705,[47] Bihbihānī emigrated to Karbala in his early youth, where he studied under his father, Mullā Muḥammad Akmal. He was reputedly dissuaded from leaving Karbala at the end of his studies by the appearance of the Imam

---

manshah and other towns of western Iran before continuing to Iraq, for example, Ṣadr ud-Dīn Qumī (see *RJ*, p. 232).

40 See the introduction by 'Abbās Iqbāl to his brief biography of "Ḥujjat ul-Islām Ḥājj Sayyid Muḥammad Bāqir Shaftī," in *Yādgār*, V (1327 Sh/1948–1949), 28.

41 For an account of his life see *Q'U*, p. 196. His *Kashkūl* was in imitation of the celebrated work of the same title by Shaykh Bahā'ī (d. 1621).

42 Accounts of Bihbihānī are given in *Q'U*, pp. 147–152, and *RJ*, pp. 122–124.

43 One of his titles was *ṣūfīkush* (Sufi-killer).

44 *al amr bi-l-ma'rūf wa-n-nahy 'an il-munkar*. A constant theme of the Quran (see, for example, 3:104; 7:157; 9:67).

45 See Bīdābādī, *op. cit.*, I, 224.

46 *Q'U*, p. 152; *RJ*, p. 122.

47 In 1118/1706–1707, according to *Q'U*.

Ḥusayn in a dream, instructing him to stay. The implication is clear: his task was to strengthen the faith of the Imam in the place where he had met his martyrdom. His enemies in controversy, the Akhbārīs, were so assured in their dominance that anyone carrying with him books of Uṣūlī fiqh was obliged to cover them up for fear of provoking attack.[48] Yet ultimately Bihbihānī was able to denounce the Akhbārīs as infidels, and when he died in 1208/1803, hardly a trace of their former dominance remained. When Mīrzā Muḥammad the Akhbārī was exiled from Iran to the 'atabāt in the 1820's,[49] he found himself isolated.

Although the Akhbārī school had been founded earlier by Shaykh Muḥammad Sharīf Astarābādī (d. 1033/1624), it is significant that the period of its greatest influence was when the ulama were excluded from participation in the affairs of a Shi'i state, namely the interregnum between Safavid and Qajar rule. Its whole tendency was to deny the function of the mujtahid and to restrict the role of the ulama, both doctrinally and practically. Ijtihād was considered an innovation in Shi'ism, dating from the time of al-Kulaynī (d. 329/941);[50] and the mujtahids were accused of adopting Sunnite positions of rationalistic, Hanafi type. Total precedence was given to *naql* (transmitted doctrine) over *'aql* (exertion of the reason), and the heavy reliance placed on the sunnat of the Prophet and the Imams led to the ulama becoming mere traditionalists, and to the simple division of the traditions themselves into two classes: *ṣaḥīḥ* (sound) and *ḍa'īf* (weak). Rather than the believers consisting of mujtahids and muqallids, all believers should be muqallid to the Imams.[51]

The means employed by Bihbihānī against the Akhbārīs were varied, and on occasion the controversy led even to violence. His pronunciation of takfīr seems almost inevitably to have implied violence. Shaykh Ja'far Najafī, one of his pupils, records that Bihbihānī was constantly accompanied by a number of *mīrghaḍab*'s

48 *RJ*, p. 123.

49 See below, p. 65.

50 See *Dānishnāma-yi Shāhī* of Muḥammad Amīn Akhbārī, son of Muḥammad Sharīf and principal theologian of Akhbārism, quoted in *RJ*, p. 33. In the period of the Lesser Occultation, the method of the Akhbārīs in fiqh was that followed by all the Shi'is. For an account of his life see Mīrzā Muḥammad 'Alī Kashmīrī, *Nujūm us-Samā* (Lucknow, 1303 Q/1885–1886), p. 41. His father's *al-Fawā'id al-Madanīyya* was answered by Bihbihānī with his *Fawā'id al-Uṣūlīyya* (see *RJ*, p. 359).

51 Thirty points of difference are listed by Khvānsārī (*RJ*, p. 36). Another summary is given by Scarcia in "Intorno alle Controversie," pp. 244–245.

(executors of corporal and capital punishment).[52] The doctrinal consequences of the controversy were important: Shaykh Ja'far's *Kashf al-Ghiṭā' 'an Mubhamāt ash-Sharī'at al-Ghurrā* (*Unveiling of Obscurities Concerning the Refulgent Divine Law*),[53] which was, in intention, partly a refutation of Akhbārism, became one of the most important works on fiqh of the whole Qajar period.

Although controversy between Akhbārīs and Uṣūlīs continued in Iran in the reign of Fatḥ 'Alī Shāh, and although the grotesque incident of Tsitsianov's head[54] lent the Akhbārīs a brief renewal of prominence, their defeat in the 'atabāt was complete and probably inevitable. The institution of the mujtahid provided for a greater flexibility of doctrine and a living, continuous leadership of the believers. Scarcia has suggested a typological contrast between Akhbārīs and Uṣūlīs: the former nonsystematic, dominated by purely doctrinal considerations; the latter institutional and organized, and as such bound to prevail.[55] That such a clear contrast existed shows that Shi'ism, at the end of the twelfth Hijri century, was undergoing a period of differentiation and definition. Neither the Akhbārī nor the Uṣūlī position was new, but the bitterness of the controversy, ending in a triumph for the mujtahids, established a clearer concept of orthodoxy, centered on and expounded by the ulama. To regard the controversy as exclusively a struggle for leadership of the community or as exclusively doctrinal would be wrong: it concerned both the very nature of that leadership and its doctrinal basis. Settlement in favor of the Uṣūlīs enabled the institution of mujtahid to survive and to lead the community in the period of Qajar rule.

Conflict with Sufism

Bihbihānī's other target, the Sufis, had suffered from similar insecurity in Safavid times. His efforts against them did not achieve so definitive a success as his attacks on the Akhbārīs. This was so partly because mysticism and theology—attachment to the esoteric and attachment to the Law—represent two constant and comple-

[52] *Q'U*, p. 148.

[53] See *RJ*, p. 151. Āqā Sayyid Muḥammad Ṭabāṭabā'ī, another pupil of Bihbihānī, also wrote a refutation of the Akhbārīs (*RJ*, p. 659). See also Kashmīrī, *op. cit.*, p. 342.

[54] See below, p. 65.

[55] Scarcia, *op. cit.*, p. 223.

mentary forms of expression of the Islamic faith, despite the frequent reciprocal hostility of their adherents. While Ghazzālī succeeded to a large extent in creating a synthesis of mysticism and theology for Sunni Islam, in Shi'ism the issue was never fully resolved. The esoterism of Sufism clashed with the monopoly of true esoteric knowledge held by the Imams, who alone might legitimately be regarded as guides to spiritual truth.

Nonetheless, Sufi orders with a Shi'i loyalty arose, the most important among them being that founded by Shāh Ni'matullāh Valī (d. 834/1431).[56] This order began to gain strength in Iran toward the end of the eighteenth century and, like Akhbārism, to pose a threat to the position of the ulama. The Ni'matullāhī reply to the exponents of the Law took the form of a counterattack, one denying the pretensions of the ulama and claiming that the Sufis were themselves the true exponents of Shi'ism, for Sufi doctrine was identical with the esoteric knowledge of the Imams. "The Sufis are the true Shi'a: the Path (*ṭarīqat*) of the Immaculate Imams is outwardly the *sharī'at* (Law) of the Imami Shi'a, but inwardly one of the divine truths of Sufism."[57] At the same time, the validity of fatvās delivered by mujtahids was denied on the basis of a tradition of the Imam 'Alī. Their validity was made doubtful by the contradictions existing among them; for God, the Prophet, and the Quran are all one, and similarly the judgment given by the ulama should be one. Moreover, dispute (*ikhtilāf*) is forbidden. Finally, Islam, being perfect, stands in no need of the ulama; and if it were not perfect, this would imply God's need of assistance in perfecting it, or the Prophet's negligence in propagating it, both of which implications constitute a proof of disbelief.[58] Any "interference" of the ulama in worldly affairs (one liable to be harmful for Sufis) was represented as a danger to the faith itself.[59] Thus Sufism, in its Ni'matullāhī form, presented a direct challenge,

56 See Jean Aubin, *Matériaux pour la biographie de Shah Ni'matollāh Walī Kermānī*, Bibliothèque Iranienne, Vol. VII (Paris, 1956), and Richard Gramlich, *Die schiitischen Derwischorden Persiens, erster Teil: die Affiliationen*, *AKM*, XXXVI, 1 (Wiesbaden, 1965), p. 29.

57 Ma'ṣūm 'Alī Shāh (Nā'ib uṣ-Ṣadr), *Ṭarā'iq ul-Ḥaqā'iq* (Tehran, 1318 Q/1900–1901), I, 104.

58 *Ibid.*, p. 23.

59 "The *fuqahā* are the trusted ones of the Prophet, if they do not intervene in worldly affairs. The Prophet was asked, 'And if they do?' He replied, 'They follow the king, and if they do that, then protect your faith from them' " (quoted by Zayn ul-'Ābidīn Shīrvānī in *Būstān us-Siyāḥa* [Tehran, 1315 Q/1897–1898], p. 35).

based on Shi'ism, to the authority of the mujtahids. In an attempt to meet the challenge, many ulama of the early thirteenth Hijri century wrote works in refutation of Sufism.[60]

A more immediate threat was at times presented by the emergence of a Sufi capable of attracting religious loyalty away from the ulama, thus provoking conflict. One such conflict took place in a long-established center of Sufism, Kirman, five years before the coronation of Āghā Muḥammad Khān in 1785. During the Safavid period, many dervishes had fled to India, particularly the Deccan, and in the interregnum the direction of the traffic was reversed.[61] A certain Ni'matullāhī dervish by the name of Ma'ṣūm 'Alī Shāh had come to Shiraz in the time of Karīm Khān Zand and soon succeeded in gaining a large following.[62] At the urging of the ulama he was banished to a village near Isfahan. After the death of Karīm Khān, Ma'ṣūm 'Alī Shāh moved to Isfahan itself, and together with Fayyāḍ 'Alī Shāh, his chief disciple, again attracted many followers. 'Alī Murād Khān Zand, at the instigation of the ulama, gave orders that the noses and ears of the dervishes be cut off.[63] The son of Fayyāḍ 'Alī Shāh, Nūr 'Alī Shāh, together with another dervish, Mushtāq 'Alī Shāh, fled to Kirman.[64] Here they attracted a large following, whose size aroused the envy of the ulama. Every Thursday evening, thousands would accompany their pilgrimage to the shrine of Shah Ni'matullāh Valī at Māhān.[65] The influence attained by the dervishes was such that the application of the sharī'at, and hence the position of the mujtahids, seemed in danger.[66] On Ramaḍān 21, 1205/May 24, 1790, Mullā 'Abdullāh Mujtahid had Mushtāq 'Alī Shāh put to death.[67] Nūr 'Alī Shāh fled, first to Isfahan and then by way of Kirmanshah to Iraq. He died in Mosul, in 1215/1800–1801, probably poisoned

---

60 E.g., Muḥammad 'Alī Bihbihānī, from whose ugly and violent treatise entitled *Khayrātīya* extracts are given in Sa'īd Nafīsī's *Tārīkh-i Ijtimā'ī va Siyāsī-yi Īrān dar Daura-yi Mu'āṣir* (Tehran, 1344 Sh/1965), II, 43–44.

61 See Muḥammad Hāshim Kirmānī, "Tārīkh-i Madhāhib-i Kirmān," in *MM*, I (1335 Sh/1956), 129.

62 For an account of Ma'ṣūm 'Alī Shāh, see Shīrvānī, *op. cit.*, pp. 77–84.

63 Malcolm, *op. cit.*, II, 417–420.

64 Aḥmad 'Alī Khān Vazīrī, *Tārīkh-i Kirmān*, ed. H. Farmānfarmā'īān (Tehran, 1340 Sh/1962), p. 348.

65 Kirmānī, *op. cit.*, p. 130.

66 Vazīrī, *op. cit.*, p. 349.

67 *Ibid.*, p. 350.

by two agents of the rabidly anti-Sufi Muḥammad 'Alī Bihbihānī,[68] the eldest son of Sayyid Muḥammad Bāqir, who at about the same time was responsible for the execution in Kirmanshah of Ma'ṣūm 'Alī Shāh and was later able to persuade Fatḥ 'Alī Shāh to expel all the dervishes from Tehran.[69]

The energy shown by the ulama against the Sufis in the early part of the nineteenth century at any rate preserved the primacy of the exponents of Law over the adherents of the Path. But if violence was not again to characterize so prominently the clash between the ulama and the Sufis, nonetheless the rivalry persisted throughout the century. Further struggles took place in the time of Fatḥ 'Alī Shāh,[70] and the direct involvement of the court and government in the time of his successor, Muḥammad Shāh, gave the old conflict a new dimension of importance.[71] Ṣafī 'Alī Shāh, a Sufi poet of much talent and originality, later in the century found himself confronted with the hostility of the ulama.[72] But the conflict, in its outward forms of expression, was unresolvable. Kirman,[73] Shiraz,[74] and Hamadan continued to be important Ni'matullāhī centers, and instances of members of the ulama adopting Sufism, or even ideally combining *'ilm* (knowledge of the Law) with *'irfān* (gnosis) were not unknown.[75] Nor were the Ni'matullāhīs the only order in Iran: the Dhahabīs, claiming as the first link in their chain of *irshād* (instruction) the Imam 'Alī b. Mūsā ar-Riḍā, recognized only eight Imams and were regarded by the ulama with at least as much hostility as were the Ni'matullāhīs.[76]

68 Nafīsī, *op. cit.*, II, 44; Shīrvānī, *op. cit.*, p. 86; Muḥammad 'Alī Tabrīzī Khiābānī, *Rayḥānat ul-Adab* (Tehran, 1326 Sh/1947–1948), II, 245–247.

69 Gramlich, *op. cit.*, p. 31. The account of Ma'ṣūm 'Alī Shāh's death given by Malcolm (*op. cit.*, II, 421) is somewhat different, but that of Gramlich, based on Ni'matullāhī sources, is to be preferred.

70 Malcolm, *op. cit.*, II, 422; Kirmānī, *op. cit.*, p. 130.

71 See below, pp. 105–108.

72 Safī 'Alī Shāh had composed a commentary in verse on the Quran, an act held to be impious by some of the ulama. See his letter to Ẓahīr ud-Daula in the introduction to his *Dīvān* (Tehran, 1336 Sh/1957–1958), p. 26.

73 Kirmānī, *op. cit.*, p. 130.

74 Shīrāzī, *op. cit.*, pp. 473, 544 n. 1.

75 E.g., Muḥammad Riḍā Hamadānī (see Shīrvānī, *op. cit.*, p. 613) and Sayyid Mihdī Kāẓimī (see Muḥammad Mihdī Kāẓimī, *Aḥsan al-Wadī'a* [Baghdad, 1374 Q/1928–1929], I, 27).

76 See Iḥsānullāh Iṣṭakhrī, "Taṣavvuf-i Dhahabīya," in *MM*, I (1335 Sh/1956), 15 ff.

While the Ni'matullahīs represented an aristocratic order, especially in the latter part of the Qajar period, other orders were closely bound to the guilds. The Mullā Sulṭānī and Gūnābādī orders, the latter an offshoot of the Ni'matullāhīs,[77] included in their ranks many petty traders and artisans. This differentiation within Sufism, no less than the appearance of schools within Shi'i theology, and the extraordinary growth and development of Babism and its successors, is a sign of the remarkable vitality of religious interest in the thirteenth Hijri century.[78] But Sufism, being less organizational in spirit than scholastic orthodoxy, never seriously threatened the position of the ulama, despite its lasting denials of their worth and necessity.

The reassertion and the rise of the Qajars

Thus there occurred, at the turn of the nineteenth century, a surge of Shi'i religious activity marked above all by an assertion of the position and function of mujtahid. That this took place at approximately the same time as the establishment of Qajar power leads to the question of whether there was an interrelation between the two phenomena. Both were in essence restorations: the first of the prominence and cohesiveness of Shi'ism, and the second of the Iranian national state that was to some extent associated with Shi'ism. Scarcia has compared Bihbihānī's attacks on Sufism and on the Akhbārīs with the persecution of Sunnis by Shah Ismā'īl.[79] The rise of the Qajars, however, merely coincided with a reformulation of Shi'i orthodoxy; the Qajars did not participate in or depend on it. The most that can be said is that, with varying de-

77 Shīrāzī, *op. cit.*, p. 544 n. 1.

78 W. Ivanow (*Ismaili Literature: A Bibliographical Survey* [Tehran, 1963], pp. 183–184) suggests that not only was Sufism in post-Timurid Iran opposed to Ithnā'asharī Shi'ism, but also leaned increasingly to extremist Shi'ism, and in particular to Ismā'īlism. In the Qajar period, contacts continued. Abū-l-Ḥasan Khān, governor of Kirman under the Zands and forty-second Imam of the Nizārī Ismā'īlīs, was one of the *murīds* of Mushtāq 'Alī Shāh (see Ma'ṣūm 'Alī Shāh, *op. cit.*, III, 84–85). Maḥallāt, the most important post-Mongol Ismā'īlī center in Iran, was also a Sufi stronghold (see Ṣafī 'Alī Shāh, *op. cit.*, introduction, p. 30). There are also traces of Sufi involvement in the rising of Āqā Khān Maḥallātī and his emigration to India (see A. J. Chunara, *Noorum Mubin, or the Sacred Cord of God: A Glorious History of Ismaili Imams* [Bombay, 1951], pp. 414 ff. [in Gujarati]).

79 G. Scarcia, "Kerman 1905: La 'guerra' tra Šeiḫī e Bālāsarī," in *Annali del Istituto Universitario Orientale di Napoli*, XIII (1963), 199.

grees of success, they attempted to identify themselves with it, at different times for different reasons. The Qajar dynasty was tribal in its origins; whereas the Safavids claimed descent from the Imams, the Qajars could point only to the Mongols for the origin of their line.[80] They raised no religious claims, even if they inherited, consciously or unconsciously, many of the assumptions concerning regal power implicit in the Safavid monarchy. Under the Safavids, a close alliance of the state and the religious body had existed, with the former as the dominant partner; under the Qajars, there would never be more than an uneasy and fitful coalition. The relative security achieved by the early Qajars, combined with a revival of urban life, commerce, and administration, provided the necessary setting for the activities of the ulama: to this extent, the governmental aspect of the national revival influenced the religious one. But, until the latter part of the nineteenth century, we never see more than a series of contacts between the ruler and the ulama: contacts undertaken by the ruler to provide a justification for his rule, or for reasons of personal piety; undertaken by the ulama to assert their own prerogatives or to lessen those of the state. These relations between state and ulama grow in importance and volume throughout the period.

Āghā Muḥammad Khān Qājār and the ulama

Āghā Muḥammad Khān Qājār at his coronation in 1200/1785, although refusing the crown of Nādir Shāh, with its four plumes symbolic of Afghanistan, India, Turkistan, and Iran, "consented to gird on the royal sabre, which was consecrated at the tomb of the holy founder of the Suffavean family; and he became, by that act, pledged to employ the sacred weapon in the defence and support of the Sheah faith."[81] Thus explicit was the restoration and the proclamation of the Shi'i character of the new dynasty. In the reign of Āghā Muḥammad Khān we see the beginning of a connection between the ulama and the affairs of state and the monarchy; but its extent was limited by the personal disposition of the monarch and the conditions of his reign.

[80] The Qajar genealogy starts traditionally with Qarāchār Nūyān, fourth ancestor of Timur Lang (see Jalāl ud-Dīn Mīrzā, *Nāma-yi Khusruvān* [Bombay, n.d.], pt. 4, p. 3; I'timād us-Salṭana, *Mir'āt ul-Buldān-i Nāṣirī* [Tehran, 1294 Q/1877], I, 50).

[81] Malcolm, *op. cit.*, II, 287–288.

In the complex psychology of Āghā Muḥammad Khān, there appears to have been an element of intense religiosity, tending to obscurantism.[82] He is reputed to have said that he once saw a man dressed in the habit of the ulama; their eyes met; and only after being pierced by that glance did he feel himself truly Shah and capable of fulfilling the tasks of monarchy.[83] Generally he refrained from ordering executions on Thursday evenings (a time worthy of respect because of its proximity to Friday), and the story of the elaborate stratagem whereby he avoided breaking an oath taken on the Quran, is well known.[84] He regularly performed prayer and fasted; when the annalist Riḍā Qulī Khān claims that his approaching the shrine at Mashhad on foot was not merely an imitation of Safavid practice but a genuine expression of piety, it is probably with justice.[85] He strictly prohibited wine-drinking; he had Bābā Khān (later Fatḥ 'Alī Shāh) enforce the same ban in Shiraz, a city accustomed to a less strict moral regime under the Zands.[86] When this prohibition came indirectly to encourage the use of opium, he invited the mullās to preach against narcotics also.[87] At a critical point in his campaign against Luṭf 'Alī Khān Zand, he gave orders for the construction of a golden tomb-railing for the shrine at Najaf.[88] Later he dispatched the shaykh ul-Islām of Isfahan to supervise the work of gilding the dome at Karbala.[89] When his mother went on pilgrimage to the 'atabāt, he had the remains of his ancestors disinterred from Asterabad and sent with her for reburial at Najaf.[90]

Despite these many signs of piety, no close relations bound him to the ulama, even though he had been born in the house of a mullā, Āqā Sayyid Mufīd.[91] He was generous to the ulama, and on

82 See Pakravan, *op. cit.*, p. 14.

83 *RSN*, IX, 281.

84 Āghā Muḥammad Khān had sworn not to detain Ja'far Qulī Khān, a Zand prince, beyond one night in Tehran; the oath was technically kept, for his dead body was removed from the city before night fell for the second time (Malcolm, *op. cit.*, II, 299, 304).

85 *RSN*, IX, 281.

86 Sir J. Malcolm, *Sketches of Persia* (London, 1845), p. 60.

87 Olivier, *op. cit.*, III, 157.

88 Lisān ul-Mulk, Mīrzā Muḥammad Taqī Sipihr, *Nāsikh ut-Tavārīkh* (Tehran, n.d.), I, 43.

89 Guillou, *op. cit.*, p. 142; 'Imād ud-Dīn Iṣfahānī, *Tārīkh-i Jughrāfīyā'ī-yi Karbalā-yi Mu'allā* (Tehran, 1326 Sh/1947), p. 113; Brydges, *op. cit.*, p. 74 n. 1.

90 *MN*, III, 54.

91 *RSN*, IX, 85.

occasion accepted their intercession, but by no means always.[92] The intervention of Mīrzā Mihdī Mujtahid (himself to be martyred later by Nādir Mīrzā) on behalf of Shāhrukh the Afshār was unsuccessful.[93] Nor was Āghā Muḥammad Khān's respect for the ulama constant: the memory of a slight of many years' standing had him rip open the belly of a mullā in Shiraz.[94] Some idea of the contempt in which many of the ulama, for their part, held the monarch is given by the story of Mullā Muḥammad 'Alī Muẓaffar Iṣfahānī, who, despite the awesome reputation of Āghā Muḥammad Khān, persisted in washing his clothes when the monarch came to visit him.[95]

The only one of the ulama, apart from Mullā Muḥammad Ḥusayn Māzandarānī Mullābāshī, with whom Āghā Muḥammad Khān had any personal relationship seems to have been Mīrzā Muḥammad 'Alī Bihbihānī.[96] According to the *Qiṣaṣ ul-'Ulamā'*,[97] the Shah encountered him at Shāh 'Abd ul-'Aẓīm, the popular shrine to the south of Tehran, and remembering some mark of disrespect Bihbihānī had shown him in the presence of Karīm Khān Zand, forbade him to enter Tehran. But on seeing him prepare to leave in the direction of Tehran, in defiance of his order, the Shah decided to make his peace with him. Another account gives the more probable version that Āghā Muḥammad Khān, while engaged in his Azerbayjan campaign of 1205/1791, sent Mullā Muḥammad Ḥusayn to meet Bihbihānī at Kirmanshah and to instruct him to go to Tehran.[98] Since we later find Bihbihānī in Kirmanshah again, his stay in the capital cannot have been permanent.[99]

In general, the initial tribal basis of Qajar rule was too marked in the reign of Āghā Muḥammad Khān for the ulama to gain any great influence. With the ruler himself performing much of the business of state, the administration consisted of only two main

92 Shaykh Muḥammad Aḥsā'ī was able to ransom some of the women of Kirman (Malcolm, *History of Persia*, II, 310).

93 *NT*, I, 41.

94 'Abdullāh Mustaufī, *Tārīkh-i Idārī va Ijtimā'ī-yi Daura-yi Qājārīya yā Sharḥ-i Zindagānī-yi Man* (Tehran, 1321 Sh/1942–1943), I, 6 n. 1.

95 Bīdābādī, *op. cit.*, I, 70.

96 *RSN*, IX, 241. Muḥammad Bāqir Bihbihānī himself seems to have had no relations with potentates other than Hidāyatullāh Khān, ruler of Gilan and a contemporary of Ṣādiq Khān Zand, but neither a Zand, nor a Qajar, nor an Afshar (*ibid.*, p. 204).

97 *Q'U*, p. 149.

98 *MN*, III, 54.

99 See above, p. 39.

officials: the *mustaufī* (treasurer) and the *lashkarnavīs* (clerk of the army).[100] The khans surrounding the court were largely illiterate,[101] and the army was the most favored section of the population.[102] Although in accordance with tradition, the monarch appointed the imām jum'a and shaykh ul-Islām of each town, the ulama for the most part played no great role in affairs.[103] The religious classes in the country had, however, again become numerous,[104] and against the background of security and the reestablishment of a Shi'i dynasty, were, in the reign of Āghā Muḥammad Khān's successor, to dominate events almost as completely as they had done in the time of Shāh Sulṭān Ḥusayn. The legacy of Sayyid Muḥammad Bāqir Bihbihānī was to come to fruition.

100 Mustaufī, *op. cit.*, I, 11; A. K. S. Lambton, "Persian Society under the Qajars," *JRCAS*, XLVIII (1961), 132.

101 Mustaufī, *op. cit.*, I, 11.

102 Malcolm, *op. cit.*, II, 309.

103 H. Dunlop, *Perzië: Voorheeren en Thans* (Haarlem, 1912), p. 426.

104 Olivier, *op. cit.*, III, 163.

III

The Clerical Policy of Fatḥ 'Alī Shāh

The reign of Fatḥ 'Alī Shāh (1797–1834) witnessed an expansion of court and administrative life, and the intervention in public life of many prominent ulama, either themselves pupils of Bihbihānī, such as Mīrzā Abū-l-Qāsim Qumī and Sayyid Mihdī Baḥr ul-'Ulūm, or of those he had taught, such as Mullā 'Alī Nūrī and Ḥājjī Muḥammad Ibrāhīm Kalbāsī. Throughout the reign, their influence on events was extensive, and the solicitude of the monarch in cultivating their goodwill encouraged their assertiveness. Their intercession on behalf of rebellious princes or the oppressed inhabitants of a province was frequent and generally successful. The religious character of Fatḥ 'Alī Shāh's rule was marked. Mosques were built and shrines embellished. Works of theology were often commissioned by the monarch or dedicated to him. Ulama were encouraged to settle in various parts of the country, especially the capital, to be frequently visited by the Shah and to be given assurances of his devotion and submission. The princes and ministers used the behavior of the Shah as a model; they likewise sought the favor of the ulama, trying to attract them to their seats of government, or ensuring that the ulama knew of their piety.

Thus there existed the paradoxical situation of an actual tyranny professing submission to a class that largely scorned the pious intentions expressed. Precisely when the tyranny and the submission came into open contradiction, the ulama would force the proclaimed devotion to become a real, if at times somewhat reluctant, acceptance of their ultimate supremacy. Thus it was with the expulsion of numerous provincial governors from their seats of government and the declaration of the Second Perso-Russian War. Nonetheless the state was not a power to despise; and the fact that it had chosen to patronize the ulama inevitably gave it some influence among them. This, apart from the varying religious interests of the sovereign and his governors and ministers, tended outwardly to give the monarchy almost the role of a de facto arbiter in sectarian disputes. This we see in the final stages of the conflict between the Akhbārīs and the Uṣūlīs, the succeeding one between Shaykhīs and Bālāsarīs, and the continuing persecution of Sufis. Intense religious interest on the one hand, and the search for religious allies in political affairs and political allies in religious affairs on the other, brought about a close interaction between the two spheres of events.

At the very outset of his reign, Fatḥ 'Alī Shāh sought to establish his reputation among the ulama as that of a pious sovereign by embellishing and repairing shrines and constructing mosques. In the second year of his reign alone, more than 100,000 tomans was spent on the shrines of Iraq, Qum, and Shāh Chirāgh in Shiraz.[1] In accordance with a vow made before succeeding to the throne, he paid special attention to Qum[2] where resided a large number of ulama and in particular Mīrzā Abū-l-Qāsim (Fāḍil-i Qumī), a mujtahid in whom he placed great trust.[3] In Rabī' ul-Avval, 1214/ August, 1799, shortly after returning from his first campaign against Nādir Mīrzā in Mashhad, he allotted money for repairing the dome of the shrine of Fāṭima in Qum and for erecting a new

1 *MN*, III, 69. The figure of 100,000 tomans occurs so frequently in connection with endowments and similar expenditure that it is probably no more than a general indication of a large amount.

2 Entitled by him Dār ul-Īmān (the Realm of Faith). See 'Abdullāh Mustaufī, *Tārīkh-i Idārī va Ijtimā'ī-yi Daura-yi Qājāriya ya Sharḥ-i Zindagānī-yi Man* (Tehran, 1321 Sh/1942–1943), I, 30.

3 J. Morier, *A Journey through Persia, Armenia and Asia Minor to Constantinople* (London, 1812), p. 180; *RSN*, X, 135.

golden grill around the tomb.[4] The shrine was also embellished with a golden gate.[5] Further repairs were carried out in 1249/1833, when the *ayvān* (archway) was covered with marble and tile-work.[6] The inhabitants of Qum were exempted from taxation, and a large madrasa, known as the Fayḍīya, was built near the shrine.[7] Later another madrasa was erected and endowed.[8] The mosque of Imam Ḥasan al-'Askarī was repaired, and a *dar ush-shifā* (dispensary), caravanserais, and *hammām*'s (bathhouses) were built.[9] The treasury of the shrine was constantly enriched by gifts from the king himself and members of the royal family.[10] From Sha'bān, 1213/January, 1799 onward, he visited Qum almost yearly, approaching the shrine on foot as a sign of becoming humility.[11] While Āghā Muḥammad Khān's body had been sent to Najaf for burial, Fatḥ 'Alī Shāh, by contrast, toward the end of his life prepared a tomb for himself in Qum.[12] Such constant devotion can hardly have failed to produce a favorable impression the ulama.[13]

Fatḥ 'Alī Shāh likewise regarded Mashhad—a city sanctified by the shrine of the Imam Riḍā—with respect. Twice the ulama were able to dissuade him from attacking the town, which was still occupied by Nādir Mīrzā Afshār. On the first occasion, he was reminded of the respect shown to Mashhad by the Safavid monarchs, Shāh Ṭahmāsp and Shāh 'Abbās, and urged to follow their example.[14] At his second attempt to dislodge Nādir Mīrzā, he was met by Mīrzā Mihdī Mujtahid, who requested him to lift the siege and refrain from bombarding the town; for, were he not to do so, "what difference would there be between him and the Uzbeks [who constantly raided Khurasan]?" So telling an argument was not lost on Fatḥ 'Alī Shāh; he explained that the sole purpose of his campaign

4 *NT*, I, 57.
5 Sir Harford Jones Brydges, *The Dynasty of the Kajars* (London, 1833), p. 70.
6 *MN*, III, 157; *NT*, I, 255.
7 Morier, *op. cit.*, p. 180; *NT*, I, 70.
8 Brydges, *op. cit.*, p. 124.
9 *NT*, I, 70; Morier, *op. cit.*, p. 180.
10 J. Morier, *A Second Journey through Persia, Armenia and Asia Minor to Constantinople* (London, 1818), p. 165. Thus the news of an Iranian victory in the Second Perso-Russian War impelled Muḥammad 'Alī Mīrzā to present the shrine with a jewel-encrusted candelabra (*NT*, I, 216).
11 *NT*, I, 70, 255; *MN*, III, 106, 112, 120, 144, 149, etc.; Mustaufī, *op. cit.*, I, 35.
12 *NT*, I, 260. A photograph of his tomb is contained in A. Godard, *The Art of Iran* (New York, 1965), pl. 168.
13 Morier, *op. cit.*, p. 166.
14 *RSN*, IX, 351.

was to punish Nādir Mīrzā for the disrespect he had shown to the shrine and the ulama.[15]After eventually taking the town, he undertook repairs on the shrine of the Imam Riḍā[16] and went there on pilgrimage in 1234/1817.[17] Among the improvements were a new courtyard and a jewelled door costing 10,000 tomans.[18] He also donated golden candelabra for the interior of the shrine.[19] Other shrines within Iran to the improvement of which Fatḥ 'Alī Shāh contributed were those of Shāh 'Abd ul-'Azīm and Imāmzāda Sayyid Aḥmad, where he was a constant pilgrim.[20]

He made numerous contributions to the shrines of Arab Iraq. Initially he had the domes at Karbala and Kāẓimayn repaired as an act of thanksgiving after his defeat of Ja'far Qulī Khān Zand.[21] The gilding of the dome at Karbala by Āghā Muḥammad Khān had been so ineffective that it turned black; and Fatḥ 'Alī Shāh decreed that a new one, made entirely of gold bricks, be constructed.[22] A new railing to surround the tomb of Ḥusayn was also given to the shrine at Karbala; and later the minarets were gilded on Fatḥ 'Alī Shāh's orders.[23] Shortly before his death he had a silver railing made for the tomb of 'Abbās b. 'Alī at Karbala.[24] In order that Mecca itself might not be deprived of some token of his munificence, in 1238/1822 he dispatched Mullā 'Alī Muḥammad Kāshānī with a commemorative plaque to be attached to the wall of the Masjid al-Ḥarām.[25]

Apart from providing such liberal and constant proof of his devotion to the holy places of Shi'i Islam, Fatḥ 'Alī Shah also constructed a number of mosques as a further expression of piety. The Masjid-i Jum'a (congregational mosque) in Tehran (also called Masjid-i Shāh), begun by Āghā Muḥammad Khān, was completed.[26] A congregational mosque and adjoining madrasa were

15 *Ibid.*, p. 377; Brydges, *op. cit.*, p. 158.
16 *RSN*, IX, 345; X, 106.
17 *MN*, III, 118.
18 *Ibid.*, p. 121.
19 *Ibid.*, p. 159.
20 *Ibid.*, p. 159; Mustaufī, *op. cit.*, I, 35.
21 R. G. Watson, *A History of Persia from the Beginning of the Nineteenth Century to the Year 1858* (London, 1866), p. 121.
22 Brydges, *op. cit.*, p. 74 n. 1; 'Imād ud-Dīn Ḥusayn Iṣfahānī, *Tārīkh-i Jughrāfīyā'ī-yi Karbalā-yi Mu'allā* (Tehran, 1326 Sh/1947), p. 130.
23 *Ibid.*, pp. 126, 148.
24 *NT*, I, 260; *MN*, III, 158.
25 *NT*, I, 186.
26 *MN*, III, 159.

built in Samnān,[27] and another mosque was started but never finished in Hamadan.[28] In Kashan, the Madrasa-yi Khāqānī was built in the name of the Shah.[29]

Another method whereby the Shah might hope to gain the sympathy of the ulama, or even to influence them, was the regular allotting of sums of money among them and granting other material signs of goodwill. Early in his reign, he appointed as *qāsim uṣ-ṣadaqāt* (distributor of offerings) Mullā Ismā'īl Māzandarānī, among whose duties was the distribution of pensions to deserving members of the religious classes.[30] According to the *Rauḍat uṣ-Ṣafā-yi Nāṣirī*,[31] every year 100,000 tomans in cash and more than 100,000 *kharvār* (a unit of weight equivalent to approximately 300 kilograms) of grants in kind were distributed to sayyids and ulama. Thus for example the Taqavī sayyids of Tehran were supported entirely by the royal bounty.[32] Apart from these regular payments, Fatḥ 'Alī Shāh granted, throughout his reign, marks of favor to various of the ulama. Mirzā Aḥmad Mujtahid, who in the course of his flight from Russian-occupied Tabriz had been plundered by Kurds, was given money and a house in the capital.[33] Ḥājj Mullā Muḥammad Taqī Burghānī received a number of villages near Qazvin as a fief which he later sold for a considerable sum, claiming that as *majhūl ul-mālik* (of unidentified ownership), they were anyhow at his disposal in his capacity of shar' judge.[34] On one of his visits to Isfahan, Fatḥ 'Alī Shāh offered to remit taxation on villages owned by Sayyid Muḥammad Bāqir Shaftī, but the latter refused, ostensibly since the amount would have to be made up by others, more probably because it would have made no difference to his vast wealth.[35] By way of contrast, we may note the case of a sayyid who permitted the Shah to settle all his debts on his behalf.[36]

Not only did Fatḥ 'Alī Shāh have in the distribution of largess a means of showing his devotion to the ulama, but also through

27 *RSN*, IX, 137.

28 Aḥmad Mīrzā 'Aḍud ud-Daula, *Tārīkh-i 'Aḍudī*, ed. Ḥusayn Kūhī Kirmānī (Tehran, 1327 Sh/1948), p. 38.

29 *RSN*, IX, 137.

30 *Ibid.*, p. 345.

31 *Ibid.*, X, 105; see n. 1 above.

32 Mustaufī, *op. cit.*, I, 35.

33 Nādir Mīrzā, *Tārīkh va Jughrāfī-yi Dār us-Salṭana-yi Tabrīz* (Tehran, 1323 Q/1905), p. 118.

34 *Q'U*, p. 20.

35 *Ibid.*, p. 104.

36 Sir William Ouseley, *Travels in Various Countries of the East* (London, 1821), III, 367.

the appointment of shaykh ul-Islāms and imām jum'as and encouraging the settlement of ulama in various parts of the country, he was able to bind himself more closely to them. Some shaykh ul-Islāms had already been appointed by Āghā Muḥammad Khān Qājār; others were appointed by Fatḥ 'Alī Shāh, such as Muḥsin b. Abī-l-Ḥasan Jazā'irī in Shushtar[37] and Mullā 'Abd ul-Aḥad Kazāzī in Kirmanshah.[38] In Tabriz Fatḥ 'Alī Shāh appointed Mirzā Luṭf 'Alī Mujtahid as imām jum'a.[39] On completing the Masjid-i Jum'a of Tehran, he wrote to Mirzā Abū-l-Qāsim Qumī, asking him to recommend a suitable person as imam. He suggested Sayyid Muḥammad Bāqir Shaftī, who was at that time little known; but the sayyid refused to comply with the royal order, despite the persistent urgings of the governor of Isfahan.[40] Here we notice already the marked distaste for involvement with the government and reluctance to act on its behalf shown by the ulama, a natural consequence of the fundamental illegitimacy of the whole apparatus of the state. Their preferred role was rather to mediate between it and others.

In the reign of Fatḥ 'Ali Shāh, the shaykh ul-Islāms, although appointed and paid by the state, were generally chosen in accordance with the wishes of the inhabitants of their areas of jurisdiction, and enjoyed a reputation for strict honesty.[41] The shaykh ul-Islām of Shiraz supplied a proof of his independence in the events of Jumādī ul-Ūlā, 1225/June, 1811, which included the first of the many bread riots to disfigure the period of Qajar rule. The exactions of Nabī Khān, the minister of Fars, had led to a rise in the price of bread. The people in desperation demanded of the shaykh ul-Islām a fatvā proclaiming lawful the killing of Mīrzā Hādī, one of the chief agents of Nabī Khān, and Mīrzā Bāqir Khabbāzbāshī, head of the bakers' guild. The fatvā was granted; and the men whose lives were thus endangered took refuge in the palace of the governor, Ḥusayn 'Alī Mīrzā Farmānfarmā. To appease the population, Nabī Khān had the price of bread immediately lowered, and all bakers publicly bastinadoed.[42]

37 Muḥammad 'Alī Kashmīrī, *Nujūm us-Samā* (Lucknow, 1303 Q/1885–1886), p. 333.

38 *Ibid.*, p. 367.

39 Mihdī Mujtahidī, *Rijāl-i Ādharbāyjān dar 'Aṣr-i Mashrūṭīyat* (Tehran, 1327 Sh/1948–1949), p. 23.

40 *Q'U*, p. 105.

41 Sir J. Malcolm, *A History of Persia* (London, 1815), II, 405.

42 Morier, *op. cit.*, p. 102; and Ouseley, *op. cit.*, II, 209–210. The annual salary

The appointment of ulama to the positions of imām jum'a and shaykh ul-Islām did not, in the reign of Fatḥ 'Alī Shāh, imply any identification with the state, as it was to in the time of Nāṣir ud-Dīn Shāh. Similarly, when ulama were invited to reside in the capital by the Shah, the favor was bestowed not by the Shah, but rather by the ulama who accepted his invitation. Even if some prestige may have been attached to a direct relationship with the monarch, the general purpose of his invitations may be deduced from the tone of a letter addressed to Āqā Sayyid Muḥammad b. Sayyid 'Alī Yazdī, inviting him to come to Tehran, and "bestow upon the generality of believers a thousand varieties of happiness . . . and fill the Masjid-i Jum'a with the pleasing sound of his worship and prayer."[43] His correspondence with Shaykh Aḥmad Aḥsā'ī was even more self-effacing in tone.[44]

Among the ulama invited to reside in Tehran was Mullā Muḥammad 'Alī Jangalī, one of the teachers of Ḥājjī Muḥammad Ṣāliḥ Burghānī, whom Fatḥ 'Alī Shāh met while on a visit to Qazvin.[45] Ḥājji Mullā Muḥammad Ja'far Astarābādī was similarly induced to settle in Tehran, where he was visited by Fatḥ 'Alī Shāh at least once a month.[46] Sayyid Ḥasan Vā'iẓ Shīrāzī, passing through Tehran on his return from a pilgrimage to Mashhad, was invited by the Shah to settle in the capital. With Fatḥ 'Alī Shāh's approval, he converted some of the numerous *takya*'s (centers for the performance of the Shi'i passion play) of Tehran into centers for religious instruction. He then summoned five of his brothers from Shiraz and, keeping two of them to assist him in Tehran, dispatched the other three to Qazvin to found similar centers of instruction.[47] That residence of the ulama in the capital was a mark of favor shown to the monarch is indicated by the fact that disagreement with him, or displeasure at his actions, was signaled

---

of the shaykh ul-Islām of Shiraz was 2,000 tomans (see Malcolm, *op. cit.*, II, 472). E. Scott Waring (*A Tour to Sheeraz, by the Route of Kazroon and Feerozabad* [London, 1807], p. 74) gives a favorable picture of his impartiality. On the shaykh ul-Islāms of Shiraz see also Furṣat Shīrāzī, *Āthār-ī 'Ajam* (Tehran, 1314 Q/1896–1897), p. 511.

43 Muḥammad Ṣādiq Ḥusaynī, *Makhzan ul-Inshā* (Tabriz, 1274 Q/1857), p. 134 (margin).

44 See below, p. 67.

45 *Q'U*, p. 21.

46 Muḥammad 'Alī Mu'allim Bīdābādī, *Makārim ul-Āthār dar Aḥvāl-i Rijāl-i Daura-yi Qājār* (Isfahan, 1337 Sh/1958), I, 85.

47 Muḥammad Ḥusayn Ādamīyat, *Dānishmandān va Sukhansarāyān-i Fārs* (Tehran, 1338 Sh/1959), II, 249.

by leaving the city. Thus Ḥājji Mullā Muḥammad Taqī Burghānī left Tehran and settled in Qazvin as a result of some dispute with the Shah.[48] Possibly we see here the remote ancestor of the mass emigrations of ulama during the Constitutional Revolution.

Not only did Fatḥ ʻAlī Shāh seek to adorn his capital with the presence of the ulama, but he also entrusted them with government missions and appointments. The shaykh ul-Islām of Khūy, Āqā Muḥammad Ibrāhīm, was sent to Istanbul in 1222/1798 bearing a letter of congratulation to Sultan Muṣṭafā IV on his accession.[49] Later in his reign, he appointed Mullā ʻAlī Aṣghar Mullābāshī to accompany Hulāgū Khān as minister to Kirman.[50]

Far more frequently, however, it was the ulama who took it upon themselves to intervene in the business of the state. In the unsettled and decentralized condition of the administration, caused in part by the vastness of distances, one of the most common forms of their intervention was mediation between the central government and rebellious towns, khans, or governors, requesting pardon for them. Usually this intercession was successful. On the death of Āghā Muḥammad Khān, Muḥammad, a nephew of Karīm Khān Zand, had taken possession of Isfahan, and had been well received by the inhabitants. Fatḥ ʻAlī Shāh was deterred from wreaking his vengeance on the town only by the intercession of the imām jumʻa of Isfahan, Mīr Muḥammad Ḥusayn.[51] As a token of submission at the end of his prolonged rebellion, Jaʻfar Qulī Khān Zand sent his son to Tehran in the company of the shaykh ul-Islām of Khūy, who was to give weight to his pleas for forgiveness.[52]

Among other uprisings during the reign of Fatḥ ʻAlī Shāh was that of Ḥusayn Qulī Khān, governor of Kashan. A certain Muḥammad Qāsim Bīralvandī and a Kashani sayyid claiming to be the deputy of the Hidden Imam urged the governor to seize the throne.[53] After a brief uprising in the course of which he sacked

48 *Q'U*, p. 16.

49 *NT*, I, 93; *RSN*, IX, 440.

50 *RSN*, X, 44. Mullā ʻAlī Aṣghar was also given one of the granddaughters of Fatḥ ʻAlī Shāh, Āghā Bīgum Khānum, in marriage. According to ʻAḍud ud-Daula (*op. cit.*, p. 37), "he drank wine and was illiterate, but had a long beard." His qualities were summarized by the poet Nashāṭ in the following line of verse: "Two-voiced; two-faced; two-hearted: God saw his faith to be such, and gave him a beard to match."

51 *RSN*, IX, 325; Watson, *op. cit.*, p. 113.

52 *RSN*, IX, 347.

53 Brydges, *op. cit.*, p. 135.

Naṭanz and Isfahan, he accepted defeat and sought refuge in Qum. There his oppressive behavior toward pilgrims to the shrine of Fāṭima caused the ulama to send a complaint to Tehran; but it was also one of their number, Mīrzā Abū-l-Qāsim Gīlānī who, by his intercession, saved the governor from death and persuaded Fatḥ 'Alī Shāh to content himself with blinding him instead.[54] The intervention of Mīrzā Sulaymān Ṭabāṭabā'i on behalf of 'Abd ur-Riḍā Khān, governor of Yazd, who had committed some minor act of disobedience, was more effective: the governor was neither punished, nor even deprived of his post.[55]

As has been suggested previously, the influence of the ulama was primarily on urban populations and exercised in an urban environment. Certain contacts, however, between the ulama and the tribes, especially in Khurasan, indicate that at least a limited respect for the ulama existed among the tribes, and they valued the ulama's capacity to intervene on their behalf. In 1244/1829 the ulama of Mashhad successfully defended the action of several khans who had risen in protest against excessive taxation.[56] Less successful was the intervention of Mullā Ḥusayn Kūchik Sabzavārī on behalf of Riḍā Qulī Khān, a persistent rebel.[57] Nor did the ulama limit themselves to intercession on behalf of the khans; they attempted also to dissuade them from purposeless revolt. Thus Mirzā Hidāyatullāh, son of the martyred Mirzā Mihdi Mujtahid, appealed to the Kurdish khans of Khurasan to put an end to their continuous risings.[58] In Fars, the shaykh-ul-Islām of Shiraz, Shaykh Muḥammad Amīn, went to the camp of Muḥammad 'Alī Khān, chieftain of the Qashqai, in order to persuade him to offer his submission to Ḥusayn 'Alī Khān Farmānfarmā.[59]

For Iran in the early years of the Qajar period, Arab Iraq was still a cause of minor friction with the Ottoman Empire. Iran had traditionally had some say in appointing the governors of Baghdad, which led to a continuous involvement in the affairs of the region.[60] This offered the ulama a further field of mediation and intervention. Iranians were predominant among the Shi'i ulama

54 *Ibid.*, p. 143; *RSN*, IX, 371.
55 *NT*, I, 215.
56 *Ibid.*, pp. 210–211.
57 *Ibid.*, p. 240.
58 *RSN*, IX, 497.
59 *NT*, I, 246; *MN*, I, 153.
60 Mustaufī, *op. cit.*, I, 32.

of the shrines, and they generally enjoyed good relations with the governors of Baghdad.[61] When Iranian involvement expressed itself in war, they were able to intervene with effect. Thus in 1219/1804, when in the course of hostilities the Iranian army was approaching Baghdad, 'Alī Pasha, the governor of the city, dispatched Shaykh Ja'far Najafī to meet Muḥammad 'Alī Mīrzā, commander of the advancing troops. His mission was successful—the advance on Baghdad was halted and Turkish and Arab prisoners released.[62] He performed a similar task in 1227/1812.[63] When in 1234/1818 hostilities broke out again, this time occasioned by differences over the Bābān region of Kurdistan, Āqā Aḥmad Kirmanshahi, a mujtahid resident at Karbala, mediated between Sulaymān Pasha, governor of Baghdad, and Muḥammad 'Alī Mīrzā.[64] In 1236/1821 it was Shaykh Mūsā Najafī, one of the sons of Shaykh Ja'far, who was sent by Dā'ūd Pasha, the new governor, to hold back the Iranian troops.[65] Use was also made of Iranian ulama resident in the 'atabāt to promote general Iranian interests in Arab Iraq.[66]

Although such participation in political matters was permitted even to obscure members of the religious classes, there were occasions when their actions were swiftly repressed. Toward the end of Muḥarram, 1229/January, 1814, a certain Mullā Muḥammad Zanjānī, who acted as *pīshnamāz* (prayer-leader) in one of the mosques of the capital, was accosted by a troublesome drunkard. Using the incident as a pretext, he gathered a number of his followers together and proceeded to attack Armenian houses, breaking the wine vats.[67] This act, designed probably to gain fame and attention, led to his expulsion from the capital. The Shah ordered

61 Friendly relations also existed with the Sunni ulama of Baghdad. See *Q'U*, p. 136.

62 Mīrzā Ja'far Khān Haqā'iqnagār, *Ḥaqā'iq-i Akhbār-i Nāṣirī* (Tehran, 1284 Q/1867–1868), p. 15; *MN*, III, 99; *NT*, I, 122; Brydges, *op. cit.*, p. 263. (In this last, instead of Najafī, "Khazzai" is given, presumably a misreading of the Persian text from which the work was translated). Shaykh Ja'far was himself an Arab, and on first coming to Iran knew little Persian. This did not lessen the enthusiasm of his reception. See *Q'U*, p. 42.

63 *NT*, I, 137.

64 *Ibid.*, p. 169; *RSN*, IX, 430; *MN*, III, 119.

65 *NT*, I, 177; *RSN*, IX, 600; *MN*, III, 126.

66 See letter of 'Abd ul-Vahhāb Mu'tamad ud-Daula to Sayyid 'Alī Karbalā'ī, in Ḥusaynī, *op. cit.*, p. 135.

67 *NT*, I, 145. According to *RSN* (IX, 514) and *MN* (III, 110), churches were also attacked.

that compensation be paid by Ḥasan 'Alī Mīrzā, governor of Tehran, for "this community [the Armenians] is under the protection of the Muslims, and is reckoned as *ahl-i dhimmat* (people enjoying contractual rights); that they should endure loss is repugnant to the sharī'at."[68] The mullā, together with his followers, was obliged to leave Tehran.[69]

A similar incident, more important in its consequences, took place in Yazd. Shāh Khalīlullāh, imam of the Nizārī Ismā'īlīs and eldest son of Sayyid Abū-l-Ḥasan Khān, who had governed Kirman under the Zands, normally resided in Maḥallāt, surrounded by followers who had come from India and Turkestan to serve him. In 1230/1815 he went to live in Yazd, which was situated on the route to Baluchistan, possibly to have a more convenient center for communication with India.[70] Here, two years later, some of his followers became engaged in a dispute with shopkeepers, using violence to settle the argument.[71] They then took refuge in the house of Shāh Khalīlullāh, refusing to emerge. One of the mullās of the town, Mullā Ḥusayn, collected a mob and on arriving at Khalīlullāh's house found his supporters armed and ready to defend themselves.[72] In the ensuing uproar, Khalīlullāh and two of his followers were killed. Ḥājjī Muḥammad Zamān Khān, governor of Yazd, sent Mullā Ḥusayn and some of his followers to Tehran. Then he was bastinadoed and had his beard plucked out; but neither he nor any of his followers were executed, either because the actual murderer of Shāh Khalīlullāh could not be ascertained,[73] or because of the intercession of Ḥājjī Muḥammad Ḥu-

68 *NT*, I, 145; *RSN*, IX, 514. In the reign of Fatḥ 'Alī Shāh, importance given to the sharī'at generally safeguarded the religious minorities. See below, p. 75.

69 This episode inspired Muḥammad Mihdī Khān Māzandarānī "Shaḥna" with the following quatrain: "An ascetic, in his rawness, broke the vinevats; the means of the winebibbers' joy were removed./If he broke them for the sake of God, woe upon us; but if he broke them for the sake of hypocrisy, then woe upon him!" (Quoted in *MN*, III, 110, and *RSN*, IX, 514).

70 *RSN*, IX, 552; *NT*, I, 158.

71 *RSN*, IX, 552; *NT*, I, 158. *MN* (III, 126) places these events one year later, in 1233/1817.

72 J. N. Hollister (*The Shia of India* [London, 1953], p. 337) drawing on Ismā'īlī sources, suggests that the jealousy of the ulama had been aroused by the popularity of Shāh Khalīlullāh in Yazd, a popularity confirmed by *RSN* (IX, 552). According to Watson (*op. cit.*, p. 192), the mullā responsible was called Ḥasan, not Ḥusayn.

73 *RSN*, IX, 553.

sayn Khān Niẓām ud-Daula.[74] Sayyid Ja'far, Mullā Ḥusayn's chief accomplice, escaped all punishment on the payment of a bribe.[75] As some token of compensation, Fatḥ 'Alī Shāh presented Āqā Khān Maḥallātī, son and successor of Shāh Khalīlullāh, with one of his daughters, Sarv-i Jahān Khānum, in marriage,[76] added to the family lands at Maḥallāt,[77] and appointed him governor of Qum.[78] It has been suggested that Fatḥ 'Alī Shāh was motivated by memories of the Assassins, and "fear of the deadly vengeance of the sect."[79] At this stage in Ismā'īlī history, it seems unlikely that such possibilities of vengeance existed. More probably, Fatḥ 'Alī Shāh remembered Abū-l-Ḥasan Khān's refusal to admit Luṭf 'Alī Khān to Kirman, and the debt the Qajars thus owed the Ismā'īlīs.[80] As in the incident of Mullā Muḥammad Zanjānī, the absolute power of the monarchy was affronted by a minor member of the religious classes, acting for personal reasons and without any tenable religious motive; hence reaction could be decided and swift.

We see, then, the appearance of a constant policy of favoring clerical influence, winning their approval by pious acts, and accepting their mediation. The motives for this policy, and the contradictions inherent in it, will be better understood from an examination of Fatḥ 'Alī Shāh's personal relations with the principal mujtahids of his day. The general tone was indicated at the very beginning of his reign when Shaykh Ja'far Najafī "permitted him to mount the throne and appointed him his deputy (*nā'ib*), on condition that a muezzin be appointed to each brigade of the army, and a prayer-leader to each battalion; and that the troops listen to a preacher once a week."[81] When accepting the pleas of Mīrzā Mihdī Mujtahid to lift the siege of Mashhad, Fatḥ 'Alī Shāh is reputed to have replied that so far from intending any insult to the shrine, "we consider our kingship to be exercised on behalf of (*ba niyābat-i*) the mujtahids of the age; and our constant endeav-

74 *NT*, I, 158.
75 *RSN*, IX, 554.
76 'Aḍud ud-Daula, *op. cit.*, pp. 9, 69.
77 *RSN*, IX, 554.
78 *NT*, I, 159.
79 Hollister, *op. cit.*, p. 337.
80 'Aḍud ud-Daula, *op. cit.*, p. 9.
81 *Q'U*, p. 141. The post of Qāḍī 'Askar also continued to exist. In the time of Fatḥ 'Alī Shāh, it was occupied by Mullā Malik Muḥammad Chārmaḥallī (*RSN*, IX, 412). The nature of his functions, however, is not clear.

our is to attain the beatitude of serving the right-guiding Imams."[82] The author of *Qiṣaṣ ul-'Ulamā'* writes that: "Fatḥ 'Alī Shāh was entirely devoted to Āqā Sayyid Muḥammad Ṭabāṭabā'ī, and obeyed him in all matters."[83]

This devotion and submission, notwithstanding the absolute nature of his power, determined the attitude of the monarch to assertions of clerical influence. Among the principal mujtahids of his reign was Mullā Aḥmad Narāqī, who had studied at Najaf under Sayyid Mihdī Baḥr ul-'Ulūm, generally accounted the most learned of the ulama at the 'atabāt after the death of Sayyid Muḥammad Bāqir Bihbihānī.[84] He had returned to Iran and taken up residence in Kashan. Here he found a tyrannical governor oppressing the populace, and he took it upon himself to expel him from the town. The account given in *Qiṣaṣ ul-'Ulamā'*,[85] even if possibly fictitious in detail, illustrates clearly the contradiction between the actual tyranny of the monarch and his proclaimed devotion to the ulama, and how the latter ultimately predominated. Fatḥ 'Ali Shāh summoned Mullā Aḥmad Narāqī to Tehran and angrily reproached him for what he had done. The mullā, far from showing repentance, lifted his hands up and tearfully exclaimed: "O God! This unjust king appointed an unjust governor over the people. I put an end to his oppression; and now this oppressor is angry with me." Fatḥ 'Alī Shāh, afraid of being further condemned, requested his pardon and appointed a new governor for Kashan in accordance with the mullā's wishes.[86]

In Yazd, Ākhūnd Mullā Ḥusayn similarly caused the people to expel an oppressive governor. He was summoned to Tehran, and in the presence of the Shah, his feet were tied to the bastinado,

82 *RSN*, IX, 327.

83 P. 93. This statement needs qualification in regard to the events leading up to the Second Perso-Russian War. See below, pp. 87–89.

84 *RJ*, p. 676; *Q'U*, pp. 124–125. Baḥr ul-'Ulūm appears never to have visited Iran, but his influence there was nonetheless great. See below, p. 70.

85 Pp. 93–94.

86 Mullā Aḥmad Narāqī also wrote poetry under the pseudonym of Ṣafā'ī (see Riḍā Qulī Khān Hidāyat, *Majma' ul-Fuṣaḥā* [Tehran, 1288 Q/1871–1872], II, 330–332), and in contrast with the severity of his attitude to the monarch, he thought it justifiable to protect the satirical poet Yaghmā, after he had been denounced as an infidel by the imām jum'a of Kashan (see Majd ul-'Alī Khurāsānī, "Raf'-i Ishtibāh-i Nabdhī az Ḥālat-i Ḥājj Mullā Aḥmad Narāqī," *Armaghān*, VII [1304 Sh/1925–1926], 604; and Muḥammad 'Alī Tabrīzī Khiābānī, *Rayḥānat ul-Adab* [Tehran, 1326 Sh/1947–1948], IV, 183–196).

ready to be beaten. The Shah and his minister, both reluctant to see the punishment carried out, tried to persuade him that in fact he had had no hand in the matter. Angrily he replied: "Why does the Shah lie? I expelled the governor because of his oppression and his extortions from the poor." Nonetheless, the Shah ordered him to be released and, according to *Qiṣaṣ ul-'Ulamā'*, that night saw the Prophet in a dream, rebuking him for the disrespect he had shown the mullā. Whether or not Fatḥ 'Alī Shāh had such a dream is immaterial: the point intended is that he showed disrespect to a member of the ulama, and came to regret having done so.[87]

The same point emerges more forcefully from an anecdote concerning Shaykh Ja'far Najafī. The Shaykh was in the habit of visiting Iran annually, to collect alms and distribute them to the poor. On one occasion when he arrived in Tehran, Fatḥ 'Alī Shāh, being angered by some action of the Shaykh, announced his intention of not receiving him. Despite the orders of the Shah, his servants and courtiers respectfully admitted the Shaykh to the palace, and when Fatḥ 'Ali Shāh heard him call out "Yallāh!" instinctively he rose and went forward to greet him. Habit proved stronger than intention.[88]

The chief concentration of mujtahids within Iran was at Isfahan, not only the former Safavid capital, but which also in a sense remained the religious capital of the country until the early part of the reign of Nāṣir ud-Dīn Shāh, attracting ulama from other parts of the country. Most of the clerical prominence of Iran resided there;[89] we can gain some idea of their numerical strength in the reign of Fatḥ 'Alī Shāh from the fact that more than four hundred

87 *Q'U*, pp. 71–73. It is not clear whether the Mullā Ḥusayn of this incident was also the leader of the mob that killed Shāh Khalīlullāh (see above, p. 55). *Q'U* makes no reference to the affair; and although the matter of bastinadoing is common to both incidents, it seems unlikely that the Shah should have wished to honor, not only the son of the murdered man, but also the son of the murderer. For he offered his daughter Ḍiyā us-Salṭana in marriage to the son of Mullā Ḥusayn, Āqā Sayyid Muḥammad Mihdī. The offer was declined. See *Q'U*, p. 89; and Kashmīrī, *op. cit.*, p. 419.

88 *Q'U*, pp. 141–142.

89 Mīrzā Muḥammad Ḥasan Khān I'timād us-Salṭana (*Mir'āt ul-Buldān-i Nāṣirī* [Tehran, 1294–1297 Q/1877–1880], I, 65) gives a list of fifteen of the ulama of Isfahan whom he considers to have "reached the highest degree of perfection in ijtihād"; and adds that the generality of the ulama of that city is without number.

ulama went to welcome him on his final visit to Isfahan in 1250/1834.[90] Particularly after the death of Mīrzā Abū-l-Qāsim Qumī,[91] it was with the mujtahids of Isfahan that he was chiefly concerned. Among them, three stand out as particularly influential: Mullā 'Alī Nūrī (d. 1246/1830), Ḥājj Muḥammad Ibrāhīm Kalbāsī (d. 1262/1846), and Sayyid Muḥammad Bāqir Shaftī Ḥujjat ul-Islām.

Mullā 'Alī Nūrī was a pupil of Mīrzā Abū-l-Qāsim Qumī, and to him he owed his initial success in establishing himself in Isfahan.[92] Like Bihbihānī, he was violently opposed to the Sufis and refused to sit with them in the same room when in Shiraz.[93] He appears to have enjoyed cordial relations with Fatḥ 'Alī Shāh, possibly because of his connection with Fāḍil-i Qumī, and was one of the notables to greet him on his entry to Isfahan in 1245/1829.[94]

Ḥājj Muḥammad Ibrāhīm Kalbāsī (*sic*)[95] had studied in the 'atabāt both under Sayyid Muḥammad Bāqir Bihbihānī and under Sayyid Mihdī Baḥr ul-'Ulūm.[96] His power in Isfahan was considerable. It came to his notice that some incautious person had delivered himself of the opinion that "the mullās have no religion." Kalbāsī spared his life only on hearing his plea that he was subject to recurring insanity, and that his disrespectful words had been uttered during one such attack. Nonetheless, he banished him for more than a year to Najafābād, a small town twenty-five kilometers to the southeast of Isfahan. Only the intercession of Sayyid Muḥammad Bāqir Shaftī could persuade Kalbāsī to allow his return to Isfahan.[97] The respect shown him by Fatḥ 'Alī Shāh is indicated by the fact that the monarch went to visit him during one of his sojourns in Isfahan.[98] Kalbāsī's relations with secular power, however, were not always untroubled: one of the governors of Isfahan aroused his anger, and he prayed for his dismissal. Shortly afterward, the governor was in fact recalled to Tehran, and Ḥājj Mu-

[90] A. von Tornau, "Aus der neuesten Geschichte Persiens: Die Jahre 1833–1835," *ZDMG*, II (1848), 420.

[91] D. 1221/1806 according to *RJ* (p. 519); but as early as 1213/1798 according to *MN* (III, 117).

[92] *RJ*, p. 517.

[93] *Q'U*, p. 111.

[94] *MN*, III, 147; *RSN*, IX, 721.

[95] Usually thus, but in *RJ* (p. 10) "Karbāsī."

[96] *RJ*, p. 10.

[97] *Q'U*, p. 84.

[98] *Ibid.*, p. 86.

ḥammad Ibrāhīm sent him a letter concluding with this distich of Sa'dī: "You see that the blood of the moth, unjustly shed by the candle, did not permit it to burn even until dawn."[99]

Of the three, Sayyid Muḥammad Bāqir Shaftī Ḥujjat ul-Islām was by far the most important. In him we see the first example of the wealthy, assertive mujtahid, whose power—judicial, economic, and political—exceeds that of the secular government, which functions, indeed, only with his consent and subject to his ultimate control. Whereas later in the century, Āqā Najafī, who attained a similar position of wealth and power, was restricted in the scope of his activities by the existence of a determined rival, Mas'ūd Mīrzā Ẓill us-Sulṭān, Sayyid Muḥammad Bāqir was able effectively to dominate the life of Isfahan until his death in the reign of Muḥammad Shāh.

Born in Shaft, a village near Rasht, in 1180/1766–1767, he traveled to the 'atabāt in 1197/1783, where he studied under Sayyid Muḥammad Bāqir Bihbihānī and Shaykh Ja'far Najafī.[100] He came to settle in Isfahan in 1216/1801–1802, and though initially poor and obscure, eventually attained a wealth and influence that the author of *Qiṣaṣ ul-'Ulamā'* describes as a "manifestation of the power of God."[101] The means by which he attained his wealth are clear; nonetheless, an element of wonder always was attached to it and doubtless contributed to the awe in which he was held. Some thought that he had mastered the art of alchemy.[102] In fact the foundations of his fortune were laid by a khan of his native village, who, impressed by his piety, presented him with a sum of money (not specified, but presumably large) to invest in property and trade. He was to divide the proceeds between charitable purposes and his own expenditure. He would offer property on terms of revocable sale, and on the expiry of the period reoccupy it, either keeping it or selling it. In a short time he was able to reap large profits and accumulate considerable property: four hundred caravanserais, two thousand shops in Isfahan alone, and many villages, not only near Isfahan, but also in the regions of Burūjird, Yazd, and Shiraz. From his holdings around Burūjird

99 *Ibid.*, p. 85.

100 *RJ*, p. 125.

101 *Q'U*, p. 103.

102 'Abbās Iqbāl, "Ḥujjat ul-Islām Ḥājj Sayyid Muḥammad Bāqir Shaftī," p. 37. Muḥammad Bīdābādī (d. 1197/1783), imām jum'a of Isfahan, had been renowned for his interest in alchemy (*RJ*, p. 651).

alone he had a yearly income of 6,000 tomans. Each of his seven sons had a separate house, and within his own house there lived more than a hundred people.[103]

This accumulation of wealth, however, far from decreasing the respect in which he was held, added to his fame. Not only did he devote part of his income to charitable expenditure,[104] but he was considered worthy of being entrusted by others with the distribution of their alms. The merchants of Isfahan, on the day of ʿĪd-i Ghadīr, customarily presented him with money to distribute among the poor.[105] From other parts of the country, and even from as far as India, alms would arrive to pass through his hands to those of the deserving poor.[106]

Apart from his imposing wealth, which seemed like a divine reward for his piety, and the influence gained through receiving and distributing zakāt, his supremacy in Isfahan had another source: his full and unhesitating exercise of the judicial functions of mujtahid. His teacher, Sayyid Muḥammad Bāqir Bihbihānī, had reasserted the functions of mujtahid, and his judgments had been carried out by mīrghaḍabs.[107] Ḥūjjat ul-Islām was no less eager in pronouncing judgment and performing his duty of "enjoining good and forbidding evil." He composed a treatise on the necessity for applying the sharīʿat during the occultation of the Imam, and undertook himself to inflict the prescribed penalties. He is reputed to have condemned between eighty and one hundred offenders to death. Frequently they were buried in a graveyard adjoining his house.[108] Such was his severity that once he was imprisoned himself until the imām jumʿa of Isfahan interceded on his behalf. With all his severity, he enjoyed a reputation for justice.[109] The Russian traveler, de Bode, visiting Isfahan in 1840, remarked that he was "distinguished for the spirit of toleration, justice and impartiality with which he treats the Christian population of Julfa."[110]

103 These details are taken from *Q'U*, pp. 104–105, and if possibly inaccurate, nonetheless convey some idea of the wealth of Sayyid Muḥammad Bāqir.

104 According to *Q'U* (p. 109), he regularly provided two thousand families with bread and meat.

105 *Ibid.*, p. 109.

106 *Ibid.*, p. 104.

107 See above, p. 36.

108 *RJ*, p. 125.

109 *Q'U*, p. 106.

110 C. A. de Bode, *Travels in Luristan and Arabistan* (London, 1845), I, 47.

The governors of Isfahan were obliged to treat with respect and submissiveness so formidable a figure. If they wanted to meet him, they had no choice but to go to his house and wait silently and respectfully until he chanced to notice their presence.[111] So complete was his control of the finances of Isfahan that governors frequently found themselves in his debt.[112] Such was the popular concern at his death that the bazaar was closed for several days.[113]

The widespread respect and devotion accorded to this mujtahid are significant. In his person, which combined weath and piety and severity, the power of the sharīʻat was elevated; its outward dominion was made clear and symbolized. This probably was the ultimate reason for the awe in which he was held, rather than his riches or even the harshness of his verdicts. The tendency to identify the actions of one mujtahid, or a group of mujtahids, with the interests of Islam can be held to account for much of the political influence of the ulama among the urban masses, particularly in the period of the Constitutional Revolution. This point emerges with great clarity, however, much earlier in the Qajar period, and particularly in the events leading up to the Second Perso-Russian War.

Fatḥ ʻAlī Shāh made repeated efforts to gain the favor of Sayyid Muḥammad Bāqir Shaftī. His failure in persuading him to come to Tehran has already been mentioned. When visiting Isfahan, he pressed him to make some request of him; but eventually all he would ask for was the abolition of the royal *naqqāra khāna* (drummers attached to the palace).[114] The Shah referred to him various disputes for settlement in accordance with the sharīʻat, such as that between the inhabitants of Malāyir and their governor, Shaykh ʻAlī Mīrzā,[115] and that between two warring tribal groups of ʻIrāq-i ʻAjam.[116] The Shah also begged the mujtahid to

---

Later in the century, when the imām jumʻa of Isfahan wielded an influence similar to that of Ḥujjat ul-Islām, the Catholics of Julfa were put under his protection with the agreement of the Apostolic Delegate. See A. de Gobineau, *Dépêches Diplomatiques,* ed. A. D. Hytier (Geneva, 1959), p. 115; and H. Brugsch, *Reise der königlichen preussischen Gesandtschaft nach Persien* (Leipzig, 1862), II, 99.

111 *QʻU*, p. 106.

112 Iqbāl, *op. cit.*, p. 34.

113 *RJ*, p. 125.

114 *QʻU*, p. 105.

115 *NT*, I, 225.

116 *RSN*, IX, 713.

be allowed to share in the cost of the mosque being built by him in Bīdābād in order to be associated with this pious act, and even more with this sacred personage. His request was refused.[117]

This may be held to symbolize the inner nature of Fatḥ 'Alī Shāh's policy of close relations with the ulama: an attempt to be accepted by them as a legitimate ruler and, in some measure, to identify the state with the sanctity they represented. The motives for this attempt, and the degree to which it succeeded, will be discussed after consideration of other aspects of relations between the ulama and the state in his reign.

If Fatḥ 'Alī Shāh willingly consented to clerical participation in state affairs, indeed to a degree even sought it, he possessed at the same time certain influence among the ulama. His interests extended to doctrinal matters, beyond personal contacts with individual members of the religious classes. This interest, insofar as it touched on controversial matters, inevitably affected the position of certain of the ulama. Nonetheless, he appears to have exerted no lasting influence upon any of the doctrinal disputes, nor to have deviated from the orthodox Uṣūlī position.

His interest in theological matters appears in the works he commissioned from various of the ulama. Mullā Aḥmad Narāqī translated for him into Persian an Arabic work on ethics, the *Mi'rāj as-Su'āt*.[118] From Muḥammad Lāhījī he requested a commentary on the *Nahj al-Balāgha*.[119] Similarly, he showed a distinct liking for *munāẓara*, disputation between two mullās. Thus he confronted Mullā Muḥammad 'Alī Jangalī with Ḥājj Mullā Muḥammad Ṣāliḥ Burghānī in Tehran.[120] On occasion he himself also ventured to enter into controversy: hearing that a certain Mīrzā Muḥammad Taqī Nūrī had declared that smoking the *qalyān*, or water-pipe, did not constitute a breaking of the fast of Ramāḍān, he summoned him to Tehran and argued the point with him, as being contrary to ijmā'.[121]

The ulama for their part appear to have valued his actions against the Sufis. Two devotees of Nūr 'Alī Shāh who fell into his grasp were surrendered to Āqā Muḥammad 'Alī Bihbibānī; he

117 *Q'U*, p. 110. The whole quarter of Bīdābād where the Sayyid lived was *bast*. See de Bode, *op. cit.*, I, 50–51.

118 *Q'U*, p. 93.

119 *RJ*, p. 661.

120 *Q'U*, p. 21.

121 *Ibid.*, p. 107.

promised at the same time to instruct his governors to punish other offenders.[122] Muḥammad Riḍā Mīrzā, governor of Gilan, and his vazīr, 'Alī Khān Iṣfahānī, were sympathetically inclined toward the Ni'matullāhīs, and as a result dervishes of that order began to collect in Gilan. The situation began to resemble that in Kirman in 1205/1790; and in 1235/1819, the ulama of Rasht protested to Fatḥ 'Alī Shāh. He dismissed 'Alī Khān Iṣfahānī, and fined Ḥājji Muḥammad Ja'far Qarāgūzlī, quṭb of the order.[123]

Thus the suppression of Sufism in the reign of Fatḥ 'Alī Shāh was in part the work of the sovereign himself. By way of contrast, the prominence attained by the Sufis in the reign of Muḥammad Shāh, showed how effective was encouragement by the state. In the time of Fatḥ 'Alī Shāh, of the Qajar princes only Allāhyār Khān Āṣaf ud-Daula appears to have had lasting Sufi inclinations.[124]

While Fatḥ 'Alī Shāh was clearly at one with the ulama in his hostility to the Sufis, his role in the controversy between the Akhbārīs and Uṣūlīs is somewhat ambiguous. It appears that the Uṣūlī ulama suspected him of being favorably disposed to the Akhbārīs. Had their suspicions been justified, the favored position of the mujtahids would immediately have been endangered. Thus it was that Iran saw the final stages of the conflict whose outcome had already been made clear in the 'atabāt. The two chief participants were Shaykh Ja'far Najafī and Mīrzā Muḥammad Akhbārī,[125] and into the conflict between them the Shah was drawn. Shaykh Ja'far, in his treatise refuting the teachings of Mīrzā Muḥammad, accuses him of having composed an anonymous commentary in the margins of a book written for the monarch, designed to lessen his respect for the ulama.[126] The sharpness of Mīrzā Muḥammad's invective in controversy aroused the ulama of the 'atabāt against him, and Shaykh Ja'far was able to pro-

[122] Malcolm, *op. cit.*, II, 422–423.

[123] *RSN*, IX, 581–582; *NT*, I, 170. In Kirman itself, Sufi influence was still strong enough to affect the choice of a governor. See Aḥmad 'Alī Khān Vazīrī, *Tārīkh-i Kirmān*, ed. H. Farmānfarmā'īān (Tehran, 1340 Sh/1962), p. 533.

[124] 'Aḍud ud-Daula, *op. cit.*, p. 16.

[125] Born Dhū-l-Qa'da 21, 1178/May 13, 1765 in India (according to *RJ*, p. 653) or Bahrayn (according to *Q'U*, p. 131). He first passed through Iran on his way to the 'atabāt during the reign of Āghā Muḥammad Khān. He is not to be confused with Muḥammad Amīn Akhbārī or Muḥammad Sharīf Akhbārī' (see above, p. 35).

[126] *RJ*, p. 153.

nounce him an infidel.[127] Fleeing to Tehran, he sought the protection of Fatḥ 'Alī Shāh, whereupon Shaykh Ja'far sent the monarch a copy of his polemical work *Kashf al-Ghiṭā 'an Ma'ā'ib Mīrzā Muḥammad 'Adūww al-'Ulamā* (*Unveiling of the Vices of Mīrzā Muḥammad, the Enemy of the Ulama*), pointing out the errors of Mīrzā Muḥammad's doctrine, and warning the Shah of his dangerous nature.[128]

The incident of the "Inspector's head" demonstrated the danger more effectively. Hoping presumably to avenge himself on his enemies, Mīrzā Muḥammad offered to obtain, by supernatural means, the death of Tsitsianov, commander of the Russian forces at that time besieging Baku.[129] If he were to succeed, Fatḥ 'Alī Shāh would undertake to make the Akhbārī madhhab the official one of the state. [130] The Shah accepted his offer and the condition attached to it; whether because he earnestly desired the death of Tsitsianov or the dominance of a madhhab by means of which he might destroy the power of the mujtahids, or whether he was motivated by nothing more than curiosity as to the outcome of the affair, is unknown. The last suggestion seems the most plausible. At the end of a forty-day period spent by Mīrzā Muḥammad in the shrine at Shāh 'Abd ul-'Aẓim, the head of Tsitsianov was in fact brought to Tehran and presented to the Shah. [131]

Fatḥ 'Alī Shāh refrained from fulfilling his promise, both because he was doubtless reluctant, even if able, to impose the Akhbārī madhhab on Iran, and moreover because he feared that the supernatural powers of Mīrzā Muḥammad might be turned against him. So Mīrzā Muḥammad was exiled to Arab Iraq. Fearing to enter the 'atabāt and face the hostility of the pupils of Shaykh Ja'far,[132] he went instead to Baghdad, where he became involved in a contest for the governorship. One of the contestants,

127 *Ibid.*, p. 55.

128 *Ibid.*, p. 152.

129 *Q'U*, p. 132. According to *NT* (I, 79), it was Fatḥ 'Alī Shāh's courtiers who suggested to Mīrzā Muḥammad that he bring about the death of Tsitsianov. Since he was renowned for his skill in geomancy and divination, and the court for their part were much interested in astrology and all forms of superstition (see Morier, *op. cit.*, p. 387), this seems equally likely.

130 *Q'U*, p. 132.

131 *NT*, I, 80; *Q'U*, p. 132. According to *RSN* (IX, 415), it was only the hand of Tsitsianov that was severed from his dead body and sent by way of Ardabīl to Tehran.

132 When Shaykh Ja'far died, Mīrzā Muḥammad's comment was: "One of the swine has died" (*Q'U*, p. 132).

As'ad Pasha, requested his help against the other, Dā'ūd Pasha, who, afraid of sharing the fate of Tsitsianov, incited a mob to attack Mīrzā Muḥammad's house in Kāẓimayn and kill him.[133]

Hereafter, Akhbārism scarcely reappears in Iranian history. Kirman, once largely Akhbārī, became predominantly Shaykhī;[134] only for a time did Akhbārism survive in Hamadan.[135] The controversy had already been decided in the 'atabāt, and the apparent identification of Fatḥ 'Alī Shāh with the Akhbārīs was only incidental and passing. The fact that he did not attempt to promote Akhbārism shows indeed how little he thought of restricting the power of the mujtahids.

His relations with Shaykh Aḥmad Aḥsā'ī were far more intimate than those with Mīrzā Muḥammad, and the controversy aroused by the teachings of the Shaykh, was more far-reaching in its effects than the dying struggle of Akhbārī and Uṣūlī. Bālāsarī and Shaykhī replaced Uṣūlī and Akhbārī as designations of loyalty,[136] and the controversy was pursued bitterly down to the early years of the twentieth century.

Shaykh Aḥmād Aḥsā'ī, born in Bahrayn in 1154/1741–1742, left there for the first time in 1176/1762–1763, and traveled to Karbala and Najaf, where he studied under Sayyid Muḥammad Bāqir Bihbihānī and Sayyid Mihdī Baḥr ul-'Ulūm.[137] An outbreak of the plague compelled him to return to Bahrayn, but after four years, in 1212/1798, he again set out for Iraq and settled in Basra.[138] In 1221/1806–1807, he decided to visit the shrine of the Imam Riḍā.[139] On his way to Mashhad, he stopped in Yazd, and such was the reception accorded him by both ulama and

[133] See Anonymous, "Fāji'a-yi Qatl-i Muḥammad-i Akhbārī," *Iṭṭilā'āt-i Māhāna*, IV (1330 Sh/1951), 31, and *MN*, III, 116. *Q'U* attributes his death to the ulama of Kāẓimayn (p. 132). See too Ḥājj Shaykh 'Abbās 'Alī Kayvān, *Kayvānnāma* (Tehran, 1340 Sh/1961), p. 127.

[134] Muḥammad Hāshim Kirmānī, "Tārīkh-i Madhāhib-i Kirmān," *MM*, I (1335 Sh/1956), 133.

[135] A. de Gobineau, *Les Religions et les Philosophies dans l'Asie Centrale* (Paris, 1865), p. 30. According to G. Scarcia ("Intorno alle Controversie tra Aḫbārī e Uṣūlī presso gli Imamiti di Persia," *RSO*, XXXIII [1958], 245–246), today Akhbārism survives only in Khurramshahr and Abadan.

[136] Kayvān, *op. cit.*, p. 131.

[137] 'Abdullāh b. Aḥmad al-Aḥsā'ī, *Sharḥ-i Ḥālāt-i Shaykh Aḥmad ul-Aḥsā'ī* (Bombay, 1310 Q/1892–1893), p. 23; and Murtaḍā Mudarrisī Chahārdihī, *Shaykh Aḥmad Aḥsā'i* (Tehran 1344 Sh/1955), p. 5.

[138] al-Aḥsā'ī, *op. cit.*, p. 25.

[139] Chahārdihī, *op. cit.*, p. 7.

people, that on his return from the pilgrimage he took up residence there.[140] His fame attracted ulama from other towns and ultimately reached the knowledge of Fatḥ ʿAlī Shāh himself.[141] In accordance with his usual practice, he invited the Shaykh to Tehran. The tone of the letter is even more devoted and submissive than that of his other communications to the ulama, and it appears in fact that "the Shah was convinced that obedience to the Shaykh was obligatory, and that opposition to him constituted unbelief."[142] He apologized for his inability to visit the Shaykh in Yazd, as it was incumbent upon him to do; he pointed out that his invitation to come to Tehran should in no way be interpreted as a sign of false pride; and he concluded by saying that should the Shaykh fail to accept his invitation, he would himself have to abandon the affairs of state and go to Yazd.[143] On the envelope containing his letter, he wrote the following distich: "I desire a confidant who will convey a message; who will mention an obscure one in the presence of the Beloved."[144] Although the Shaykh wrote a treatise in reply to several questions of theology put to him by Fatḥ ʿAlī Shāh, he initially refused his invitation to Tehran.[145] When the monarch persisted, he made preparations to leave Iran altogether and to return to Basra.[146] Ultimately, however, he was persuaded to stay in Iran and even to visit Tehran. He was received with great courtesy by Fatḥ ʿAlī Shāh, but he refused to take up residence in the capital, for "in my opinion, all kings and governors enforce their edicts and orders by means of oppression; and since the people consult me and take refuge with me in all matters, and the defence of the Muslims and provision for their needs is incumbent upon me, my intervention with the king can have only one of two results: either he will accept it, and thus his rule will be suspended; or he will reject it, and I will be humiliated."[147] Although Fatḥ ʿAlī Shāh was temporarily able to dissuade him from returning to Basra, he attempted to return to Iraq later. Despite the pleas of Amīn

140 al-Aḥsāʾī, *op. cit.*, p. 29.
141 *Ibid.*, p. 29.
142 Chahārdihī, *op. cit.*, p. 8.
143 Text of the letter given in al-Aḥsāʾī, *op. cit.*, p. 31.
144 ʿAḍud ud-Daula, *op. cit.*, p. 69.
145 *QʿU*, p. 31.
146 al-Aḥsāʾī, *op. cit.*, p. 32.
147 *Ibid.*, pp. 35–36; Chahārdihī, *op. cit.*, pp. 8–9.

ud-Daula, governor of Yazd, he finally left the town from which his fame had spread, and traveling by way of Isfahan, reached Kirmanshah in Rajab, 1229/May–June, 1814.[148] Here he was persuaded to stay for two years by the governor of the town, Muḥammad 'Alī Mīrzā, eldest son of Fatḥ 'Alī Shāh. Even after leaving Kirmanshah, he enjoyed the bounty of this prince, who sent him a yearly allowance of 700 tomans.[149] Returning from the Hijaz and Iraq in 1234/1818–1819, he stayed again in Kirmanshah until the death of Muḥammad 'Alī Mīrzā.[150] Thereafter he traveled to Mashhad, Qum, and Isfahan.[151]

In all these places he was well received, both by the ulama and the governors. Possibly the constant devotion shown to him by the monarch and his family aroused the envy of some of the ulama and was instrumental in his takfīr. Rumor had it that the Shah had spent 100,000 tomans in paying the Shaykh's debts and given him a cloak encrusted in pearls.[152] He presented him with a village near Kirmanshah.[153] Nonetheless, the doctrinal grounds for his takfīr appear to be clear: his denial of the resurrection of the material body, and of the material nature of the *mi'rāj*, the Prophet's Ascension.[154]

The close and devoted association of Fatḥ 'Alī Shāh with one who was declared an infidel, and from among whose followers emerged many of the early Bābīs, should not be taken to imply

148 al-Aḥsā'ī, *op. cit.*, pp. 44–47; Chahārdihī, *op. cit.*, p. 9.

149 *RJ*, p. 25; *Q'U*, p. 28; Kashmīrī, *op. cit.*, p. 368.

150 al-Aḥsā'ī, *op. cit.*, p. 48.

151 *Ibid.*, pp. 49–52.

152 Muḥammad Hāshim Kirmānī, "Ṭā'ifa-yi Shaykhīya," *MM*, II (1337 Sh/1958), 252.

153 al-Aḥsā'ī, *op. cit.*, p. 52.

154 See *Q'U*, p. 31. Apart from Mullā Muḥammad Taqī Burghānī, Mullā Āqā Darbandī and Ibrāhīm b. Sayyid Muḥammad Bāqir were instrumental in the takfīr of Shaykh Aḥmad. The doctrines of Shaykhism have not yet been adequately examined and remain obscure in many respects. Here no detailed examination will be attempted; Shaykhī doctrine insofar as it touches on the position of the mujtahid has been mentioned above (see p. 7). Among the apparent contradictions we see in Shaykhism are a use of mystical terminology coupled with a strong rejection of Sufism (see *RJ*, p. 25, and Kirmānī, *op. cit.*, p. 246); and a tendency to allegorical explanation combined with an extension of the traditional cosmology (see A. Bausani, *Persia Religiosa* [Milan, 1959], p. 404). The most systematic account of Shaykhism is Henry Corbin's "L'Ecole Shaykhie en Théologie Shî'ite," *Annuaire de l'Ecole Pratique des Hautes Etudes. Section des Sciences Religieuses*, 1960–1961, pp. 1–60. See too the same author's "Pour une Morphologie de la Spiritualité Shî'ite" in *Eranos-Jahrbuch*, Zurich, XXIX (1960), 57–107.

any lack of orthodoxy on his part. Shaykh Aḥmad had studied under two of the greatest Shi'i theologians of the thirteenth century A.H.; and among those mujtahids who in turn received ijāza from him were Ḥājj Mullā Ibrāhīm Kalbāsī and Mullā 'Alī Nūrī.[155] He was held in high respect by Sayyid Mihdī Baḥr ul-'Ulūm.[156] It is true that Bābism had many of its roots in Shaykhism; but Shaykhism was not bound inevitably to develop in the direction of Bābism. Indeed, the direction it took under Ḥājjī Muḥammad Karīm Khān was strongly opposed to Bābism.[157] Even if we dismiss later Shaykhī attempts to minimize the heterodox elements in Shaykh Aḥmad's teaching as taqīya,[158] it still seems true that only his takfīr established Shaykhism as a separate madhhab.[159] Thus in no sense can Fatḥ 'Alī Shāh be held to have encouraged a heterodox movement.

Indeed, when Ḥājj Mullā Muḥammad Taqī Burghānī declared the Shaykh an infidel in Qazvin, the governor of the town, 'Alī Naqī Mīrzā, attempted to effect a reconciliation in order that the Shah might not be disquieted by this dispute between the ulama.[160]

Thus neither in the case of the Akhbārīs nor of the Shaykhīs did Fatḥ 'Alī Shāh play a decisive role in theological controversy; but through his interest in theological matters, and his habit of personal contact with the ulama, he gained momentary and indecisive influence over a section of the religious classes. This did not contradict the general tendency of relations between the monarch and the ulama: favor dispensed by the latter, and sought by the former.

As the monarch acted, so did his princes. Many of the provincial governors of his reign cultivated personal relations with the ulama, either out of genuine devotion and piety or to avoid being

155 *Q'U*, p. 27, and *RJ*, p. 26.

156 al-Aḥsā'ī, *op. cit.*, p. 22.

157 See below, p. 149.

158 See for example Shaykh Abū-l-Qāsim Kirmānī, *Fihrist-i Kutub-i Marḥūm Shaykh Aḥmad-i Aḥsā'ī va Sharḥ-i Ḥāl-i Sā'ir-i Mashāyikh-i 'Iẓām* (Kirman, 1337 Sh/1958–1959).

159 Muḥammad Hāshim Kirmānī (*op. cit.*, p. 350) suggests that it was only takfīr that prevented Shaykh Aḥmad from being accorded the status of a Mullā Muḥsin Fayḍ-i Kāshānī or a Mullā Ṣadrā, i. e., that of a philosopher outwardly at peace with orthodoxy. The religious content of his thought was, however, considerably more pronounced than that of Mullā Ṣadrā (see Bausani, *op. cit.*, p. 404).

160 *Q'U*, pp. 31–32.

expelled from their seats of government. That Shaykh Aḥmad was respectfully treated by the governors of Yazd, Kirman, Isfahan, Mashhad, and Kirmanshah, we have already seen. It was Ibrāhīm Khān Ẓahīr ud-Daula who first drew Fatḥ 'Alī Shāh's attention to Shaykh Aḥmad,[161] and his son Ḥājjī Muḥammad Karīm Khān Qājār later became leader of the sect. Muḥammad 'Alī Mīrzā, governor of Kirmanshah, "bought" from Shaykh Aḥmad one of the gates of Paradise, and another from Sayyid Riḍā, son of Baḥr ul-'Ulūm. He gave orders that both deeds of sale be wrapped up with him in his shroud.[162] Less forthcoming than Shaykh Aḥmad and Sayyid Riḍā was Sayyid Muḥammad 'Alī Māzandarānī, who after accepting the invitation of the governor of Qumīsha to reside in his town, stayed not more than a few months.[163] Muḥammad Amīn Khān, governor of Hamadan, corresponded with Mīrzā Muḥammad Akhbārī concerning Akhbārī teachings.[164] Purely mundane motives accounted for the great respect accorded by the princes to Sayyid Mihdī Baḥr ul-'Ulūm, for they were convinced that his influence might determine the choice of a successor to Fatḥ 'Ali Shāh.[165]

Members of the government and court also sought contact with the ulama. 'Abd ul-Vahhāb Mu'tamad ud-Daula (whose pen name was Nashāṭ) wrote to Shaykh Aḥmad inviting him on his own behalf to Tehran.[166] Mīrzā Shafī' was once offered 5,000 tomans by the Shah to drink a cup of wine; he refused and took care to inform Abū-l-Qāsim Qumī of his refusal.[167] Amīn ud-Daula informed the ulama that he endeavored to avoid anything contrary to the sharī'at in the course of his duties, which indeed he had accepted only under duress.[168]

Such instances typify the relations between the government and the ulama; the case of 'Abbās Mīrzā and Qā'im Maqām involves other factors and will be treated separately.

Thus we see throughout the reign of Fatḥ 'Alī Shāh a constant deference of the monarch to the ulama, a close and lasting asso-

161 Kirmānī, *op. cit.*, p. 252.
162 *Q'U*, p. 26.
163 *Ibid.*, p. 98.
164 *RJ*, p. 656.
165 *Q'U*, p. 129.
166 Ḥusaynī, *op. cit.*, p. 134.
167 'Aḍud ud-Daula, *op. cit.*, p. 49.
168 *Ibid.*, p. 53.

ciation with many of their number, and his consent to their participation in matters of government. Despite this, he was and remained a tyrant with virtually unfettered powers; so we are bound to ask whether his professed submission to the ulama was anything more than a pretense, and if not, what motivated the pretense.

It must at the outset be noted that the revival of religious interest and religious influence was only one aspect of what might be termed a minor renaissance, one consciously promoted by the monarch. If he sought to adorn his capital with the presence of mujtahids, he similarly sought to gather together the literary talent of the period in the Anjuman-i Khāqānī (the Imperial Society).[169] Apart from building mosques and endowing shrines, he made himself the subject of a bas relief carved, in Sasanid style, in the rock near Shahr-i Ray.[170] Most important of all, he envisaged a restoration of the Safavid state, and as a part of this restoration some form of close association between the state and the religious classes was necessary. More simply, the appearance of piety was useful, even necessary, in gaining popular respect.[171]

So much for reasons of state. Added to these, halfway, one might say, between sincerity and insincerity, was the eternal Iranian interest in religious and spiritual matters, and therefore in those whose chief concern they were—the ulama. To deny or ignore the validity of this factor would seem to be a self-defeating exercise in the explanation of historical phenomena. The very multiplicity of doctrine prevailing suggests, as Gobineau noted later, a high degree of activity in that interest, and in the ruler no less than in the rest of the nation. The manner and circumstances of expression of doctrines or beliefs, the degree to which they find acceptance, the identity of those who choose to accept them—all these might be explicable in social or even political terms. But the evolution of the doctrine or belief itself, though to an extent influenced and shaped by outward circumstances, is not wholly explicable in terms of them, and in fact acts deeply and pervasively upon them. Both

169 See Introduction to Hidāyat, *op. cit.*, (Vol. I) and J. Rypka, *Iranische Literaturgeschichte* (Leipzig, 1959), p. 311. Morier (*A Journey through Persia*, p. 286) notes that apart from members of the royal family and foreign envoys, only poets and "learned and holy men" were permitted to sit in the presence of the Shah.

170 I'timād us-Salṭana, *op. cit.*, IV, 241.

171 Malcolm, *op. cit.*, II, 559.

causatively and temporally, belief precedes expression or exploitation of itself. Bearing this in mind, and the unity of all spheres of human existence in Islam, to maintain that essentially political issues are, in the Islamic world, bound to express themselves religiously, does not seem a true or adequate analysis of the situation.

Moreover, the existence of a conflict in Fatḥ 'Alī Shāh—between raison d'état and devotion to the ulama—as noted above, points to the reality of that devotion. Thus Fatḥ 'Alī Shāh is to be regarded both as a monarch—an autocratic one—and as a believing Shi'i Muslim.[172] The Shi'ism of his age was marked by a reassertion of the power of the mujtahid, judicially and socially. Shar' courts, if not absolute, were strong, their verdicts severe;[173] and the collection of zakāt took place even by coercion.[174] On the other hand, the state he headed was not only tyrannical, but totally excluded from the system of belief. It seems likely that the contradiction between these two powers was reflected both in the sovereign himself and his manner of life: thus to his state belonged the astrologers, but their very existence was condemned by the mujtahids whose regent he proclaimed himself to be.[175] Assertions of power by the ulama might initially be resented but were finally accepted.

Ultimately, therefore, we see the question not as one of the reasons of state on the one hand and religious sincerity on the other, but rather as an attempt, largely unsuccessful, to reconcile the two. When the mother of Fatḥ 'Alī Shāh went on pilgrimage to the 'atabāt, she met Shaykh Ja'far in Najaf, and begged him to pray for her and her son: "Since my son is king, he commits much oppression and cruelty towards his subjects. I beg of you, contrive somehow that God Almighty may forgive our sins and resurrect us with Haḍrat Fāṭima [i.e., among the righteous]."[176]

172 Ouseley (*op. cit.*, III, 367) suggests that Fatḥ 'Alī Shāh was "as little influenced by religious bigotry as the most enlightened of his subjects"; but the very assumptions implicit in the wording of this observation lead one to doubt the competence of the writer to judge such matters.

173 Malcolm, *op. cit.*, II, 429–430.

174 *Q'U* says of Shaykh Ja'far: "He obtained God's right by whatever means necessary" (p. 143).

175 M. Tancoigne, *Narrative of a Journey into Persia* (London, 1820), p. 173.

176 *Q'U*, p. 141. If the story were apocryphal, its point would hardly be reduced.

IV

‘Abbās Mīrzā, Qā’im Maqām, and the Ulama

The religious attitudes of ‘Abbās Mīrzā, heir apparent to Fatḥ ‘Alī Shāh until his death in 1249/1833, and his relations with the ulama deserve separate attention. His importance in the events of Fatḥ ‘Alī Shāh's reign, in particular those concerning relations with Russia, was hardly less than that of the monarch himself. Moreover, with the military reforms of ‘Abbās Mīrzā started that process of transformation variously known as reform, westernization, and modernization, which was increasingly to preoccupy Iran throughout the century. Many of the elements in the confusion of response which it evoked can already be discerned in the reception accorded to the Niẓām-i Jadīd or "New Army."

The general climate of the reign favored the influence of the ulama and the deference of the state to them. In Tabriz, seat of government of ‘Abbās Mīrzā, no less than elsewhere, this influence was apparent. ‘Abbās Mīrzā wrote to his vazīr, Mīrzā Abū-l-Qāsim Qā'im Maqām, shortly after the surrender of Tabriz to the Russians in the Second Perso-Russian War, that "never have the ulama of Tabriz enjoyed as much respect, deference, honour and obedience as they have in this age."[1] Among the ulama of Tabriz, however, there appears to have been no individual with whom 'Abbās Mīrzā enjoyed close and devoted relations.[2] Although he was reputed to be regular in performing his basic religious duties,[3] he was more interested in practical and immediate matters than in theology. This determined the nature of his relations with the ulama, and limited them to matters of state. He attended Friday prayer in the congregational mosque of Tabriz;[4] and every Thursday evening the ulama would meet at his invitation in one of the mosques of Tabriz to discuss the implementation of the sharī'at. Any case that had not reached settlement elsewhere was referred to these meetings for an authoritative judgment.[5] Usually these meetings were attended by Mīrzā Abū-l-Qāsim Qā'im Maqām, and sometimes 'Abbās Mīrzā himself would participate in the discussions. Similar sessions were held in other parts of Azerbayjan.[6] That 'Abbās Mīrzā expected or hoped for a practical result from these meetings is apparent from the bitter disappointment he later expressed to Mīrzā Abū-l-Qāsim when ordering him to sever all contact with the ulama.[7]

Like a later reformer, Amīr Kabīr, he also tried to ensure that the shar' courts were administered by honest and capable judges.[8] The successive shaykh ul-Islāms of Tabriz, Ḥājji Mīrzā Mihdī and Mīrzā 'Ali Aṣghar, appear to have enjoyed his particular confidence.[9] In Tabriz, a new *divānkhāna* (the highest organ of secular jurisdiction) was established, and qadis subordinate to it were appointed to the other towns of Azerbayjan. Tax assessments were submitted to this dīvānkhāna for approval.[10]

1 Muḥammad Ṣādiq Ḥusaynī, *Makhzan ul-Inshā* (Tabriz, 1274 Q/1857), p. 324.

2 According to Muḥammad Hāshim Kirmānī ("Ṭā'ifa-yi Shaykhīya," *MM*, II [1337 Sh/1958], 247), 'Abbās Mīrzā was one of the many princely devotees of Shaykh Aḥmad Aḥsā'ī; but no contemporary or later Qajar source makes any mention of a meeting or correspondence between them.

3 G. Drouville, *Voyage en Perse* (Paris, 1825), I, 248.

4 'Abd ur-Razzāq Dunbulī, *Ma'āthir-i Sulṭānīya* (Tabriz, 1242 Q/1826), p. 138.

5 *Ibid.*, p. 139.

6 *Ibid.*; Nāṣir Najmī, *Irān dar Miān-i Ṭūfān, yā Sharḥ-i Zindagī-yi 'Abbās Mīrzā dar Janghā-yi Īrān va Rūs* (Tehran, 1337 Sh/1958–1959), p. 29.

7 See below, p. 80.

8 Najmī, *op. cit.*, pp. 29, 198.

9 Nādir Mīrzā, *Tārīkh va Jughrāfī-yi Dār us-Salṭana-yi Tabrīz* (Tehran, 1323 Q/1905), p. 244.

10 Najmī, *op. cit.*, p. 198; Bāqir Qā'im Maqām, *Qā'im Maqām dar Jahān-i Adab va Sīyāsat* (Tehran, 1320 Sh/1941–1942), p. 19.

'Abbās Mīrzā showed special concern for the religious minorities, and sought the cooperation of the ulama in securing for them the rights accorded by the sharī'at. In 1821, a Muslim child was lost in Urumiya, and suspicions arose that he had been kidnapped or murdered by certain Jews. Hence the entire Jewish community of that town was imprisoned. When 'Abbās Mīrzā was petitioned by the Jews of Tabriz to intervene, he submitted the matter to a mujtahid. The mujtahid ruled that if two witnesses to the murder of the child could be found, then the murderers must be punished and the rest of the community set free; whereas if no witnesses existed, there was no basis for acting against any of the Jewish community. 'Abbās Mīrzā informed the governor of Urumiya of this fatvā and ordered the immediate release of the Jews.[11]

He similarly extended his patronage to the Christians of Azerbayjan and the Caucasus, possibly to lessen the attractions of Russian rule.[12] Assistance was given to missionaries working among the Nestorians of Urumiya,[13] and 'Abbās Mīrzā was prepared to sanction a missionary school in Tabriz itself, to be attended by Muslims as well as Nestorians and Armenians.[14] Even more remarkable was his attempt in 1242/1826 to attract, through advertisements in the London press, English agricultural colonists for the Sāvujbalāgh (present-day Mahābād) region of Azerbayjan.[15] How widely these friendly contacts with foreigners and Christians were known is not clear; but it seems probably that they provided a background against which accusations of unbelief connected with the Niẓām-i Jadīd could be made more plausible.

The military reforms of 'Abbās Mīrzā were not in themselves of a nature to arouse wide hostility, nor were they applied throughout the Iranian army. In brief, they consisted of recruiting a number of troops on a permanent basis, with fixed and regular pay, dis-

11 Ḥabīb Levi, *Tārīkh-i Yahūd-i Īrān* (Tehran, 1339 Sh/1960–1961), III, 553, quoting from the travels of Rabbi David d'Beth Hillel. The identity of the mujtahid concerned is not given.

12 Tsitsianov attempted to promote antagonism between Muslims and Christians in the Caucasus. (See E. Pakravan, *Abbas Mirza, Prince Réformateur* [Tehran, 1958], I, 80.)

13 J. Perkins, *A Residence of Eight Years in Persia among the Nestorian Christians with Notices of the Muhammadans* (Andover, 1843), p. 165.

14 J. Wolff, *Missionary Journal* (London, 1829), III, 128.

15 See S. Nafīsī, "Jalb-i Muhājirīn-i Urūpā'ī dar Sāl-i 1242," *Sharq*, I (1310 Sh/1931–1932), 57–64, 125–127; and *Tārīkh-i Ijtimā'ī va Sīyāsi-yi Īrān dar Daura-yi Mu'āṣir* (Tehran, 1340–1344 Sh/1961–1965), II, 144 ff.

ciplining them according to contemporary European (particularly French and Russian) models, and equipping them with modern weapons and firearms.[16] The necessary training was carried out initially by fugitive Russian officers, and later by the French military mission under General Gardane.[17]

Opposition to these measures was deep and persistent. It may, in large part, be ascribed to the hostility of the brothers of 'Abbās Mīrzā, and their choice of religious means to attack his position. Here we see for the first time a phenomenon recurring throughout the Qajar period: the use for political or personal purposes of the threat of clerical opposition, which, although potentially existent, might never express itself but for encouragement or, in some instances, never even exist. It was a pretext for refusing or resisting measures of reform or even of administrative reorganization, a threat to suspend over the heads of enemies, one capable of fulfillment but equally capable of being fictitious. It was this that later impelled Malkum Khān, himself no sincere friend of the ulama, to write: "These accusations have long grown stale; don't accuse the wretched mujtahids!"[18]

It is significant that no individual from among the ulama is recorded as having been opposed to the Niẓām-i Jadīd or preached against it. According to von Kotzebue,[19] Muḥammad 'Alī Mīrzā, who as eldest son of Fatḥ 'Alī Shāh considered his claim to the succession stronger than that of 'Abbās Mīrzā, was his chief antagonist and responsible for representing the Niẓām-i Jadīd as contrary to Islam.[20] The enmity and jealousy of his other brothers, which later became apparent, were doubtless already active.[21]

'Abbās Mīrzā's response was clear: he presented the Niẓām-i Jadīd as being not merely compatible with the sharī'at, but deriving in fact from the forgotten and neglected practice of the Prophet himself. In order to counteract hostile rumors, and to pre-

16 Najmī, *op. cit.*, pp. 31–34.

17 Pakravan, *op. cit.*, I, 78; Drouville, *op. cit.*, II, 105–106.

18 Mīrzā Malkum Khān, *Majmū'a-yi Āthār*, ed. Muḥammad Muḥīṭ Ṭabāṭabā'ī (Tehran, 1327 Sh/1948–1949), p. 14.

19 Moritz von Kotzebue, *Narrative of a Journey into Persia in the Suite of the Imperial Russian Embassy in the Year 1817* (London, 1819), pp. 160–161.

20 See also J. Morier, *A Second Journey through Persia, Armenia and Asia Minor to Constantinople* (London, 1818), p. 213. According, however, to Paul Amédée Jaubert (*Voyage en Arménie et Perse* [Paris, 1821], p. 280), Muḥammad 'Alī Mīrzā later followed 'Abbās Mīrzā's initiative and founded a corps of Niẓām-i Jadīd.

21 Pakravan, *op. cit.*, I, 67.

vent the threat of clerical opposition from becoming a reality, "I ['Abbās Mīrzā] caused a passage in the Koran that is favourable to the improvement of the means of attack in the cause of religion, to be copied, to be sealed and approved by the chiefs of the law in Persia, and disseminated throughout the country."[22] The discipline of the Niẓām-i Jadīd was held to be that which was instrumental in the early conquests of Islam. It had then penetrated to Europe and simultaneously declined in the Muslim East. Thus far from being a suspect innovation, the Niẓām-i Jadīd was to be regarded as a return to the beginnings of Islam.[23] Here again is the earliest example of a recurring phenomenon of the Qajar period: the attempt, marked by varying degrees of sincerity and accuracy, to present apparently European importations as forgotten products of Islamic thought and civilization, and thus to ease the path of reform. The extent to which the motivation of this attempt may be regarded as genuinely Islamic is of little relevance here.

This justification of the Niẓām-i Jadīd was chiefly 'Abbās Mīrzā's retort to his brothers. It seems almost definite that he had in mind the Ottoman example and borrowed from Sultan Selīm both the term used to designate the new corps and its theological justification. Sultan Selīm had obtained support for his military reform among a minority of the higher ulama, who quoted in its defense several Quranic verses, among them that recorded by Riḍā Qulī Khān in his discussion of the Iranian Niẓām-i Jadīd (61:4).[24] The medium of transmission is unknown. Possibly the Ottoman envoys who came to Tehran to suggest the formation of a common front against Russian expansionism were one channel whereby the Ottoman example was communicated.[25] The founder of the Ottoman Niẓām-i Jadīd was deposed by the Janissaries in June,

22 Quoted in Morier, *op. cit.*, p. 213. Riḍā Qulī Khān Hidāyat, when discussing the Niẓām-i Jadīd (*RSN*, IX, 436), quotes the verse: "Truly God loves those who fight in ranks in His path, as if they were a firm foundation" (61:4), and compares a disciplined rank of men in battle with a line of believers engaged in congregational prayer. It is presumably to this verse that allusion is made.

23 Sir Harford Jones Brydges, *Dynasty of the Kajars* (London, 1833), pp. 307–310; Dunbulī, *op. cit.*, p. 132. *RSN* (IX, 436) suggests an even older precedent for the Niẓām-i Jadīd: the military organization of the Achaemenids.

24 See Uriel Heyd, "The Ottoman 'Ulema and Westernisation in the Time of Selīm III and Maḥmūd II," *Scripta Hierosolymitana*, IX (1961), 69, 74.

25 *RSN*, IX, 436. Awareness of events in the Ottoman Empire played a continuous role in Iran; and parallels between Iranian and Ottoman history in the nineteenth century are many.

1807, after the shaykh ul-Islām had been persuaded to issue a fatvā to the effect that the military reforms were contrary to the sharī'at.[26] Although no military elite comparable with the Janissaries existed in Iran, the princes attempted to make a similar use of religious pretexts in their intrigues against 'Abbās Mīrzā. By borrowing the theological arguments of the Ottoman reform, he was largely able to counter them.

While religious opposition to the Niẓām-i Jadīd was thus chiefly a product of the jealousy and hostility of 'Abbās Mīrzā's brothers, their decision to use religious pretexts shows that widespread and deep objections to the Niẓām-i Jadīd existed, independent of any agitation. When 'Abbās Mīrzā began himself to learn military drill in Tabriz, he chose to do so in secret in order to avoid the attentions of the ulama.[27] Most of the European travelers of the period comment, without being more specific, on "religious obstacles" to military reform,[28] and Mirzā Abū-l-Qāsim Qā'im Maqām himself testifies to the widespread hostility to 'Abbās Mīrzā and himself. "They say, 'This man is a Christian, and wishes to make up Christians. It is for this reason that he gives currency to the customs of the Christians, and causes us to wear their dress.' "[29] This, it would seem, was the basic objection to the Niẓām-i Jadīd: the simulation of the dress of a non-Muslim nation. The uniform of the Niẓām-i Jadīd closely resembled that of the Russian army;[30] only the Iranian fur hat remained as a sign, not so much of nationality, as of religious allegiance.[31] The subtle, intricate relationship between outward signs and inner beliefs was added to the confusion between religion and national custom, a confusion that determined many later attitudes to innovation. Although no specific instances of objections by the ulama to the uniform can be found, they were voiced in other quarters and doubtless also among the ulama. Drouville remarks that 'Abbās Mīrzā's opponents held him unworthy of the succession, "for he has become a Farengi and wears

26 Enver Ziya Karal, *Osmanlı Tarihi* (Ankara, 1947), V, 81–88.

27 Pakravan, *op. cit.*, I, 78.

28 E.g., Jaubert, *op. cit.*, p. 280; von Kotzebue, *op. cit.*, p. 160; Morier, *op. cit.*, p. 213.

29 Qā'im Maqām, *op. cit.*, p. 19.

30 J. Morier, *A Journey through Persia, Armenia and Asia Minor to Constantinople* (London, 1812), p. 184.

31 Najmī, *op. cit.*, p. 33. Pakravan (*op. cit.*, I, 203) suggests that discipline was conceived of as contrary to pious acceptance of the divine will; but no evidence of this is to be found in contemporary sources, whether Persian or European.

Farengi boots."[32] Finally, any attempt at modernization implied a strengthening of the state, and this in turn an extension of its prerogatives—an extension bound to be resisted by the ulama. Their opposition was able to prevent the introduction of conscription.[33]

That the sum of these objections succeeded in casting doubt on the faith of 'Abbās Mīrzā, is seen in various of the writings of Mīrzā Abū-l-Qāsim Qā'im Maqām.[34] Not only did he defend his master against the charge of unbelief, but threw it back at those who made it: "Without doubt, he has not the faith of the Prophet and the Valī ['Alī] who has not in his heart loyalty to the Crown Prince."[35] In defending 'Abbās Mīrzā, he was also defending himself, for he too was the target of countless accusations: "Not a day passes without this recluse being accused of a hundred foul deeds from every quarter."[36] Both the first Qā'im Maqām, Mīrzā Buzurg Farāhānī, and the second, his son, Mīrzā Abū-l-Qāsim, were closely identified with the policies of 'Abbās Mīrzā, and it is not always possible to determine their shares in the measures taken by the crown prince. They maintained similarly close relations with the ulama. In one instance, however, the initiative can clearly be seen to be that of Mīrzā Buzurg: the proclamation of jihad during the First Perso-Russian War. He dispatched Ḥājji Mullā Bāqir Salmāsī and Ṣadr ud-Din Muḥammad Tabrīzī to the 'atabāt and Isfahan to procure fatvās declaring the war against Russia to be jihad. Shaykh Ja'far Najafī, Āqā Sayyid 'Alī Iṣfahānī, Mīrzā Abū-l-Qāsim Gīlānī, Mullā Aḥmad Narāqī, Mīr Muḥammad Ḥusayn, the imam jum'a of Isfahan, and many others delivered the required fatvās, or composed treatises setting out the conditions and duties of jihad.[37] These were all sent to Tabriz, where Mīrzā Buzurg, on the instructions of 'Abbās Mīrzā, collected them together into a volume called *Risāla-yi Jihādiya*.[38]

32 Drouville, *op. cit.*, I, 241.

33 Jamīl Qūzānlū, *Tārīkh-i Niẓāmī-yi Īrān* (Tehran, 1315 Sh/1936–1937), II, 687.

34 E.g., *Risāla-yi Shakvā'īya* in *Munsha'āt*, ed. Jahāngīr Qā'im Maqāmī (Tehran, 1337 Sh/1958–1959), p. 338.

35 *Ibid.*, p. 466.

36 *Ibid.*, p. 438.

37 *NT* (I, 94) places the declaration of jihad in 1223/1808–1809, shortly after the arrival of Sir Harford Jones in Tehran; *MN* (III, 93) in 1224/1809; Dunbulī (*op. cit.*, pp. 144–145) in 1228/1813; while *RSN* (IX, 456) suggests no date.

38 See introduction to *Risāla-yi Jihādīya-yi Ṣaghīra* in Ḥusaynī, *Makhzan ul-Inshā*, p. 217. This introduction, as also that to *Risāla-yi Jihādiya-yi Kabīra*

The motives for this proclamation of jihad deserve examination. The war with Russia had already been in progress for some years. According to 'Abd ur-Razzāq Dunbulī, it occurred to the court that "since all the Muslims were engaged in fighting the Russian army, it was no longer possible to distinguish the war from jihād."[39] *Nāsikh ut-Tavārīkh* suggests that it was Fatḥ 'Ali Shāh who conceived the idea of proclaiming jihad, and who entrusted Mīrzā Buzurg with obtaining fatvās.[40] Since, however, the collection of fatvās began in Tabriz, it appears more likely that this use of religious motive was planned by Mīrzā Buzurg himself, with the agreement of 'Abbās Mīrzā. We have already seen how they sought to identify the ulama with various aspects of their policy, and how the brothers of 'Abbās Mīrzā sought to arouse religious suspicions against him. It appears possible that now with the declaration of jihad, 'Abbās Mīrzā sought to turn the weapon of religious pressure against his brothers. Despite repeated appeals to the capital for help and reinforcements, the princes had failed to come to his aid, and effectively prevented Fatḥ 'Ali Shāh from realizing the difficulty of his position.[41] By the proclamation of jihad, he may have hoped to force his brothers into action, leaving them the choice of openly neglecting their religious duties or abandoning their intrigues against him. The ulama for their part could have had little objection to the declaration of jihad against an aggressive infidel power.

Ultimately, 'Abbās Mīrzā came to regret bitterly his policy of close association with the ulama. Writing to Mīrzā Abū-l-Qāsim Qā'im Maqām after the surrender of Tabriz to the Russians by Mīr Fattāḥ, he ordered him to cease all association with the ulama to "shake himself free of their dust," and instead to cultivate the company of capable men of affairs. The ulama were no more useful "than overfed horses who have forgotten their function of running."[42] Mīrzā Abū-l-Qāsim himself can have held no favorable opinion of the ulama and their pretensions. The sentiments expressed in these verses also suggest, behind the conventionalism of

---

(in *ibid.*, pp. 192–212), was written and added later to the collected fatvās and treatises by Mīrzā Abū-l-Qāsim, although in the name of Mīrzā Buzurg.

39 Dunbulī, *op. cit.*, p. 144.

40 *Loc. cit.*

41 Najmī, *op. cit.*, pp. 55, 60.

42 Ḥusaynī, *op. cit.*, pp. 324–326.

the imagery, a disappointment at the results of clerical influence in political matters:

> In my belief, if there is any faith in the world, it is in the infidelity of the chainlike tresses of the idols.
> If the preacher in the mosque says other than this, heed him not: how should that poor idiot know? he is but an animal!
> Do not be deceived by mosque and prayer-mat, for the ascetic is a wolf, and wishes it to be said that he is the shepherd.
> Say: come to the head of this alley, for here the seller of asceticism has set up shop.
> In our quarter it is a strange custom that faith should be sold so cheaply, and justice be so dear.
> If the religion of Islam is indeed as he says, then the wine-dispensing youth at the Magian's temple is in the right.[43]

This first attempt at associating the ulama with a reformist policy failed. The failure was not realized by its chief protagonist, however, until after the greatest display of clerical power before the agitation against the tobacco monopoly—the proclamation of the Second Perso-Russian War.

[43] Qā'im Maqāmī, *op. cit.*, p. 443.

V

The Ulama and the Early Foreign Impact

The distant and immediate causes of any war are numerous and complex, and it is seldom that one of them may be separated from the mass of contributory factors and regarded as the ultimate origin of the conflict. Thus it is with the Second Perso-Russian War: the stern determination of the ulama to lead Iran into war cannot be detached from other considerations—personal and political motives and ambitions. But all these were ultimately absorbed into the movement for jihad, and the final steps to war were taken under the pressure of religious impulse and enthusiasm. The ulama came to express and enforce the will of the Iranian nation, however short-lived and ill-defined that will may have been.

The tension that erupted into war was expressed chiefly in the form of frontier disputes. The Treaty of Gulistān (1228/1813) had left certain areas ill-defined, and it was ultimately the Russian occupation of Gökcha in the Khanate of Erivan and refusal to negotiate withdrawal which led to the beginning of hostilities. 'Abbās Mīrzā sought repeatedly to achieve a negotiated demarcation, but was unsuccessful. Yermelov, Russian commander in the Caucasus, insisted on his own competence to deal with all matters concerning

Iran, and prevented Iranian envoys from traveling beyond Tiflis to St. Petersburg.[1] The utmost he would agree to was that Mazarovich, Russian chargé d'affaires in Iran, should convey Iranian representations to St. Petersburg.[2] 'Abbās Mīrzā then attempted to send an envoy by way of Istanbul, and thus avoid Yermelov; but by the time he had reached the Ottoman-Russian frontier, Iran and Russia were already on the verge of war, and the envoy was turned back.[3]

Although 'Abbās Mīrzā thus sought a solution of frontier disputes, it is clear that at the same time a renewal of war with Russia, at some date and under some pretext, was constantly in his mind. His defeat in the First Perso-Russian War had been caused more by the hostility of his brothers and inept organization than by Russian superiority; and it was the same coalition that defeated him in the second war.[4] His own position as heir-apparent, moreover, had been threatened by Russia: his enmity to Russian interests impelled Yermelov after his embassy to Iran in 1817 to suggest Muḥammad 'Alī Mīrzā as a more pliable candidate for the succession.[5] Thus 'Abbās Mīrzā hoped both to regain the lost provinces and to win a personal triumph. Already in 1825 Drouville wrote that 'Abbās Mīrzā was awaiting an opportunity to reopen hostilities and was making extensive military preparations.[6] The possibility of forming a common front with the Ottoman Empire against Russian expansion was also investigated.[7] No precise plan for leading up to a war with Russia seems to have existed; it was only after a certain point had been reached in the frontier negotiations that 'Abbās Mīrzā appeared determined on war. A provisional settlement reached in Tiflis in February, 1825 by Fatḥ 'Alī Khān, *bīglarbīgī* (constable) of Tabriz, envisaged Russian occupation of the disputed area of Gökcha. 'Abbās Mīrzā dissuaded the

1 Sharaf ud-Dīn Mīrzā Qahramānī, "Yak Silsila Asnād-i Tārīkhī, yā 'Ilāl-i Vāqi'ī-yi Jang-i Duvvum-i Rūs-Īrān," *Sharq*, I (1310 Sh/1931–1932), 525, 440, 556.

2 *Ibid.*, p. 320.

3 *Ibid.*, p. 628.

4 Muḥammad Amīn Riyāḍī, "Dau Nāma-yi Muhimm-i Sīyāsī va Tārīkhī az 'Abbās Mīrzā Nā'ib us-Salṭana," *Yādgār*, IV (1327 Sh/1948–1949), 20.

5 'Abd ul-Ḥusayn Hazhīr, "Dar Rāh-i Valī-'Ahdī-yi 'Abbās Mīrzā," *Mihr*, I (1313 Sh/1934–1935), 707.

6 G. Drouville, *Voyage en Perse* (Paris, 1825), I, 248.

7 Nāṣir Najmī, *Īrān dar Miān-i Ṭūfān yā Sharḥ-i Zindagī-yi 'Abbās Mīrzā dar Janghā-yi Īrān va Rūs* (Tehran, 1337 Sh/1958–1959), p. 196.

Shah from ratifying the agreement, and no longer showed any signs of interest in a negotiated settlement.[8] He was no less eager than the ulama in taking the final steps to war and many of these steps he in fact coordinated with them.

Despite this, many writers attribute to him continued opposition to the renewal of hostilities, and instead accuse other individuals or groups of intrigues that forced him reluctantly into battle.[9] In these theories of intrigue, the ulama play an important role. Most prominent among those who allegedly used the ulama as their instrument were the Caucasian khans who had fled to Iran. The khans of Shīrvān and Qarābāgh had been dispossessed of their lands by Yermelov and taken refuge with 'Abbās Mīrzā in Tabriz.[10] He resettled them near the new frontier with Russia, clearly hoping to make use of their presence in the event of hostilities, while at the same time restraining them from acting prematurely and independently.[11] Their interest in a renewal of hostilities was clear: to regain their lost possessions. According to the *Tārīkh-i Nau*, they proceeded to forge letters from the inhabitants of the occupied provinces, describing Russian oppression, and to send them to 'Abbās Mīrzā, Fatḥ 'Alī Shāh, and the ulama, urging the proclamation of war.[12] Doubtless they were able to spread information about the condition of the occupied provinces, having themselves been subject to Russian rule. Article fifteen of the Treaty of Turkumānchāy, by which the Second Perso-Russian War was concluded, moreover, provided for the extradition of religious leaders or khans whose activities provoked unrest on the other side of the frontier.[13] This suggests that contact between the fugitive khans and the Muslim population of the former khanates existed and contributed to the renewal of war.[14] That the khans were alone

8 See Willock's dispatch of March 31, 1826 (F.O. 60/27). He remarks that "he ['Abbās Mīrzā] will endeavour to harry the Shah into a war." *RSN* (IX, 641) confirms that "the court of the Crown Prince, on account of certain interests, would not consent to a compromise." See also R. G. Watson, *A History of Persia from the Beginning of the Nineteenth Century to the Year 1858* (London, 1866), p. 208.

9 E. Pakravan, *Abbas Mirza, Prince Réformateur* (Tehran, 1958), II, 4; Najmī, *op. cit.*, p. 212; Jahāngīr Mīrzā, *Tārīkh-i Nau*, ed. 'Abbās Iqbāl (Tehran, 1327 Sh/1948), p. 15.

10 Najmī, *op. cit.*, p. 209; Qahramānī, *op. cit.*, p. 320.

11 Jahāngīr Mīrzā, *op. cit.*, pp. 5, 8.

12 *Ibid.*, p. 7.

13 *NT*, I, 140.

14 M. Afschar, *La Politique Européenne en Perse* (Berlin, 1921), p. 45.

in inspiring religious agitation, in opposition to the wishes of 'Abbās Mīrzā, is unproven.

The *Tārīkh-i Nau* further claims that various opponents of 'Abbās Mīrzā at court joined their efforts to those of the khans, in order to plunge 'Abbās Mīrzā into a war he was bound to lose.[15] The modern writer Pakravan mentions in this connection the long-standing enmity between 'Abbās Mīrzā and Allāhyār Khān Āṣaf ud-Daula, at that time *sadr-i a'ẓam* (chief minister).[16] Yet Menshikov, last Russian envoy to Iran before the outbreak of war, reported as the chief cause of war 'Abbās Mīrzā's wish to attract the Shah's favor to his own person, and thus bring about the dismissal of Allāhyār Khān.[17] In fact, in 1244/1828 he was dismissed for his negligence in pursuing the war with Russia.[18]

Apart from the exiled khans and elements at court hostile to 'Abbās Mīrzā, Ḥusayn Khān, sardar of Erivan, was a constant enemy of the Crown Prince, and has also been suspected of attempting to push him into war.[19] Although all of these may have hoped for incidental gains from the war, and the khans have played a part in the religious agitation, nonetheless the prime mover was 'Abbās Mīrzā. The attempt of his biographers to free him from all responsibility for the outbreak of war is understandable but would appear to be unsuccessful.[20] If he had opposed the ulama when they came to Sulṭānīya to urge the Shah to war, it seems unlikely that immediately afterward he should have dis-

15 P. 9; see also Najmī, *op. cit.*, pp. 210, 214.

16 Pakravan, *op. cit.*, II, 15.

17 See Ottokar von Schlechta-Wssehrd, "Der letzte persisch-russische Krieg (1826–1828)," *ZDMG*, XX (1866), 296 n. 1, quoting from the official *Petersburgische Zeitung*.

18 *NT*, p. 141.

19 Jahāngīr Mīrzā, *op. cit.*, p. 5; Pakravan, *op. cit.*, II, 12.

20 Jamīl Qūzānlū (*Tārīkh-i Niẓāmī-yi Īrān* [Tehran, 1315 Sh/1936–1937], II, 848, and *Jang-i Īrān va Rūs* [Tehran, 1314 Sh/1935–1936], p. 2) suggests that Britain, anxious to defend India against a possible Russian attack, impelled the ulama to drive Iran into war, and thus divert Russian attention. No evidence of this, however, appears in contemporary British documents; in fact, Willock, the British ambassador, urged Fatḥ 'Alī Shāh to accept a compromise over Gökcha (see Qahramānī, *op. cit.*, p. 625; von Schlechta-Wssehrd, *op. cit.*, p. 295). A variation on the theme is provided by Najmī (*op. cit.*, p. 217), according to whom the British wished to divert an impending Russian attack on the Ottoman Empire to Iran and used Allāhyār Khān and the ulama to bring Iran into war, promising the former Khurasan as a reward. No supporting evidence is offered. A. Reza Arasteh (*Man and Society in Iran* [Leiden, 1964], p. 99) claims on the contrary that it was the Russians who were pushed into war by British intrigue and encouragement.

patched mullās to various parts of Azerbayjan to prepare the people for war.[21] The note of bitter regret apparent in his letter to Qā'im Maqām, previously referred to, suggests a personal identification with the campaign waged for jihad by the ulama.[22] While it is probable that the exiled khans disseminated reports of Russian oppression, the only definite indication as to the source of these accounts is contained in the *Rauḍat uṣ-Ṣafā-yi Nāṣirī*.[23] According to this account, Mīrzā Ṣādiq Vaqāyi'-Nagār, who had been sent to Tiflis by 'Abbās Mīrzā in an attempt to find a favorable solution to the frontier problem,[24] sent accounts of excesses committed by the Russians during the occupation of Gökcha. These accounts presumably reached the knowledge of the ulama, or may even have been forwarded to them directly by 'Abbās Mīrzā.[25]

The pretext for the declaration of jihad was Russian oppression of the Muslim population of the Caucasus. While specific charges relating to the occupation of the former khanates beyond theft and rape[26] are not mentioned, it seems probable that it too was marked by the sporadic savagery of Russian expansion in the Caucasus. Yermelov, both commander-in-chief of the Russian forces and head of the administration of the Caucasus, used to sell Chechen women captives at one ruble each, and slaughtered whole villages of Circassians.[27] His barbarity alarmed even so ruthless a tyrant as Nicholas I,[28] and Paskievich, Yermelov's successor, attributed the disaffection existing in the former khanates to his indiscriminate slaughter of rebels.[29] British envoy McNeill wrote on September 5, 1826 that "the population of territories taken from Persia . . . is now with almost no exception hostile to Russia."[30] As soon as the troops of 'Abbās Mīrzā attacked, the Muslim population arose against the Russians in their midst.[31] Yermelov himself considered

21 Najmī, *op. cit.*, p. 216.
22 See above, p. 80.
23 *RSN*, IX, 641.
24 Qahramānī, *op. cit.*, p. 566.
25 Von Schlechta-Wssehrd, *op. cit.*, p. 295. According to *NT* (p. 192) certain of 'Abbās Mīrzā's courtiers communicated directly with Āqā Sayyid Muḥammad Iṣfahānī Mujtahid in Karbala.
26 *RSN*, IX, 641; *NT*, p. 192.
27 J. N. Baddeley, *The Russian Conquest of the Caucasus* (London, 1908), pp. 147, 153.
28 *Ibid.*, p. 162 n. 1.
29 *Ibid.*, pp. 159–160.
30 J. McNeill, *Memoir of the Right Hon. Sir John McNeill* (London, 1910), p. 86.
31 Watson, *op. cit.*, p. 212; Baddeley, *op. cit.*, p. 154.

both this uprising and the Iranian attack to be the product of "religious fanaticism."[32] Thus the grounds for jihad were existent and valid. Yet, paradoxically, the declaration of jihad, the duty of defending Islam and the Muslims, was initially a weapon directed against Fatḥ 'Alī Shāh.

Although 'Abbās Mīrzā was prominent in the political maneuverings that culminated in war and was himself to lead the attack on the occupied provinces, the decision to go to war rested, at least formally, with Fatḥ 'Alī Shāh. Though doubtless hoping eventually, by some means, to regain territory lost in the first war with Russia,[33] he appears to have been continually reluctant to reopen hostilities. 'Abbās Mīrzā, having himself decided on war, had only the weapon of clerical pressure to compel Fatḥ 'Alī Shāh's agreement. We have already seen than an adequate pretext for jihad existed, and it is possible that the inhabitants of the occupied provinces themselves communicated with the 'atabāt; but it seems probable that 'Abbās Mīrzā at least encouraged the religious agitation and sought to direct it against the monarch's reluctance and temporizing.

The direct intervention of the ulama brought the agitation to a new stage of enthusiasm, where it no longer required stimulation, and absorbing all lesser motives, showed the ulama as the de facto leaders of the nation. Reports of Russian barbarity had reached Āqā Sayyid Muḥammad Iṣfahānī Mujtahid, a grandson of Sayyid Muḥammad Bāqir Bihbihānī, in Karbala. Initially he sent a representative, Mullā Riḍā Qulī, to Tehran, to inquire of Fatḥ 'Alī Shāh whether it was his intention to declare jihad.[34] Although the reply was affirmative, evidently Āqā Sayyid Muḥammad considered its sincerity doubtful. Such by now was the temper of the ulama that they declared themselves ready to go to war even without the consent or participation of the Shah.[35] Realizing that the seeming compliance was motivated by a fear of popular indignation, Āqā Sayyid Muḥammad decided to set out in person for Iran

[32] Baddeley, *op. cit.*, p. 156. It is worth noticing that Yermelov himself considered necessary the extension of Russian rule throughout the Caucasus (*ibid.*, p. 162). In fact, neither side was disinclined to war, as is pointed out by H. Rawlinson (*England and Russia in the East* [London, 1875], p. 40) and Aḥmad Tājbakhsh (*Tārīkh-i Ravābiṭ-i Īrān va Rūsīya dar Nīma-yi Avval-i Qarn-i Nūzdahum* [Tabriz, 1337 Sh/1958–1959], p. 67).

[33] Baddeley, *op. cit.*, p. 100.

[34] *RSN*, IX, 642.

[35] Muḥammad 'Alī Kashmīrī, *Nujūm us-Samā* (Lucknow, 1303 Q/1885–1886), p. 364; *RSN*, IX, 641.

and reached Tehran toward the end of Shavvāl, 1241/June, 1826.[36] There he was received with the greatest respect by all classes of the population, in particular by the princes and the ulama. The tanks in which he performed his ablutions were constantly emptied of the water that was thought to have acquired miraculous properties from contact with his person.[37] Fatḥ 'Alī Shāh appointed 'Abdullāh Khān Amīn ud-Daula as the Sayyid's *mihmāndār* (official host); and in order to lend his intention of declaring war more credibility, allotted 300,000 tomans for military expenditure.[38]

Āqā Sayyid Muḥammad, however, remained unconvinced: from Tehran he wrote to the ulama of the provinces, urging them to preach the necessity for jihad and to join him in the capital.[39] When Fatḥ 'Alī Shāh left Tehran on Shavvāl 26, 1241/June 3, 1826, for his summer residence at Sulṭānīya, he was pursued by Āqā Sayyid Muḥammad and a number of other ulama who had meanwhile arrived from the provinces.[40] Accompanied by Ḥājj Mullā Muḥammad Ja'far Astarābādī, Āqā Sayyid Naṣrullāh Astarābādī, Ḥājj Sayyid Muḥammad Taqī Burghānī, Sayyid 'Azīzullāh Tālishī, and a number of other ulama, Āqā Sayyid Muḥammad reached Sulṭāniya on Dhū-l-Qa'da 4, 1241/June 11, 1826, shortly after the arrival of the monarch and his retinue.[41] Their arrival had, however, been preceded by that of an envoy sent by Alexander I, who had recently succeeded to the Russian throne, bearing the good wishes of the new Tsar.[42] Thus the fears of the ulama, far from being allayed by Fatḥ 'Alī Shāh's proclaimed warlike inten-

36 *Ibid.*, p. 642; *Q'U*, p. 93; *NT*, p. 193; Jahāngīr Mīrzā, *op. cit.*, p. 14. According to *RJ* (p. 659), Fatḥ 'Alī Shāh had already determined to go to war with Russia and requested Sayyid Muḥammad to "favour Iran with his auspicious presence" in the first stages of the war. The mounting pressure exercised on Fatḥ 'Ali Shāh shows that his inward consent to war and participation in the religious enthusiasm came considerably later.

37 Kashmīrī, *op. cit.*, p. 364.

38 *RSN*, IX, 643.

39 *Ibid.*, p. 642; *NT*, p. 193.

40 *RSN*, IX, 644; *NT*, p. 193.

41 *RSN*, IX, 645; *NT*, p. 193; *Q'U*, p. 15; *RJ*, p. 659. The date here quoted is that given by Willock in his dispatch from Sulṭānīya of July 15, 1826 (F.O. 60/27). *MN* has Dhūl-Qa'da 17, 1241/June 23, 1826, and *RSN* has Ṣafar 17, 1241/October 1, 1825. The latter is patently wrong and contradicts the date given on p. 644 of the same work for the Shah's departure from Tehran; while to the former Willock's evidence is to be preferred as that of a contemporary eyewitness.

42 That the terms of his mission in fact left no room for negotiation appears not to have been known or overlooked. See Willock's dispatch of July 18, 1826 (F.O. 60/27) and Watson, *op. cit.*, p. 211.

tions, were redoubled, and the religious pressure increased noticeably. Fatḥ 'Alī Shāh found himself even more isolated than did Nāṣir ud-Din Shāh during the agitation against the tobacco monopoly; of his courtiers, only 'Abd ul-Vahhāb Mu'tamad ud-Daula and Mīrzā Abū-l-Ḥasan Khān Shīrāzī sought to resist the demand for jihad. They were silenced by a fatvā that opposition to jihad constituted a sign of unbelief.[43] The religious enthusiasm, born out of the communications between 'Abbās Mīrzā and his courtiers with the ulama, and disseminated by Āqā Sayyid Muḥammad throughout Iran, now reached its peak. Willock had witnessed Āqā Sayyid Muḥammad's arrival at Sulṭānīya: "Much enthusiasm was manifested by the populace. To the Sied's person they could get no access, but they kissed the litter, kissed the ladder by which he had ascended to it, and collected the dust which had the impressions of the mule's feet which bore him."[44] Eventually the sovereign himself appears to have submitted to the emotional influences surrounding him: he assigned to the service of each of the ulama one of the princes[45] and was seen to weep bitterly "in speaking of the misfortunes of the faithful under the Russian Government."[46] A second group of ulama including Mullā Aḥmad Narāqī and Mullā 'Abd ul-Vahhāb Qazvīnī arrived at the royal camp clad in shrouds as a sign of their preparation for jihad and martyrdom.[47] It was then that the Shah finally submitted. On Dhū-l-Qa'da 24/July 1, Menshikov, the Russian envoy, was given permission to leave,[48] and the Shah demanded of Āqā Sayyid Muḥammad written testimony as to his zeal for jihad to show to the interrogating angels, Nākir and Munkir.[49] "The Shah was committed to the nation";[50] hostilities started.

43 *RSN*, IX, 646; *NT*, p. 194. Jahāngīr Mīrzā (*op. cit.*, p. 15) interprets the fatvā as being directed against the continued opposition of 'Abbās Mīrzā. This appears improbable for reasons already stated. Qā'im Maqām, however, did oppose the decision to go to war (see Baqīr Qā'im Maqām, *Qā'im Maqām dar Jahān-i Adab va Sīyāsat* [Tehran, 1320 Sh/1941–1942], p. 22).

44 Dispatch of July 15, 1826 (F.O. 60/27).

45 *Q'U*, p. 21.

46 Willock's dispatch of July 5 (*op. cit.*).

47 *Ibid.*, and *RSN*, IX, 645.

48 *Ibid.*, p. 646; and Willock's dispatch of July 18 (*op. cit.*).

49 Dispatch of July 15. If later Fatḥ 'Alī Shāh complained to McNeill that "I did not want war with Russia; the mollahs brought me into it" (quoted by J. Wolff, *Researches and Missionary Labours among the Jews, Mohammadans, and Other Sects* [London, 1835], p. 45), it does not disprove that his commitment to war ultimately came to be inward.

50 Thus Willock in his dispatch of July 18 (*op. cit.*).

The enthusiasm encouraged in the first place by 'Abbās Mīrzā by no means subsided now that Fatḥ 'Alī Shāh was committed to war. The feelings that had been aroused were of a violent nature and more easily encouraged than discouraged. It was, moreover, only the second time since the Mongol invasion that Iran had been in direct conflict with a non-Muslim power (if we except the skirmishings with the Portuguese in the Persian Gulf in the sixteenth century and Peter the Great's invasion of Gilan in 1722); and the shock produced by Russian triumphs in the first war cannot have been forgotten. Despite Fatḥ 'Alī Shāh's belated decision to go to war, the effective leadership of the people was still in the hands of the ulama. "Affairs reached such a point that the rulings of the ulama were given precedence over the commands of the king. . . . Were he to have opposed their policy, the people of Iran would have destroyed the monarchy."[51] The wave of enthusiasm, however temporary, was significant: it was strong enough to determine state policy, and it showed clearly the close connection between religious and national feeling. The organ and director of this feeling was the ulama; their directives were interpreted as those best designed to defend Islam. Here we see in an as yet undefined form the conviction that the survival of Iran as a nation was equivalent to its survival as an Islamic nation, the same conviction that was voiced with great clarity and insistence in the latter part of the century. The agitation showed also the fundamental alienation between the state and the nation, one that increased, and the difference of interest between the two. In this alienation, the ulama embodied the aspirations of the people. The adulation accorded to their persons proves this more even perhaps than their voicing of demands popularly felt, demands that were in any event seldom conscious and frequently stimulated. The strength of the religious appeal was such as to overcome other considerations; and how this strength was used depended on the character and desires of the ulama themselves.

If they were able to impel Fatḥ 'Alī Shāh into war, they were unable to have any influence on its outcome. Initially they appear to have participated in the hostilities, but their participation did not last long. Āqā Sayyid Muḥammad accompanied 'Abbās Mīrzā

51 *RSN*, IX, 647.

in the early successful stages of his campaign, but evidently some serious disagreement caused his return. According to Mīrzā Muḥammad 'Alī Kashmīrī, 'Abbās Mīrzā was afraid of his successes being attributed to the presence of Āqā Sayyid Muḥammad, and therefore he slowed the tempo of his advance.[52] The *Qiṣaṣ ul-'Ulamā'* simply says that brokenhearted at the defeats suffered by the Iranians and the disrespectful treatment that the Shah saw fit to bestow upon him, Āqā Sayyid Muḥammad returned to Iran and died of grief.[53] In addition to these explanations, it seems probable that not only the Shah but 'Abbās Mīrzā was interested in reducing the dangerously elevated stature attained by Āqā Sayyid Muḥammad, the more so since he had fulfilled his purpose.[54]

An indication of the retort that may have been made by the ulama to this reassertion by the state of its control over the nation's affairs is given in an anecdote related about Ḥājj Mullā Muḥammad Taqī Burghānī. After the end of the Perso-Russian War, he was asked by Fatḥ 'Alī Shāh why the jihad had been unsuccessful. He replied, "Because of the insincerity of 'Abbās Mīrzā's intentions."[55]

That 'Abbās Mīrzā leveled the same charge against the ulama, we have already seen; nor is this surprising, for the fall of Tabriz was largely the work of one of their number, Mīr Fattāḥ. He was the son of a respected mujtahid of Tabriz, Mīrzā Yūsuf, who had died as the Russian troops were crossing the Aras into Azerbayjan.[56] Inheriting his father's position of influence and respect, Mīr Fattāḥ used it to gain control of the town in the absence of 'Abbās Mīrzā. The Crown Prince had entrusted the defense of Tabriz to an army of Mazandaranis, under the command of Allāhyār Khān Āṣaf ud-Daula, arousing the people's anger by so doing, and it was of this anger that Mīr Fattāḥ made use.[57] Ḥājji 'Alī 'Askar Khvāja,

52 Kashmīrī, *op. cit.*, pp. 364–365.

53 P. 93. *NT* (p. 199) attributes his death to dysentery, and places it in the first year of the war.

54 See *RJ*, p. 659. Qā'im Maqām, angered at his humiliation by the ulama at Sulṭānīya, may have had a hand in the matter.

55 *Q'U*, pp. 19–20.

56 Nādir Mīrzā, *Tārīkh va Jughrāfī-yi Dār us-Salṭana-yi Tabrīz* (Tehran, 1323 Q/1905), p. 250.

57 Mīrzā Muḥammad Ḥasan Khān I'timād us-Salṭana, *Mir'āt ul-Buldān-i Nāṣirī* (Tehran, 1294–1297 Q/1877–1880), I, 405; *RSN*, IX, 674.

the only one of 'Abbās Mīrzā's courtiers left in Tabriz, attempted unsuccessfully to satiate Mīr Fattāḥ's ambitions with cash.[58] Mīr Fattāḥ plotted with the khans of Marand, who for their own reasons were ill-disposed toward 'Abbās Mīrzā, to surrender Tabriz to a detachment of the advancing Russian forces.[59] His motives were probably those of simple ambition and personal gain, though Riḍā Qulī Khān implies that he imagined surrender to be in the best interests of the Tabrizis,[60] and Nādir Mīrzā attributes to him a personal enmity with the Qā'im Maqām.[61] The Russians held out to him the promise of appointing him governor of occupied Azerbayjan.[62] He read the *khuṭba* (sermon) in the name of the Tsar,[63] and such was the hatred of the Tabrizis for Āṣaf ud-Daula that when the Russians had been guided to the town by the rebellious khans of Marand, under the direction of Mīr Fattāḥ they proceeded to cast down the defenders of the town from the walls and silence the cannons that had been directed against the Russians.[64] Mīr Fattāḥ then caused the town gate to be opened and went out in person to welcome the Russians.[65] Of the ulama of Tabriz, only Mīrzā Aḥmad Mujtahid refused to deal with the Russians.[66] On Rabī' uth-Thānī 3, 1242/October 24, 1827, the Russians entered the town.[67] Mīr Fattāḥ's triumph was short-lived; the Russians were reluctant to garrison so large a town that quickly became hostile, and soon withdrew their troops.[68] After the conclusion of the Treaty of Turkumānchāy, Mīr Fattāḥ was obliged to go into exile in the Caucasus.[69]

Nor was the treachery of Mīr Fattāḥ and the ulama of Tabriz

58 Jahāngīr Mīrzā, *op. cit.*, p. 88; Najmī, *op. cit.*, p. 239.

59 One of their number, Naẓar 'Alī Khān, had been executed by 'Abbās Mīrzā for treason (see *RSN*, IX, 674).

60 *Ibid.*, p. 675.

61 Nādir Mīrzā, *op. cit.*, p. 250.

62 *Loc. cit.*

63 Von Schlechta-Wssehrd, *op. cit.*, p. 305; *NT*, I, 205.

64 Von Schlechta-Wssehrd, *op. cit.*, pp. 305–306.

65 *RSN*, IX, 676.

66 Nādir Mīrzā, *op. cit.*, p. 251.

67 *RSN*, IX, 677.

68 *Ibid.*, p. 678; Najmī, *op. cit.*, p. 242.

69 See V. Minorsky, *Tārīkh-i Tabrīz*, trans. 'Abd ul-'Alī Kārang (Tabriz, 1337 Sh/1959), p. 69. R. Wilbraham in October, 1837, came across the residence of a mujtahid near Tiflis: "He receives a large pension from the Russian gov-

the only incident to make 'Abbās Mīrzā regret his policy of using clerical pressure. If earlier he had used this weapon to force Fatḥ 'Alī Shāh into war, it was now used by his enemies among the princes to prevent him from terminating it. While the preliminary peace negotiations were being carried on at Dihkhāraqān, Ḥasan 'Alī Mīrzā Shujā' us-Salṭana set out from Mashhad carrying four black standards, which, so he claimed, had been miraculously given him by the Imam Riḍā to bear triumphantly into battle against the Russians.[70] In January, 1828, he arrived at Tehran and announced that he would replace 'Abbās Mīrzā as heir apparent. "The evening before H.R.H. arrived, a meeting of the mullahs was held to arrange the manner in which the sacred banner of Meshed was to be brought into the town, and it was carried by acclamation that he who should recommend the Shah to pay money to the unbelievers should be announced as an enemy of the true faith."[71] Fatḥ 'Alī Shāh was reluctant to accept the loss of the Caucasian provinces and the payment of reparations and blamed 'Abbās Mīrzā for his predicament.[72] An army was gathered in Tehran to proceed to the front in the Caucasus.[73] Ultimately, the pressure of realities was too strong for the agitation to be successful: the provinces were lost and the humiliating Treaty of Turkumānchāy was concluded.

Thus disastrously ended the Second Perso-Russian War. The ulama had been used initially as instruments for the arousing of religious emotions; but their success in arousing these emotions revealed their potential strength as leaders of the nation. The contradiction between the nation and the state rendered them powerless to affect the course of the war; the ever-increasing foreign influence that followed its unfavorable outcome gave a new dimension to their role of leading the nation against the state.

---

ernment for his services in the war between Russia and Persia" (*Travels in the Transcaucasian Provinces of Russia* [London, 1839], p. 256). His exile was not permanent: he returned to Tabriz where he died in 1269/1852–1853 (see Nādir Mīrzā, *op. cit.*, p. 256). His descendants are mentioned by Aḥmad Kasravī in *Zindagānī-yi Man* (Tehran, 1323 Sh/1944), p. 25.

70 Jahāngīr Mīrzā, *op. cit.*, p. 102; Najmī, *op. cit.*, p. 251.

71 McNeill, *op. cit.*, p. 103.

72 'Abbās Iqbāl, "Ghurāmāt-i Mu'āhada-yi Turkumānchāy," *Yādgār*, I (1324 Sh/1945–1946), 22.

73 Jahāngīr Mīrzā, *op. cit.*, p. 103.

POSTSCRIPT TO THE WAR: THE MURDER OF A. S. GRIBOYEDOV

Not long after the conclusion of the Second Perso-Russian War, an incident occurred in Tehran which threatened to plunge Iran into renewed disaster. Again the national honor seemed affronted; and again it was the ulama who were called upon to reject the affront. Although some of the relevant facts are disputed, complicating theories of intrigue appear to be unjustified: Griboyedov was the victim of his own behavior and the reaction it aroused.

The Russian poet and dramatist, A. S. Griboyedov, was not unfamiliar with Iran when he came on his mission to Tehran in Rajab, 1244/January, 1829.[74] In 1820 he had acted as secretary to the Russian legation. Willock, after attending a meeting between him and 'Abbās Mīrzā, observed: "M. Gribayedoff has a rooted aversion to the Persians which he has taken no pains to conceal."[75] In addition to this "rooted aversion to the Persians," he had marked sympathies toward the Georgians. While serving in the Caucasus, he had married Nina Chavchavadze, daughter of the Georgian poet Aleksandr Chavchavadze, and he was also related to Paskievich.[76] These emotions, and the position of strength he enjoyed as Russian envoy at a time when Russian troops were occupying Khūy and other towns of Azerbayjan, infused his conduct in Tehran with a careless arrogance. He chose to disregard court protocol and refused to remove his boots for an audience with the Shah.[77] His entourage committed offenses for which no redress was given, and drunken Cossacks roamed the streets.[78] Similar occur-

[74] *RSN*, IX, 705. He had reached Tabriz in October, 1828, where he had left his wife and part of his suite before continuing to Tehran (Watson, *op. cit.*, p. 247).

[75] Quoted by D. P. Costello in "Griboyedov in Persia in 1820: Two Diplomatic Notes," *Oxford Slavonic Papers*, V (1954), 87–88.

[76] Article on Griboyedov in *Bol'shaya Sovyetskaya Entsiklopediya* (Moscow, 1952), XII, 583.

[77] *RSN*, IX, 706; *NT*, I, 222. Though D. P. Costello ("The Murder of Griboyedov," *Oxford Slavonic Papers*, VIII [1957], 66) characterizes Griboyedov's conduct as "dignified and firm," we may imagine that it left a less favorable impression on Iranians.

[78] Watson, *op. cit.*, p. 250.

rences had taken place in Qazvin as the legation passed through on its way to Tehran.[79]

The aim of Griboyedov's mission was as unpalatable to the Iranians as was his conduct: to secure the ratification and application of the Treaty of Turkumānchāy, and the payment of war reparations to the Russian government.[80] Among the articles of the treaty was one providing for the return of all prisoners, and on the basis of it Griboyedov proceeded to search Tehran for all Georgian or Armenian women. His men forcibly entered homes looking for women of Georgian or Armenian extraction. They were then taken to the residence of the envoy near Darvāza-yi Shāh 'Abd ul-'Aẓīm to be interrogated as to whether they wished to stay in Iran or return to the Caucasus. At times they were allegedly detained there overnight.[81] The anger of the people at the violation of their homes by armed foreigners could, by itself, have produced the riot that ended in the massacre of the Russian legation; but the question is complicated by Mīrzā Āghā Ya'qūb Khān, a eunuch of Armenian origin, who fled the royal palace and took refuge with Griboyedov. According to the Iranian accounts, Mīrzā Ya'qūb had been entrusted with a large amount of money belonging to the royal household, and being unwilling or unable to return it, fled to Griboyedov's residence.[82] The sole member of the Russian legation to survive the massacre, Maltsov, writes, however, that financial claims were not preferred against Mīrzā Ya'qūb until some days after his flight from the palace. Only receipts could be presented for the money he was alleged to have misappropriated; and the money was intended to be spent on the royal household in accordance with the Shah's instructions.[83] Whether or not the charges against Mīrzā Ya'qūb were justified, Fatḥ 'Alī Shāh cannot but have resented one acquainted with the details of court life fall-

79 Qā'im Maqām, *op. cit.*, p. 27, quoting from the work of a French traveler I have been unable to trace, Louis Dubois. This account differs in several details from others.

80 Baddeley, *op. cit.*, p. 202; *MN*, III, 144.

81 Jahāngīr Mīrzā, *op. cit.*, p. 121.

82 *RSN*, IX, 707; Jahāngīr Mīrzā, *op. cit.*, p. 120. Both speak of "a considerable amount." Najmī (*op. cit.*, p. 277) mentions the figure of 40,000 tomans; Qā'im Maqām (*op. cit.*, p. 27), 50,000; and Aḥmad Mīrzā 'Aḍud ud-Daula (*Tārīkh-i 'Aḍudī*, ed. Ḥusayn Kūhī Kirmānī [Tehran, 1327 Sh/1948], p. 28), 30,000.

83 Quoted by Costello in "The Murder of Griboyedov," pp. 74–75.

ing into Russian hands.[84] It seems highly unlikely that the loss of Mīrzā Ya'qūb was so important as to cause the Shah to plot the death of Griboyedov. The agitation against the Russian minister also threatened the throne with its violence, as had the movement leading to jihad, and rather than encourage any such danger, Fatḥ 'Alī Shāh must have sought to avoid it. That he realized the possibility of Russia making war on Iran again if provoked is also clear from his horrified reaction to the murder.[85]

In fact, Griboyedov's fate was not determined by Mirzā Ya'qūb, but by two Georgian women from the house of Allāhyār Khān Āṣaf ud-Daula. According to *Rauḍat uṣ-Ṣafā-yi Nāṣiri*,[86] it was Mīrzā Ya'qūb who brought their existence to the notice of Griboyedov; it is possible that on account of some enmity, he wished to cause Āṣaf ud-Daula discomfort and humiliation. It appears, however, more probable that Griboyedov was seeking to punish him for his hostility to Russia, a hostility that had hardly been lessened by his captivity in Russian hands from October, 1827 to July, 1828.[87] Āṣaf ud-Daula, fearing to provoke an incident, dispatched the women accompanied by a number of servants. The latter were refused entry to the Russian envoy's house, but the women were detained.[88] The Russians claimed that the women, who had embraced Islam and borne children to Āṣaf ud-Daula, wished to leave Iran;[89] but the rumor spread that they were being held against their will and were being forced to renounce Islam.[90] According to one account, they conveyed their unwillingness by reciting the Quran loud enough for those outside to hear.[91]

It was at this point that the ulama intervened. It is not clear whether Āṣaf ud-Daula was alone in asking for their assistance; doubtless he was at least the most prominent to do so. The people of Tehran, despairing at the acquiescence of the government in

84 Mīrzā Ya'qūb had been one of the eunuchs charged with the care of Fatḥ 'Alī Shāh's private chambers ('Aḍud ud-Daula, *op. cit.*, p. 28).

85 Watson, *op. cit.*, p. 252.

86 *RSN*, IX, 708.

87 Watson, *op. cit.*, p. 249; Costello, *op. cit.*, p. 76 n. 3.

88 *NT*, I, 222; Jahāngīr Mīrzā, *op. cit.*, p. 122.

89 See Maltsov's account quoted by Costello, *op. cit.*, p. 78.

90 *Ibid.*, p. 77; Watson, *op. cit.*, p. 250; *RSN*, IX, 708.

91 *NT*, I, 222. The account quoted by Qā'im Maqām (*op. cit.*, p. 27) says that the women were not Georgians, but Armenians, from the eastern provinces of the Ottoman Empire; and that they succeeded in escaping from Griboyedov's house and incited the people against him. This information is in contradiction to all other available accounts.

Griboyedov's high-handedness, may have seen in the affliction of Āṣaf ud-Daula a means to avenge themselves on the Russian envoy.[92] The ulama of Tehran, headed by Ḥājjī Mīrzā Masīḥ, a pupil of Mīrzā Abū-l-Qāsim Qumī,[93] initially sent a message to Griboyedov, demanding the release of the women and pointing out the dangers of his refusing to do so.[94] The women were not released, and a representative sent to Griboyedov by the ulama was turned back without having seen him.[95] Ḥājjī Mīrzā Masīḥ thereupon delivered a fatvā to the effect that the rescue of Muslim women from the hands of unbelievers was lawful.[96] The day after the fatvā was delivered, the bazaars were closed, and a number of townspeople made their way to Griboyedov's house.[97] Maltsov maintained that the ulama urged them to "go to the house of the Russian minister, remove the captives and kill Mīrzā Ya'qūb and Rustam [a Georgian in Griboyedov's retinue]."[98] It seems unlikely, however, that the intention of the ulama was more than to curb Griboyedov's activities and to secure the release of the women. Ḥājjī Mīrzā Masīḥ repeated his appeal twice but without effect.[99] In any case, the number of rioters now assembled was so great as to be beyond control.[100] The two women were released, but as the mob demanded Mīrzā Ya'qūb, the Cossacks opened fire, and a boy of fourteen was killed.[101] There followed a general attack on Griboyedov's residence, in which Mīrzā Ya'qūb and the entire Russian mission, with the exception of Maltsov, who happened to be elsewhere at the time, were massacred.[102]

In order to placate the Russian government and save Iran from the ordeal of another war, Khusrau Mīrzā, one of the sons of

92 *RSN*, IX, 708.

93 *Q'U*, p. 108.

94 *RSN*, IX, 708.

95 *Ibid.*, p. 708; Jahāngīr Mīrzā, *op. cit.*, p. 122.

96 Watson, *op. cit.*, p. 251.

97 *Ibid.*, p. 252.

98 Costello, *op. cit.*, p. 77.

99 Jahāngīr Mīrzā, *op. cit.*, p. 122.

100 *RSN*, IX, 708.

101 *Ibid.*, p. 709. Najmī (*op. cit.*, p. 277), without giving his source, states that the first attack on Griboyedov's house was made before the delivery of the fatvā, and that in the course of it six people were killed. See also Qā'im Maqām (*op. cit.*, p. 27), who says that the corpse of each was borne to a separate mosque, from which the rioters then set out in greater numbers.

102 *RSN*, IX, 709. The number of dead among the rioters is given by Riḍā Qulī Khān as approximately eighty; by Jahāngīr Mīrzā as approximately eighty (*op. cit.*, p. 216); and by Watson (*op. cit.*, p. 252) as thirty-five.

'Abbās Mīrzā, was sent on a mission to St. Petersburg in the company of Maltsov.[103] The Tsar, being preoccupied by a war with the Ottoman Empire, was not reluctant to overlook the affair but stipulated that the chief instigator of the disturbances, Ḥājjī Mīrzā Masīḥ, be banished from Tehran. Fatḥ 'Alī Shāh hesitated in complying with this condition, for, according to the *Nāsikh ut-Tavārīkh*,[104] "he suspected it to be contrary to the sharī'at." His doubts were probably inspired by the resistance of Ḥājjī Mīrzā Masīḥ to any attempt to expel him. After some delay, he was persuaded by Ḥājjī Muḥammad Ibrāhīm Kalbāsī to leave for the 'atabāt and not make himself responsible for a new war with Russia. As he was preparing to depart, certain of his followers convinced him that once he left Tehran he would be sent to Tiflis for execution by the Russians; again he refused to leave Tehran.[105] Eventually, on Ṣafar 8, 1244/August 29, 1829, he was brought by force to the Masjid-i Shāh, and compelled to take leave of his family and followers in view of the public.[106] This was the sign for further disorder and rioting, more serious than that which ended in the sack of the Russian legation, and this time directed solely against the government. The gates of the citadel were closed, and cannon mounted on its walls; Fatḥ 'Alī Shāh, no longer anxious to comply with the desires of the ulama, threatened a general massacre. Finally, again with the intervention of Ḥājjī Muḥammad Ibrāhīm Kalbāsī, Ḥājjī Mīrzā Masīḥ was escorted peacefully out of Tehran in disguise.[107]

Thus ended the Griboyedov episode. Though many details are unclear, it appears unnecessary to search here for hidden motives. If, as some writers imply,[108] Āṣaf ud-Daula was interested in a renewal of the war with Russia, it remains unexplained how he succeeded in persuading Griboyedov to demand the two Georgian women from his household, and that such a stratagem could even have occurred to an Iranian nobleman, jealous of his honor (*ghayrat*), is highly questionable. On the basis of the available evidence, it is not possible to assert that the massacre was brought

103 *NT*, I, 208.
104 P. 209.
105 *Ibid.*, p. 209; *RSN*, IX, 712.
106 *NT*, I, 209.
107 *Loc. cit.*; *RSN*, IX, 713.
108 Costello, *op. cit.*, p. 78. Najmī (*op. cit.*, p. 277) also attributes the whole affair to enemies of 'Abbās Mīrzā.

about "not by a spontaneous outburst of mob violence, but by a plot, in which the conspirators were leading members of the Persian government";[109] at the most, it could be said that such a plot could have existed, but that final evidence remains to be found. Soviet historians, for their part, attribute the murder to British intrigue.[110]

The episode appears above all as a confrontation between people and government, in which the ulama act as inspirers and leaders of popular feeling and defenders of the national honor. "The common people clearly said that if the government gave orders contrary to their will, they would ignore them and fight against it."[111] The closing of the bazaar, the gathering in the Masjid-i Shāh, the use of martyrs' corpses to inspire violent anger, the fury of the people when threatened with the removal of their leaders—all these are elements of Iranian history which recur in later, more serious situations. The episode provided the first clear confrontation between the government and the people; that the confrontation was religiously motivated and centered on the person of a mujtahid was not coincidental. The government became increasingly suspected of treason and cooperation with foreign, non-Muslim powers; the ulama were the natural leaders of opposition to it. The events connected with the murder of Griboyedov were without immediate consequences of any importance; but they gave a foreboding of many later developments.

THE ULAMA AND THE MISSIONARY: THE REACTION TO HENRY MARTYN

In the events leading to the Second Perso-Russian War and the murder of Griboyedov, we see the ulama formulating the national reaction to the aggressive impact of the northern neighbor. In the reign of Fatḥ 'Alī Shāh, a close involvement of British policy with Iran also begins, one which in many of its aspects was to elicit a strong reaction from the ulama. At this stage, however, no such reaction is to be observed, nor does there appear to have been any

109 Costello, *op. cit.*, p. 66.

110 See D. P. Costello, "A Note on 'The Diplomatic Activity of A. S. Griboyedov' by S. V. Shostakovich," *Slavonic and East European Review*, LX (1961–1962), 235–244. The *Bol'shaya Sovyetskaya Entsiklopediya* (XII, 583) attributes Griboyedov's death to "British agents and reactionary circles."

111 *RSN*, IX, 709.

direct contact between agents of British policy and members of the clerical classes: only a handful of travelers met and recorded their impressions of some of the prominent ulama.[112] Nonetheless, the activities of an English missionary, Henry Martyn, did not go unnoticed by the ulama; and despite their minimal effect, as indeed that of all proselytism among Muslims, they deserve examining, for to counteract them was peculiarly the concern of the ulama.

Martyn (who came to be known as the "*pādrī*") arrived in Shiraz from India in June, 1811, and it was chiefly in that town that he engaged in controversy.[113] According to the *Ma'āthir-i Sulṭānīya*,[114] he pretended to adopt Islam, and taking the name of Yūsuf, studied the religious sciences at the madrasas of Shiraz. Mīrzā Abū-l-Qāsim Qā'im Maqām, in the introduction to his *Miftāḥ un-Nubūwwa*, written in refutation of Martyn's polemics against Islam, says that Martyn, on arriving in Shiraz, made a show of being favorably inclined toward Islam. He then encouraged "a simple-minded ascetic" to write a vindication of the prophecy of the Prophet Muḥammad, which by its inadequacy would tend to discredit Islam.[115] It is clear, however, that an exchange of polemical tracts started soon after his arrival, a fact that makes at least the first accusation appear improbable. On Jumādī ul-Ukhrā 23, 1226/July 26, 1811, a certain Mīrzā Ibrāhīm, "the preceptor of all the moolas," delivered himself of a treatise on the prophetic mission of the Prophet Muḥammad, dealing chiefly with the inimitability (*i'jāz*) of the Quran.[116] At the beginning of this risāla, Mīrzā

[112] E.g., J. B. Fraser (*A Winter's Journey from Constantinople to Teheran* [London, 1838], I, 483); A. Conolly (*A Journey to the North of India Overland from England, through Russia, Persia and Affghaunistaun* [London, 1834], I, 265, 296, 333); and A. Burnes (*Travels into Bukhara* [London, 1834], II, 81), all of whom visited Mashhad and wrote favorably of the mujtahids they encountered. Beyond these casual contacts, Maḥmūd Maḥmūd (*TRS*, I, 337) claims that Conolly made use of the ulama for purposes of espionage in Khurasan, but offers no evidence. Similarly he suggests (*ibid.*, I, 88 n. 1) that the British obtained the dismissal of Mīrzā Ibrāhīm Khān Shīrāzī by mounting against him a campaign of clerical pressure. This suggestion, too, is unsupported.

[113] See introduction by S. Lee to Henry Martyn, *Controversial Tracts on Christianity and Mohammedanism* (Cambridge, 1824), p. cxv.

[114] 'Abd ur-Razzāq Dunbulī, *Ma'āthir-i Sulṭānīya* (Tabriz, 1242 Q/1826), p. 147.

[115] Contained in Muḥammad Ṣādiq Ḥusaynī, *Makhzan ul-Inshā* (Tabriz, 1274 Q/1857), p. 176.

[116] Martyn, *op. cit.*, p. cxv. A translation of the treatise is given on pp. 1–39 of the same work. J. Wolff (*Missionary Journal* [London, 1829], III, 67) mentions

Ibrāhīm states that "a certain Christian priest has requested me to set down proofs upon which I rely respecting the mission of our Prophet after Christ";[117] but treatises on the same theme quickly multiplied, and these were probably in response to some printed polemic against Islam circulated by Martyn.[118] Mullā Aḥmad Narāqī called together ten of the rabbis of Kashan, and with their help translated into Persian a number of passages from the Old Testament and Jewish theological works, which he included in his tract refuting Henry Martyn, entitled *Sayf ul-Umma.*[119] Other treatises were produced by Mullā 'Alī Nūrī,[120] Mullā 'Alī Akbar b. Muḥammad Bāqir Iṣfahānī,[121] Ḥājj Mullā Taqī Burghānī, Sayyid Muḥammad Karbalā'ī, Mullā Ibrāhīm Kalbāsī, Ḥājj Mullā Mūsā Najafī, and Mīrzā Muḥammad Akhbārī.[122]

It is therefore surprising to find Qā'im Maqām writing that Martyn's polemics had not been considered worthy of an answer until the matter reached the knowledge of Fatḥ 'Alī Shāh.[123] Possibly he meant that the answers given had all appeared ineffectual; but such an admission, even by implication, would be even more surprising, for among those who wrote in reply to Martyn were some of the most eminent ulama of the age. It might be thought that these risālas were composed later, on royal instructions, but the only tract of which this is recorded is that of Ḥājj Mullā Riḍā Hamadānī.[124] 'Abbās Mīrzā, in his angry letter to Qā'im Maqām at the end of the Second Perso-Russian War, accuses the ulama of not being able to refute the *pādrī* successfully; whether this accu-

---

among those who wrote refutations of Martyn, Mīrzā Ibrāhīm Fasā'ī; it is possibly to him that the reference is made. Furthermore, his treatise, weak in reasoning, may be that mentioned unfavorably by Qā'im Maqām; though a tendentious translation may have shorn it of some of its force.

117 Martyn, *op. cit.*, p. 1. The use of the word "our" before "Prophet," the projection of a non-Muslim conviction, strengthens the suspicion of tendentious translation.

118 According to Morier (*A Second Journey*, p. 224), Martyn's real purpose in Iran was to produce a Persian translation of the Bible; and while engaged in this task, was drawn into controversy and impelled to publish a tract. His translation was published at Calcutta in 1816.

119 *Q'U*, pp. 93–94; *RJ*, p. 27.

120 *Q'U*, p. 122; *RJ*, p. 417; Wolff, *op. cit.*, III, 67.

121 *RJ*, p. 416.

122 Wolff, *op. cit.*, III, 156.

123 Introduction to *Miftāḥ un-Nubūwwa*, in Ḥusaynī, *op. cit.*, p. 187. Qā'im Maqām's tract itself may also have been designed for royal perusal, if not directly commissioned.

124 *Ibid.*, p. 188; Martyn, *op. cit.*, p. 161; Wolff, *op. cit.*, III, 67.

sation is motivated simply by his anger at the treachery of Mīr Fattāḥ, is difficult to tell.[125]

The volume of the response aroused by Martyn's polemics, whatever its quality, does not in itself point to any positive impact made by his attacks on Islam. It was an age of intense theological activity, and polemical tracts against Sufism and Akhbārism, as well as Christianity, were a commonplace. The enjoyment of disputation for its own sake cannot be discounted: Wolff relates a meeting with a mujtahid of Shiraz, who admitted liking conversation with foreigners, for, he said, "it sharpens the understanding."[126] If Wolff also found frequent occasion during his wanderings to exclaim, "Martyn! Oh! my Martyn! thou hast kindled a light in Persia which will never go out!"[127] it is hard to discern any lasting effect of Martyn's activities in Iran. Indeed, after his departure from Iran, we find few, if any, examples of open proselytism among Muslims in Iran; although many of the later ulama, in particular Āqā Najafī, clashed with missionaries, these clashes were only an aspect of the general, external impact of the West on Iran. The ideological threat implicit in this impact was different from that of missionary polemics, and the nature of the ulama's response more complex and far reaching in its consequences.

In the reign of Fatḥ 'Alī Shāh we see then already developing the dual role of the ulama, that of opposing the state, and that of countering the impact of foreign powers. This role was to become more explicit and active as the century progressed. Fatḥ 'Alī Shāh's policy, based partly on personal piety and partly on considerations of state, was able to restrict the expression of the contradiction between state and ulama. His efforts could not, in the nature of things, have been successful, and when his successors failed to make such efforts, the contradiction became more apparent and immediate in its effects.

125 See above, pp. 80, 91.
126 Wolff, *op. cit.*, III, 52.
127 *Ibid.*, p. 46 and *passim*.

VI

The Reign of Muḥammad Shāh

In the reign of Muḥammad Shāh, relations between the state and the ulama entered a new phase of conflict and hostility. If Fatḥ 'Alī Shāh had sought, however erratically and unsuccessfully, to reconcile the demands of piety and the tasks of absolute ruler, the attempt was largely abandoned by Muḥammad Shāh. The heterodox nature of his religious beliefs and those of his vazīr, Ḥājjī Mīrzā Āqāsi, did not provide for even a theoretical acknowledgment of the Shah's submission to a marja'-i taqlīd. Although the Bābī insurrections might have been expected to bring together ulama and monarchy against a common enemy, they revealed themselves ultimately as events of passing and marginal importance, despite their violent and spectacular appearance. In the reign of Nāṣir ud-Dīn Shāh, intermittent attempts were again made to restore some kind of viable relationship between the ulama and the state, but in vain: to the inherent incompatibility between Shi'i doctrine and monarchy had been added an intense and specific hatred of the Qajar dynasty.

Certain aspects of Fatḥ 'Alī Shāh's clerical policy may again be discerned in the events of Muḥammad Shāh's reign. He, too, as a sign of piety, extended his patronage to the shrines of Arab Iraq: he had the golden dome at Karbala restored after its destruction by the Wahhābī raiders in 1216/1801,[1] and in 1252/1836–1837, sent Mīrzā Ḥasan Rashtī to supervise repairs undertaken on his orders at Kāẓimayn.[2] Mosques were again built in the name of the sovereign, notably the Masjid-i Jāmi' in Khūy.[3] Early in his reign he entrusted the distribution of the royal bounty among the ulama and sayyids to Mīrzā Naṣrullāh Ardabīlī, and the sum given away yearly amounted to 100,000 tomans.[4] Ḥājj Mullā Muḥammad Ja'far Astarābādī, first invited to settle in Tehran by Fatḥ 'Alī Shāh, was in 1255/1839–1840 again summoned to the capital by Muḥammad Shāh.[5] On occasion, clerical intercession on behalf of rebels was accepted; thus the ulama of Shushtar obtained pardon for Muḥammad Taqī Khān, a rebellious Bakhtiyārī chieftain.[6] One of the ulama, Ḥajj Mullā Aḥmad Kirmānshāhī, was even appointed governor of Dizful.[7] While Fatḥ 'Alī Shāh, for all his show of piety, had not prohibited the sale of alcohol, his successor did so, and was himself an abstainer.[8] He directed, moreover, that all lands seized by Nādir Shāh should be restored to their original owners, if proof of ownership could be provided to a shar' court.[9] Considering the length of time that had elapsed since the death of Nādir, it seems probable this measure was intended to lessen the enmity of the ulama: clearly Fatḥ 'Alī Shāh had never found it necessary. Whether it was any longer possible to determine the ownership of the confiscated lands, seems in any event questionable.

Such expressions of orthodox piety and deference to the ulama appear, however, as isolated elements in contradiction to the general tendencies of their reign—partly as habits inherited from

1 'Imād ud-Dīn Ḥusayn Iṣfahānī, *Tārīkh-i Jughrāfīyā'ī-yi Karbalā-yi Mu'allā* (Tehran, 1326 Sh/1947), p. 150.

2 *NT*, I, 341.

3 Mīrzā Muḥammad Ḥasan Khān I'timād us-Salṭana, *Mir'āt ul-Buldān-i Nāṣirī* (Tehran, 1294–1297 Q/1877–1880), IV, 102.

4 *RSN*, X, 169, 171.

5 Muḥammad 'Alī Mu'allim Bīdābādī, *Makārim ul-Āthār dar Aḥvāl-i Rijāl-i Daura-yi Qājār* (Isfahan, 1337 Sh/1958), I, 85. He died in 1263/1846–1847. (*RSN*, X, 241).

6 *NT*, I, 402.

7 *MN*, III, 179.

8 W. K. Stuart, *Journal of a Residence in Northern Persia and the Adjacent Provinces of Turkey* (London, 1854), p. 206; *NT*, I, 476.

9 *Ibid.*, 477.

Fatḥ 'Alī Shāh, and partly as unimportant and incidental concessions. Muḥammad Shāh's devotion to Sufism, and more particularly to the eccentric person of his preceptor and vazīr, Ḥājjī Mīrzā Āqāsī, tended to override other loyalties. In the ancient conflict between Sufi and faqīh, the monarch was now involved; and the precarious balance between the monarchy and the ulama preserved by Fatḥ 'Alī Shāh was virtually destroyed.

Muḥammad Shāh appears to have been inclined from his earliest youth to seek the company of dervishes, and his acquaintance with Ḥājjī Mīrzā Āqāsī confirmed these early tendencies. One of the Ni'matullāhī order, Muḥammad Riḍā Hamadānī ("Kauthar 'Alī Shāh"), had taken refuge with 'Abbās Mīrzā from the persecutions of the ulama and was an honored figure at the Crown Prince's court.[10] It is reasonable to suppose that Muḥammad Shāh came under his influence while in Tabriz. Not only Ḥājjī Mīrzā Aqāsī, but also a certain Pir Ḥājjī 'Abd ul-Vahhāb Nā'īnī prophesied that among all the Qajar princes, Muḥammad would succeed to the throne. While Ḥājjī Mīrzā Āqāsī was rewarded with the control of Iran, Pir Ḥājjī 'Abd ul-Vahhāb received a more modest token of gratitude in the shape of a shrine erected for him in Nā'īn.[11]

It was, however, Ḥājjī Mīrzā Āqāsī who ultimately gained the devotion of Muḥammad Shāh. Born in Erivan, he was taken in his youth by his father, Mīrzā Muslim to the 'atabāt, where he studied under the celebrated Sufi, 'Abd uṣ-Ṣamad Hamadānī.[12] When his master was killed in the Wahhābī attack on Karbala, Ḥājjī Mīrzā Āqāsī left the 'atabāt, and for some time worked as clerk to the Armenian patriarch of Erivan.[13] After further wanderings in the guise of a dervish, he joined the court of 'Abbās Mīrzā in Tabriz,

[10] Zayn ul-'Ābidīn Shīrvānī, *Būstān us-Siyāḥa* (Tehran, 1315 Q/1897–1898), p. 614; Aḥmad 'Alī Khān Vazīrī, *Tārīkh-i Kirmān*, ed. H. Farmānfarmā'īān (Tehran, 1340 Sh/1962), p. 350. Even before Mullā Riḍā fled from Hamadan, one of the women in 'Abbās Mīrzā's household, Jānbājī Khānum, had been sending him a regular allowance (Aḥmad Mīrzā 'Aḍud ud-Daula, *Tārīkh-i 'Aḍudī*, ed. Ḥusayn Kūhī Kirmānī [Tehran, 1327 Sh/1948], p. 13).

[11] P. M. Sykes, *Ten Thousand Miles in Persia* (London, 1902), p. 345. According to *RSN* (X, 150–151), the dervish was called Ḥājjī Muḥammad Ḥasan Nā'īnī, and others made the same prediction.

[12] *RSN*, X, 168. For a brief biography of 'Abd uṣ-Ṣamad Hamadānī, see Muḥammad 'Ali Tabrīzī Khīābānī, *Rayḥānat ul-Adab* (Tehran, 1326 St/1947–1948), IV, 326.

[13] W. R. Holmes, *Sketches on the Shore of the Caspian* (London, 1845), p. 357.

where he established himself as tutor and companion to Muḥammad Mīrzā.[14]

According to the *Nāsikh ut-Tavārīkh*, Muḥammad Shāh considered Ḥājjī Mīrzā Aqāsī to be "the pole of the firmament of both sharī'at and ṭarīqat," and was strengthened in his conviction by the wondrous deeds which Ḥājjī Mīrzā Aqāsi performed.[15] Thus he was reputed to have once alleviated the ferocity of the summer heat for the sake of the Shah's well-being.[16] It would seem that the relation between the monarch and his minister was even more than of disciple and spiritual guide. Muḥammad Shāh "did not doubt that . . . Ḥājjī Mīrzā Aqāsī had direct and frequent communications with the divinity, and that he was himself a being of far from ordinary nature."[17]

After the disgrace of Qā'im Maqām early in the reign of Muḥammad Shāh (1251/1836), the affairs of Iran were controlled until 1848 by this dervish of whom an English observer remarked that "his words and actions are strongly tinctured with real or affected insanity."[18] Amidst the eccentricity of his rule, however, one constant element is visible: patronage of Sufis and their shrines. Whereas Fatḥ 'Alī Shāh lavished his attentions on the shrines of Qum, Mashhad, and Arab Iraq, Muḥammad Shāh, guided by Ḥājjī Mīrzā Āqāsī, preferred to attend to the tombs of Farīd ud-Dīn 'Aṭṭār and Shaykh Maḥmūd Shabistarī.[19] Other places of Sufi pilgrimage were erected or repaired in Kirman,[20] Nā'īn, Bisṭām,[21] and Turbat-i Shaykh Jām.[22] A number of lands round Kirman were assigned as vaqf to the shrine of Shāh Ni'matullāh Valī in

14 *MN*, III, 78; *RSN*, X, 168.

15 *NT*, I, 333.

16 *Ibid.*, p. 336.

17 A. de Gobineau, *Trois Ans en Asie* (Paris, 1859), p. 336. Even in relation to Ni'matullāhī Sufism, Ḥājjī Mīrzā Āqāsī appears to have been of heterodox belief, if indeed holding any belief at all. Together with Riḍā Qulī Khān Hidāyat, he was one of the "spiritual progeny" of Zayn ul-'Ābidīn Shīrvānī (Mast 'Alī Shāh), author of the *Bustān us-Siyāḥa* (see Khiābānī, *op. cit.*, I, 406; and Bīdābādī, *op. cit.*, I, 20), but according to Mas'ūd Mīrzā Ẓill us-Sulṭān (*Tarīkh-i Sargudhasht-i Mas'ūdī* [Tehran, 1325 Q/1907], p. 197), his claim to be successor of Zayn ul-'Ābidīn was not generally accepted.

18 R. Wilbraham, *Travels in the Transcaucasian Provinces of Russia* (London, 1839), p. 19.

19 *NT*, I, 477.

20 Vazīrī, *op. cit.*, p. 126.

21 *NT*, I, 477.

22 *RSN*, X, 204.

Mahan.[23] Sufis were given posts at court and entrusted with government missions: Mīrzā Mihdī Khū'ī, a *murshid* (spiritual guide) of the Ni'matullāhī order, was chief scribe to the Shah;[24] a dervish, 'Abd ul-Muḥammad Maḥallātī, was once dispatched to Herat to negotiate with the Amir.[25]

It was inevitable that these predilections of the monarch and his vazīr should alienate the ulama. While Sufis were thus favored and their shrines as freely endowed as those of the Imams, it was no longer possible to suppress all manifestations of Sufism, much less to enjoy the support of the monarch and his ministers in so doing. The open profession of Sufism became common,[26] and thus the standing and influence of the ulama among the masses was endangered. Their rivals in directing the religious emotions of the nation were protected, and throughout the reign of Muḥammad Shāh we encounter no mujtahid daring to emulate the example of Mīrzā Muḥammad 'Alī Bihbihānī in the killing of Sufis. The ground thus gained by the Sufis was never entirely lost, and they enjoyed a position of security and even respect in the reign of Nāṣir ud-Dīn Shāh. Not even with the patronage of the monarch and his minister, however, did they represent anything more than a mild irritant for the ulama: the institutionalized nature of the power of the latter, and its greater breadth and acceptance, made it virtually invulnerable.

There were other, more serious, political consequences of Muḥammad Shāh's mystical beliefs. That the country should be ruled by a king of unorthodox belief was in itself scandalous. Moreover, his submission to Ḥājjī Mīrzā Āqāsī as murshid excluded the possibility of any direct influence by the ulama on the conduct of affairs. Ultimately, the monarch, no less than any other Shi'i, was bound to conform, in matters of practice, to the rulings of a learned mujtahid, as marja'-i taqlīd. In the case of Fatḥ 'Alī Shāh, this conformity had sometimes been enforced. But Muḥammad Shāh's unquestioning devotion to Ḥājjī Mīrzā Āqāsī left no room for the consultation of religious authority. "The deeds of one who has a

23 Sykes, *op. cit.*, p. 149.

24 Riḍā Qulī Khān Hidāyat, *Majma' ul-Fuṣaḥā* (Tehran, 1288 Q/1871–1872), II, 439.

25 *RSN*, X, 237.

26 C. A. de Bode, *Travels in Luristan and Arabistan* (London, 1845), I, 47.

king for disciple will appear pleasing, even if they are all evil."[27] Not only were the monarch and his minister unamenable to clerical direction, but also throughout the country intercession by the ulama and pressure on local governors became less successful. The gap between doctrinal conceptions of authority and the realities of monarchical power could be partially offset only by a policy of careful accommodation on the part of the monarch, and such a policy was never undertaken by Muḥammad Shāh. This, together with certain tendencies toward strengthening the central power of the state, made conflict between the state and the ulama inevitable.

The conflict began at the very outset of the reign. On the death of Fatḥ 'Alī Shāh, Mīrzā Abū-l-Qāsim Qā'im Maqām summoned together the ulama of Tabriz, among them Mīrzā Aḥmad Mujtahid and Mīrzā 'Alī Aṣghar Shaykh ul-Islām, requested them to break the news of his accession to Muḥammad Shāh—then Crown Prince and Governor of Azerbayjan—and to cooperate in maintaining order during the transfer of rule to the new monarch.[28] But even before the new monarch left for the capital, he had clashed with the ulama and ordered the execution of one of their number. In July, 1834, he was confronted with a riot occasioned by a shortage of corn and a consequent rise in the price of bread. The townspeople, holding his entourage responsible, gathered in front of his palace to protest, led by a mullā. When they refused to disperse, he gave orders that the mullā be seized and hanged in full view of the public.[29] Other disturbances in which the ulama participated occurred in Tehran,[30] but Muḥammad Shāh on arriving there was greeted by many of the ulama, and temporary peace prevailed.[31]

Considerably more serious was the prolonged reign of anarchy in Isfahan where Fatḥ 'Alī Shāh died, in which Ḥājjī Sayyid Muḥammad Bāqir Shaftī played a leading part. On the death of Fatḥ 'Alī Shāh, Ḥusayn 'Alī Mīrzā Farmānfarmā had proclaimed himself Shah in Shiraz, taking the name of 'Alī Shāh, and dispatched his brother, Ḥasan 'Alī Mīrzā Shujā' us-Salṭana, in the direction of

27 A verse from chapter five of Sa'dī's *Gulistan* quoted in *RSN*, X, 174.
28 *RSN*, X, 308.
29 A. von Tornau, "Aus der neuesten Geschichte Persiens: Die Jahre 1833–1835," *ZDMG*, II (1848), 415; Gobineau, *op. cit.*, p. 315.
30 J. McNeill, *Memoir of the Right Hon. Sir John McNeill* (London, 1910), p. 195.
31 *NT*, I, 319.

Isfahan to gain the obedience of the province of Iraq.[32] In Isfahan itself his claim was supported by 'Abdullāh Khān Amīn ud-Daula, the last minister of Fatḥ 'Alī Shāh, and by Ḥājjī Sayyid Muḥammad Bāqir Shaftī.[33] Their motives in so doing are of some interest: Amīn ud-Daula, a long-standing enemy of Allāhyār Khān Aṣaf ud-Daula, was unwilling to see his sister's son mount the throne. Beyond this, however, his alliance with Ḥājjī Sayyid Muḥammad Bāqir is indicative of religious motive. Even in the atmosphere of pious devotion to the ulama created by Fatḥ 'Alī Shāh, Amīn ud-Daula had been renowned for his attempts to win their favor.[34] It is possible that he may already have been aware of the threat posed to their influence by the Sufi inclinations of the new monarch. Ḥusayn 'Alī Mīrzā had, shortly before the death of Fatḥ 'Alī Shāh, expelled the Sufi Ḥājjī Mīrzā Zayn ul-'Ābidīn Shīrvānī from Shiraz at the request of the ulama.[35] Although Abū-l-Qāsim Qā'im Maqām was still Muḥammad Shāh's minister, his closest confidant and subsequent vazīr, Ḥājjī Mīrzā Āqāsī, was one of the "spiritual progeny" of Mīrzā Zayn ul-'Ābidīn. Thus Ḥusayn 'Alī Mīrzā might reasonably have been thought to be more amenable to clerical pressure, and therefore a more desirable occupant of the throne.

For Ḥājjī Sayyid Muḥammad Bāqir, such considerations were doubtless also of importance. In his case, however, we see personal ambitions of a more marked nature. His effective dominance of the affairs of Isfahan in the reign of Fatḥ 'Alī Shāh has already been described, and that sovereign, in the course of one of his later visits to Isfahan, is reputed to have noticed a change in his character—a greater interest in personal power.[36] This would seem to be borne out by his relations with the lūṭīs, a kind of secret society that at times engaged in brigandage on its own account and at times acted as the executive arm of clerical authority.[37] On the

32 Jahāngīr Qā'im Maqāmī, "Tauṭi'a-yi Ḥusayn 'Alī Mīrzā Farmānfarmā-yi Fārs," *Yaghmā*, V (1328 Sh/1949–1950), 37; *MN*, III, 162.

33 R. G. Watson, *A History of Persia from the Beginning of the Nineteenth Century to the Year 1858* (London, 1866), p. 283; *RSN*, X, 157; J. B. Fraser, *Travels in Koordistan, Mesopotamia, etc.* (London, 1840), II, 253. Fraser writes that the Farmānfarmā was crowned by Amīn ud-Daula in Isfahan, but in fact he never left Shiraz (see *NT*, I, 301).

34 See *Q'U*, p. 72; 'Aḍud ud-Daula, *op. cit.*, p. 53.

35 Bīdābādī, *op. cit.*, I, 18.

36 *Q'U*, p. 105.

37 See Heinz-Georg Migeod, "Die Lutis: Ein Ferment des städtischen Lebens in Persien," *Journal of the Economic and Social History of the Orient*, II (1959), 82–91.

death of Fatḥ 'Alī Shāh, they immediately began to plunder Isfahan, storing their spoils in the Masjid-i Jum'a.[38] Their leader, Ramaḍān Shāh, became virtual ruler of the town and had coins struck in his own name.[39] Evidence of Ḥājjī Muḥammad Bāqir's involvement in these activities is contradictory: Fraser claims that he encouraged the lūṭīs,[40] while von Tornau writes that on the contrary he attempted to restrain them.[41] According to the *Nāsikh ut-Tavārīkh*,[42] Amīn ud-Daula sent a message to the ulama, in which he recalled the respect they had enjoyed under Fatḥ 'Alī Shāh, and asked them, as a sign of gratitude, to restrain the lūṭīs from excessive plundering. In response, Ḥājjī Sayyid Muḥammad Bāqir and Mīr Muḥammad Mihdī, the imām jum'a, gave orders that a number of the brigands be delivered to Sulṭān Muḥammad Mīrzā, and have their hands and feet severed. It thus appears possible that both Amīn ud-Daula and Ḥājjī Sayyid Muḥammad Bāqir sought to allow the destructive energies of the lūṭīs only so much scope as was compatible with their own purposes. In one sense, the lūṭīs were merely one element of disorder in the chaos accompanying the change of ruler; but, as we shall see, in Isfahan there was a continuing relationship between the lūṭīs and high religious authority. They represented a force that might be pitted against the government; and the sanctuary afforded by mosques and the residences of the ulama was their ultimate protection against retaliation.

Behind Ḥājjī Sayyid Muḥammad Bāqir's use of the lūṭīs, there is visible an attempt to restore to Isfahan its former rank of religious and political centrality. This attempt was continuous, and accounts in large part for the fact that, until the reign of Nāṣir ud-Din Shāh, it was in Isfahan that the chief clashes between the ulama and the state took place. The central authority and its representatives were never more than grudgingly accepted, and resistance to them never ceased. In this sense too, the Qajar attempt at a restoration of the Safavid state was a failure. It is significant that we find the *navvābs* (descendants of the Safavids) of Isfahan involved together with the lūṭīs and Ḥājjī Sayyid Muḥammad Bāqir in the disturbances of Muḥammad Shāh's reign.[43]

38 Fraser, *op. cit.*, II, 283.
39 De Bode, *op. cit.*, I, 49.
40 Fraser, *op. cit.*, II, 283.
41 Von Tornau, *op. cit.*, p. 422.
42 P. 302.
43 Ẓill us-Sulṭān, *op. cit.*, p. 184.

Thus it was that when the Farmānfarmā's claims finally collapsed, and Manūchihr Khān Mu'tamad ud-Daula, supported by a number of British officers, took possession of Isfahan on behalf of Muḥammad Shāh, the resistance of Ḥājjī Sayyid Muḥammad Bāqir to the dictates of secular authority continued unaffected.[44] As mujtahid, his own person was inviolable, and he extended his protection to Amīn ud-Daula. Sheltering him in his house in Bīdābād, he interceded on his behalf with the Shah until it was conceded that Amīn ud-Daula might proceed untroubled to either Mashhad or the 'atabāt.[45] He remained in Isfahan, however, and under the protection of Ḥājjī Sayyid Muḥammad Bāqir was able to act freely. A letter from Abū-l-Qāsim Qā'im Maqām to Ḥājjī Sayyid Muḥammad Bāqir, reproaching him for his persistent encouragement of Amīn ud-Daula, suggests a survival of the coalition between Ḥājji Sayyid Muḥammad Bāqir, Amīn ud-Daula, and the lūṭīs, and ends with an appeal to Ḥājjī Sayyid Muḥammad Bāqir no longer to impede the restoration of peace: "It has repeatedly been rumoured that in the course of this period he [Amīn ud-Daula] has not been inactive, nor considered idleness permissible. Your excellency is better aware of how much of the property of the people of Isfahan has until now been destroyed, how much blood been spilt, how many souls borne on the wind of extinction, both in that province and elsewhere. . . . If he [Amīn ud-Daula] disregards our wishes, which are motivated solely by concern for the welfare of the people, and magnanimity towards his own person, we desire of you that you may not admit him to your presence."[46] Finally, in Shavvāl, 1251/January-February, 1836, Muḥammad Shāh dispatched one of his courtiers to Isfahan to escort Amīn ud-Daula from the town.[47] At the same time, a number of lūṭīs were sent to Tehran, where they were punished with the severance of their hands.[48]

Still, Ḥājjī Sayyid Muḥammad Bāqir persisted in his opposition to Muḥammad Shāh and his agents. In 1253/1837–1838, together with Mīr Muḥammad Mihdī, imām jum'a, he directed an open revolt against the governor of Isfahan, Khusrau Khān, who had

44 *MN*, III, 162; Fraser, *op. cit.*, II, 282.

45 'Abbas Iqbāl, "Ḥujjat ul-Islām Ḥājj Sayyid Muḥammad Bāqir Shaftī," *Yādgār*, V (1327 Sh/1948–1949), 37.

46 Muḥammad Ṣādiq Ḥusaynī, *Makhzan ul-Inshā* (Tabriz, 1274 Q/1857), p. 359.

47 Iqbāl, *op. cit.*, p. 39.

48 *NT*, I, 329.

shown himself disinclined to accept the intervention of the ulama in the affairs of the city.[49] Thus he refused to accept Mīr Muḥammad Mihdī's pleas on behalf of a trader, Āqā Shafī' Najafābādī, who was remiss in his payment of taxes. It was this refusal that provided the immediate pretext for the revolt. Khusrau Khān took refuge in his palace, and Farrukh Khān Kāshī Ghaffārī was sent from Tehran to negotiate between the governor and the ulama. He was met at the gates of Isfahan by a crowd of townspeople who obliged him to take up residence in the house of the imām jum'a, and to acquiesce in the expulsion of Khusrau Khān.[50] Farrukh Khān then remained temporarily as governor until the appointment of Faḍl 'Alī Khān.

Encouraged by this success, Ḥājjī Sayyid Muḥammad Bāqir and his allies among the lūṭīs extended their activities. At night the lūṭīs would emerge from bast and engage in murder, robbery, and rape with impunity. "The next day, they would wash their swords, which were red with the blood of Muslims, in the water-tanks of the mosques."[51] Finally in 1255/1839–1840, an army under Manūchihr Khān Mu'tamad ud-Daula was dispatched to put a definite end to the chaos in Isfahan.[52] More than 150 of the lūṭīs were executed, and a similar number banished to Ardabil.[53] Others who had taken refuge in Qum were promised safety if they surrendered; but on emerging from the sanctuary, they were slaughtered.[54]

On this occasion, Muḥammad Shāh himself accompanied his army to Isfahan, and met his chief antagonist, Ḥājjī Sayyid Muḥammad Bāqir.[55] The *Qiṣaṣ ul-'Ulamā'* contains a highly significant account of their meeting: although the whole expedition had been undertaken to break the power of the sayyid, and his following had been forcibly dispersed, he was able to preserve an attitude

49 *MN*, III, 169. *NT* (I, 358) places these events in 1254/1838–1839. Later, Ḥājjī Sayyid Muḥammad Bāqir appears to have quarreled with Mīr Muḥammad Mihdī (see Ẓill us-Sulṭān, *op. cit.*, p. 185).

50 *NT*, I, 358.

51 *Ibid.*, p. 385.

52 *MN*, III, 172.

53 *Ibid.*, p. 173.

54 H. Rawlinson, *England and Russia in the East* (London, 1875), p. 344.

55 According to Gobineau (*op. cit.*, p. 315) Muḥammad Shāh on this occasion expelled a mujtahid from Isfahan. Presumably Ḥājjī Sayyid Muḥammad Bāqir is meant; but the Persian sources make no mention of such an expulsion, and it seems unlikely, even in the bitterness of the struggle between the two men, that the monarch would have dared to commit so sacrilegious an act, at least so early in the century.

of arrogant and righteous contempt toward Muḥammad Shāh, one which onlookers evidently felt to be justified. Mounted on a mule, he went to the palace of Haft Dasht, where the monarch had taken up residence. In front went an Arab, 'Ali Naqī, reciting the Quran. On arriving at the palace, he reached, whether by intention or chance, the following verse (27:18): "Till, when they reached the Valley of the Ants, an ant exclaimed: O ants! Enter your dwellings lest Solomon and his armies crush you."[56] The soldiers and courtiers at the palace thronged around his sacred personage, but so dense was the crowd of townspeople that many, unable to gain access to him, had to content themselves with kissing the hooves of his mule.[57]

Although the outward tokens of Hājjī Sayyid Muḥammad Bāqir's exalted power thus remained, Manūchihr Khān's energetic governorship of Isfahan deprived it of much of its reality. A traveler, on visiting Isfahan in 1840, found the power of the lūṭīs broken and Bīdābād, the quarter of Isfahan where Ḥājjī Sayyid Muḥammad Bāqir resided, no longer enjoying the quality of bast.[58] Although Muḥammad Shāh in Shavvāl, 1258/November-December, 1842, found it necessary to come to Isfahan and regulate its affairs yet again, the sayyid was by now old, and on hearing the drumbeats of Muḥammad Shāh's procession approaching his house, merely lifted up his hands in supplication, and said: "O Lord! Desire no longer the humiliation of the descendants of Fāṭima!" Shortly after, he died, and Isfahan was deprived of its spiritual and temporal ruler.[59]

Thus ended the career of Ḥājjī Sayyid Muḥammad Bāqir. It is a clear demonstration of the unconditional power residing in the person of the mujtahid. If, in fact, as was suggested above, a change or development in his motives took place, and his interest in personal power for its own sake became greater than his concern with the fulfillment of religious duty, it is nonetheless clear that his standing was in no way diminished thereby. Even while he condoned bloodshed and plunder, he remained an object of respect. This unquestioning loyalty to the person of the mujtahid, already noticed in connection with the Second Perso-Russian War, enabled

56 The implication is that Muḥammad Shāh, a being as insignificant as an ant, should retreat warily from the approach of one as august as Solomon.

57 *Q'U*, p. 106.

58 De Bode, *op. cit.*, I, 49–51.

59 *Q'U*, p. 123; *MN*, III, 183.

the ulama to arouse and use religious emotions for purposes of a personal, even illegitimate, nature. As the enmity between ulama and state developed, the ulama increasingly exploited this source of power until it found its greatest application in the Constitutional Revolution.

The struggle in Isfahan had been bitter—according to one source,[60] attempts were even made to have the sayyid poisoned or assassinated—and since it was not merely a struggle for the control of Isfahan, it influenced other aspects of Muḥammad Shāh's reign. Prominent among these was the "Karbala affair," which again brought Iran to the edge of war. Fatḥ 'Alī Shāh, who sought an accommodation with the sayyid, had allowed himself to be impelled into war by clerical pressure. Muḥammad Shāh, who by contrast clearly and openly opposed the sayyid was bound also to resist his attempts to force Iran into another war on religious pretexts.

For some time, Karbala had, by virtue of its sanctity, been a place of refuge for thieves and brigands both from Iran and Arab Iraq.[61] Such were their numbers that they could plunder without fear, and the continual stream of pilgrims from Iran provided them with ever new booty. A certain Sayyid Ibrāhīm Qazvīnī Mujtahid was robbed, for instance, of four thousand *qirān*'s.[62] The Ottoman government was thus faced with a problem similar to that which confronted Muḥammad Shāh in Isfahan, but one complicated by the fact that the majority of Karbala's inhabitants were Iranian, and that any attempt to deal with it would risk provoking Iranian reaction. An autonomous Iranian enclave threatened to come into being on Ottoman territory. Successive pashas of Baghdad attempted to reduce Karbala to obedience, but Dā'ūd Pasha's siege of 1239/1824 could secure no more than the partial payment of overdue taxes.[63] Finally Najīb Pasha, in Dhū-l-Qa'da, 1258/December, 1842—January, 1843, decided to take more energetic measures: by now the name of the Sultan was being omitted from the khuṭba, and Ibrāhīm Za'farānī, a lūṭī of Iranian origin, was in complete control of the town.[64] Najīb Pasha's object in attacking

60 *Q'U*, p. 124.

61 *NT*, I, 426.

62 'Abbās al-'Azzāwī, *Tārīkh al-'Irāq bayn Iḥtilālayn* (Baghdad, 1373 Q/1953–1954), VI, 288.

63 *Ibid.*, 289.

64 See Najīb Pasha's letter to the Iranian consul in Baghdad, attached in translation to Sheil's dispatch of March 9, 1843 (F.O. 60/96); and al-'Azzāwī, *op. cit.*, VII, 65 n. 1.

Karbala appears to have been clear: to restore it to the effective control of the Ottoman government. According to Taylor, the British consul in Baghdad, he had sought the cooperation of the mujtahids of Karbala in suppressing the lūṭīs,[65] who for their part could have had no liking for the brigands who terrorized them. Yet the activities of the lūṭīs were a means for securing some kind of independence for Karbala. When a Sunni army attacked a Shi'i holy place, moreover, the reaction of the Shi'i ulama could have been none other than the instinctive one to resist. On Dhū-l-Ḥijja 11, 1258/January 13, 1843, Najīb Pasha's troops entered Karbala and were fired upon by the inhabitants. There followed a general massacre, in which not even those taking refuge in the shrine itself were spared.[66] Estimates of the number killed ranged from 4,000 to 18,000.[67]

The news reached Tehran early in Muḥarram, 1259/February–March, 1843, but was kept secret by Ḥājjī Mīrzā Āqāsī until the end of 'Āshūrā.[68] Muḥammad Shāh was ill at the time, and it is possible that his minister did not wish to inform him until his recovery.[69] It seems more likely that Ḥājjī Mīrzā Āqāsī was reluctant to release such inflammatory information at a time when anti-Sunni feelings were peculiarly excitable. The inevitable outburst of indignation came nonetheless, and its chief spokesman was Ḥājjī Sayyid Muḥammad Bāqir. Ḥājjī Mīrzā Āqāsī found himself caught between two conflicting pressures: that of the ulama, headed by Ḥājjī Sayyid Muḥammad Bāqir, demanding war against the Ottoman Empire, and that of Russia and England, urging a peaceful settlement. Even if it had been possible, it is unlikely that Ḥājjī Mīrzā Āqāsī would have attempted to suppress all reaction to the Karbala massacre, for some temporary diversion to another

65 Report dated February 16, 1843, sent to Sheil in Tehran (F.O. 60/96).

66 *NT*, I, 327; al-'Azzāwī, *op. cit.*, VII, 66. It is a remarkable fact, for which no immediate explanation offers itself, that no Shaykhī houses were attacked, and all those who took refuge in the house of Sayyid Kāẓim Rashtī, Shaykh Aḥmad Aḥsā'ī's successor as head of the sect, were safe. It might be thought that Najīb Pasha made a distinction between Shaykhīs and non-Shaykhīs, holding the latter to be responsible for Karbala's resistance to Ottoman control; but Ibrāhīm Za'farānī was himself a Shaykhī (see al-'Azzāwī, *op. cit.*, VII, 65 n. 1).

67 *Ibid.*, p. 66: 4000; report of an English eyewitness quoted by Sheil in dispatch of March 3, 1843; 5000; *NT*, I, 328: 9000; other rumors mentioned by Sheil: 15,000 to 18,000.

68 Watson, *op. cit.*, p. 340.

69 al-'Azzāwī, *op. cit.*, VII, 68.

target of the religious odium in which the government was held, was doubtless welcome.[70] On the other hand, Ḥājjī Sayyid Muḥammad Bāqir, in April, 1843, informed the Russian ambassador in Tehran, Count Medem, that he would dispatch an army against Baghdad, "whatever the intentions of the Shah."[71] These were ominous words, reminiscent of those used in the events leading up to the Second Perso-Russian War. Ḥājjī Mīrzā Āqāsī, not pursuing a policy of submission to clerical pressure, could hardly have wished for an outcome similar to that of the agitation of Āqā Sayyid Muḥammad in 1826. Thus, with typical cynicism, he made apparent preparations for an attack on Baghdad, in order to appease popular feeling led by the ulama, while at the same time avoiding any commitment to go to war.[72] Sheil, the British ambassador, reported "it appears to me to be in the power of this government, in conjunction with the priesthood, to raise a general ferment throughout the country by proclaiming a religious war against Turkey"; but by March 29 he had reached the conclusion that "the Haji is disposed to avoid hostilities."[73] By the time the indignation subsided, it had become possible to negotiate terms with the Ottoman Empire at Erzerum, with the participation of the British and Russian governments.[74]

Earlier, in 1216/1801, the Wahhābīs had similarly sacked Karbala, killing about two thousand people, and allegedly grinding their coffee on the tomb of 'Abbās b. 'Alī.[75] Apart from the destruction of a shrine that was, by Wahhābī standards, idolatrous, the raiders were seeking revenge for the murder of the Amir 'Abd ul-'Azīz āl-Sa'ūd by an Afghan resident in Karbala.[76] It is worth noting that this outrage did not produce a reaction in Iran comparable

[70] The Herat campaigns to an extent fulfilled a similar purpose. Stuart wrote on April 26, 1836: "The Shah has endeavoured to turn to account the excited and bigoted feelings against the Sunnis, which this season [Muḥarram] always awakens. This morning the officers of the garrison were desired to accompany Kuhurman [*sic*] Mirza to the principal mosque, where Hajee Ibrahim preached a religious war against the hostile sect; the number of Sheahs enslaved by the Afghans and Turkomans was mentioned, and all the Persians were exhorted to march, without pay, but certain of eternal reward, against the enemies of their religion and country" (*Journal of a Residence in Northern Persia*, p. 296).

[71] A. Denis, "Affaire du Kerbela," *Revue de l'Orient*, I (1843), 139.

[72] Holmes, *op. cit.*, pp. 361–362; Watson, *op. cit.*, p. 342.

[73] Dispatches in F.O. 60/96.

[74] *NT*, I, 329.

[75] al-'Azzāwī, *op. cit.*, VI, 144; *Q'U*, p. 92.

[76] al-'Azzāwī, *op. cit.*, VI, 160.

with that provoked by Najīb Pasha forty years later. Fatḥ 'Alī Shāh protested to the Ottoman government,[77] but the ulama are not recorded as having urged warlike action on him. The enemy was not a familiar one,[78] whereas in the case of Najīb Pasha, traditional feelings of hostility to the Sunnis were awakened. It is moreover probable that Ḥājjī Sayyid Muḥammad Bāqir welcomed the discovery of a further field where he might do battle with the government.

In this battle, he was not alone. Although he did not enjoy the status later accorded to Shaykh Murtaḍā Anṣārī and Mīrzā Ḥasan Shīrāzī, as the most prominent mujtahid of his time, he had wide influence among the ulama and many of them sought their ijāzas from him.[79] His influence made itself felt, for instance, in Qazvin. Sayyid Muḥammad Bāqir Qazvīnī Mujtahid, on returning from his studies at the 'atabāt, spent some time with Ḥājjī Sayyid Muḥammad Bāqir Shaftī in Isfahan before taking up residence again in Qazvin. There he encouraged the townspeople to expel an oppressive governor and was banished by Muḥammad Shāh to Najaf for so doing. The intervention of Shaykh Murtaḍā Anṣārī persuaded the Shah to permit his return, but again he insisted on intervening in public affairs. The author of the *Qiṣaṣ ul-'Ulamā'*, Muḥammad b. Sulaymān Tunukābunī, attempted to dissuade him from so doing, but was told: "When I desired to take my leave of Ḥujjat ul-Islām Sayyid Muḥammad Bāqir he enjoined me not to be idle in matters concerning the needs of the Muslims, and to exert myself in promoting their affairs. For Shaykh Kulaynī[80] has included in his work *Uṣūl-i Kāfī* a chapter on this subject, and quoted many sayings of the Immaculate Imams relevant to it. Therefore I allow myself not a moment's respite in the protection of the poor and the weak."[81]

[77] *NT*, I, 67.

[78] If some Shi'is compared the Wahhābī raid with the tragic martyrdom of the Imam Ḥusayn (see Ibrāhīm al-Wā'ilī, *ash-Shi'r as-Sīyāsī al-'Irāqī fī-l-Qarn at-Tāsi'-'ashar* [Baghdad, 1381 Q/1961–1962], p. 123), others considered it a merited punishment for the sinfulness into which Karbala had fallen. One historian wrote: "It became necessary for the Almighty . . . to purify the holy soil by the edge of the sharp, terror-exciting sword of the barbarous Saud" (Sir Harford Jones Brydges, *The Dynasty of the Kajars* [London, 1833], pp. 149–150).

[79] A. Sepsis, "Quelques mots sur l'état religieux actuel de la Perse," *Revue de l'Orient*, III (1844), 99.

[80] Muḥammad b. Ya'qūb al-Kulaynī Thiqat ul-Islām, d. 329/941.

[81] *Q'U*, pp. 48–50.

Whereas Sayyid Muḥammad Bāqir Qazvīnī was able to return to Qazvin, a mujtahid expelled from Kirman was permanently prohibited from returning there by Muḥammad Shāh. Mullā 'Alī Akbar, imām jum'a of Kirman, under the pretext of "enjoining good and forbidding evil" was continually disturbing the life of the town and showed special enmity to the Shaykhīs.[82] He was brought under escort to Tehran, and from there sent to Mashhad, where he remained until the end of his life.[83]

If these disturbances might be held to be the natural outcome of Ḥājjī Sayyid Muḥammad Bāqir's ambition and the traditional rivalry between the ulama and provincial governors, manifestations of clerical hostility to the monarchy in the capital—more direct and more threatening—were largely provoked by Ḥājjī Mīrzā Āqāsī's policies. Partly this was the result of his Sufism. He appears deliberately to have cultivated the enmity of the ulama, as if he were seeking to avenge the dervishes killed at their hands. "The policy of this prime minister, with regard to the mullas whom he detests, is to suppress them by all possible means."[84] It was natural that the chief weight of his hostility should be directed against Ḥājjī Sayyid Muḥammad Bāqir, and he showed himself completely unamenable to his suggestions and intercession.[85] He clashed also with Ḥājjī Mullā Muḥammad Taqī Burghānī (known as Shahīd-i Thālith, "The Third Martyr," after his assassination by a Bābī), trying to deprive him of his lands and even to expel him from Iran.[86] That the ulama should react outspokenly was natural.

Stuart wrote in his journal on January 11, 1836: "The anniversary of the murder of Ali. This long fast of Ramazan creates a great deal of religious ferment. . . . The Soofies are frightened. At the commencement of the fast some soldiers were sent into the principal mosque to make a row, and prevent the anti-Soofie doctrines of the Imam Jooma from being listened to. The Imam, by nature a weak and submissive man, was indignant, but prudently desired the orthodox to remain quiet. Subsequently, however, he armed them with clubs, and the next time the soldiers attempted to enter the mosque, they were well thrashed. A few days ago the

82 'Alī Muḥammad Kashmīrī, *Nujūm us-Samā* (Lucknow, 1303 Q/1885–1886), p. 419.

83 Vazīrī, *op. cit.*, p. 387.

84 Sepsis, *op. cit.*, p. 105.

85 *Ibid.*, p. 104.

86 *Q'U*, pp. 20–21.

Imam Jooma, in Hajee Meerza Aghassee's presence, denounced the Soofies from his pulpit, called them 'sons of burnt fathers' and 'defiled mothers,' recommended their immediate extermination, and devoted them to future damnation. The Hajee foolishly sent a message to the Imam, asking whom he alluded to, when he particularly censured some who did not believe in the Koran. The chief priest answered that it was not then the time to tell him, but that he would write and explain. The 'lion-pilgrim' [?] was so frightened that he has abandoned his own house, and sleeps in the Ark, under the wing of his royal pupil, whose real or reputed Soofieism renders him also obnoxious to his people."[87]

Other of the ulama arrived from the provinces to participate in the agitation against Muḥammad Shāh. Stuart mentions the coming of a certain Ḥājjī Ibrāhīm, who spent his energies in quarreling with the imām jum'a.[88] Āqā Sayyid Muḥammad Mihdī, imām jum'a of Isfahan, came to Tehran and, claiming that the Jews of the city had acted in contradiction to the conditions of *dhimmat* (contractual protection), gave orders that their water supply should be cut off. Muḥammad Shāh countermanded his orders, and in protest he left the city for Shāh 'Abd ul-'Aẓīm, where shortly afterward he died.[89] As in the case of the Karbala affair, the occasion for opposition to the government was probably here also less important than the desire to oppose.

That clerical agitation, explicitly against the policies of the monarch, took place in Tehran, was possibly the most portentous feature of Muḥammad Shāh's reign. Although clashes between the ulama and secular authority continued to occur in the provinces, occasioned by the oppressiveness of governors and the ambitiousness of the ulama, the basic contradiction between state and ulama received its clearest expression in Tehran. It was in Tehran that, despite the loose structure of government, the intrigues constituting the nation's political processes were worked out and the largest concentration of population was at the disposal of the ulama.

Even in the time of Ḥājjī Mīrzā Āqāsī, we can discern attempts at strengthening and centralizing the state. Provincial governors were subjected to closer control,[90] and military reform continued.

87 Stuart, *op. cit.*, pp. 219–220.

88 *Ibid.*, p. 245.

89 *Q'U*, pp. 89–90.

90 See "S," "De l'état administratif et politique de la Perse," *Revue de l'Orient*, IV (1844), 114.

The delicate question of uniform received attention, and again religious sanction was sought for introducing what was apparently European dress.[91] One of the earliest attempts at settling the tribes was made: seven tribal groups were alloted land in the neighborhood of Qum, and each was attached to the following of one of the ulama of that city.[92] In general the process of strengthening the state was one tending to restrict the prerogatives of the ulama. Ḥājjī Mīrzā Āqāsī attempted to extend ʿurf jurisdiction by removing cases from sharʿ courts,[93] and to weaken another aspect of the power of the ulama by abolishing bast. Ironically, he was himself obliged on the death of Muḥammad Shāh to avail himself of the facility he had sought to abolish;[94] but the restriction of the right of sanctuary was a permanent element in the attempts of the state at self-assertion.

These tendencies were confirmed by the acquisition by the state, under Nāṣir ud-Dīn Shāh, of certain western appearances: thus the ulama came to see in innovation the means whereby their traditional enemy was strengthened, and their own freedom of action limited.

We see then that the rivalry between ulama and state, resting on a firm doctrinal basis, but held somewhat in check by the policies of Fatḥ ʿAlī Shāh, became bitter and explicit in the time of Muḥammad Shāh. His heterodox tendencies, and the slow, almost unconscious, attempts at strengthening the central secular authority, exacerbated the inherent hostility of the ulama. While their power in the provinces continued undiminished, they became a constant and formidable force in the politics of the capital.[95] Hardly a single major event of Nāṣir ud-Dīn Shāh's reign is free from the imprint of their intervention, either threatened or actual.

Already the ulama were treating the Qajars as usurpers and—final condemnation—gave prominence to rumors that "their tribe

91 *NT*, I, 378.

92 A. K. S. Lambton, *Landlord and Peasant in Persia* (London, 1953), p. 141.

93 Sepsis, *op. cit.*, p. 105.

94 Watson, *op. cit.*, p. 357.

95 Gobineau (*op. cit.*, p. 315) writes that Muḥammad Shāh made of the ulama "powerless and humble officials of the state," but it would seem that he is exaggerating his success in combating the ulama. He also writes that the Shah assigned to himself the appointment of mujtahids, which, for obvious reasons, cannot have been the case. It should be remembered that here Gobineau is dealing with a period of history he did not himself witness in Iran, and that his remarks do not therefore possess any special authority.

assisted Yazīd in his wars against the sons of 'Alī."[96] Thus bitter was the hatred; and the reign of Nāṣir ud-Dīn Shāh confirmed and amplified it, until it became one of the chief elements in the Constitutional Revolution.

[96] Similar rumors as to the unholy ancestry of the Qajars were current in the Constitutional Revolution. See below, p. 252.

VII

The First Four Years of Nāṣir ud-Dīn Shāh's Reign and the Ministry of Mīrzā Taqī Khān Amīr Kabīr (1264/1848–1268/1851)

Despite the apparent continuity of power, the long reign of Nāṣir ud-Dīn Shāh (1848–1896) saw the development of all the factors that went to make up the period of turmoil and confusion known as the Constitutional Revolution. The ulama and their enmity to the state without doubt were among the most important of these, and the nature of their power and influence was diversified and extended throughout the reign. Although it is not possible to discern any constant policy or ultimate aim on the part of Nāṣir ud-Dīn Shāh after the early years of his reign, there was a continuing tendency for the conflict between ulama and state to expand and deepen. Intermittent attempts at westernizing certain aspects of the state necessarily pushed forward the line of demarcation between clerical and monarchical power into the realms of the former. Admittedly, this line had never been explicitly recognized and was often subject to dispute; but as the state advanced far-reaching claims, the dispute inevitably became more bitter. Reform offered tyranny, at least in theory, the possibility of imposing itself more efficiently, and innovation was thus an object of mistrust for the ulama. The tyranny, however, far from becoming more efficient, simply became more oppressive. When the proceeds of oppression failed to satisfy the needs of the ruler and his government, they encouraged the increasing penetration of the nation's life by foreign powers and individuals, securing ready cash in return. Again this penetration—apart from being in itself a reprehensible innovation—was expressed in forms of economic and commercial activity unfamiliar to the Perso-Muslim mind. Thus the ulama, who had already in the Second Perso-Russian War taken upon themselves the duty of defending the national honor against infidel aggression, found this function now joined with their other traditional preoccupation—opposition to the assertion by the state of its claims. The internal and external enemy represented two aspects of the same danger, namely the disappearance of Iran as a Muslim country.[1]

The prevention of this danger came to be seen as the chief duty of the ulama, and throughout the reign of Nāṣir ud-Dīn Shāh direct clashes between the ulama and the state, primarily in Tehran but also in the provinces, increased in frequency. As the importance and scope of the ulama's function increased, so too did their involvement in affairs, and the composition of the clerical estate underwent modification as a result. If earlier certain of the ulama (notably Ḥājjī Sayyid Muḥammad Bāqir Shaftī) had exercised a purely personal power, cases of mujtahids motivated by no more than transparent ambition are many in the reign of Nāṣir ud-Dīn Shāh and later. Although the foundations of monarchical and clerical power continued to be widely different, a similarity arose in the uses to which they were put: the corruption of the court and government was matched by that of some of the more powerful ulama. The power they enjoyed, political and economic, despite the tyranny of Nāṣir ud-Dīn Shāh, increased rather than decreased, for a number of reasons; it was natural that those seeking to partake in it should be many, and should on occasion clash with each other in bitter and personal enmity. Such tendencies were accentuated by the state enrolling in its service certain of the ulama in an attempt to control indirectly religious jurisdiction and patronage, and by the persistence, on the other hand, of many ulama in their traditional reluctance to be polluted by the touch of royal power. The

[1] I.e., one in its cultural and religious traditions overwhelmingly Islamic. Iran in Qajar times was never an Islamic state in any sense of the term, no consistent effort being made to enforce the sharī'at.

power of the state was thus on occasion supported by certain ulama, while the state intervened among them in matters of precedence. This, although a consequence of the continuing struggle between ulama and state, tended to obscure it. The equivocal role of the imām jum'a of Tehran is the clearest example of this contradiction.

A further element gaining prominence in the events of Nāṣir ud-Dīn Shāh's reign was the hesitant growth and expansion of what, for convenience, will be called liberal ideas. The response to the impact of Europe was not merely the negative one indicated above; others considered it worthy of at least a partial welcome, and planned to give lasting effect to some of its aspects. The questions of which aspects these were to be, to what degree they were in accord with Islam, and what should be the relationship between them and traditional ways of thought and life—all these inevitably involved the liberal thinkers with the ulama. Above all, they were in an infinitesimal minority; to secure acceptance for their ideas, it was essential to gain the cooperation of the ulama, who alone could rouse the greater part of the nation.

Thus we see everything in the reign of Nāṣir ud-Dīn Shāh tending to reinforce the importance of the ulama as leaders of the nation against the state. It would doubtless be an exaggeration, the result of ideologically determined hindsight, to regard the Constitutional Revolution as inevitable. Nāṣir ud-Dīn Shāh was lavishly and ostentatiously pious, and on occasion sought good relations with the ulama. His piety, nonetheless, was not that of Fatḥ 'Alī Shāh, who sought submissively to gain the favor of the ulama; rather he attempted to transfer to his own person something of the religious dignity and sanction attaching to the ulama. His attempts were unsuccessful. The Constitutional Revolution came—in part an expression of the confused response to the impact of the West, and in part a continuation of the traditional conflict between ulama and state. In both these aspects, the ulama were of central importance, and the roles they filled in regard to them can be seen developing in the reign of Nāṣir ud-Dīn Shāh.

The interval between the death of Muḥammad Shāh and the establishment of Nāṣir ud-Dīn Shāh on the throne in Tehran was marked, according to precedent, by the loosening of central control and by temporary chaos, both in the capital and the provinces. The ulama again played an important role in the situation, either making use of it for their own purposes, or seeking on the contrary to preserve some kind of order and stability. Thus in Tehran, the fury unleashed against Ḥājjī Mīrzā Āqāsī and his followers after the death of Muḥammad Shāh was repressed by the efforts of the imām jum'a.[2] Similarly the imām jum'a of Shiraz gave refuge to the governor, Niẓām ud-Daula, when his life was threatened by a popular uprising.[3] The *Rauḍat uṣ-Ṣafā-yi Nāṣirī* claims that "the ulama empowered the Crown Prince to mount the throne,"[4] but this would seem to be an exaggeration. It is significant that in Tehran it was the imām jum'a, a figure increasingly connected with the state, who exerted himself on behalf of order.

Elsewhere the ulama participated enthusiastically in the promotion of disorder. In Tabriz, fighting broke out between various of their number, after Mīrzā Aḥmad Mujtahid had pronounced the Shaykhīs to be infidels. Ultimately order was restored by the governor, Malik Qāsim Mīrzā.[5] More serious were the prolonged disturbances in Mashhad. Again the town threatened to withdraw itself totally from the control of the Qajars. In the latter part of Muḥammad Shāh's reign, a son of Allāhyār Khān Āṣaf ud-Daula, known as the Sālār, had taken refuge in the shrine of the Imam Riḍā, whence the troops of Ḥamza Mīrzā Ḥishmat ud-Daula, governor of Mashhad at the time, had attempted to expel him. They were prevented from fulfilling their sacrilegious undertaking by the resistance of the ulama. On the death of Muḥammad Shāh, the Sālār disputed the possession of the town with Ḥishmat ud-Daula. He was supported in his claims by the ulama, whose indignation had been aroused by the violation of the shrine.[6] A majority of the townspeople also responded to clerical encouragement and ceased paying taxes to Ḥishmat ud-Daula. Although the governor caused a cannonball to be dropped on the head of Ḥājjī Mīrzā Hāshim Mujtahid, severely wounding him,[7] resistance was not easily suppressed, and an army coming to reduce Mashhad to obedience was

[2] R. G. Watson, *A History of Persia from the Beginning of the Nineteenth Century to the Year 1858* (London, 1866), p. 358.

[3] *HAN*, p. 44.

[4] *RSN*, X, 358.

[5] Mīrzā Muḥammad Ḥasan Khān I'timād us-Salṭana, *Mir'āt ul-Buldān-i Nāṣirī* (Tehran, 1294–1297 Q/1877–1880), II, 9; *al-Ma'āthir va-l-Āthār* (Tehran, 1306 Q/1889), p. 38. The life of Tabriz was frequently interrupted down to the eve of the Constitutional Revolution by clashes between Shaykhīs and Bālāsarīs. See Aḥmad Kasravī, *Zindagānī-yi Man* (Tehran, 1323 Sh/1944), p. 13.

[6] Watson, *op. cit.*, p. 363.

[7] *HAN*, p. 52.

met by an armed concourse of citizens led by mullās and religious students.[8]

Nor was Isfahan showing signs of greater tranquillity in the new reign. In 1264/1848, the agitation of the imām jum'a secured the dismissal of Mīrzā 'Abd ul-Vahhāb, who had been appointed minister to the governor, Sulaymān Khān Afshār.[9] The following year, he clashed with Sulaymān Khān's successor, Ḥusayn Khān Sipahdār. It appears that one of the imām jum'a's retinue was insulted by a soldier, and the imām jum'a considered himself personally affronted. After consulting Ḥusayn Khān Sipahdār, he agreed to overlook the matter if the guilty soldier and his accomplices were punished next day in the square known as Maydān-i Shāh.[10] There were, however, those in Isfahan who looked forward to a revival of the disorder they had profited by so richly in the reign of Muḥammad Shāh. Among them were the remnants of the lūṭīs, and one of the navvābs, Aḥmad Mīrzā Ṣafavī.[11] While some of the lūṭīs and townspeople took up quarters in the Masjid-i Shāh (the royal mosque), the majority gathered in the Masjid-i Jum'a (the Friday mosque) and declared noisily their intention of avenging the imām jum'a's affronted dignity.[12] The Sipahdār sent a certain Muḥammad Ḥusayn Khān to disperse them, but he was overpowered and pitched into the tank of the mosque.[13] Two days later, he died of his wounds. Thereupon large-scale fighting broke out between Aḥmad Mīrzā Ṣafavī and Ḥusayn Khān Sipahdār for the possession of the town. Aḥmad Mīrzā, emerging from the Masjid-i Jum'a, took refuge in the house of Mīrzā Zayn ul-'Ābidīn Mujtahid, one

8 *RSN*, X, 396.

9 *HAN*, p. 61.

10 *Ibid.*, p. 85; I'timād us-Salṭana, *Mir'āt ul-Buldān-i Nāṣiri*, II, 22.

11 *Ibid.* The participation of the navvābs in the disturbances of Muḥammad Shāh's reign has already been mentioned. Evidently their open hostility to the Qajars continued in the time of Nāṣir ud-Dīn Shāh: "The Safavi *sayyids* are like a disease battening on the faith and behaviour of the Iranians. Even now they consider it a duty and incumbent upon them to pray for that vanished dynasty from their pulpits. . . ." (I'timād us-Salṭana, *al-Ma'āthir va-l-Āthār*, p. 121).

12 See the letter of Amīr Kabīr to Nāṣir ud-Dīn Shāh quoted by Ḥusayn Makkī in *Zindagānī-yi Mīrzā Taqī Khān Amīr Kabīr* (Tehran, 1327 Sh/1948–1949), p. 118, one remarkable for the informality of its tone: "You have written: is there any news? Certainly, what is newer than this, that through the auspicious fortune of your relatives the Isfahanis have gathered in the Masjid-i Shāh and have started behaving like lūṭīs? About a thousand men and women are shouting their protests, with five thousand spectators calling out: O God! O God! Indeed, God only knows how it will all end."

13 I'timād us-Salṭana, *Mir'āt ul-Buldān-i Nāṣirī*, p. 23.

of the sons of the formidable Ḥājjī Sayyid Muḥammad Bāqir Shaftī.[14] It would appear, however, that the traditional alliance between the lūṭīs and the ulama had been, at least temporarily, broken. Mīrzā Asadullāh, who as eldest son of Ḥājjī Sayyid Muḥammad Bāqir had succeeded to his position of eminence and respect, even went so far as to advise his brother to cease protecting Aḥmad Mīrzā.[15] Together with Āqā Muḥammad Mihdī, the son of and successor to Ḥājjī Muḥammad Ibrāhīm Kalbāsī, he presented Ḥusayn Khān Sipahdār with a fatvā to the effect that the shedding of the rebels' blood was lawful.[16] He was unable, however, to persuade his brother of his error in supporting Aḥmad Mīrzā and left Isfahan to visit the 'atabāt. At the request of the government, he turned back on reaching Gulpāyagān and consented to accompany his brother and Aḥmad Mīrzā to Tehran, where he would intercede for them at court.[17] Despite these cooperative gestures on the part of the ulama, the governor of Isfahan arranged for the party to be attacked on the road to Qum, and others of the ulama of Isfahan, notably Mīrzā Muḥammad Ḥasan, son of Mullā 'Alī Nūrī, were arrested and their houses plundered on the governor's orders.[18]

The role of the ulama in this episode is ambiguous. Only Mīrzā Zayn ul-'Ābidīn appears to have been directly involved in the rebellion, but Ḥusayn Khān Sipahdār's apparent treachery may have been motivated by the suspicion that the ulama were insincere in their cooperation, acting only under duress. On the other hand, we have already seen that differences existed between Ḥājjī Sayyid Muḥammad Bāqir and the imām jum'a in the previous reign, and it is possible that these differences, inherited by the next generation, may have prevented the formation of a common front against the Sipahdār. Moreover, it is unlikely that the ulama, at so early a point in the reign, should have cherished any immediate enmity to the monarch, or the governor he had appointed. The replacement of a heterodox ruler by one at least outwardly pious was probably welcomed; and in fact Nāṣir ud-Dīn Shāh protected the ulama of Isfahan against Ḥusayn Khān Sipahdār, whatever his reasons may

[14] *Ibid.*, p. 23. According to *HAN* (p. 86), the navvāb in question was called Muḥammad, not Aḥmad.

[15] *Ibid.*

[16] I'timad us-Salṭana, *op. cit.*, p. 24.

[17] *Ibid.*, p. 25.

[18] *HAN*, p. 87.

have been in so doing.[19] If on certain occasions the actions of the ulama were motivated predominantly by religious emotion, on others they acted with the prudence dictated by immediate interest, and it is probable that on this occasion they thought support of Aḥmad Mīrzā unprofitable. As the power and ambitions of many of the leading ulama became more strictly personal in nature and more firmly based on foundations of personal wealth, their policies became more deliberate and, when necessity dictated, prudent. The involvement of the ulama in political affairs was lasting and intimate, and thus their actions too were overshadowed by the ambiguity of intrigue. On occasion, even Āqā Najafī saw fit to conclude a truce with Mas'ūd Mīrzā Ẓill us-Sulṭān in his struggle for the control of Isfahan.

The unrest in Isfahan was finally settled in 1267/1850–1851, the penultimate year of Mīrzā Taqī Khān Amīr Kabīr's short ministry. His policy toward the ulama was more far-reaching than the mere suppression of open rebellion. Although the poet Qā'ānī greeted Mīrzā Taqī Khān Amīr Kabīr's appointment as minister with a qasida containing the line: "In the place of an impious tyrant sits one just and pious, of whom the believers are exceedingly proud,"[20] his policies were not totally dissimilar from those of Ḥājjī Mīrzā Āqāsī. Although he did not share his predecessor's Sufi sympathies, he surpassed him in his devotion to the state. His overriding concern was the strengthening of the state, and in this he combined the enmity to the ulama shown by Ḥājjī Mīrzā Aqāsī with reformist tendencies acquired from his preceptor, Mīrzā Abū-l-Qāsim Qā'im Maqām. The place occupied by Amīr Kabīr in the history of reform in Iran is paradoxical: while he is accorded a justly eminent place in that history, his sole aim was the promotion of the state to a position of effective control of the nation's life. The reforms he worked for were designed to make existing administrative organisms function better, rather than to change these functions or introduce new organisms. Most of his few permanent achievements, however, were used by others to further corruption. Although his intentions differed markedly from those of most of his successors in the post of ṣadr-i a'ẓam to Nāṣir ud-Dīn Shāh, the ultimate effect of his policies was in many respects the same.

[19] *Ibid.*

[20] Qā'ānī, *Dīvān*, ed. Muḥammad Ja'far Maḥjūb (Tehran, 1336 Sh/1957), p. 47.

This is clearly seen in his policy toward the ulama, which was not based on any ideal conception of their role in affairs but evolved according to his concern with asserting the power of the state wherever possible. Thus he attempted to abolish certain aspects of the power of the ulama, such as the right to grant asylum, and to weaken their juridical functions by expanding the range of 'urf jurisdiction, and at the same time establishing a loose control over the shar' courts. Even though in doing so he sought the sanction and cooperation of the leading ulama, there can be little doubt that his aim was to break clerical power, or at least to reduce it to a point where it was no longer able to challenge the state.[21] His clashes with the ulama occurred when he disputed the validity of certain of their functions and the manner in which others were exercised.[22]

His relations with Mīrzā Abū-l-Qāsim, imām jum'a of Tehran, are illustrative of this pragmatism. Mīrzā Abū-l-Qāsim had succeeded his uncle and father-in-law, Mīr Muḥammad Mihdī, as imām jum'a in 1263/1846–1847, near the end of Muḥammad Shāh's reign.[23] Clearly he hoped to maintain the prestige gained for the office by his predecessor's resistance to Ḥājjī Mīrzā Āqāsī, and his own efforts to pacify Tehran during the transfer of rule.[24] In the Masjid-i Shāh, he sheltered thieves and brigands to act as the executive arm of his authority.[25] When in Jumādī ul-Ukhrā, 1265/March, 1849, a mutinous company of Azerbayjani troops garrisoned in Tehran forced Amīr Kabīr temporarily to resign, Mīrzā Abū-l-Qāsim, together with Ḥājjī Shaykh Riḍā, Shaykh 'Abd ul-Ḥusayn Shaykh ul-'Irāqayn, and others of the ulama, was again instrumental in the restoration of peace to the capital. He ordered the merchants to close the bazaar and to arm themselves against the mutineers.[26] If he considered himself thereby deserving of Amīr Kabīr's unconditional gratitude, he was mistaken: Mīrzā Taqī Khān granted no favors in return. Simultaneously, the imām jum'a had been maintaining contact with foreign powers, as an

21 Amīr Kabīr once remarked to Stevens, British consul in Tabriz, that the Ottoman government had begun to recover its lost importance only after the reduction of the power of the mullās (see Stevens' dispatch to Sheil, dated June 15, 1849, in F.O. 60/153).

22 'Abbās Iqbāl, *Mīrzā Taqī Khān Amīr Kabīr* (Tehran, 1340 Sh/1961), p. 163.

23 *Ibid.*, p. 171; I'timād us-Salṭana, *al-Ma'āthir va-l-Āthār*, p. 141.

24 See above, p. 125.

25 Iqbāl, *op. cit.*, p. 172.

26 *RSN*, X, 401; Watson, *op. cit.*, p. 377; Iqbāl, *op. cit.*, p. 374.

additional ramification to his influence. This Amīr Kabīr refused to tolerate, considering the regulation of foreign affairs to be the exclusive concern of the state.[27] When the Tsar sent Mīrzā Abū-l-Qāsim a diamond-encrusted snuffbox bearing his portrait, Amīr Kabīr demanded to know what had occasioned this gift, and the imām jum'a was obliged to submit the Tsar's letter for inspection.[28] Mīrzā Abū-l-Qāsim also communicated with Palmerston and tried to obtain the support of the British ambassador against Amīr Kabīr, but Sheil was unable to achieve anything on his behalf.[29] He was even deprived of his judicial functions by the Amir for suspected dishonesty in performing them and was ultimately restricted to leading the prayer at the Masjid-i Shāh.[30] Nonetheless, Mīrzā Taqī Khān accepted the demand of the imām jum'a for the dismissal of the governor of Naṭanz, after assuring himself that the demand was justified;[31] and a less hostile relationship between the two men appears to have established itself gradually, as the imām jum'a resigned himself to defeat. Later, the imām jum'a, in the person of Mīrzā Zayn ul-'Ābidīn, who was given one of the daughters of Nāṣir ud-Dīn Shāh,[32] became closely identified with the monarch and his policies. It is ironic that Amīr Kabīr's success in obtaining the submission of so important a member of the clerical estate should have resulted later in strengthening the opposition to reform.

The threat to governmental authority in Tabriz was more explicit, and Amīr Kabīr dealt with it with corresponding firmness. Ḥājjī Mīrzā Bāqir Mujtahid, Mīrzā 'Alī Aṣghar Shaykh ul-Islām, and his son Mīrzā Abū-l-Qāsim had among them deprived Ḥamza Mīrzā Ḥishmat ud-Daula (now transferred to Tabriz) of all but the nominal governorship of the town. Ḥājjī Mīrzā Bāqir's rulings were immediately enforced, while Mīrzā 'Alī Aṣghar, encouraged by the promptings of his son, allowed his residence to shelter an armed following, constantly prepared for battle.[33] In the first year

27 According to Makkī (*op. cit.*, p. 47), Amīr Kabīr founded a special office whose task it was to report on contacts between the ulama and foreign powers. Intimate relations between the ulama and foreign embassies do not appear to have existed until considerably later.

28 See Sheil's dispatch of June 16, 1849 (F.O. 60/154), and Firīdūn Ādamīyat, *Amīr Kabīr va Īrān* (Tehran, 1334 Sh/1955), p. 186.

29 *Ibid.*, p. 187.

30 Iqbāl, *op. cit.*, p. 175.

31 *Ibid.*, p. 174.

32 I'timād us-Salṭana, *al-Ma'āthir va-l-Āthār*, p. 142.

33 Iqbāl, *op. cit.*, p. 175; Nādir Mīrzā, *Tārīkh va Jughrāfi-yi Dār us-Salṭana-yi Tabrīz* (Tehran, 1323 Q/1905), pp. 118, 244.

of Nāṣir ud-Dīn Shāh's reign, Amīr Kabīr dispatched Sulaymān Khān Afshār to Tabriz in order to arrest the three and bring them to Tehran.[34] After some resistance, Mīrzā 'Alī Aṣghar and his son surrendered, but it took longer to persuade Ḥājjī Mīrzā Bāqir. Every night his house was guarded by a thousand armed Tabrizis, until finally he too consented to accompany Sulaymān Khān to Tehran.[35] All three were kept in the capital until the fall and disgrace of Amīr Kabīr. Such disrespectful treatment of prominent members of the ulama cannot have failed to leave a deep impression. If before certain mullās had been punished or even killed and pressure brought on mujtahids, indirectly and under various pretexts, no monarch, vazīr, or governor of the Qajar period had presumed to expel a mujtahid or shaykh ul-Islām from any town merely on account of the rule to which he was theoretically entitled. The impious nature of Qajar rule was now tacitly admitted. Disrespect toward the ulama aroused feelings of indignation not necessarily connected with the person or character of the divine insulted: the offense was against something deeper and more sacred. As suggested above, the outward power and dignity of the ulama symbolized the dominion of the sharī'at and provided a focal point for collective loyalties. Thus when the government, in the person of 'Ayn ud-Daula, later chose lightheartedly to offend against this dignity, its alienation from the people was complete. We see already the various elements in the motivation of the Constitutional Revolution taking shape at the beginning of Nāṣir ud-Dīn Shāh's reign.

The complexities of the problem which faced Amīr Kabīr are apparent in his attempts to reform the legal system, if one may call "system" an uncodified and fluctuating set of partly contradictory practices. Ḥājjī Mīrzā Āqāsī's attempts to extend 'urf jurisdiction have already been mentioned, and Amīr Kabīr followed a similar policy. He sought for a time even to supersede the shar' courts of the capital by sitting in judgment himself on cases brought before him. He abandoned the attempt when he realized that the inadequacy of his juridical knowledge had caused him to pronounce incorrect verdicts.[36] Instead, he established indirect control over the shar' courts by giving prominence to one enjoying his special

[34] *Ibid.*, p. 119; H. Dunlop, *Perzië: Vorheeren en Thans* (Haarlem, 1912), p. 425.
[35] Iqbāl, *op. cit.*, p. 176.
[36] *Ibid.*, p. 166.

patronage. Cases concerning the government would be referred to it for decision, and its prestige was thus enhanced.[37] While later the association of the principal shar' court of the capital with the interests of the court became yet another instrument of oppression and corruption, it is clear that Amīr Kabīr's purpose in establishing state supervision of religious jurisdiction was of a different nature. The imām jum'a of Tehran was deprived of his judicial functions for suspected dishonesty, and the partiality of Mīrzā 'Alī Aṣghar in giving judgments was doubtless one of the reasons that caused Amīr Kabīr to expel him from Tabriz.[38] The principal shar' court in Tehran was occupied by a certain Shaykh Mullā 'Abd ur-Raḥīm Burūjirdī until on one occasion he offered to settle a case involving one of Mīrzā Taqī Khān's servants to the Amīr's satisfaction.[39] He was obliged to leave Tehran immediately, and in his place Shaykh 'Abd ul-Ḥusayn Ṭihrānī Shaykh ul-'Irāqayn was invited to the capital. Shaykh 'Abd ul-Ḥusayn retained the trust of the Amīr and presided over the principal shar' court until his patron's downfall.[40]

Beyond this indirect control of shar' jurisdiction, Amīr Kabīr also laid down certain principles intended to restrict its scope. The issuing of *nāsikh* judgments (i.e., reversing earlier pronouncements, a device frequently used to gain possession of land and other property) was forbidden.[41] Cases involving the religious minorities were to be referred to the dīvānkhāna in Tehran for judgment, and thus removed from the possible religious prejudices of provincial mujtahids and governors.[42] The dīvānkhāna, the highest instance

[37] Ādamīyat, *op. cit.*, p. 134.

[38] Makkī, *op. cit.*, p. 148.

[39] Iqbāl, *op. cit.*, p. 168; Ādamīyat, *op. cit.*, p. 134; Makkī, *op. cit.*, p. 46; I'timād us-Salṭana, *op. cit.*, p. 159.

[40] Iqbāl, *op. cit.*, p. 169. He was one of the ulama who supported Amīr Kabīr during the mutiny of the Azerbayjani garrison. He was later entrusted by Nāṣir ud-Dīn Shāh with supervising repairs to the Shi'i shrines in Arab Iraq (I'timād us-Salṭana, *op. cit.*, p. 139; Muḥammad Mihdī Kāẓimī, *Aḥsan ul-Wadī'a* [Baghdad, 1347 Q/1928–1929], I, 75–76).

[41] Ādamīyat, *op. cit.*, p. 136.

[42] *Ibid.*, p. 133. 'Abbās Mīrzā's concern for the religious minorities in Azerbayjan was noted above (p. 75). In the reign of Nāṣir ud-Dīn Shāh, foreign interest was shown not only in the position of Armenian and Nestorian Christians, but also in that of Jews and Zoroastrians, and Amīr Kabīr may have been influenced, like 'Abbās Mīrzā, by the fear of foreign interference on religious pretexts, a misfortune that plagued the Ottoman Empire throughout the nineteenth century.

of 'urf jurisdiction, still had no properly defined functions, and it was not until 1279/1863 that its exercise was regulated according to rules of procedure.[43] Amīr Kabīr appears to have assured the dīvānkhāna a more prominent place in the legal system. A case would be referred in the first instance to it, and then passed on to a shar' court. The judgment pronounced by the latter was valid only if confirmed by the dīvānkhāna, which was in any event entrusted with its execution.[44] Although ultimately the signature or seal of the mujtahid presiding over the shar' court was also essential for the execution of any judgment, and the system was still flexible enough to operate to the advantage of shar' jurisdiction, 'urf was significantly strengthened. The reference of a case in the first instance to the dīvānkhāna enabled the government to pass it on to a shar' court enjoying its special patronage and favor. Thus the state was able to trespass on one of the chief domains of clerical power.

The confusion surrounding or, it might almost be said, inspiring the entire Iranian legal system, persisted for many years. Not only was there no attempt at a consistent application of the religious law, and no demarcation of the spheres of shar' and 'urf, but the introduction of Western legal and political concepts in the latter part of the century added to the prevailing complexity. It was this confusion that, in part, produced an alliance of interest between the westernizing liberals and the ulama in the Constitutional Revolution—and also destroyed it, as the differing aims and purposes became apparent. We see Amīr Kabīr, then, in his legal policy taking up certain elements of reform, first put forward by 'Abbās Mīrzā and Mīrzā Abū-l-Qāsim Qā'im Maqām, and repeating them to no great effect. His intentions, however, were clearly hostile to the prerogatives of the ulama, and doubtless the response evoked was the confirmation of existing enmity.

Amīr Kabīr's attempts to restrict bast to shrines were similarly motivated and similarly inconclusive in their outcome. In Isfahan, Tabriz, and Tehran, he had seen mosques sheltering the armed followers of the ulama, a constant threat to order and government authority. In the capital, the imām jum'a, Mīrzā Abū-l-Qāsim, ultimately had no choice but to consent in 1266/1850 to the "break-

43 See *Rūznāma-yi Daulat-i 'Alīya-yi Īrān*, 1279 Q/1862–1863, no. 935; 'Abdullāh Mustaufī, *Tārīkh-i Idārī va Ijtimā'ī-yi Daura-yi Qājārīya yā Sharḥ-i Zindagānī-yi Man* (Tehran, 1321 Sh/1942–1943), I, 99.

44 Ādamīyat, *op. cit.*, p. 133.

ing" of the bast of the Masjid-i Shāh.[45] In Tabriz, however, opposition was more serious and imaginative and was doubtless one of the reasons for the subsequent expulsion of the imām jum'a. In the middle of Tabriz is a shrine known as Buq'a-yi Ṣāḥib ul-Amr, where visions of the Hidden Imam have reputedly been vouchsafed to various pious persons.[46] In the early summer of 1850, "a cow being conducted to the slaughter house in passing by the noted shrine . . . twice took refuge in the holy spot. On the third repetition of the disregard of this appeal to the power of the defunct saint, the butcher was struck dead."[47] Miracles followed, and the hairs of the cow were plucked out by the eager Tabrizis on account of the sacred character that the beast's anatomy had acquired.[48] The imām jum'a delivered a fatvā to the effect that anyone found drinking or gambling in the vicinity of the shrine would be executed.[49] Mīr Fattāḥ, perhaps anxious in his old age to regain something of his former eminence by exploiting the religious fervor, donated an embroidered cloak to adorn the cow,[50] while the British consul, Stevens, endowed the shrine with a crystal candelabra.[51] Significant rumors arose that "Tabriz has become the property of the Hidden Imām, and is exempt from taxation and rule by governors."[52] This spectacular attempt to draw attention to bast failed, and the immediate instigators were brought to Tehran,

45 I'timād us-Salṭana, *al-Ma'āthir va-l-Āthār*, p. 131; Ādamīyat, *op. cit.*, p. 190. The imām jum'a had evidently asked Sheil to intervene with Amīr Kabīr and prevent the abolition of bast in the Masjid-i Shāh. See Sheil's letter to Amīr Kabīr, dated Rajab 25, 1266/June 6, 1849, given in translation in F.O. 60/154.

46 I'timād us-Salṭana, *Mir'āt ul-Buldān-i Nāṣirī*, I, 347; Nādir Mīrzā, *op. cit.*, p. 110.

47 Lady Sheil, *Glimpses of Life and Manners in Persia* (London, 1856), p. 165. She writes of intelligence of the event reaching Tehran in early June, 1850, i.e., late Shavvāl, 1266; hence the date given by Nādir Mīrzā (*op. cit.*, p. 111) of 1265 must be wrong.

48 Watson, *op. cit.*, p. 392.

49 Ādamīyat, *op. cit.*, p. 188.

50 Nādir Mīrzā, *op. cit.*, p. 111.

51 *Ibid.*, p. 111; Ādamīyat, *op. cit.*, p. 188. Stevens' policy appears to have been consonant with Sheil's attempts to maintain bast at the Masjid-i Shāh in Tehran, and Amīr Kabīr complained accordingly in a letter to Sheil (see Ādamīyat, *op. cit.*, p. 188). Although the implication is clear that the British wished for some kind of base from which the agents of their policy might work, it is not clear from contemporary diplomatic and consular documents whether in fact bast was so used. It is possible that the aim was rather to earn the goodwill of the ulama by championing their cause, a goodwill that might be made use of in later contingencies.

52 Nādir Mīrzā, *op. cit.*, p. 111.

while soon after the imām jum'a and the shaykh ul-Islām were expelled.[53]

This restriction of bast, a recurring element in the state's attempts at self-assertion, was only partial, and the Constitutional Revolution was to witness the most extensive and successful use made of the right of sanctuary in the Masjid-i Shāh itself.

Even less capable of fulfillment was the Amīr's desire to abolish ta'zīya, public mourning by various kinds of dramatic display, of the martyrdom of the Imam Ḥusayn. Ta'zīya gained widely in popularity in the reign of Nāṣir ud-Dīn Shāh.[54] The material of the dramas was expanded and supplemented, and takyas multiplied. On occasion, foreigners were permitted, or even invited, to witness the proceedings,[55] and as the fictitious material in the ta'zīya increased, it appeared to be about to develop into a purely theatrical form of entertainment.[56] Particularly in its less formal aspect, rauḍakhvānī (recitations of elegiac verse), it was still a powerful instrument for the arousing of religious emotions, and as such an element of clerical strength. In his attempts at the abolition of ta'zīya, Amīr Kabīr again sought and obtained clerical sanction, notably that of the imām jum'a of Tehran.[57] It is probable that on this occasion his support was more spontaneous than his consent to the abolition of bast, for many of the ulama had traditionally been opposed to ta'zīya.[58] Not only did they realize its incompatibility with the sharī'at, but saw in the rauḍakhvāns competitors in the excitement and control of religious emotion.[59] The deep and widespread attachment to ta'zīya, however, as a means of expressing loyalty to Shi'ism was too strong to be broken by the Amīr, even

53 Lady Sheil, *op. cit.*, p. 166; Watson, *op. cit.*, p. 392. Watson attributes the whole affair to a desire to counteract the rise of Bābism; but the motivation suggested by Lady Sheil ("restoring the right of bast to its ancient vigour") appears more probable.

54 See I'timād us-Salṭana, *al-Ma'āthir va-l-Āthār*, p. 96. The monarch himself was particularly attached to ta'zīya. On Nāṣir ud-Dīn Shāh's religious proclivities, see below, pp. 156–160.

55 E.g., R. Wilbraham, *Travels in the Transcaucasian Provinces of Russia* (London, 1839), p. 420. Later the diplomatic corps would attend performances at the royal takya. See below, p. 158.

56 See 'Abd ul-Ḥusayn Zarīnkūb, "Yāddāshtī dar bāra-yi Ta'ziya-yi Māh-i Muḥarram," *Sukhan*, IX (1337 Sh/1958–1959), 314.

57 Ādamīyat, *op. cit.*, p. 189; Watson, *op. cit.*, p. 373.

58 A. de Gobineau, *Les Religions et les Philosophies dans l'Asie Centrale* (Paris, 1865), p. 67.

59 Hermann Vambéry, *Meine Wanderungen und Erlebnisse in Persien* (Pest, 1867), p. 82.

with the sanction of some of the ulama; and in the face of strong opposition, particularly from Isfahan and Azerbayjan, he was obliged to relent.[60] Here again, the object of Amīr Kabīr's distaste was to play a role in the Constitutional Revolution: when refuge was taken, first in the Masjid-i Shāh and then in the grounds of the British embassy, rauḍakhvānī was used to inspire and maintain enthusiasm.

Thus, in sum, the ministry of Mīrzā Taqī Khān Amīr Kabīr effected little change in the power and influence of the ulama. He is, on occasion, reckoned among the precursors of the Constitutional Revolution, but the effect of his policies contributed to the development of revolutionary factors primarily by their failure. After his fall, only Mīrzā Ḥusayn Khān Sipahsālār among Qajar ministers contemplated any serious reform, and the demand for reform was to become associated with that for a form of government consultative at least in appearance. The ulama, traditionally opposed to monarchical power, were inevitably involved in this demand. The identification of certain of the ulama with the state, brought about by Amīr Kabīr's legal policy and by his relations with the imām jum'a of Tehran, was unable to reduce the power of the majority, while the effect of his other measures was to confirm existing hostility. If certain concerns were common to both state and ulama, the approach of each to them was different. The ulama demanded of Amīr Kabīr that he prohibit the sale of alcohol; he agreed only to punish open drunkenness.[61] The sin against the sharī'at was of less importance than the offense against public order. It might have been thought that despite these many differences of interest, the danger of Bābism, made manifest during the ministry of Amīr Kabīr, would bring together the ulama and the state. The basic hostility, however, was never lost sight of; and if for Amīr Kabīr the execution of the Bāb was made necessary by reasons of state,[62] for the ulama the issue was more serious. Precisely this gravity of approach became a new source of conflict with the state, and together with other aspects of the reaction of the ulama to Bābism and its effects on the subsequent course of Iranian history, it deserves detailed examination.

60 Watson, *op. cit.*, p. 373.
61 Makkī, *op. cit.*, p. 192.
62 Iqbāl, *op. cit.*, p. 164.

VIII

Bābism, Bahā'ism, and the Ulama

The rise of Bābism and its successor Bahā'ism was swift and accompanied by much bloodshed; it seemed at least initially to be of great importance for the history of Iran, and even, it was thought, for the whole of the Middle East. As such, it has received much attention, and several attempts at interpretation have been made. In these, the reaction of the ulama to the appearance of Bābism has not been closely studied. It was, however, the ulama who formulated the most explicit reaction to Bābism and its claims, and in this case as in others we see the ulama functioning as de facto leaders of the nation, concerned on this occasion to preserve its religious uniformity. Both Bābīs and Bahā'īs recognized the ulama as among their chief adversaries, and this recognition was expressed in word and deed.

That this should be so was perhaps inevitable. Bābism, at all stages of its doctrinal development, was of necessity opposed to Islam, for its claim to validity presupposed the supersession of Islam. The coming of a new revelation would have destroyed the worth of the existing one, which regarded itself as final. The ulama, on the other hand, were the institutional expression of the power of Islam, the expositors and guardians of its doctrine and the enforcers of its law, and among their functions was the rebuttal of heresy and innovation.

The sources for the history of Bābism are opposed in emotional and religious emphasis; yet if Bābī accounts are stripped of their hagiographical elements, and state chronicles of their polemical fervor, a fairly reliable narrative can be established. It is clear that when Sayyid 'Alī Muḥammad, in 1259/1843, first claimed to be the Bāb, the "gateway" to the Hidden Imām, he clashed immediately with the ulama. One of the earliest writers on the history of Bābism, Comte Arthur de Gobineau, suggests that anticlerical themes formed a large part of his early preaching, and that their acceptability was an important element in the earliest conversions to the new faith.[1] More significant a cause for the hostility of the ulama to the Bāb was doubtless provided by the realization that his doctrines constituted *bid'at,* i.e., reprehensible innovation in matters of faith. Mullā 'Alī Akbar Ardistānī, one of the early converts, appended to the *idhān* (call to prayer) he proclaimed from the mosque of Āqā Qāsim in Shiraz: "I bear witness that 'Alī Muḥammad is the 'remnant' (*baqīya*) of God."[2]

The governor of Shiraz, Ḥusayn Khān Niẓām ud-Daula (also entitled Ājūdānbāshī) had been absent from the town. After his return, the ulama persuaded him, on Sha'bān 16/September 11, to punish Mullā 'Alī Akbar, Mullā Muḥammad Ṣādiq, and other followers of the Bāb.[3] Some were whipped, others, such as Muḥammad 'Alī Bārfurūshī, were paraded around the bazaar with blackened faces and burnt beards.[4] On Ramaḍān 15/October 9, Sayyid 'Alī Muḥammad was brought to Shiraz from Bushire, where he had first publicly announced his claims. In Shiraz, he was confronted for the first time with the ulama.[5] Accounts given of this confrontation by sources hostile to the Bāb contain two elements recurring in later interrogations—his deficient knowledge of Arabic and

1 A. de Gobineau, *Les Religions et les Philosophies dans l'Asie Centrale* (Paris, 1865), pp. 148–149.

2 E. G. Browne, ed., *Tārīkh-i-Jadīd or New History of Mīrzā 'Alī Muḥammad the Bāb* (Cambridge, 1893), p. 200. According to Khan Bahadur Agha Mirza Muhammad ("Some New Notes on Babism," *JRAS*, n.v. [July 1927], 451), Mullā Muḥammad Ṣādiq was the first to proclaim this deformed idhān.

3 Browne, ed., *op. cit.*, p. 200; *RSN*, X, 311; *MN*, III, 184.

4 E. G. Browne, *A Traveller's Narrative, Written To Illustrate the Episode of the Bab* (Cambridge, 1891), II, 7.

5 *MN*, III, 185; *RSN*, X, 311.

the traditional religious sciences, and his recantation.[6] While it is legitimate to question the accuracy of these accounts, and details may have been invented or emphasized to discredit the Bāb, the silence of Bābī sources on the course of the confrontations suggests that the Bāb was in fact worsted by the ulama in debate. The confrontations demonstrate the role of the ulama in refuting Bābism: by employing that scholastic knowledge which was one of their chief qualifications, they questioned the legitimacy of his claims; and by accepting his recantation, visibly asserted their own authority. At the end of his interrogation, the Bāb was beaten and then conducted by 'Abd ul-Ḥamīd Khān Kalāntar to the Masjid-i Vakīl, where he publicly repeated his recantation.[7] Bābī accounts agree that a meeting between the Bāb and the ulama took place, without offering any detail, and that it was attended by Sayyid Yaḥyā Dārābī, who was subsequently to lead the Bābī insurrection at Nayrīz.[8]

Although thus far Ḥusayn Khān Niẓām ud-Daula appears to have acted in cooperation with the ulama, differing approaches by the state and the ulama to the problem of Bābism can be detected. According to Gobineau, both the ulama of Shiraz and Ḥusayn Khān wrote to Tehran explaining the situation; and their example was followed by the Bāb.[9] It seems entirely possible that at this stage the Bāb hoped to secure his position by winning the support of Muḥammad Shāh and his minister. Even when imprisoned in Mākū, the Bāb still considered it worth his while to compose a risāla dedicated to Ḥājjī Mīrzā Āqāsī.[10] Although Bābī political theory left little room for the exercise of regal power,[11] Sayyid 'Alī Muḥammad may have sought to make use of the conflict between ulama and state by presenting himself as an instrument for the destruction of clerical power. Gobineau writes that he asked for permission to come to Tehran, and that Ḥājjī Mīrzā Āqāsī was

6 *MN*, III, 184.

7 Muhammad, *op. cit.*, pp. 452–454. According to this account, the Bāb was interrogated twice by the ulama in Shiraz, the second meeting being caused by the rashness of his followers. If this is so, we see here already how the development of Bābism as a movement of revolt proceeded more or less independently of the Bāb and his pronouncements.

8 Browne, ed., *Tārīkh-i-Jadīd*, p. 203; Browne, ed., *Traveller's Narrative*, I, 10.

9 Gobineau, *op. cit.*, p. 151.

10 Browne, ed., *op. cit.*, II, 274.

11 Gobineau, *op. cit.*, p. 335.

initially disposed to let him come.[12] One of such heterodox outlook as Ḥājjī Mīrzā Āqāsī can scarcely have been scandalized by the Bāb's claims; more probably he hoped for some amusement from the spectacle of the Bāb's clash with the ulama, and even for an amount of support in his own constant struggle with the clerical class. The opposition of Shaykh 'Abd ul-Ḥusayn Mujtahid forced him to change his intentions. He pointed out that if the ulama were to be obliged to defend themselves against the government and the Bāb, they were capable of doing so.[13] As in the case of the demand for war against the Ottoman Empire, Ḥājjī Mīrzā Āqāsī appears to have made all unavoidable outward concessions, while being careful not to encourage the expression of clerical power. He sent orders to Ḥusayn Khān prohibiting further discussion between the Bāb and the people of Shiraz.[14] The Bāb was confined to his house, but evidently his confinement was not strict, for it was in Shiraz that Mullā Ḥusayn Bushravayh, on his way from Arab Iraq to Kirman, accepted the Bāb's claims.[15] He it was who, on being converted, organized the insurrections in Khurasan and Mazandaran. Thus far-reaching were the consequences of the Bāb's residence in Shiraz. The ulama protested against the inefficacy of his confinement, but without success.[16] The danger of Bābism, not only to orthodoxy but also to the state, was not yet apparent. The failure to isolate the Bāb completely represented not only the customary inefficiency of the administration, but also its indifference to the support of orthodoxy. The ulama, for their part, although dissatisfied with the laxity of the measures taken against the Bāb, do not yet appear to have demanded his death.[17] The imām jum'a of Shiraz considered his release from prison permissible if he recanted;[18] and others of the ulama considered the Bāb insane and therefore neither responsible for his words, nor liable to the punishment they would otherwise bring him.[19] Despite all this,

[12] *Ibid.*, p. 153.
[13] *Ibid.*, p. 154.
[14] *Ibid.*, p. 155.
[15] *Ibid.*, p. 157.
[16] *Ibid.*, p. 155.
[17] The *Traveller's Narrative* (ed. Browne, I, 7, 14) claims that the ulama of Shiraz issued a fatvā for the killing of the Bāb. It should be remembered that the Bahā'ī histories lay great emphasis on the role of the ulama. This is largely justified; but in this case events appear to have been anticipated.
[18] Muhammad, *op. cit.*, p. 453.
[19] *RSN*, X, 311.

an ambiguity in the attitude of the state is observable, and the ultimate execution of the Bāb was preceded by several fatvās declaring him deserving of death.[20]

Mullā Ḥusayn Bushravayh, on his way from Shiraz to Khurasan, had passed through Isfahan and informed the governor, Manūchihr Khān Mu'tamad ud-Daula, of the appearance of the Bāb.[21] Both Bābī and other Persian sources agree that Manūchihr Khān was favorably inclined to the Bāb and had him brought to Isfahan to satisfy his personal curiosity.[22] With Manūchihr Khān, the identification of the Bāb with the state almost became a reality. In order, presumably, to conceal his inclinations and to nullify any possible agitation, Manūchihr Khān caused the Bāb to be accommodated in the residence of the imām jum'a, and after a period of forty days, to be publicly confronted with the ulama of Isfahan, gathered in the Masjid-i Shāh.[23] It is clear that the ulama suspected the nature of Manūchihr Khān's intentions. By again confronting the Bāb with the ulama, he may have hoped to erase the impression left by his experience in Shiraz, or at least to provide a pretext for postponing any final decision. Most of the ulama refused to attend the confrontation saying that as the incompatibility of the Bāb's pretensions with the sharī'at was "clearer and brighter than the sun," any further discussion was superfluous, and all that remained to be done was to enforce the relevant provision of the law.[24] This appears to have been the first clear demand by the ulama for the execution of the Bāb. Only the imām jum'a, Āqā Mir Muḥammad Mihdī, and Mīrzā Ḥasan Nūrī, son of Mullā 'Alī Nūrī, attended

20 A. K. S. Lambton ("Persian Society under the Qajars," *JRCAS*, XLVIII [1961], 136) writes that in Qajar times as earlier, movements of social revolt tended to take on a religious coloring "because orthodoxy was associated with the ruling institution," and that "because there was no separation between Church and State, unorthodoxy was almost automatically regarded as a threat to the existing régime"; and cites Bābism as the chief example. We have already noted, however, the alienation of the ulama from the state; and in the case of Bābism, the danger was initially only to orthodoxy. The state reacted seriously only when its own security was affected. The most significant movements of social revolt in the Qajar period took place precisely within an "orthodox" frame of expression, drawing on a long tradition in so doing.

21 Gobineau, *op. cit.*, p. 15.

22 Browne, ed., *op. cit.*, II, 15; Browne, ed., *Tārīkh-i-Jadīd*, p. 208; *RSN*, X, 312; *NT*, p. 426; *MN*, III, 185. The last three imply that Manūchihr Khān was deceived as to the nature of the Bāb's claims.

23 Browne, ed., *Traveller's Narrative*, II, 16; Browne, ed., *Tārīkh-i-Jadīd*, p. 210.

24 Browne, ed., *Traveller's Narrative*, II, 16.

the meeting in the Masjid-i Shāh.[25] Mīr Muḥammad Mihdī inquired of the Bāb what was the source of his certainty, for after the occultation of the Twelfth Imam, certain knowledge on any point of religious law was to be had only by a pronouncement of the Hidden Imam, vouchsafed in a vision. Mīrzā Ḥasan Nūrī asked him to describe the circumference of the earth, since the knowledge of this, among other matters, was a sign of the Mahdī.[26] Both questions he was unable to answer, and the meeting was dissolved without conclusive result.[27] Manūchihr Khān protected the Bāb until his death, and again the Bāb appears to have had enough freedom to maintain and even expand contact with his followers.[28] The ulama protested to Ḥājjī Mīrzā Āqāsī, but received only a noncommittal reply.[29]

On the death of Manūchihr Khān in 1263/1847, Ḥājjī Mīrzā Āqāsī gave orders that the Bāb be brought to Tehran.[30] According to the *Traveller's Narrative,* the Bāb, when a few stages distant from Tehran, wrote a letter to Muḥammad Shāh, asking to be granted an audience.[31] Ḥājjī Mīrzā Āqāsī, anxious neither to arouse the opposition of the ulama, nor to give them an opportunity of asserting themselves, refused his consent.[32] Instead the Bāb was sent in chains to be imprisoned at Mākū in Azerbayjan. En route, he spent forty days in Tabriz, but the ulama refused to meet him.[33] From Mākū, he was transferred to the fortress at Chihrīq near the Ottoman border. Here again he appears to have been able to maintain contact with his disciples, who were by now engaged in revolt in Mazandaran.[34] The disquiet caused by the Bābī uprisings, together with the continuing agitation of the ulama, led Ḥājjī Mīrzā Āqāsī, three months after the Bāb had been brought to Chihrīq, to have recourse again to the device of a confrontation, one little more conclusive that the preceding ones in Shiraz and

25 *Ibid.*, II, 17.

26 *NT*, p. 427. The *Tārīkh-i-Jadīd* (Browne, ed., p. 209) claims that Mīr Muḥammad Mihdī accepted the claims of the Bāb.

27 *NT*, p. 428.

28 Browne, ed., *Traveller's Narrative*, II, 15.

29 Text given in Aḥmad Kasravī, *Bahā'īgarī* (Tehran, n.d,). p. 26; Firīdūn Ādamīyat, *Amīr Kabīr va Īrān* (Tehran, 1334 Sh/1955), p. 202.

30 Browne, ed., *op. cit.*, II, 18.

31 *Ibid.*, II, 20.

32 *Ibid.*, II, 19. There may be some truth in the suggestion that Ḥājjī Mīrzā Āqāsī was afraid of Muḥammad Shāh transferring his spiritual loyalties to the Bāb. See Browne, ed., *op. cit.*, II, 21.

33 *Ibid.*, II, 22.

34 Gobineau, *op. cit.*, p. 274.

Isfahan. The *Traveller's Narrative* represents Ḥājjī Mīrzā Āqāsī as being still reluctant to conform with the wishes of the ulama;[35] but on this occasion, the ulama of Tabriz, hoping possibly for a definitive solution of the problem, consented to meet the Bāb in the presence of Nāṣir ud-Dīn Mīrzā, at the time heir apparent and governor of Azerbayjan. The Bāb was brought from Chihrīq by Sulaymān Khān Afshār, and the day after his arrival in Tabriz was interrogated by Mullā Muḥammad Mamaqānī, chief of the Shaykhī ulama of Tabriz;[36] Ḥājjī Mullā Maḥmūd Niẓām ul-'Ulamā;[37] Mīrzā 'Alī Aṣghar Shaykh ul-Islām; Mīrzā Aḥmad Mujtahid Imām Jum'a; and Ḥājjī Murtaḍā Qulī Marandī.[38] Various questions were put to the Bāb, concerning Arabic grammar and syntax, and the signs traditionally associated with the coming of the Hidden Imam.[39] Unable to answer them, he again recanted, and after being beaten by the shaykh ul-Islām in person, was sent back to Chihrīq.[40] Still, then, the Bāb was left alive; and it was only when Amīr Kabīr thought the state endangered that the penalty for apostasy was applied. Religious duty had to wait on the state for its fulfillment. The episode of the Bāb provided one of the clearest examples of the dependence of shar' law on the state for the execution of its judgments. The shaykh ul-Islām of Tabriz wrote to the Bāb that only doubts concerning his sanity prevented his immediate execution,[41] but it is difficult to see in what manner these doubts

35 Browne, ed., *op. cit.*, II, 25.

36 Nādir Mīrzā, *Tārīkh va Jughrāfī-yi Dār us-Salṭana-yi Tabrīz* (Tehran, 1323 Q/1905), p. 117.

37 Mullā Maḥmūd was tutor to Nāṣir ud-Dīn, and when his pupil mounted the throne, he occupied a position of some importance at court. See below, p. 160.

38 Browne, ed., *op. cit.*, II, 20; Browne, ed., *Tārīkh-i-Jadīd*, p. 285; Kasravī, *op. cit.*, p. 29; *RSN*, X, 423; *NT*, p. 470. According to the *Tārīkh-i-Jadīd*, the Bāb was lodged in the house of Mīrzā Aḥmad; according to *NT*, in that of Kāẓim Khān Farrāshbāshī.

39 The substance of this examination of the Bāb is not seriously disputed by either the *Traveller's Narrative* or the *Tārīkh-i-Jadīd*, both Bahā'ī sources. Riḍā Qulī Khān claims to base his account on the information of Ḥājjī Mullā Maḥmūd (*RSN*, X, 423). Together with the versions given in *Q'U* (p. 46) and *NT* (pp. 470–472), it corresponds in detail with the report sent to Tehran by Nāṣir ud-Dīn Mīrzā (original in Majlis library, Tehran; text reproduced by Ādamīyat, [*op. cit.*, p. 202], Kasravī, [*op. cit.*, pp. 30–32] and E. G. Browne [*Materials for the Study of the Babi Religion* (Cambridge, 1918), pp. 253–256]).

40 Browne, ed., *Traveller's Narrative*, II, 27; Browne, ed., *Tārīkh-i Jadīd*, p. 290.

41 Kasravī, *op. cit.*, p. 34. The fact that the Bāb was a sayyid (Gobineau [*op. cit.*, p. 143] considers his claim weak) may have been a further cause for delaying his execution, and also for choosing Armenian troops to shoot him.

were dispelled before the execution of the Bāb in 1266/1849. On the other hand, the threat posed to secular authority became ever clearer.

Mullā Ḥusayn Bushravayh had gone from Shiraz by way of Tehran to Khurasan, and there attempted to secure acceptance of the Bāb's claims. He met with partial success in Nayshapur, and then moved to Mashhad, where in the last years of Muḥammad Shāh's reign, the Sālār and Ḥamza Mīrzā Ḥishmat ud-Daula were struggling for the possession of the town.[42] However, Mullā Ḥusayn was repulsed by both of them, and Ḥamza Mīrzā imprisoned him at the bidding of the ulama.[43] Escaping, he moved in the direction of Sabzavar, where he and his followers were armed by a certain Mīrzā Taqī Juvaynī.[44] At this point, the rebellion against the state began. This fact was obscured by the death of Muḥammad Shāh, and the Bābī revolt became one element in the chaos surrounding the succession. Mullā Ḥusayn, together with Mullā Muḥammad 'Alī Bārfurūshī and Qurrat ul-'Ayn, moved into Mazandaran, and here the first battles between Bābism and the state took place. The immediate threat was, however, to the ulama, just as the claims of the Bāb appeared initially to endanger only religion. The ulama of Bārfurūsh (modern Bābul) were threatened by Mullā Muḥammad 'Alī who marched through the streets of the town at the head of three hundred men with drawn swords: "le clergé jugea qu'il était grandement temps d'engager la lutte si l'on ne voulait pas courir le risque d'être un plus peu tard anéanti sans combat."[45] Sa'īd ul-'Ulamā Bārfurūshī led the resistance to the Bābīs, constantly pleading for troops to be sent against them.[46] Nāṣir ud-Dīn Shah was preparing to leave for Tehran, and evidently the matter was thought too trivial to warrant serious attention.[47] At the request of Sa'īd ul-'Ulamā, however, 'Abbās Qulī Khān, governor of Lārījān, sent three hundred troops to Bārfurūsh,

[42] See above, p. 125.
[43] *NT*, p. 473; *RSN*, X, 422; Gobineau, *op. cit.*, p. 171.
[44] *Ibid.*, p. 173.
[45] *Ibid.*, p. 185.
[46] Browne, ed., *Tārīkh-i-Jadīd*, p. 52. The same work (p. 91) claims that Sa'īd ul-'Ulamā' was a Jewish convert to Islam, implying, perhaps, that his resistance to Bābism was inspired by the enthusiasm of a proselyte. The short biographical notice of Sa'īd ul-'Ulamā' in Mīrzā Muḥammad Ḥasan Khān I'timād us-Salṭana, *al-Ma'āthir va-l-Āthār* (Tehran, 1306 Q/1889, p. 150) makes no mention of any Jewish origin.
[47] Muhammad, *op. cit.*, p. 457.

and Mullā Ḥusayn and his followers withdrew from the town.[48] There then followed the siege of the Bābī stronghold at Shaykh Ṭabarsī. In the course of the repeated defeats suffered by government troops, Sa'īd ul-'Ulamā exhorted them constantly to persist against the Bābīs; when ultimately Shaykh Ṭabarsī fell, he executed some of the survivors with his own hands in the marketplace at Bārfurūsh.[49] As the most important of the ulama of Mazandaran, he thus played a central role in combating Bābism.

Whereas the Bābīs in Mazandaran established themselves in a stronghold at some distance from the main towns of the region, the insurrection in Zanjān was a more direct challenge to governmental authority. There it was led by Mullā Muḥammad Zanjānī, who before adopting Bābism had followed the Akhbārī madhhab. It appears that even before his conversion to Bābism, he had constantly been in dispute with both state and ulama.[50] When visiting the governor of Zanjān, he was always accompanied by a group of armed followers.[51] His disputes with the Uṣūlī ulama of Zanjān became so acrimonious that they wrote to Tehran requesting his removal from the town.[52] He was banished on several occasions; it was on one of these, toward the end of the reign of Muḥammad Shāh, that he met Mullā Ḥusayn Bushravayh in Tehran.[53] In the confusion following the death of Muḥammad Shāh and the fall from power of Ḥājjī Mīrzā Āqāsī, he returned to Zanjān, where he was enthusiastically received by his former followers.[54] He proclaimed that he had become a Bābī, and his followers decided also to adopt the new faith. Initially, his violence was directed only against the ulama; a Bahā'ī source records that a mullā was dragged down from his *minbar* (pulpit),[55] and the son of the shaykh ul-Islām was murdered.[56] The ulama informed the capital

48 Gobineau, *op. cit.*, pp. 186–187.

49 Browne, ed., *Tārīkh-i-Jadīd*, pp. 58, 72, 88; *RSN*, X, 446.

50 Gobineau (*op. cit.*, p. 233) writes: "A s'en faire une idée tout a fait impartiale, on peut voir en lui un de ces nombreux musulmans qui, au vrai, ne le sont pas du tout, mais que pressent un fond très ample et très vivace de foi et de zèle religieux dont ils cherchent l'emploi avec passion." The analysis does not, however, give an immediate impression of impartiality.

51 *RSN*, X, 448.

52 Gobineau, *op. cit.*, p. 234; Browne, ed., *Traveller's Narrative*, II, p. 13; Browne, ed., *Tārīkh-i-Jadīd*, p. 135.

53 Browne, ed., *Traveller's Narrative*, II, 12.

54 Gobineau, *op. cit.*, p. 235.

55 Browne, ed., *Tārīkh-i-Jadīd*, p. 371.

56 Gobineau, *op. cit.*, p. 238.

of what was happening, but it was not until one of the Bābīs was arrested that fighting broke out. He was arrested for nonpayment of fiscal arrears, and Mullā Muḥammad 'Alī attempted to free him by force.[57] Although the insurrection was in the name of Bābism and was pursued with great ferocity, we see here a repetition of one of the traditional motives for movements of disobedience led by the ulama: in particular it may be compared with the rising of 1253/1837–1838 in Isfahan.[58] One of the many motives that led to the dissemination of Bābism was thus the readiness of a devoted following to obey the directives of a mullā, even after his conversion to Bābism. Here, one aspect of clerical power is reflected in Bābism; but the case of Zanjān, with the exception of that of Nayrīz, is isolated.

Sayyid Yaḥyā Dārābī, as mentioned above, attended the first interrogation of the Bāb in Shirāz, doing so, according to Bahā'ī sources, on behalf of Muḥammad Shāh.[59] From Shiraz he had gone to Yazd, whence he was expelled for preaching Bābism in 1850.[60] Reaching Nayrīz, he enclosed himself in the citadel from which he was driven after a prolonged siege.[61] His father, Sayyid Ja'far, had enjoyed wide popularity which was transferred to him, while a dispute between the townspeople and their governor, Mīrzā Zayn ul'Ābidīn, supplied an additional reason to welcome him.[62] Here again it is evident that loyalty to the person of a powerful mullā survived his conversion to Bābism, when he fulfilled the traditional role of opposition to the oppression of the governor. The *Tārīkh-i-Jadīd* confirms that Sayyid Yaḥyā relied on the faithfulness of his father's followers.[63]

The insurrection in Zanjān at last decided Amīr Kabīr to do away with the Bāb, as ultimate source of the unrest.[64] Again he was brought from Chihrīq to Tabriz, and fatvās were delivered by

[57] Browne, ed., *Tārīkh-i-Jadīd*, p. 140; Gobineau, *op. cit.*, p. 238.

[58] See above, pp. 111–112.

[59] Browne, ed., *Traveller's Narrative*, II, 10; Browne, ed., *Tārīkh-i-Jadīd*, p. 113.

[60] Browne, ed., *Traveller's Narrative*, II, 254.

[61] *Ibid.*, p. 254.

[62] *RSN*, X, 457.

[63] P. 118. See, too, Muhammad, *op. cit.*, p. 466. It is questionable how well the participants in Bābī-led revolts were acquainted with Bābī tenets. Browne (introduction to *Tārīkh-i-Jadīd*, p. xxvii)points out that the devotion of the Bābīs was, in general, more to leaders than to books and precepts.

[64] *RSN*, X, 456. The *Tārīkh-i-Jadīd* (p. 292) bears witness to Amīr Kabīr's reluctance, and to his being motivated solely by reasons of state.

various of the ulama condemning him to death. The *Traveller's Narrative* mentions Mullā Muḥammad Mamaqānī, Mīrzā Bāqir Mujtahid, and Mullā Murtaḍā Qulī Marandī.[65] At last, the state decided to enforce the penalty for apostasy; but the offense causing it to do so was one in nature less religious, and more directly threatening itself. On Sha'bān 27, 1266/July 8, 1850, the Bāb was shot dead in the citadel of Tabriz.[66]

This ended the first stage in the development of the religious movement resulting in the syncretist doctrines of Bahā'ism.[67] It was the ulama who were first threatened by it and often suffered from its violence. In Qazvin, Ḥājjī Mullā Muḥammad Taqī Burghānī was killed in the *miḥrāb* (niche) of a mosque by Mīrzā Ṣāliḥ Shīrāzī for his persistent denunciation of Bābism.[68] The Bāb himself, though largely remote from the activities of his followers, indicated his attitude to the ulama by breaking a stick over the chief mullā of Mākū.[69] Furthermore, it was the ulama who throughout encouraged the state to suppress the movement, and their resistance to it was more consistent than that of either Ḥājjī Mīrzā Āqāsī or Amīr Kabīr. Their function of defending the religio-national community was, then, again exemplified in the struggle against Bābism, while in this struggle the role of the state appeared to them, at best, as lacking in enthusiasm and, at worst, as ambiguous.

It is, nonetheless, necessary to recall that many of the leading Bābīs were drawn from the ulama, though only one mujtahid, Āqā Sayyid Ḥusayn Turshīzī, appears to have joined their ranks.[70] The majority of these were Shaykhīs, and in the light of the expectations implicit in Shaykhī teaching, their conversion is not remarkable.[71] We have seen that, on the other hand, Mullā Muḥammad 'Ali Zanjānī was an Akhbārī before his conversion, but it appears possible that he was attracted above all by the insurrectionary as-

65 II, 55. Gobineau (*op. cit.*, p. 260) says that another discussion between the ulama and the Bāb was provided for, which most of them refused to attend. It is probable, however, that he is confusing these events with the earlier bringing of the Bāb from Chihrīq.

66 Gobineau, *op. cit.*, p. 263; *NT*, p. 489.

67 It is arguable that the movement began with Shaykh Aḥmad Aḥsā'ī, or even earlier. See Kasravī, *op. cit.*, pp. 2–20.

68 *Q'U*, p. 22.

69 Browne, ed., *Tārīkh-i-Jadīd*, p. 352.

70 Browne, ed., *Traveller's Narrative*, II, 212.

71 A list of some Shaykhī mullās who accepted Bābism is given in *ibid.*, p. 6.

pects of the new faith. The *Tārīkh-i-Jadīd* estimates the number of ulama to have accepted Bābism at 400, and claims that they occupy "the position of a touchstone or measure for the proving of his [the Bāb's] claims, which distinguishes base metal from true."[72] That indeed the vast majority of the ulama rejected the Bāb's claims was probably the most important single factor working against their acceptance. Had the Bāb in fact been acknowledged as the Hidden Imam, the function of the ulama would have ceased to exist. It may be conceded that they thus had a vested interest in the continued occultation of the Hidden Imam; but even Bahā'īs realized that the ulama had only two possible courses of action: to reject as false the Shi'i traditions considering the manner of the appearance of the Hidden Imam, or to consider the Bāb a blasphemous apostate.[73]

Bābism had certain consequences for the ulama and for Iran as a whole, many of which are suggested by a comparison with Ismā'īlism. The comparison was made in the Qajar period and has been repeated by later investigators.[74] Both Ismā'īlism and Bābism were heresies of Shi'ite origin seeking to overthrow orthodoxy (Sunni and Ithnā'asharī respectively) by violence, and spreading their doctrines by secret instruction.[75] Doctrinally, too, there were similarities: the title of Bāb was given in Ismā'īlism to one of the seven grades of the esoteric hierarchy.[76] The Bābīs for their part revived the mystic use of the numeral seven with the theory of the seven letters (*ḥurūf*) by means of which God accomplished the task of creation.[77] As Bābī-Bahā'ī doctrine lost its Shi'ite tinge, it tended to attract the religious minorities, particularly the Zoroastrians[78]

72 Pp. 231–235.

73 Browne, ed., *Traveller's Narrative*, II, 32.

74 *Q'U*, p. 46; article on Bābism by Jamāl ud-Dīn Asadābādī in *Dā'irat al-Ma'ārif*, ed. Buṭrus Bustānī (Beirut, 1881), V, 26; Jamāl ud-Dīn Asadābādī, "Radd-i Naycharīya," in *Ārā va Mu'taqadāt-i Sayyid Jamāl ud-Dīn-i Afghānī*, ed. M. Chahārdihī (Tehran, 1337 Sh/1958), p. 49; 'Abd ar-Razzāq al-Ḥasanī, *al-Bābīyūn wa-l-Bahā'īyūn fi Ḥāḍirihim wa Māḍīhim* (Sidon, 1376 Q/1956–1957), p. 10; G. Scarcia, "A Proposito del Problema della Sovranità presso gli Imamiti," *Annali del Istituto Orientale di Napoli*, VII (1957), 121 (Bābism a "neo-Ismā'īlī interpretation of Shaykhī Imāmism").

75 On Ismā'īlī use of violence, see Marshall G. Hodgson, *The Order of Assassins* ('s-Gravenhage, 1955), pp. 110–115.

76 H. Corbin, *Histoire de la Philosophie Islamique* (Paris, 1963), p. 131.

77 Gobineau, *op. cit.*, p. 314. No complete analysis of the doctrines of Bābism and its successors is attempted here.

78 E. G. Browne, *A Year amongst the Persians* (new ed., London, 1950), p. 430.

in much the same way as Ismā'īlism had proclaimed "interconfessionalism" in its attempts to subvert orthodoxy.[79] The threats presented by Bābism and Ismā'īlism, being both pervasive and hidden in their nature, permitted accusations of allegiance to heresy to become means of controversy and enmity. This was particularly the case with Bābism, after the attempted assassination of Nāṣir ul-Dīn Shāh.[80]

Taqīya, the prudent concealment of belief in circumstances of danger, was both a cause and a result of this pervasive fear and suspicion. The original justification of taqīya, self-protection from Sunni intolerance, had virtually ceased to exist,[81] but the habits of concealment and ambiguity it engendered lived on. Many of the Bābīs who remained in Iran found themselves obliged to practice taqīya, as the violence of the early Bābīs was paid back to their successors by the ulama and the state. Taqīya at the same time enabled them to continue in, or penetrate, the ranks of the ulama, and the discontent of Bahā'īs and Azalīs added a further element to the opposition to the Qajar monarchy, one that became entwined with the ulama themselves.

Probably the emergence of Bābism affected the Shaykhīs more than other sections of the ulama, and taqīya was in practice forced on them too. The process had started when Sayyid Kāẓim Rashtī, successor to Shaykh Aḥmad Aḥsā'ī as leader of the sect, was obliged to confess that the apparent meaning of certain of Shaykh Aḥmad's doctrines constituted misbelief.[82] On the death of Sayyid Kāẓim, not only the Bāb, but two other rival successors emerged, both hostile to the pretensions of Sayyid 'Alī Muḥammad.[83] Mullā Muḥammad Mamaqānī, a follower of Mirzā Shafī' Tabrīzī, one of the claimants to the succession, was among the ulama who condemned the Bāb to death in Tabriz. Ḥājjī Muḥammad Karīm Khān, the other claimant, was not less decisive in his reaction to Bābism. In Kirman, he gave a fatvā for the killing of two Bābī missionaries.[84] He wrote a treatise refuting the Bāb's claims, allegedly at the request of Nāṣir ud-Dīn Shāh, but more probably to

79 B. Lewis, *The Origins of Ismā'īlism* (Cambridge, 1940), pp. 93–96.

80 Gobineau, *op. cit.*, p. 304.

81 See below, p. 228.

82 *Q'U*, p. 31.

83 Kasravī, *op. cit.*, pp. 19–20.

84 Browne, ed., *Tārīkh-i-Jadīd*, p. 200.

establish a distance between himself and the Bāb.[85] In his treatise *Sī Faṣl,* he later claimed that, far from suffering from Bābī inclinations, he was the first to pronounce the Bāb an infidel.[86] It is clear that a certain similarity existed between the initial claims of the Bāb and the Shaykhī concept of the *shī'a-yi kāmil* (the perfect shi'a) as human intermediaries between the community of believers and the Hidden Imam. Therefore, the followers of Ḥājjī Muḥammad Karīm Khān found it prudent to reexplain the concept as no more than an idea, not to be identified with any one person.[87] When he wrote a treatise summarizing Shaykhī beliefs, significantly such typical Shaykhī concepts as the *jism-i hūrqalīyā'ī*[88] received no mention.[89] A successor of Ḥājjī Muḥammad Karīm Khān even went so far as to suggest that the differences between Uṣūlīs and Shaykhīs were purely terminological.[90] Thus did the emergence of Bābism force one section of the ulama to resort to taqīya in its struggle with the majority. This struggle, though secondary to that between ulama and state, continued until the Constitutional Revolution and was another element in the confusion of motive surrounding that event.

The development of Bābism into Bahā'ism confirmed the existing hostility to the ulama.[91] Thus Mīrzā Jānī Kāshānī, author of the *Nuqṭat ul-Kāf,* looked forward to the beheading of 70,000 mullās by the Hidden Imam on his emergence,[92] and thought them less valuable than the carcass of a dog.[93] The attempt on the life on Nāṣir ud-Dīn Shāh was preceded by a similar plot against the imām jum'a of Tehran, which however was not put into operation. The Bahā'īs dissociated themselves from the attack on the Shah,

[85] Browne, *A Year amongst the Persians,* p. 608; 'Abd ul-Ḥusayn Navā'ī, "Ḥājj Muḥammad Karīm Khān Kirmānī," *Yādgār,* V (1328 Sh/1949–1950), 117.

[86] *Ibid.,* IV, 72.

[87] Alessandro Bausani, *Persia Religiosa* (Milan, 1959), p. 406.

[88] *Jism-i hurqalīyā'ī*: "Hurqalyan body," the subtle body in which the Hidden Imam subsists in the realm of Hurqalīyā, a region intermediate between spirit and matter (see Henry Corbin, *Terre Celeste et Corps de Résurrection* [Paris, 1960], pp. 99–164).

[89] Navā'ī, *op. cit.,* IV, 68.

[90] Shaykh Abū-l-Qāsim Kirmānī, *Fihrist-i Kutub-i Marḥūm Shaykh Aḥmad-i Aḥsā'ī va Sā'ir-i Mashāyikh-i 'Iẓām* (Kirman, 1337 Sh/1958–1959), p. 105.

[91] Azalism, the other successor to Bābism, becomes of importance later than Bahā'ism.

[92] Browne, ed., *Tārīkh-i-Jadīd,* p. xvii. In one sense, a curious sentiment to entertain, for the Bāb had claimed precisely to be the Hidden Imam.

[93] *Ibid.,* p. 15.

and in fact sought to achieve with Nāṣir ud-Dīn Shāh what the Bāb had failed to accomplish with Muḥammad Shāh: to present themselves as allies of the state against the ulama. 'Abd ul-Bahā wrote in this vein to Nāṣir ud-Dīn Shah.[94] Not only was the role of the ulama in suppressing Bābism emphasized, but they were held responsible for preventing Nāṣir ud-Dīn Shah from introducing a policy of toleration.[95] The charge was hardly justified; in reality the Bahā'īs came to occupy something of a position between the state and the ulama, not one enabling them to balance the two sides, but rather exposing them to blows each side was aiming at the other. The government, interested in maintaining order, would resist persecution of Bahā'is by the ulama, but would equally, when occasion demanded, permit action against the Bahā'īs.

Despite these consequences of the rise of Bābism, the contradiction between ulama and state, its origins and its results, remained largely unchanged. Not long after the execution of the Bāb, Amīr Kabīr expelled the shaykh ul-Islām and the imām jum'a from Tabriz. Even while Sayyid Yaḥyā Dārābī was leading the Bābī insurrection in Nayrīz, a not less violent conflict was raging in Isfahan between clerical and secular power. Bābism was ultimately no more than a side issue in the Qajar history.

[94] Text and Arabic translation in al-Ḥasanī, *op. cit.*, pp. 132–164.
[95] Browne, ed., *Traveller's Narrative*, II, 149.

IX

Between Two Reformers, Mīrzā Taqī Khān Amīr Kabīr and Mīrzā Ḥusayn Khān Sipahsālār (1268/1851–1288/1871)

During the ministry of Mīrzā Āqā Khān Nūrī, Amīr Kabīr's successor, the struggle between ulama and state lessened in intensity. The state attempted to buy the favor of the ulama, and while the growing entanglement of Iran with foreign powers and their rivalries was becoming ever more apparent, the government seemed to be seeking the cooperation of the ulama in dealing with the problem. Although Nāṣir ud-Dīn Shāh was later to undertake other, halfhearted, uncoordinated attempts at reform, attempts that were to arouse clerical opposition, no such innovations were seen in the time of Mīrzā Āqā Khān. On the other hand, the ground that the state had won in its struggle with the ulama was not given up, and their independent participation in affairs was discouraged. Administrative changes introduced by Nāṣir ud-Dīn Shāh on the dismissal of Āqā Khān Nūrī repeated this tendency, and together with the demonstrations of unorthodox ostentation particularly marked during the twenty years from 1850 to 1870 supplied the enmity of the ulama with continuing justification. This hostility found sporadic expression and carried the seed of later, more far-reaching clashes.

While Amīr Kabīr had, by his reforms, attempted to reduce clerical power, Mīrzā Āqā Khān saw in the ulama, on the contrary, a means of supporting his own position. While the ulama do not appear to have played any immediate role in the disgrace of Amīr Kabīr, the policy followed by his successor toward the ulama was in many respects a reversal of his own. Mīrzā Āqā Khān increased payments made to various of the ulama (as well as princes and courtiers), designed to gain their goodwill.[1] Mīrzā Bāqir Mujtahid and Mīrzā 'Alī Aṣghar, son of the imām jum'a, expelled from Tabriz by Amīr Kabīr, were able to return to an enthusiastic welcome from their followers.[2] Mīrzā Faḍlullāh Mustaufī Vazīr Niẓām, who was appointed vazīr to the governor of Tabriz, Amīr-i Niẓām, in 1269/1852–1853, was instructed to care for the well-being of the ulama of that town.[3] It is clear, however, that the prerogatives won for the central power by Amīr Kabīr were not entirely ceded. The dīvānkhāna, as primary organ of jurisdiction, was strengthened under the direction of Mīrzā Ṣādiq Rashtī, and the ultimate decision regarding any case was reserved to the Amīr-i Niẓām himself.[4] It is likely that the initiative was that of the Amīr-i Niẓām, for he later showed great firmness against the ulama, and in the first year of Mīrzā Faḍlullāh's appointment, he had Mīrzā 'Alī Aṣghar expelled again from Tabriz for his part in clashes with the Shaykhīs.[5] Nonetheless, Mīrzā Āqā Khān Nūrī, while attempting to gain the goodwill of the ulama by gifts, opposed their participation in affairs of state: when in 1274/1857–1858, a group of ulama from Yazd came to denounce the oppression of the governor of that town to the Shah, he forbade them to proceed beyond Qum.[6]

Apart from general gestures of goodwill to the ulama, an attempt appears to have been made to associate them with the foreign policy of the government, which at that time was concerned chiefly with the reconquest of Herat and British objections to this plan. When Herat fell in 1273/1856, Nāṣir ud-Dīn Shāh gave orders for

[1] *HAN*, p. 124.

[2] Nādir Mīrzā, *Tarīkh va Jughrāfī-yi Dār us-Salṭanā-yi Tabrīz* (Tehran, 1323 Q/1905) pp. 118, 244.

[3] *HAN*, p. 146.

[4] *RSN*, X, 526.

[5] Nādir Mīrzā, *op. cit.*, p. 118. At the same time, he used the ulama in his intrigues against Mīrzā Āqā Khān Nūrī. See A. de Gobineau, *Dépêches Diplomatiques*, ed. A. D. Hytier (Geneva, 1959), p. 77.

[6] *HAN*, p. 251.

3,000 tomans to be distributed among the ulama, ostensibly as a token of gratitude for the efficacy of their prayers, and a further 10,000 tomans was sent to the 'atabāt to be spent on repairs.[7] The British reaction to the fall of Herat was to declare war on Iran, and the cooperation of the ulama was sought in declaring jihad against the enemy, who attacked first Bushire and then Muhammara.[8] Orders were given throughout the country that jihad against the British was to be preached, and volunteers and monetary contributions collected. Gobineau, at the time French minister in Tehran, wrote on January 3, 1857 that several mullās had started preaching jihad, but without being able to arouse popular enthusiasm.[9] A week later, after Bushire had been occupied by a British force, Mīrzā Āqā Khān himself decided to address the population of Tehran on the subject of jihad. The bazaar was closed by government order, and the populace obliged to gather in the Masjid-i Shāh.[10] After Mīrzā Āqā Khān had spoken on the necessity of jihad, the proclamation was formally read out.[11] There was virtually no response.[12] The failure of this plan to arouse religious emotion is significant. Presumably, the examples of the First and Second Perso-Russian Wars were remembered, and although the agitation in neither case was productive of military success, it did produce, especially in the second war, a wave of enthusiasm decisively influencing events. Similarly, earlier campaigns against the Sunnis of Herat had been sanctioned by the declaration of jihad.[13] Now, however, the tested device proved worthless. It is probable that British operations against seaports in the Persian Gulf seemed considerably more remote than Russian aggression in the Caucasus, and therefore the national-religious existence less endangered. In

7 *RSN*, X, 700.

8 'Abdullāh Mustaufī, *Tārīkh-i Idārī va Ijtimā'ī-yi Daura-yi Qājārīya yā Sharḥ-i Zindagānī-yi Man* (Tehran, 1321 Sh/1942–1943), I, 83.

9 Gobineau, *op. cit.*, pp. 46–47. *RSN* (X, 731) says that on the contrary the ulama wrote from every part of the country to Nāṣir ud-Dīn Shāh, proposing the declaration of jihad, but that he rejected their suggestion. This would appear to be a discreet manner of recording the failure of the agitation. Gobineau's evidence may in this case be regarded as decisive.

10 Gobineau, *op. cit.*, p. 53; *Trois Ans en Asie* (Paris, 1859), p. 292. *RSN* (X, 731) gives the date of Jumādī ul-Ulā 11, 1273, corresponding to January 8, 1857, i.e., two days earlier than that given by Gobineau.

11 Gobineau, *Dépêches Diplomatiques*, p. 53; *Trois Ans en Asie*, p. 294.

12 *Ibid.*, p. 294; H. Brugsch, *Reise der königlichen preussischen Gesandtschaft nach Persien* (Leipzig, 1862), I, 220; R. G. Watson, *A History of Persia from the Beginning of the Nineteenth Century to the Year 1858* (London, 1866), p. 434.

13 See above, p. 116 n. 70.

any event, Gobineau records that many "honourable mullās" refused to participate in the agitation.[14] Above all, its failure lay in its artificiality, in the fact that it was instigated by the state rather than by the ulama. It was rumored, even, that the idea first occurred to an Armenian Catholic, drawing on the examples of Shamyl in Daghistan and 'Abd ul-Qādir in Algeria.[15] Although successful deceptions in the course of nineteenth-century Iranian history were not infrequent, religious agitation initiated by the state had little chance of making itself credible. Usually the target of such agitation was the state itself, and we have seen that even when it was directed against a foreign target, the state tended to become a second objective for the popular anger. The initiators of the plan clearly realized that the agitation, if successful, might spontaneously expand its scope, and gave explicit instructions that Ottoman, Russian, and French subjects were not to be harmed.[16]

In the spring of 1857, one of the subsidiary motives for the attempt to arouse religious enthusiasm became apparent. Arbitrary taxes were imposed under the guise of a war levy. In Qazvin, the population took refuge from the governor's rapacity in the Masjid-i Jum'a, whence he expelled them by force. The imām jum'a was bastinadoed for his support of the people.[17] The ulama, then, fulfilled their political duty in the traditional context: in opposition to the state, not in cooperation with it.

While Mīrzā Āqā Khān Nūrī attempted to appease the ulama by payments of money, the religiosity of Nāṣir ud-Dīn Shāh might have been thought at least as capable of placating their inherent hostility to the throne. He was reputedly conscientious in fulfilling his religious duties,[18] and among the flattering remarks addressed to him was one to the effect that his religious knowledge was such as befitted a mujtahid.[19] The ulama regularly participated in court ceremony, and petitions might be presented to him through the

14 Gobineau, *Trois Ans en Asie*, p. 292.

15 *Ibid.*, p. 295; R. G. Watson, *op. cit.*, p. 434.

16 Gobineau, *Dépêches Diplomatiques*, p. 53.

17 *Ibid.*, p. 95.

18 Dūst 'Alī Khān Mu'ayyir ul-Mamālik, *Yāddāshthā'ī az Zindagānī-yi Khuṣūṣī-yi Nāṣir ud-Dīn Shāh* (Tehran, n.d.), p. 63; G. Curzon, *Persia and the Persian Question* (London, 1892), I, 405. According to Atrpyet (pseud.) (*Imamat': Strana Poklonnikov Imamov* [Alexandropol, 1909], p. 45), Nāṣir ud-Dīn Shāh gave himself the name of Ghulām Riḍā ("Slave of Riḍā") and refused to eat any bread unless it was baked from the wheat of the granary belonging to the shrine of the Imam Riḍā in Mashhad.

19 Mas'ud Mīrzā Ẓill us-Sulṭān, *Tārikh-i Sargudhasht-i Mas'ūdī* (Tehran, 1325 Q/1907), p. 191.

intermediary of the ulama.[20] None of this had any great effect. Even though the piety of Fatḥ 'Alī Shāh may not have been free of political considerations, it seems to have had a genuine basis; nonetheless, it was never accepted as such by the ulama. The religiosity of Nāṣir ud-Dīn Shāh, being in its manifestations essentially ceremonial and ostentatious and involving a degree of unorthodoxy, had even less chance of acceptance. Fatḥ 'Alī Shāh had sought to cover himself with the mantle of sanctity worn by the ulama by submitting to their directives; Nāṣir ud-Dīn Shāh attempted to establish his piety independently. A striking example of this was given at almost the same time as the attempt to enlist the support of the ulama for declaring jihad. In fact, the idolatrous ceremonies surrounding the portrait of 'Alī b. Abī Ṭālib may even have heightened their unwillingness to cooperate.

Information available on court ceremonial in the reigns of preceding Qajar monarchs is not detailed, but it seems probable that earlier customs were expanded and added to by Nāṣir ud-Dīn Shāh. A number of the ulama were always present at the levee on the occasion of Naurūz, the Persian New Year.[21] Headed by the imām jum'a, they would seat themselves at the side of the throne. Nāṣir ud-Dīn Shāh, out of deference to the ulama's disapproval of luxury, would content himself with sitting on a gold-embroidered throne rather than the customary jewel-encrusted one.[22] As soon as the New Year had officially begun and the ulama had been dismissed with gifts, music was played.[23] The contradiction between respect for the ulama and the practices that they condemned, and the purely formal nature of the former, is here clearly visible. Dr. Feuvrier, the monarch's French physician, witnessed a Naurūz audience in 1890, and by then Nāṣir ud-Dīn Shāh had evidently further developed the ceremony. At the moment when the New Year began, a mujtahid (unnamed) wrote verses of the Quran considered to be of good omen on the inside of a cup, which he then filled with a white liquid. When the writing had been dissolved in this liquid, he passed the cup to the Shah, who drank from it, be-

20 Mu'ayyir ul-Mamālik, *op. cit.*, p. 60; Mīrzā Muḥammad Ḥasan Khān I'timād us-Salṭana, *Mir'āt ul-Buldān-i Nāṣirī* (Tehran, 1294–1297 Q/1877–1880), III, 236.

21 Mīrzā Muḥammad Hasan Khān I'timād us-Salṭana, *Vaqāyi'-i Rūzāna-yi Darbār* (Tehran, n.d.), p. 5; J.-B. Feuvrier, *Trois Ans à la Cour de Perse* (Paris, 1899), p. 128.

22 Mu'ayyir ul-Mamālik, *op. cit.*, p. 77.

23 *Ibid.*, p. 78.

fore handing it on to those standing near him.[24] Such ceremonies, inspired by Nāṣir ud-Dīn Shāh's superstition and love of ostentation, were obviously more of a humiliation than an honor for any of the ulama participating in them and cannot have failed to intensify, rather than moderate, hostility to the throne and its occupant.

An even clearer illustration of the quality of Nāṣir ud-Dīn Shāh's religiosity was provided by ceremonies connected with the alleged portrait of 'Alī b. Abī Ṭālib. Shortly before the fall of Herat, there came into the Shah's possession a portrait of the Imam which had reputedly been painted in his lifetime. Where it originated is not clear: Riḍā Qulī Khān contents himself with mentioning "the treasuries of ancient kings,"[25] while according to Gobineau it was sent from India.[26] If its origin was in fact Indian, we may conjecture that it was a gift from one of the Shi'i princes of Oudh or Sind. Nāṣir ud-Dīn "visited" the painting daily, and gave orders that a jewel-encrusted copy be made for the adornment of his own person.[27] When Mīrzā Abū-l-Ḥasan Khān Naqqāshbāshī completed his task,[28] a favorable day was chosen by the astrologers, and certain of the ulama and the courtiers were invited to witness the Shah don the medallion for the first time. On Rabī' ul-Avval 27, 1273/November 26, 1856, they gathered in the presence of Nāṣir ud-Dīn Shāh, the ulama standing near the sovereign and the princes behind them. Mīrzā Āqā Khān brought in the medallion on a jewel-encrusted tray, and Nāṣir ud-Dīn Shāh rose and saluted it. A certain Shaykh Riḍā then hung it around the Shāh's neck, and simultaneously 120 cannon shots were fired in Tūp Khāna Square, the number 120 being the numerical value of the Arabic letters making up the name 'Alī. Gold coins were distributed among the ulama, and the ceremony ended.[29] Ḥaydar Efendi, the Ottoman ambassador, stealing a march on his colleagues, the next day hastened to congratulate the Shah on his blessed acquisition.[30]

24 Feuvrier, *op. cit.*, p. 208.

25 *RSN*, X, 702.

26 Gobineau, *Trois Ans en Asie*, p. 317.

27 *RSN*, X, 702. According to Gobineau (*op. cit.*, p. 316), Nāṣir ud-Dīn filled his apartments with images to which he addressed his prayers. It seems, however, doubtful that his idolatrous tendencies went so far.

28 Thus *RSN*, X, 702. Brugsch, who saw the medallion in 1860, says that it was painted by an Armenian from Tiflis (*op. cit.*, II, 310).

29 *RSN*, X, 702–703.

30 Gobineau, *Dépêches Diplomatiques*, p. 34.

The powerlessness of the ulama to prevent this idolatrous display, offensive to the basic spirit of Islam, and indeed their failure even to protest against it, has been interpreted as evidence of their weakness.[31] It is doubtful, however, that weakness accounted for their silence; more probably the incident was received as a further confirmation of the impious, unorthodox nature of the Qajar monarchy, and as such unworthy of reaction. The disgust felt toward the throne, nonetheless, cannot have failed to increase.

Nāṣir ud-Dīn Shāh's exaggerated veneration of the Shi'i Imams found other ways of ostentatious demonstration, some of them, though not all, equally of a nature to merit the disapproval of the ulama. Poems in praise of the Imams were attributed to the Shah.[32] For the first time, the birthdays of 'Alī b. Abī Ṭālib, Ḥusayn b. 'Alī, and the Hidden Imam, as well as the commemoration of the Day of Ghadīr[33] were, at approximately the same time, made official festivals.[34] In 1890 the birthday of 'Alī was celebrated, typically, with fireworks and a military parade.[35] The author of *al-Ma'āthir va-l-Āthār* writes revealingly that "ta'zīya was for Nāṣir ud-Dīn Shāh of the same importance as *vājibāt* and *farā'iḍ* [the basic religious duties]."[36] So that he might witness ta'zīya even if outside Tehran during Muḥarram, in 1273/1856–1857, the Shah had a takya built at Nayāvarān, in addition to extending that already existing in the capital.[37] It is indicative of the extent to which the ceremonial aspect of ta'zīya prevailed over its religious function that for a time foreign envoys accredited to the court were permitted by Mīrzā Āqā Khān to attend the performances at the government takya. At this the ulama protested, fearing that the religious purpose of ta'zīya would be totally submerged, and, paradoxically enough, only the Ottoman ambassador, as a Muslim,

31 J. E. Polak, *Persien; das Land und seine Bewohner* (Leipzig, 1865), I, 322; Gobineau, *Trois Ans en Asie*, p. 317.

32 See Nāṣir ud-Dīn Shāh, *Dīvān-i Kāmil-i Ash'ār* (Tehran, 1339 Sh/1960), pp. 59–63.

33 The day on which, according to Shi'i tradition, the Prophet designated 'Alī b. Abī Ṭālib as his successor.

34 Mīrzā Muḥammad Ḥasan Khān I'timād us-Salṭana, *al-Ma'āthir va-l-Āthār* (Tehran, 1306 Q/1889), p. 96. According to Mu'ayyir ul-Mamālik (*op. cit.*, p. 73), the birthday of Ḥusayn b. 'Alī was not made an official festival until the reign of Muẓaffar ud-Dīn Shāh. The birthday of the Hidden Imam was proclaimed as a festival in 1273/1856–1857 (*HAN*, p. 239).

35 Feuvrier, *op. cit.*, p. 205.

36 I'timād us-Salṭana, *op. cit.*, p. 96.

37 I'timād us-Salṭana, *Mir'āt ul-Buldān-i Nāṣirī*, II, 195; *RSN*, X, 782.

even though Sunni, was allowed to continue attending.[38] The ulama were also able to obtain the proscription of the traditional scenes depicting the marriage of Qāsim b. al-Ḥasan, which were judged to have no historical foundation whatsoever.[39] The performances continued, however, and were so theatrical in nature that in Muḥarram, 1299/November–December, 1881, one of the less reverent ladies of the royal household remarked that the display was more laughable than the comedies of Europe.[40] We have already remarked that many of the ulama considered ta'zīya in itself reprehensible; that the monarch should thus encourage it, and help to develop it into a kind of popular entertainment, cannot have done otherwise than to add, yet again, to their hostility.

Simultaneously, Nāṣir ud-Dīn Shāh engaged in other acts of piety, more orthodox in nature. Thus he had gilded the domes of Qum and Shāh 'Abd ul-'Aẓīm and provided for a new courtyard to be built at Mashhad, while Mīrzā Āqā Khān Nūrī paid for the construction of a mosque at Karbala and a madrasa at Najaf.[41] Such expenditure had not, in the time of Fatḥ 'Alī Shāh, been enough to establish the piety of the ruler; still less was it so in the case of Nāṣir ud-Dīn Shāh. As the reality of religious belief declined, its outward signs increased and tended toward greater unorthodoxy. Certain charges of bid'at (reprehensible innovation in matters of religious practice) and excessive preoccupation with external forms may in general be made against nineteenth-century Iranian Shi'ism. While with the generality of believers this did not necessarily mean a decline in religious enthusiasm, in the case of the sovereign such tendencies were united with his own love of pomp and ceremonial, and to indulge them became, together with hunting and travel, one of his chief pastimes and pleasures. Like them too, it was a means whereby his courtiers would distract his mind from matters of state. It is significant that many of these acts of ostentation had their origin during the ministry of a venal ṣadr-i a'ẓam, Mīrzā Āqā Khān.[42] As with Muḥammad Shāh, the religion

38 *Ibid.*, X, 788. See also Gobineau's letter to Prokosch-Osten, dated September 19, 1855, in *Correspondance entre le Comte de Gobineau et le Comte de Prokosch-Osten* (Paris, 1933), p. 43.

39 I'timād us-Salṭana, *al-Ma'āthir va-l-Āthār*, p. 124.

40 I'timād us-Salṭana, *Vaqāyi'-i Rūzāna*, p. 69.

41 *RSN*, X, 811, 817–818.

42 On his role in encouraging Nāṣir ud-Dīn's love for ceremony, see Khān Malik Sāsānī, *Siyāsatgarān-i Daura-yi Qājār* (Tehran, 1338 Sh/1959), p. 17.

of the monarch became something unorthodox and separate from that of the rest of the nation, and the pattern repeated itself to a lesser degree with Muẓaffar ud-Dīn Shāh, who was thought to be a Shaykhī. It is not therefore surprising that the monarch no longer considered himself bound, even theoretically, to accept the direction of a marja'-i taqlīd. The government was, in a sense, foreign to the people and increasingly alienated from the ulama. It was precisely the proliferation of religious ceremony that confirmed and demonstrated this alienation, and thus it was that the identification of the ulama with the national interests became ever closer.

There were, nonetheless, certain of the ulama closely associated with the court, and they played a role of some importance in the events of Nāṣir ud-Dīn Shāh's reign and that of his successor. A mujtahid, summoned to appear before Muḥammad Shāh, had lifted up with his stick the carpet polluted by royal use and taken his seat on the floor beneath it instead.[43] It is thus worth examining what kind of men were those ulama associating with one as unorthodox as Nāṣir ud-Dīn Shāh. In his youth and when governor of Azerbayjan, he had been consistently accompanied by his tutor, Mullā Maḥmūd Niẓām ul-'Ulamā (or Mullābāshī). Amīn ud-Daula wrote of Mullā Maḥmūd that "he was not fit to teach the Heir Apparent of Iran," without giving any specific grounds for his opinion.[44] We know however that Mullā Maḥmūd accompanied Nāṣir ud-Dīn, when still governor of Azerbayjan, to meet the Tsar Nicholas in 1251/1835–1836, on one of the latter's trips to his Caucasian provinces. He exchanged compliments with the Tsar, remarking that "the hearts of kings are the receptacles of inspiration," and received a ring for his son, Muḥammad Āqā, who, the Tsar hoped, would remember this gift on growing up and show proper gratitude.[45] It seems, therefore, highly likely that the piety and honesty of Mullā Maḥmūd were not superior to those of the mullā bearing the title of Niẓām ul-'Ulamā in the reign of Fatḥ 'Alī Shāh.[46] Mullā Maḥmūd died in 1271/1854–1855, and on his death the title passed to Naṣrullāh Khān and Mīrzā Muḥammad Khān in turn.[47] The

43 Gobineau, *Trois Ans en Asie*, p. 386.

44 *KhS*, p. 13.

45 *NT*, pp. 344–345. According to *RSN* (X, 197), the gift of the ring was rejected.

46 See above, p. 52.

47 *HAN*, p. 171; *RSN*, X, 603; I'timād us-Salṭana, *al-Ma'āthir va-l-Āthār*, p. 24.

first, not to be confused with Naṣrullāh Ardabīlī (also the possessor of a fanciful title, that of *Ṣadr ul-Mamālik*), who had been entrusted with the distribution of grants to the ulama in the time of Muḥammad Shāh, was one of the maternal uncles of Nāṣir ud-Dīn.[48] It is clear that this title did not imply any specific function, other than presence at court. Another frequenter of the court was the blind Shaykh Asadullāh, who recited the Quran to the women of the royal household, and of whom I'timād us-Salṭana remarked: "The foul-tongued say many things about him; God alone knows the truth."[49] In general, those ulama attached directly to the court were men of no great significance, and their titles such as *Ṣadr ul-'Ulamā, Sulṭān udh-Dhākirīn*, and so forth, were only a few among the host that were distributed as marks of royal favor.[50]

More important than any of these was the imām jum'a of Tehran. As we have seen, the connection between him and the state began during the ministry of Amīr Kabīr. Deprived of their unfettered power, the imām jum'as of Tehran sought thereafter to conserve their influence by a close association with the monarch, one which he also welcomed. The son of Mīrzā Abū-l-Qāsim, Mīrzā Zayn ul-'Ābidīn, was presented in the lifetime of his father with one of the daughters of Nāṣir ud-Dīn Shāh, Ḍiyā us-Salṭana.[51] Although Mīrzā Zayn ul-'Ābidīn was still under age, on the death of Mīrzā Abū-l-Qāsim, the Shah issued a decree appointing him imām jum'a in place of his father, with his uncle, Mīrzā Murtaḍā Ṣaḍr ul-'Ulamā, acting on his behalf until he attained maturity.[52] By this maneuver Nāṣir ud-Dīn Shāh hoped presumably to secure one connected to him by marriage in the influential post of imām jum'a. It is at the same time remarkable that not only were the claims of heredity regarded in making the appointment, but also that a minor was chosen. In the latter part of the reign of Nāṣir ud-Dīn Shāh it became a frequent practice to appoint a minor to a post he was unable to fulfill, in order to gain illicit influence and wealth. That this practice extended to religious posts (in so far as

48 *RSN*, X, 603.

49 I'timād us-Salṭana, *Vaqāyi'-i Rūzāna*, p. 87.

50 See J. Bassett, *Persia, the Land of the Imams* (London, 1887), p. 336.

51 Mu'ayyir ul-Mamālik, *op. cit.*, p. 18.

52 I'timād us-Salṭana, *al-Ma'āthir va-l-Āthār*, p. 142. Evidently Mīrzā Murtaḍā continued as acting imām jum'a at least until 1288/1871–1872, for in that year he was confirmed in his function by Nāṣir ud-Dīn Shāh. See Maḥmūd Farhād Mu'tamad, *Tārīkh-i Ravābiṭ-i Īrān va 'Uthmānī* (Tehran, n.d.), I, 146.

they were at the disposal of the monarch) is a measure of the corrupting influence of the state. On the death of Ḥājjī Mullā ʿAlī Kanī in 1306/1888–1889, the trusteeship of the Madrasa-yi Fakhrīya (or Marvī) was entrusted to the imām jumʿa, as a reward for services to the throne, much as during the Constitutional Revolution, Shaykh Faḍlullāh Nūrī was rewarded with the administration of several auqāf for his resistance to the movement.[53] The imām jumʿa, at the same time, retained a considerable standing and influence among the ulama of Tehran, and by reason of this ambiguity was in fact able to be of greater service to the monarch. Other imām jumʿas, however, notably those of Tabriz and Isfahan, though appointed by Nāṣir ud-Dīn Shāh, showed themselves by no means complacent toward government policies, as will be seen. Although apparently friendly relationships might at any time prevail between a section of the ulama and the state, this depended largely on the person of the minister or other dominant figures at court or in the provinces, and the extent to which their interests coincided with those of individuals from among the ulama. In short, a twofold division among the ulama existed: those who sought their advancement through association with the state, and the far larger group, seeing either their duty or means of worldly success in opposition to it.

At this period of Nāṣir ud-Dīn Shah's reign, then, the religious attitudes of the monarch, encouraged probably by Mīrzā Āqā Khān Nūrī, had become apparent. The subservience of a certain section of the ulama, begun during the ministry of Amīr Kabīr, was confirmed, while a policy of outward respect and liberal donations attempted to forestall open opposition. At approximately the same time, however, other developments had been taking place among the ulama themselves, which were to prove of greater importance for their role in Iranian society and their relations with the monarchy. These developments were centered on the person of Shaykh uṭ-Ṭāʾifa Murtaḍā Shushtarī Anṣārī, who may be considered the most influential figure in Shiʿism since Mīrzā Muḥammad Bāqir Bihbihānī Mujaddid. Born in 1216/1801–1802 and descended from Jābir b. ʿAbdullāh the Anṣārī,[54] he had been a pupil of the great ulama of Isfahan of the period of Fatḥ ʿAli Shāh,

[53] Iʿtimād us-Salṭana, *op. cit.*, p. 142.

[54] Āqā Buzurg Ṭihrānī, *Ṭabaqāt Aʿlām ash-Shīʿa* (Najaf, 1373 Q/1953–1954), III, 429.

notably Sayyid Muḥammad Bāqir Shaftī and Muḥammad Ibrāhīm Kalbāsī.[55] He studied also in Burūjird under a certain Ḥājjī Asadullāh Mujtahid, who laid claim to *a'lamīyat*, to being more learned than all other mujtahids, and hence exclusively deserving the taqlīd of all believers.[56] What Ḥājjī Asadullāh failed to gain, his pupil succeeded in winning. As was the custom, he left Iran for the 'atabāt in order to continue his studies. In Najaf, he perfected his knowledge of fiqh under the guidance of Shaykh Muḥammad Ḥasan Najafī, one of the sons of Shaykh Ja'far, and author of the celebrated work on fiqh, *Jawāhir al-Kalām*.[57] His fame and learning spread so quickly that soon he was recognized as sole marja'-i taqlīd for the Iranians in the 'atabāt, and through their medium for Iran itself. On the death of Shaykh Muḥammad Ḥasan Najafī, Shaykh Murtaḍā Anṣārī's supremacy was acknowledged also by Turkish, Arab, and Indian Shi'is: for the first time the whole Shi'i Muslim world had a sole marja'-i taqlīd, resident at its holiest shrine.[58] Such was his achievement in fiqh that, it was said, the task of later generations consisted simply in developing its various aspects.[59]

Through his hands passed more than 200,000 tomans in alms and voluntary contributions, and those receiving ijāza from him until his death in 1281/1864–1865 numbered more than 300.[60]

It was above all his establishing himself as sole marja'-i taqlīd that was of great consequence. The possibility of united and firm direction of the believers was thus realized, and immense power concentrated in the person of one mujtahid. Whereas before kingly power had stood as a single unit against a fragmented collection of ulama, the clerical power was now also embodied in one person. This unity, though passed on to Mīrzā Ḥasan Shīrāzī, did not survive him. Nonetheless, the memory of it—the aura cast by it—gave added strength to the directives of other powerful mujtahids, particularly those resident at the 'atabāt. Sayyid Muḥammad Bāqir Bihbihānī had reaffirmed and redefined the function of the mujtahid; Shaykh Murtaḍā Anṣārī raised that function to its highest

55 *HY*, I, 24.
56 I'timād us-Salṭana, *op. cit.*, p. 140.
57 *HY*, I, 25.
58 *Ibid.*, I, 26; I'timād us-Salṭana, *op. cit.*, p. 137.
59 Muḥammad Mihdī Kāẓimī, *Aḥsan ul-Wadī'a* (Baghdad, 1347 Q/1928–1929), I, 147.
60 I'timād us-Salṭana, *op. cit.*, p. 137.

theoretical potentiality, though he appears himself to have made little use of it.

That this sole marja'-i taqlīd arose in the 'atabāt, outside the borders of Iran, was also to be of far-reaching importance. The influence exerted by the 'atabāt before the emergence of Shaykh Murtaḍā Anṣārī is not to be underestimated. The 'atabāt had always been a center of attraction for pilgrims and students of the religious sciences from Iran and had exerted a direct influence on occasions It was there that Sayyid Muḥammad Bāqir Bihbihānī had reconstructed the theological positions of Ithnā'asharī Shi'ism, and from there Āqā Sayyid Muḥammad had set out to force Fatḥ 'Alī Shāh into war with Russia. The supremacy of Isfahan was already on the wane. The fact that Shaykh Murtaḍā finally established the 'atabāt as the most important center of religious influence in the Shi'i world had important consequences. When the conflict between Nāṣir ud-Dīn Shāh and the ulama sharpened, many of the leading mujtahids were outside Iranian territory and well able to maintain constant contact with the Ottomans who were their temporary allies. Yet, at the same time, they kept constant contact with Iran, both by means of pilgrims and agents traveling between Iran and the 'atabāt, and later through telegrams. It is not possible to claim that Shaykh Murtaḍā established himself in Najaf because of the oppressiveness of Qajar rule; but that he had done so, was highly convenient for those who followed after him. It is often said that Mīrzā Ḥasan Shīrāzī, through his breaking of the tobacco monopoly, gave one of the earliest indications as to how a constitution might be achieved. If this is so, Shaykh Murtaḍā Anṣārī too must be considered one of the principal ancestors of the Constitutional Revolution.

His career was, however, markedly unpolitical. His relations with royal power appear to have been good,[61] and such was his reluctance to involve himself in public affairs that he refused even to declare the Bābīs apostate and liable to the appropriate penalty, saying that he was inadequately informed of their doctrines.[62] It was left to his pupils, such as Ḥājjī Mīrzā Javād Tabrīzī and above

61 *Q'U*, p. 75.

62 E. G. Browne, *A Traveller's Narrative Written to Illustrate the Episode of the Bab* (Cambridge, 1891), II, 113. Mīrzā Jānī Kāshānī, author of the *Tārīkh-i Jadīd*, excludes Shaykh Murtaḍā from the general vituperation he directs against the ulama (Browne, ed., p. 187).

all Mīrzā Ḥasan Shīrāzī, to put into practice the political implications of his achievement.

In 1275/1858, Mīrzā Āqā Khān Nūrī was dismissed, and Nāṣīr ud-Dīn Shāh again turned his dilettante eye toward reform. Instead of a single ṣadr-i a'ẓam, six ministers were appointed to deal with government business, each responsible directly to the Shah.[63] This reform made little difference to the administration, and to its relations with the ulama. One of the six ministries was that of grants and endowments (*vaẓā'if va auqāf*), but in practice the payment of grants to the ulama continued to be the task of the mustaufīs, while the state, as yet, had no concern with auqāf other than those directly administered by the monarch.[64] In 1276/1859–1860, orders were given for the establishment of consultative bodies entitled *maṣlaḥatkhāna,* both in the capital and the provinces, but it is doubtful whether such bodies were ever set up, let alone able to function.[65] In the realm of law we see a further expansion of 'urf at the cost of shar'. The head of 'urf jurisdiction, the *Amīr-i Dīvān,* was instructed to draw up at the end of each year a register of cases and judgments and fatvās delivered on them.[66] This would appear to be the earliest attempt at a systematic codification of the law. A representative of the Dīvān (renamed *'Adlīya* after the formal establishment of ministries) was to be present at all sittings of shar' courts,[67] and if the case involved a foreign subject his consul might attend.[68] Thus not only did the state encroach on the preserves of the ulama, but also these were threatened by the growing entanglement with the West. Cries of protest had been raised when Nāṣir ud-Dīn, as Crown Prince, imprisoned the thieves of a dog belonging to a Russian subject.[69] The foreign penetration of Iran was to lead to much worse, and the presence of consuls at shar' courts was a foretaste of this.

At the same time, Nāṣir ud-Dīn Shāh continued the efforts made by Amīr Kabīr to restrict the right of sanctuary in mosques. In July, 1863, with the consent of the ulama (how willing their consent was, is not clear), murderers, thieves, and adulterers were

63 Mustaufī, *op. cit.*, I, 88.
64 *Ibid.*, p. 89.
65 *Ibid.*, p. 92.
66 *RSN*, X, 780.
67 Mustaufī, *op. cit.*, I, 99.
68 *Ibid.*, I, 100.
69 *NT*, p. 469.

declared prohibited from availing themselves of sanctuary in mosques.[70] Similarly, the right to claim sanctuary at the Buq'a-yi Ṣāḥib ul-Amr in Tabriz was restricted in 1275/1858.[71]

Measures such as these, together with Nāṣir ud-Dīn's display of ostentation, confirmed the hostility of the ulama to the state, but few manifestations of this hostility appear to have occurred in this period. In March, 1861, however, a scarcity of bread led to severe rioting in Tehran, in which the ulama played a considerable part, preaching against the government.[72] So serious were the disturbances that a European observer conjectured that grain-hoarding was being deliberately continued in order to provoke a full-scale revolt against the Shah.[73] If this was so, we see here already how the ulama lent their influence to other elements for the attainment of a common aim. It is also worth remarking on that the imām jum'a was by now popularly associated with the state, for he received rough handling from the rioters.[74]

Shortly after, another clerical agitator caused great excitement in the capital. Mullā Āqā Darbandī had resided for several years in Najaf, where he became well known for his vigorous manner of preaching.[75] In controversy, he was equally fearsome and is reputed once to have used a sword to emphasize the force of his argument.[76] Shortly after the dismissal of Mīrzā Āqā Khān Nūrī, he came to Tehran and started preaching to an ever-increasing audience during Muḥarram. His sermons concerned themselves chiefly with the low morality of members of the government, and so specific and detailed were his charges that Nāṣir ud-Dīn Shāh, by means of the imām jum'a, decided to put an end to his preaching. He was virtually exiled to Kirmanshah[77] but cannot have stayed there long, for it was in Tehran that he died in 1286/1869–1870.[78]

In Isfahan, the struggle between ulama and state continued, and

[70] Gobineau, *Dépêches Diplomatiques*, p. 262.

[71] Nādir Mīrzā, *op. cit.*, 232.

[72] Brugsch, *op. cit.*, II, 330.

[73] *Ibid.*, II, 342.

[74] E. B. Eastwick, *Journal of a Diplomate's Three Years' Residence in Persia* (London, 1864), I, 291.

[75] I'timād us-Salṭana, *op. cit.*, p. 139. While in Najaf, he had been the object of an attempted assassination by the Bābīs. See Muḥammad 'Alī Tabrīzī Khīābānī, *Rayḥānat ul-Adab* (Tehran, 1326 Sh/1947–1948), III, 14–15.

[76] A. de Gobineau, *Les Religions et les Philosophies dans l'Asie Centrale* (Paris, 1865), p. 107.

[77] *Ibid.*, pp. 108–110.

[78] I'timād us-Salṭana, *op. cit.*, p. 139.

one of the protagonists of the last, most bitter and protracted stage of this struggle was Mas'ūd Mīrzā Ẓill us-Sulṭān, governor of the town. No details are known of his clashes with Mīrzā Sayyid Muḥammad Imām Jum'a at this stage: in his memoirs he contents himself with accusing Mīrzā Sayyid Muḥammad of causing the ruin of the Shamsābād district of Isfahan.[79] We may conclude that a number of lūṭīs had yet again gathered under the direction of the imām jum'a to plunder and loot. A more favorable impression of Mīrzā Sayyid Muḥammad's character is given by European writers.[80] He appears to have exerted himself willingly to keep the peace between Gregorian and Catholic Armenians in Julfā, for the Tsar Nicholas awarded him a medal in recognition of his services to the former,[81] while Gobineau speaks highly of his care for the latter.[82] The other chief representative of clerical power in Isfahan at the time was Shaykh Muḥammad Bāqir, who controlled shar' jurisdiction in the town.[83] It is not however clear whether he bore the title of shaykh ul-Islām. In order to reduce his power, Ẓill us-Sulṭān encouraged his rivals, and later, using more original methods, carried his struggle against the shaykh into the latter's household.[84]

Amidst these scattered manifestations of continuing hostility to the state, in 1287/1870 Nāṣir ud-Dīn Shāh went on pilgrimage to the shrines of Arab Iraq.[85] In Kāẓimayn, Najaf, and Karbala, he was introduced to the Iranian ulama resident there, and part of his intention may have been to investigate the developments among them outlined above.[86] More significant, however, was the beginning of his association with Mīrzā Ḥusayn Khān Sipahsālār, Iranian ambassador to the Ottoman Empire, who had come from Istanbul for the occasion. He took the opportunity to demonstrate

79 Ẓill us-Sulṭān, *op. cit.*, p. 350.

80 John Ussher, on the other hand, who visited him in 1863, claims that "he was gifted with one of the very worst countenances it was possible to witness. Every low passion seemed plainly written on it. . . ." Reading on, we find a description of the Armenian archbishop as having "a kind and benevolent face, rendered venerable by a long grey beard" (*A Journey from London to Persepolis* [London, 1865], p. 593). An improbably stark contrast!

81 Brugsch, *op. cit.*, II, 99.

82 Gobineau, *Dépêches Diplomatiques*, pp. 115, 259.

83 I'timād us-Salṭana, *op. cit.*, p. 142.

84 *HY*, I, 37; and see below, p. 180.

85 'Abbās al-'Azzāwī, *Tārīkh al-'Irāq bayn Iḥtilalayn* (Baghdad, 1373 Q/1953–1954), VII, 243.

86 I'timād us-Salṭana, *Mir'āt ul-Buldān-i Nāṣirī*, III, 126–127.

to Nāṣir ud-Dīn Shāh the improvements effected in the condition of Baghdad by the efforts of Midḥat Pasha, an energetic governor.[87] His own tenure of office in Iran was also to be associated with reform and innovation, and this, together with the earliest threat of foreign economic domination, was to call forth a sustained resistance from the ulama, and thus give a direction to the hostility already so well developed.

[87] *KhS*, p. 33.

X

Mīrzā Ḥusayn Khān Sipahsālār and his Downfall

With Mīrzā Ḥusayn Khān Sipahsālār, the attempts to strengthen the central government by administrative reform entered a new and seemingly effective phase. The bases of this reform, as indeed its whole purpose, were alien and suspect to the ulama, and their opposition to it was inevitable. At the same time, in the person of the Sipahsālār, it became associated with the foreign economic penetration of Iran. Although his motives in granting concessions may have been different from those impelling later grants, in appearance and effect these concessions were similar and not less liable to arouse clerical resistance. It was not merely a case of reactionary vested interest, for innovation appeared in the suspect form of foreign exploitation. Behind these general considerations and reinforcing them, can be seen, as always, the workings of personal interests and rivalries, directing and making use of the emotions aroused in the defense of tradition.

Mīrzā Ḥusayn Khān Sipahsālār, after twelve years as Iranian ambassador to the Ottoman Empire, returned to Tehran in 1287/1871 in the company of Nāṣir ud-Dīn Shāh on the latter's return from his pilgrimage to Arab Iraq. His first appointment was to the

Ministry of Pensions and Endowments (*vaẓā'if va auqāf*) and that of Justice, both of which posts he appears to have held simultaneously.[1] The former can have made few demands on his time, while the latter gave him an opportunity to start on his program of reform. Already in Jumādī ul-Ukhrā, 1279/November-December, 1872, he had composed a *niẓāmnāma* (rules of procedure) for the judicial system, among the articles being one restricting the competence to deal with any case involving a foreigner to the Ministry of Foreign Affairs.[2] As Minister of Justice, he attempted, like his predecessor and mentor Amīr Kabīr, to ensure the appointment of reliable mujtahids to shar' courts, and thus indirectly control one of the chief branches of clerical power.[3] It is true that his strengthening of the central judicial authority also diminished the prerogatives of the provincial governors, who were themselves rivals of the ulama in the administration of justice. Nonetheless, they frequently provided the executive branch of shar' jurisdiction, and when Mīrzā Ḥusayn Khān forbade them to inflict bodily penalties and the severance of limbs, his prohibition indirectly weakened shar' courts as well.[4] We see here, moreover, one of the earliest examples of legislation directly contrary to the sharī'at: whereas before an ill-defined duality in legal matters had existed, now the state sought to extend its powers even at the cost of implicitly abandoning pretensions to religious sanction.

In Sha'bān, 1288/October-November, 1871, after a short period as Minister of War, Mīrzā Ḥusayn Khān was appointed ṣadr-i a'ẓam.[5] He increased the enmity felt toward him by insisting on the collection of taxes that had not been paid since the dismissal of Mīrzā Āqā Khān Nūrī.[6] One year after his appointment, he proposed to Nāṣir ud-Dīn Shāh the formation of a cabinet (*darbār-i a'ẓam*) of ten ministers, meeting once a week, to replace the loose body of six ministers each responsible individually to the Shah.[7]

1 Firīdūn Ādamīyat, *Fikr-i Āzādī va Muqaddima-yi Nihḍat-i Mashrūṭīyat-i Īrān* (Tehran, 1340 Sh/1961), p. 58.

2 *Ibid.*, p. 73; Maḥmūd Farhād Mu'tamad, *Mushīr ud-Daula Sipahsālār-i A'ẓam* (Tehran, 1326 Sh/1947–1948), p. 38.

3 *Loc. cit.*

4 Ādamīyat, *op. cit.*, p. 75; 'Abdullāh Mustaufī, *Tārīkh-i Idārī va Ijtimā'ī-yi Daura-yi Qājārīya ya Sharḥ-i Zindagānī-yi Man* (Tehran, 1321 Sh/1942–1943), I, 114.

5 *Ibid.*, I, 116.

6 Mu'tamad, *op. cit.*, p. 103.

7 Mustaufī, *op. cit.*, I, 120; Ādamīyat, *op. cit.*, p. 80; Mīrzā Muḥammad Ḥasan Khān I'timād us-Salṭana, *Mir'āt ul-Buldān-i Nāṣirī* (Tehran, 1294–1297 Q/1877–1880), III, 162–166.

Though this measure was not in itself of a nature to merit a hostile reception, its inspiration cannot have passed unnoticed. The Sipahsālār, when recommending the proposal to the Shah, said that "the results of these measures must be observed in the experiences of other states."[8] The style of the proclamation establishing the cabinet suggested strongly that it was a translation of foreign laws.[9] Europeanization in Iran, as elsewhere, had begun with the improvement of military techniques, no more than a detail, however important, in the national life; now the state was adopting measures touching its own organization which were of almost explicitly European origin. Not only was the purpose of these measures—the strengthening of the state—distasteful to the ulama, but also their origin was unfamiliar and alien. The traditional context for relations between the state and the ulama was being disturbed, and this disturbance was bound to lead to an intensification of hostility.

However obscure other aspects of his policy might have appeared, Mīrzā Ḥusayn Khān's attitude to the ulama was clear. Amīn ud-Daula credits him with an attempt to gain the favor of the ulama,[10] and he himself, in a letter to Nāṣir ud-Dīn Shāh, written after his dismissal in 1290/1873 following the agitation against the Reuter Concession, claims that "the mullās have never been so cherished and respected as they were during the days of my ministry." Immediately afterward he adds, however, that "I refused to permit their intervention in matters of state."[11] This article of policy was probably one of the conclusions drawn from his experiences in Istanbul, where the period of his appointment as ambassador had approximately coincided with the introduction of various reforms by Sultan 'Abd ul-'Azīz. The drawing up of the *mecelle* (codified laws) and the establishment of the *mahakim-i nizamiye* (state-administered courts) had led to the virtual seculari-

[8] Mustaufī, *op. cit.*, I, 120.

[9] *Ibid.*, I, 121. Since the influence suggested here is that of Malkum Khān, the translation would presumably have been made from French. The influence of Ottoman Turkish, however, on the political vocabulary of late nineteenth-century Persian was marked (see E. G. Browne, *The Press and Poetry of Modern Persia* [Cambridge, 1914], p. xxvii). The Sipahsālār, having witnessed reforms in Istanbul, was one of the earliest channels of this influence. Mustaufī attributes to his inspiration use of the word *'askarīya* by Nāṣir ud-Dīn Shāh in his Nauruz address of 1288 (*Tārīkh-i Idārī*, I, 114).

[10] *KhS*, p. 43.

[11] Quoted by Ibrāhīm Taymūrī in *'Aṣr-i Bīkhabarī yā Tārīkh-i Imtiyāzāt dar Īrān* (Tehran, 1336 Sh/1957), pp. 43–44.

zation of a large part of Ottoman law.[12] Of this development, among others, Mīrzā Ḥusayn Khān reported favorably to Tehran, implying the desirability of taking similar measures in Iran.[13] While his aims were not as explicitly stated as those of, for example, his "adviser" Malkum Khān, he seems to have sought reform of the state on the basis of setting up Western legislative and executive forms. No place was foreseen in these for the ulama; the only adjustment possible was the reduction of clerical power. Thus the practical disregard of the Sipahsālār for the prerogatives of the ulama stemmed from his nonrecognition of these in theory. The aim summarized by his adviser, Malkum Khān, as "the assimilation of European civilisation without Iranian adaptation" was one unacceptable to the ulama.[14] Unconditional submission to the primacy of European models would have made their religious learning irrelevant to the affairs of society and destroyed their whole raison d'être. Nonetheless, attempts were made in following years to harness their strength and influence to the realization of such an aim. This task appeared possible above all because of the persistence of the traditional rivalry between ulama and state. All these implications became clearer, however, considerably later.

In the first year of the Sipahsālār's ministry, a famine broke out in Tehran, and this tragedy provided the first battlefield for Mīrzā Ḥusayn Khān and the ulama. It is likely that accusations became more detailed and explicit after his fall from power, but they doubtless had some basis in the events of 1288/1871. His chief adversary on this occasion was, as later, Ḥājjī Mullā 'Alī Kanī, the most powerful of the ulama of the capital until his death on Muḥarram 27, 1306/October 3, 1888.[15] He gained for himself the title of *ra'īs ul-mujtahidīn* (chief of the mujtahids), but his power was not based solely on the exercise of ijtihād. He appears to have had close relations with certain of the Qajar princes, in particular with 'Abbās Mīrzā Mulkārā, a brother of Nāṣir ud-Dīn Shāh, and Farhād Mīrzā Mu'tamad ud-Daula.[16] These relations with the court doubtless influenced his role during the agitation against the Reuter Concession. Moreover, although he affected "a primitive

12 Enver Ziya Karal, *Osmanlı Tarihi* (*Ankara,* 1947–1956), VII, 167–169.

13 Ādamīyat, *op. cit.*, pp. 60–67.

14 *Ibid.*, pp. 113–114.

15 Taymūrī, *op. cit.*, p. 123 n. 1

16 See 'Abbās Mīrzā Mulkārā, *Sharḥ-i Ḥāl*, ed. 'Abd ul-Ḥusayn Navā'ī (Tehran, 1325 Sh/1946–1947), pp. 58–59; and Farhād Mīrzā Mu'tamad ud-Daula, *Hidāyat us-Sabīl* (Tehran, 1294 Q/1877), p. 1.

simplicity" and his judgments were generally reputed to be honest, he was known to possess vast wealth.[17] How, in part, he acquired these riches may perhaps be deduced from his role in the famine of 1288/1871. On Rajab 28, 1290/September 20, 1873, Mīrzā Ḥusayn Khan wrote to Nāṣir ud-Dīn Shāh that "while Ḥājjī Mullā 'Alī Kanī had a granary full of corn and the people were dying of hunger, I brought out the supplies of my family and household and distributed them among the poor. They offered him 50 tomans for each kharvār (= 1 cwt. appr.), but he refused to sell, hoping that the price would increase. Meanwhile, the people were perishing. . . . Now they [Ḥājjī Mullā 'Alī and his associates] are guardians of the Holy Law, while I am a subverter of the faith!"[18] Together with Ḥājjī Mullā 'Alī, he held Dūst 'Alī Khān Mu'ayyir ul-Mamālik, Minister of Finance, and Niẓām ud-Daula responsible for the speculation in grain and the consequent artificial shortage.[19] His charges are supported by Mukhbir us-Salṭana, who wrote that Mullā 'Alī Kanī eventually caused the price of corn to reach 64 tomans per kharvār.[20] On the other hand similar accusations were made against Mīrzā Ḥusayn Khān himself. I'timād us-Salṭana wrote in his *Khvābnāma* that the Sipahsālār imported cheap grain from the Caucasus and sold it at a large profit in the starving capital.[21] Despite his enmity to the Sipahsālār, I'timād us-Salṭana admitted elsewhere in the same work that he had "revived the justice of 'Umar,"[22] so it is difficult to decide whether the accusation against him was purely malicious. That Ḥājjī Mullā 'Alī Kanī should have engaged in grain-hoarding is, on the other hand, entirely possible. Later Āqā Najafī in Isfahan was to practice similar profitable speculation;[23] and Ḥājjī Mīrzā Javād, when reproached with grain-hoarding, is said to have retorted that he might freely dispose of his own property.[24] The rapacity of some of the ulama came to rival that of the state, but seldom to the extent of allying

17 S. G. W. Benjamin, *Persia and the Persians* (London, 1887), p. 441.

18 Quoted in Taymūrī, *op. cit.*, p. 44. His claims to have helped the poor are confirmed by *Ṣadr ut-Tavārīkh*, according to which money and bread were daily distributed to the poor (quoted in Ādamīyat, *op. cit.*, p. 75).

19 Mu'tamad, *op. cit.*, p. 116.

20 Mihdī Qulī Khān Hidāyat Mukhbir us-Salṭana, *Khāṭirāt va Khaṭarāt* (Tehran, 1329 Sh/1950), p. 10.

21 Quoted in Mu'tamad, *op. cit.*, p. 11.

22 Quoted in Ādamīyat, *op. cit.*, p. 84.

23 See below, p. 220.

24 Atrpyet (pseud.), *Imamat': Strana Poklonnikov Imamov* (Alexandropol, 1909), p. 41; *TB*, p. 195.

the two in common cause. It also contributed to the growth of anticlerical feeling in the immediate prerevolutionary period and thereafter. Until then, the basic clash between the state and the ulama reduced all others to secondary importance.

In 1299/1873, Mīrzā Ḥusayn Khān accompanied Nāṣir ud-Dīn Shāh on his first excursion to Europe.[25] If in Baghdad he had sought to demonstrate to Nāṣir ud-Dīn Shāh the advantages of Europeanization, he hoped now to impress these on him at first hand. Although the ulama were requested to instruct the people of the useful nature of the proposed journey, they appear to have objected to it.[26] Curzon praises Nāṣir ud-Dīn Shāh for paying no attention to these objections,[27] which appear to have come primarily from Ḥājjī Mullā 'Alī Kanī.[28] Their probable nature is worth considering. Nāṣir ud-Dīn Shāh would, while in Europe, be beyond the reach of their objections and remonstrations, and at the same time more amenable to the political and economic pressure of his hosts in different capitals. Hence the visit might lead indirectly to a strengthening of European influence, and in fact did become closely linked with the granting of the Reuter Concession. In addition, it may already have been realized that the educational aspects of the visit would be limited and subordinate to the demands of entertainment. The precedent established by this journey led to growing extravagance, necessitating in turn the negotiation of foreign loans, and the further penetration of the nation's economic life by foreigners.

While the Shah and Mīrzā Ḥusayn Khān were in Europe, these and other considerations on the part of the ulama and the grievances of other discontented elements, combined to bring about a powerful wave of agitation against the Sipahsālār. This agitation centered on the granting of a concession, in 1872, to Julius Reuter, a British financier, for the exploitation of all minerals and forests in Iran, and for the construction of railways.[29] The surrender of a major part of the economic resources of the nation into foreign hands was bound to be resisted by the de facto leaders of the nation—the ulama. The significance of the Reuter Concession was

25 Mustaufī, *op. cit.*, I, 125.

26 *KhS*, p. 43.

27 G. Curzon, *Persia and the Persian Question* (London, 1892), I, 405.

28 Ādamīyat, *op. cit.*, p. 89.

29 For the text of the concession see H. Rawlinson, *England and Russia in the East* (London, 1875), pp. 373–376.

more than economic. The British, seeking to maintain Iran as a buffer state against Russian southward expansion, already were planning to strengthen it by "economic regeneration," although in the case of the Reuter Concession, their diplomatic support of the speculators was by no means unconditional.[30] Mīrzā Ḥusayn Khān for his part would have welcomed foreign, particularly British, influence as a means for hastening reform, and the acquisition of economic interests was clearly the most effective basis for any political influence.[31] While in Istanbul, he had reported favorably on the pressure exerted by Britain and France on the Ottoman government to bring about reform, considering it necessary though unpleasant.[32] For the ulama, the entrenching of such foreign influence would have been particularly unpleasant, and taking place in cooperation with the state, would have strengthened their traditional enemy and thereby endangered their own influence and function.

It is at the same time interesting to note that of all the articles of the concession, the one permitting the construction of railways aroused the greatest objections. Mīrzā Ḥusayn Khān appears to have shared the nineteenth-century faith in the railway as a principal instrument of human progress; he reported enthusiastically from Istanbul of the benefits resulting from the proposed Iskenderun-Basra line.[33] The ulama's rejection of the railways was no less firm and decisive. Mīrzā Ḥusayn Khān wrote to the British chargé d'affaires on Ramaḍān 16, 1290/November 7, 1873, that "the introduction of railways has been represented to the ulama and the whole of the people as so destructive of both religion and state, and the integrity of the nation, that however much we try to explain its benefits and uses, we are, at the moment, unable to do so. . . ."[34] After his dismissal, he attributed this opposition to the building of railways to a distorted version of the concession, circulated by Mīrzā Sa'īd Khān Mu'taman ul-Mulk, Minister of Foreign Affairs, and one of the Sipahsālār's chief opponents. According to this version, the proposed railway would pass through the suburb of Tehran known as Shāh 'Abd ul-'Aẓīm, necessitating

30 See R. L. Greaves, "British Policy in Persia, 1892–1903," *BSOAS*, XXVIII (1965), 35–36.

31 Ādamīyat, *op. cit.*, p. 61.

32 *Loc. cit.*

33 *Ibid.*, p. 63.

34 Taymūrī, *op. cit.*, p. 137.

the destruction of the shrine and the tombs surrounding it.[35] Whether this was believed or not, there would appear to have been other reasons for the ulama's objections. Railways were a symbol easily understood by the popular imagination, feared as a noisy intrusion of the mechanized West, and bringing about an undesired intimacy with the outside world.[36] The deep-seated nature of these fears is apparent from a letter addressed by Ḥājjī Mullā 'Alī Kanī to Nāṣir ud-Dīn Shāh during the agitation against Mīrzā Ḥusayn Khān. After affirming the right of the ulama to intervene in matters of state, whether or not their intervention is welcome to the monarch and acted upon by him or not, he goes on to suggest that the construction of railways would bring about the descent of a horde of Europeans on Iran. "With the onslaught of the Farangis on Iran by railway, what respected influential 'ālim will remain in Iran? And if he remains will he have life and breath enough to cry even once: Alas for the faith! Alas for the nation!"[37] The presence of a large number of foreigners in Iran, in prominent or even dominating positions, was thought of as bound to affect the nature of the national life, as indeed it has since done, on an ever-increasing scale. A further withdrawal of the nation from the legitimate control of the ulama, not to a state professing at least on occasion submission to them, but to non-Muslim foreigners, was clearly intolerable for the ulama.[38] We see, therefore, that though irrationality played a part at popular levels, the attitude of the ulama was not dictated by mere obscurantism.

At the same time, other elements whose hostility Mīrzā Ḥusayn Khān had aroused made common cause with the ulama.[39] Among

[35] Letter to Mīrzā Malkum Khān, quoted in Ādamīyat, *op. cit.*, p. 90.

[36] Jane Dieulafoy (*La Perse, la Chaldée et la Susiane* [Paris, 1887], p. 139) recounts a conversation among muleteers, attributing the decline of the institution of bast to the presence of Europeans. In a sense, of course, they were right; but in another sense their attribution seems to reflect the primitive association between catastrophe and ill-fortune and the presence of strangers. This association may well have supplemented the more rational considerations of the ulama.

[37] Taymūrī, *op. cit.*, pp. 124–126.

[38] The presence of foreigners directly affected the judicial function of the ulama. When consulates were established in Isfahan, the ulama were prevented from inflicting the bodily penalties prescribed by the sharī'at. See *HY*, I, 87.

[39] According to 'Abbās Mīrzā Mulkārā (*op. cit.*, p. 88), the ulama had no part in the conspiracy against Mīrzā Ḥusayn Khān. Their role was, however, a leading one. 'Abbās Mīrzā's motives in denying this can only be guessed at.

these was Mustaufī ul-Mamālik, who felt his influence weakened by the introduction of the cabinet system;[40] Farhād Mīrzā Mu'tamad ud-Daula, who had been entrusted with the affairs of the capital during the absence of Nāṣir ud-Dīn Shāh;[41] and, finally, Anīs ud-Daula, one of the royal andarūn whom the Sipahsālār's regard for protocol had deprived of a trip to Europe.[42] The military felt offended by the introduction of shorter dress, and the provincial governors, by the stricter supervision exercised over them.[43] The Russians for their part cannot have remained indifferent to the possibility of British intrusion in regions of northern Iran hitherto considered their own preserve, but the extent and manner of their opposition to the Reuter Concession and Mīrzā Ḥusayn Khān is difficult to determine.[44] When Nāṣir ud-Dīn Shāh arrived at Anzalī on his return from Europe, telegrams were sent to him demanding the dismissal of the Sipahsālār and the cancellation of the Reuter Concession.[45] Although most of the elements mentioned sent petitions to this effect, it is significant that the coalition against Mīrzā Ḥusayn Khān was headed by the ulama, and that the objections to him were stated chiefly in religious terms. Rumors arose that the Sipahsālār wanted to christianize Iran,[46] and Ḥājjī Mullā 'Alī Kanī issued a fatvā declaring that his dismissal was vājib (religiously incumbent).[47] Of the other ulama of Tehran, Mīrzā Ṣāliḥ 'Arab was prominent in the agitation.[48] They threatened to leave the capital, or even Iran, if Nāṣir ud-Dīn should fail to dismiss Mīrzā Ḥusayn Khān.[49] Later, the mass emigration of ulama was to prove a highly effective means of influencing events. It is worth noting that the agitation, though

40 Taymūrī, *op. cit.*, p. 39.
41 Mu'tamad, *op. cit.*, p. 189.
42 Rawlinson, *op. cit.*, p. 131.
43 Mustaufī, *op. cit.*, I, 126.
44 See Maḥmūd Farhād Mu'tamad, "Qarārdād-i Reuter," *Yaghmā*, II (1328 Sh/1949–1950), 210. Malkum Khān, on November 9, 1874, informed the Foreign Office in London that the Reuter Concession was broken at the demand of the Russian government (letter contained in F. O. 60/406; see also R. L. Greaves, *Persia and the Defence of India, 1884–1892* [London, 1959], p. 96). Malkum Khān's statements were, however, generally designed to correspond to the wishes or beliefs of his hearers.
45 Mustaufī, *op. cit.*, I, 128.
46 Ādamīyat, *op. cit.*, p. 91.
47 'Abbās Iqbāl, "Sharḥ-i Hāl-i Marḥum Ḥājj Mullā 'Alī Kanī," *Yādgār*, IV (1326 Sh/1947–1948), 75.
48 Taymūrī, *op. cit.*, p. 39.
49 Mustaufī, *op. cit.*, I, 128; Mu'tamad, *op. cit.*, p. 184.

making use of significant rumors, did not lead to the takfīr of the Sipahsālār, a fate that was later to befall Mīrzā 'Ali Aṣghar Amīn us-Sulṭān.[50] It provided a precedent, however, for obtaining the dismissal of unwanted ministers.

Thus the ulama, though partly motivated by their personal interests and feelings and by those of others, appeared again as the defenders of the national interests against a treacherous government and foreign influence. Like the tobacco monopoly later, the Reuter Concession was primarily a focal point for many elements of discontent and unrest. Sectional grievances were subsumed under a single protest voiced in religious terms and led by the ulama. On this occasion, the elements involved were few in number; with the tobacco monopoly, the whole nation felt itself affronted, and the role of the ulama as national leaders received unequivocal expression.

Nāṣir ud-Dīn Shāh, bowing to the pressure, returned to Tehran, leaving Mīrzā Ḥusayn Khān behind in Gilan as governor, and advising him to treat the ulama in particular with deference and respect.[51] Still the agitation did not subside; in Tehran, some of the ulama considered not delivering the customary sermons in Ramaḍān, as a sign of dissatisfaction with the government.[52] Nonetheless, the Shah, later in 1290/1874, sought to restore some of Mīrzā Ḥusayn Khān's lost power by appointing him Minister of Foreign Affairs.[53] There then appears to have taken place a certain rapprochement between the Sipahsālār and the ulama, some of them even going so far as to claim that they had acted purely out of deference to what they had imagined the wishes of the Shah to be—a highly unlikely claim, but one that demonstrates the venality of some of the ulama.[54]

Although Mīrzā Ḥusayn Khān failed to regain his former in-

50 See below, p. 234.

51 Maḥmūd Farhād Mu'tamad, "Musāfarat-i Nāṣir ud-Dīn Shāh ba Urupā va Barkinārī-yi Mīrzā Ḥusayn Khān Sipahsālār," *Yādgār*, II (1325 Sh/1946–1947), 46. On his return to Tehran Nāṣir ud-Dīn went to pay his respects to Mullā 'Alī Kanī, an act he must have found necessary to quieten clerical discontent. See Khān Malik Sāsānī, *Siyāsatgarān-i Daura-yi Qājār* (Tehran, 1338 Sh/1959), p. 81.

52 Taymūrī, *op. cit.*, p. 121.

53 Mustaufī, *op. cit.*, I, 130.

54 *KhS*, p. 52; letter of Mīrzā Ḥusayn Khān to Nāṣir ud-Dīn dated Sha'bān 16, 1290/October 9, 1873, quoted in Taymūrī, *op. cit.*, p. 48. Mullā 'Alī Kanī persisted, however, ostracizing the Sipahsālār. See *TB*, p. 106.

fluence, and Nāṣir ud-Dīn Shāh was fast succumbing to total indifference to the affairs of Iran, again, in the period before the emergence of Mīrzā 'Alī Aṣghar Amīn us-Sulṭān in the late 1880's, certain minor attempts at reform took place. These were largely inspired by Mīrzā 'Alī Khān Amīn ud-Daula. He suggested to Nāṣir ud-Dīn Shāh that the provisions of the sharī'āt be officially codified, and the task was entrusted to Mīrzā Sa'īd Khān Mu'taman ul-Mulk. Under his chairmanship, a committee of ulama and others met, but failed to produce any result.[55] Later Amīn ud-Daula proposed the introduction of revenue stamps, so that official receipts might be issued for all sums of money paid to the government. This proposal met with clerical opposition, particularly in Tabriz, for, as Amīn ud-Daula pointed out, the ulama regarded it as one of their functions to certify and seal all kinds of documents.[56] At the same time, the measure represented potentially another means of extortion, whatever the intention behind it may have been. Nāṣir ud-Dīn Shāh abolished the revenue stamps, together with a short-lived tax on tobacco, after observing the widespread opposition to them.[57]

Amīn ud-Daula writes that at this point the ulama realized the extent of their power and the weakness of Nāṣir ud-Dīn Shāh's resolution,[58] but between the dismissal of Mīrzā Ḥusayn Khān from the ministry and the establishment of the tobacco monopoly, we find no major incident opposing the ulama to the government in the capital. In 1295/1878, Nāṣir ud-Dīn Shāh went on his second journey to Europe, and other than the first visit of Sayyid Jamāl ud-Dīn Asadābādī, it had no consequences of any importance.[59] In the capital, Mullā 'Alī Kanī continued as chief mujtahid and appears to have established a working agreement with secular authority. Thus, through the intermediary of Sayyid Bāqir Jamarānī Nāẓim ul-'Ulamā, all shar' cases concerning the government were referred to his court for judgment.[60] Once a year, he had the prostitutes of Tehran expelled from the city, so that the chief

55 *KhS*, p. 94.
56 *Ibid.*, p. 120.
57 *Ibid.*, p. 121. See also V. A. Kosogovsky, *Iz Tegeranskovo Dnevnika* (Moscow, 1960), pp. 64–65.
58 *KhS*, p. 122.
59 See below, p. 199.
60 Mīrzā Muḥammad Ḥasan Khān I'timād us-Salṭana, *Vaqāyi'-i Rūzāna-yi Darbār* (Tehran, n.d.), p. 110.

of police and Nā'ib us-Salṭana, governor of the capital, might extort money from them and then secretly permit them to return to employment.[61] On occasion conflict occurred: on Shavvāl 7, 1298/September 3, 1881, I'timād us-Salṭana, passing through the quarter of Kāmrānīya with the royal carriage, saw a crowd setting on one of the soldiers of Nā'ib us-Salṭana. It turned out that because of some offense, they had decided to slit his tongue, and they then took refuge in the house of Ḥājjī Mullā 'Alī Kanī. The Shah gave orders for the offenders to be removed by force.[62]

Events in the provinces also provided sporadic evidence of the continuing struggle between the ulama and the state. In 1300/1882–1883, Mīrzā Sayyid Muḥammad Imām Jum'a of Isfahan had died and, according to Ẓill us-Sulṭān, Nāṣir ud-Dīn Shāh exclaimed: "Praise be to God! At last I can call Isfahan my own."[63] After a protracted struggle between two brothers of the deceased imām jum'a, Mīr Muḥammad Ḥusayn and Ḥājjī Mīrzā Hāshim, the latter succeeded in inheriting the title on Jumādī ul-Ūlā 19, 1300/March 28, 1883.[64] While Mīrzā Hāshim did not offer serious opposition to Ẓill us-Sulṭān in the government of Isfahan, on the death of Shaykh Muḥammad Bāqir in 1301/1883–1884, a powerful rival to the governor arose. Ẓill us-Sulṭān had had the satisfaction of seducing Shaykh Muḥammad Bāqir's wife and seeing him powerless to react,[65] but the Shaykh's son, Muḥammad Taqī, known as Āqā Najafī, amply avenged his father and built up for himself a power hardly inferior to that of the governor. His power was largely exercised for personal gain, and the fact that he was nonetheless able to maintain a religious standing was perhaps due to the mentality of his opponent. Ẓill us-Sulṭān combined a professed belief in Islam with freely admitted dislike of the ulama.[66] According to the French traveler Dieulafoy, he had a pigsty erected in his palace garden and would force the ulama to pass through the befouled courtyard when they attended his Naurūz audience.[67]

61 *Ibid.*, pp. 76, 114.
62 *Ibid.*, p. 46.
63 Mas'ūd Mīrzā Ẓill us-Sulṭān, *Tārīkh-i Sargudhasht-i Mas'ūdī* (Tehran, 1325 Q/1907), p. 250.
64 *Loc. cit.*; I'timād us-Salṭana, *op. cit.*, p. 121.
65 Mulkārā, *op. cit.*, p. 58.
66 Ẓill us-Sulṭān, *op. cit.*, pp. 96, 173.
67 Dieulafoy, *op. cit.*, p. 253. The same traveler reports the governor of Qazvin as saying: "As for me, I am a civilized person. I don't even pray. During the three years I have spent in Qazvin, I have not set foot once in the mosque" (p. 105).

Thus the ulama of the provinces were not only aware of the impious character of the Qajar monarchy as such but were faced with individual examples of it in the conduct of provincial governors. It was this that enabled them to act as defenders of religion, despite the corruption of some of their number; this, too, partly ensured the cooperation of the ulama throughout the country during later agitation.

In Tabriz, also, a similar struggle was taking place. Mīrzā Javād Āqā, a pupil of Shaykh Murtaḍā Anṣārī whom the Shah had met during his visit to the 'atabāt, had been appointed imām jum'a.[68] The wealth he had accumulated was enormous; some reports estimated his personal wealth at 16,000 tomans, and others credited him with the possession of 200 villages.[69] On this firm basis of economic power, he threatened to paralyze the whole administration of the town. In April, 1886, he brought about the temporary exile of Amīr-i Niẓām from Tabriz, for, among other offenses, encouraging the heir apparent to wear clothes of European cut.[70] Soon after, however, his own turn came. In July, Abbott, the British consul in Tabriz, reported that the Mīrzā had been "plotting for some time against the authority of His Majesty, and was a serious obstacle to the maintenance of public order"; that he had "established at Tabriz a kind of local government board which completely swamped the efforts made by the central board to carry on the government of His Majesty." Mīrzā Javād was expelled, and his departure, says Abbott, was mourned only by a few lūṭīs and old women.[71]

The year 1306/1888–1889 witnessed a number of disturbances in the capital of a religious nature, indicating that far from a truce existing between the ulama and the state, nothing more than a hiatus had occurred. The opposition to the innovation and foreign influence increasingly associated with the state was unyielding. In Muḥarram-Ṣafar, 1306/October, 1888, Nāṣir ud-Dīn Shāh was obliged to bow again to the persuasive force of clerical objections. As a further gratification for his love of ostentation, he had caused a statue of himself to be molded and gilded in the artillery arsenal at Tehran, intending to expose it to the admiration of the popu-

68 Nādir Mīrzā, *Tārīkh va Jughrāfī-yi Dār us-Salṭana-yi Tabrīz* (Tehran, 1323 Q/1905), p. 130.
69 *Loc. cit.*; Atrpyet, *op. cit.*, p. 42.
70 Dieulafoy, *op. cit.*, p. 45.
71 Reports dated July 7 and 9, 1886, contained in F.O. 60/483.

lace in some public square. The ulama objected, the three-dimensional representation of human beings having been forbidden by Islam, and ultimately the statue had to be erected in the seclusion of the royal garden near Darvāza-yi Qazvīn.[72]

About one month later, the installations of the railway between the capital and Shāh 'Abd ul-'Aẓīm, which had been erected less than a year before,[73] were destroyed by an angry mob. According to Browne, an accident was caused when a passenger jumped out of the moving train and fell under the wheels.[74] It is possible that confused memories of the clerical agitation against the Reuter Concession also influenced the rioters as they set about their task. The outraged passengers in the confusion following the accident started to wreck the coaches and came into conflict with the Belgian officials working the line. One of the rioters appears to have been killed.[75] Mu'ayyir ul-Mamālik writes that the Belgian Embassy claimed compensation of 300,000 tomans on behalf of the company operating the railway, but that the imām jum'a then pronounced use of the railway ḥarām, thus persuading the Belgians to withdraw their claim.[76]

In 1306/1889, Nāṣir ud-Dīn Shāh left on his third trip to Europe. This journey, like the first one, became associated with the grant of economic concessions and monopolies. Among them was the monopoly for the establishment of a state lottery, given to Malkum Khān, at the time Iranian ambassador in London.[77] Soon after Nāṣir ud-Dīn Shāh's return to Iran, the concession was revoked, and in this revocation the ulama played their part. The Shah in his letter annulling the concession, refers to the incompatibility of a lottery with the sharī'at, and presumably a fatvā had been issued to that effect.[78] Suspicions have been raised that

72 J. Bleibtreu, *Persien: Das Land der Sonne und des Löwen* (Freiburg im Breisgau, 1894), pp. 124–125. See also Mīrzā Muḥammad Ḥasan Khān I'timād us-Salṭana, *al-Ma'āthir va-l-Āthār* (Tehran, 1306 Q/1889), pp. 56, 107, and dispatch of December 17, 1888, in F.O. 60/498.

73 In Dhū-l-Qa'da, 1305/July–August, 1888 (Mustaufī, *op. cit.*, I, 448).

74 E. G. Browne, *A Year Amongst the Persians*, new ed. (London, 1950). p. 98. See also I'timād us-Salṭana, *al-Ma'āthir va-l-Āthār*, p. 52. Mu'ayyir ul-Mamālik (*Yāddāshthā'ī az Zindagānī-yi Khuṣūṣī-yi Nāṣir ud-Dīn Shāh* [Tehran, n.d.], p. 179) attributes the origin of the riots to a dispute over the price of tickets.

75 I'timād us-Salṭana, *al-Ma'āthir va-l-Āthār*, p. 52.

76 Mu'ayyir ul-Mamālik, *op. cit.*, pp. 180–181.

77 Taymūrī, *op. cit.*, p. 215.

78 *Ibid.*, p. 261.

Amīn us-Sulṭān had been promised some kind of remuneration for his help in obtaining the concession, and that when this was not forthcoming, he avenged himself by applying clerical pressure against the lottery.[79]

The same pressure, more determined and persistent, was applied to Amīn us-Sulṭān himself in the case of the tobacco monopoly, another result of Nāṣir ud-Dīn Shāh's largess on his European trip. The agitation against the monopoly, however, was far more than the expression of personal or sectional discontent in religious terms, through the medium of the ulama. It exceeded, not only this, but all precedents of clerical intervention in national affairs. It was a watershed in Iranian history, a demonstration of the power of the ulama and of how it might be mobilized against the state. Popular discontent supplied the ulama with means for a direct confrontation with the traditional enemy. At the same time, a new element had emerged in opposition to the state, and before discussing the agitation against the tobacco regie, it is necessary to examine the attitudes of this element toward the ulama and its relationships with them.

[79] *Ibid.*, p. 215.

XI

Two Apostles of Change and the Ulama

The ideological background leading to the constitutional movement, and beyond it to many modern Iranian ways of thought and belief, is a subject of great complexity which has not yet been adequately examined.[1] Although no comprehensive discussion can be undertaken, the content of revolutionary thought will be examined here for its attitudes to the ulama and its effect upon them. The contribution of liberal thinkers and the ulama to the constitutional movement were, at least in the early stages of the revolution, closely linked; it is nonetheless important to separate them, so that the real aims of both may be clarified to some extent and points of interaction indicated. A beginning is made here, in reference to the early manifestations of revolutionary thought, and the attempt will be pursued in connection with the events of the Constitutional Revolution.

[1] Many of the questions involved have, however, been raised by Nikki R. Keddie in her paper "Religion and Irreligion in Early Iranian Nationalism," *Comparative Studies in Society and History*, IV (1962), 265–295.

MĪRZĀ MALKUM KHĀN

The role of Mīrzā Malkum Khān in preparing the climate of thought leading to the Constitutional Revolution is generally acknowledged to have been considerable, and his activities deserve a detailed study, not only for their influence upon Iranian history, but also for their intrinsic interest.[2] Emphasis will be placed here upon factors determining his attitude to the ulama and the extent of his influence upon them.

Born of Armenian parents in Julfā in 1249/1833–1834, Mīrzā Malkum Khān spent most of his youth in Paris, receiving his education first at Armenian schools and then at the Polytechnique, where, on the advice of Mīrzā Taqī Khān Amīr Kabīr, he studied political science.[3] Shortly after the disgrace of Amīr Kabīr, he returned to Iran and obtained a post at the Dār ul-Funūn, working both as teacher and interpreter for the foreign instructors employed there.[4] His interest was chiefly devoted, however, to establishing and running a pseudo-masonic lodge, the famous *farāmūshkhāna* ("house of forgetfulness").

It has sometimes been thought that the term "house of forgetfulness" was coined by Malkum Khān himself, and that he was the first to propagate masonic teachings in Iran.[5] Neither the concept of freemasonry nor the word farāmūshkhāna, however, was new to Iran.[6] It is possible that Malkum Khān's first knowledge of masonry was acquired in Iran, but it is clear that the main source of his information was Paris. From European examples, he came to realize the social and political potentialities of Freemasonry. "I went to Europe and studied there the religious, social and political systems of the west. I learned the spirit of the various sects of Christendom, and the organisation of the secret societies and free-

2 See my forthcoming monograph on Malkum Khān for a detailed consideration of his career.

3 Firīdūn Ādamīyat, *Fikr-i Āzādī va Muqaddima-yi Nihḍat-i Mashrūṭiyat-i Īrān* (Tehran, 1340 Sh/1961), p. 94; introduction of Muḥammad Muḥīṭ Ṭabāṭabā'ī to Mīrzā Malkum Khān, *Majmū'a-yi Āthār* (Tehran, 1327 Sh/1948–1949), I, i.

4 *Loc. cit.*

5 By, for example, A. de Gobineau in *Les Religions et les Philosophies dans l'Asie Centrale* (Paris, 1865), p. 305.

6 See my "Introduction to the History of Iranian Freemasonry," to appear in *Middle Eastern Studies*, Vol. VI (1970).

masonries, and I conceived a plan which should incorporate the practical wisdom of Europe with the religious wisdom of Asia."[7] He showed special interest in Mirabeau, and translated into Persian his address on liberty, delivered to the National Assembly.[8] Possibly he was aware, too, of Mirabeau's masonic connections, and of the influence of these on the French Revolution.[9] In any event, the genesis of Malkum Khān's projects of social and political change, and of the farāmūshkhāna, took place in Europe.

The exact nature of the farāmūshkhāna and its activities is difficult to determine. According to Gobineau, Malkum Khān represented it to Nāṣir ud-Dīn Shāh as an ideal means of securing the loyalty of all the important men in the country: the monarch himself was to be Grand Master, and those selected for membership by reason of their influence, were to be bound to him by secret oath.[10] The nominal direction of the lodge, however, was divided between one of the Qajar princes, Jalāl ud-Dīn Mīrzā, a graduate of the Dār ul-Funūn, and Mīrzā Malkum Khān's father, Mīrzā Ya'qūb, while its real administration lay in the hands of Malkum Khān himself.[11] Nāṣir ud-Dīn Shāh, even if not associated personally with the farāmūshkhāna, must at least have approved of what he supposed to be its aims. Malkum Khān, while in Paris, had learned some elementary chemistry and physics, and it was part of his duties at the Dār ul-Funūn to perform simple experiments. These attracted popular attention to him, and it is possible that Nāṣir ud-Dīn Shāh thought the function of the farāmūshkhāna to be no more than the imparting of elementary

[7] W. S. Blunt, *Secret History of the English Occupation of Egypt* (London, 1907), p. 83. Blunt reproduces in full a discourse held by Malkum Khān while in London, a remarkable mixture of fact and fancy with the latter predominating. Among his more outrageous claims are to have been the foster brother of Nāṣir ud-Dīn Shāh, and to have been prime minister of Iran, with despotic powers, at the age of twenty (*ibid.*, p. 83). E. G. Browne refers to this passage in his *Persian Revolution of 1905–1909* (Cambridge, 1910), p. 39, but without indicating its fanciful character. Blunt was greatly impressed by Malkum's words, and afterward felt "more convinced than ever of the superior intelligence of the Eastern mind" (*Secret History*, p. 85).

[8] Malkum Khān, *op. cit.*, p. 181.

[9] See *Mémoires de Mirabeau écrits par lui-même, par son père, son oncle et son fils adoptif, et précédés d'une étude sur Mirabeau par Victor Hugo* (Paris, 1834), III, 47. On the influence of illuminist masonry in general on the French Revolution, see J. J. Mounier, *De l'influence attribuée aux philosophes, aux francs-maçons et aux illuminés sur la revolution française* (Paris, 1822).

[10] Gobineau, *op. cit.*, p. 306.

[11] Ṭabāṭabā'ī's introduction to Malkum Khān, *op. cit.*, p. vii.

scientific knowledge, particularly as many of the members were either students or graduates of the Dār ul-Funūn.[12] His suspicions were ultimately aroused, stimulated, no doubt, by quarters hostile to Malkum Khān, in particular the Russian embassy.[13] On Rabī' ul-Avval 12, 1278/September 17, 1861, the farāmūshkhāna was dissolved by royal decree, and even the mention of its name was prohibited.[14] Nāṣir ud-Dīn Shāh's suspicions extended to the Dār ul-Funūn, associated through Malkum Khān with the farāmūshkhāna, and his active encouragement of that institution ceased.[15]

Inevitably, one of the suspicions raised against the farāmūshkhāna was that of Bābism, a suspicion considered groundless by Gobineau.[16] It was inevitable not only because of the pervasiveness of the Bābī danger, but also because of the obscurity of Malkum Khān's aims. It appears that the farāmūshkhāna was intended to form a nucleus of highly placed men for the dissemination and eventual application of Malkum Khān's projects of reform—political and economic reorganization according to European models.[17] These projects have been laid out in various of his writings, in particular in *Kitābcha-yi Ghaybī yā Daftar-i Tanẓīmāt* and the *Daftar-i Qānūn*.[18] They deal largely with legal, political, and administrative reform, the first being emphasized, and seem to have been of general, nineteenth-century European inspiration, rather than specifically masonic.[19]

Indeed, when the first lodge affiliated to the Grand Orient was established in the reign of Muḥammad 'Alī Shāh, it was revealed that Malkum Khān's farāmūshkhāna had never had any formal connection with the European lodges.[20] He had borrowed from them above all their form—the technique of secret organization

12 *Ibid.*, p. ix; *TB*, p. 120.

13 Tabāṭabā'ī's introduction to Malkum Khān, *op. cit.*, p. ix; Ibrāhīm Ṣafā'ī, *Rahbarān-i Mashrūṭa II: Mīrzā Malkum Khān* (Tehran, 1342 Sh/1963), p. 11.

14 Ṭabāṭabā'ī's introduction to Malkum Khān, *op. cit.*, p. ix.

15 'Abbās Iqbāl, "Ba'd az Ṣad Sāl," *Yādgār*, V (1327 Sh/1948–1949), 6; Mihdī Qulī Khān Hidāyat Mukhbir us-Salṭana, *Khāṭirāt va Khaṭarāt* (Tehran, 1329 Sh/1950), p. 75.

16 Gobineau, *op. cit.*, p. 307.

17 Ādamīyat, *op. cit.*, pp. 113–114.

18 Malkum Khān, *op. cit.*, pp. 2–52, 120–165.

19 They were probably the fruit of his studies at the Polytechnique: among the authors he quotes is John Stuart Mill (*ibid.*, p. 177).

20 Jahāngīr Qā'im Maqāmī, *Tārīkh-i Taḥavvulāt-i Siyāsī-yi Niẓām-i Īrān* (Tehran, n. d.), p. 77; Ādamīyat, *op. cit.*, p. 201.

and propaganda—doubtless finding many parallels with Iranian tradition. The similarity of the secret societies—not only those of masonic or pseudo-masonic origin—to traditional forms of politico-religious organization, was greatly to increase their effectiveness during the Constitutional Revolution.[21]

We find, nonetheless, traces of masonic ideology in Malkum Khān's attitudes to religion. He appears to have had no positive beliefs, regarding all religions as fundamentally identical, and in any event destined to be superseded by the pseudoreligion of humanity and reason, as proclaimed by the French Revolution.[22] Evidence of this is provided by Blunt, according to whom Malkum Khān claimed to have produced in Iran a new religion with 30,000 adherents. He further declared that "they gave me the title of 'Holy Ghost,' and the Shah that of 'Reformer of Islam.' I wrote a book, a bible of my creed, and enthusiasts maintained that I worked miracles. At last the Shah was alarmed at my power, which in truth had become superior to his own. . . ."[23] Allowing for exaggeration and imaginative interpretation of events, it may be deduced from this that the farāmūshkhāna was recognized, despite its outward forms, as something totally alien, if not hostile and dangerous, and this was probably the most important single factor leading to its suppression.

Further confirmation is supplied by the ambiguity of Malkum Khān's professions of religious belief. His father, if only from practical considerations, had adopted Islam, and he himself outwardly professed belief in Islam.[24] While in Istanbul, however, he is reputed to have adopted Christianity and to have married in an Armenian church there.[25] A confidential report sent from the

21 A. K. S. Lambton, "Secret Societies and the Persian Revolution of 1905–1906," *St. Anthony's Papers*, IV (1958), 60.

22 Ādamīyat *(op. cit.*, p. 103) says that Malkum "followed the religion of humanity (*dīn-i insānīyat*)." Malkum proclaimed there was no essential difference between the Quran and the Bible (see below, p. 190), and similarly said of the doctrines of the Bāb that they were "identical with those of Jesus Christ" (Blunt, *op. cit.*, p. 82).

23 *Ibid.*, pp. 82, 84. It is interesting to note that at least Mīrzā Fatḥ 'Alī Ākhūndzāda (Akhundov) addressed Malkum as Rūḥ ul-Quds, "Holy Ghost": see the Azerbayjani Turkish translation of two of his letters to Malkum Khān, printed in M. Arif and H. Hüsaynov, *Mükhtäsär Azärbayjan Ädäbiyatï Tarikhi* (Baku, 1944), II, 379–385.

24 Ṣafā'ī, *op. cit.*, p. 4; Ṭabāṭabā'ī's introduction to Malkum Khān, *op. cit.*, p. x.

25 *Loc. cit.*

British ambassador in Tehran in September, 1901, to Lord Lansdowne refers to Malkum as "a professed Christian."[26] It is highly probable that Malkum Khān, when occasion demanded, both in Europe and the East, made use of the ancient practice of taqīya, changing the nature of his pretense according to the audience he was addressing. To those whom he considered "initiates," such as Blunt, he administered a more complex mixture of fact and untruth, which nonetheless gave some hint as to his real purposes.

To Blunt he spoke of a material reform, "introduced under the name of a Reformation of Islam," and of having talked to "the chief persons of Tehran, my friends . . . in private of the need which Islam had of purer doctrine."[27] The question of whether the reform was conceived of as genuinely religious in its basis or was merely a cover for other purposes, he left carefully obscure. The same paradox is observable in various of Malkum Khān's writings. In *Naum va Yaqẓa*, he writes (though putting the words into the mouth of a fictitious character): "Those most hostile to the ordering (*naẓm*) of the country, the education and liberty of the people, are the ulama and the fanatic grandees (*akābir-i fanātīk*)."[28] In *Daftar-i Qānūn*, he proposes that the ulama and the theological colleges be subject to the control of the Ministry of Sciences (*vizārat-i 'ulūm*).[29] At the same time, he suggested that use should be made of the special knowledge of the ulama for the reformation of the legal system,[30] and in his newspaper *Qānūn* repeatedly expressed devotion to the ulama.[31]

The reasons for this paradox are not far to seek. If ultimately his aim was the assimilation of European civilization without Iranian adaptation, an aim whose realization would effectively render the ulama superfluous, their cooperation was necessary in attaining it. Mirabeau, in his *Mystères de la Conspiration*, had written of the clergy as follows: "The clergy, being the most powerful through public opinion, can only be destroyed by ridiculing religion, rendering its ministers odious, and representing them as hypocritical monsters. . . ."[32] This point of strategy,

26 Report dated September 6, 1901, contained in F.O. 60/637.
27 Blunt, *op. cit.*, pp. 83–84.
28 Malkum Khān, *op. cit.*, p. 174.
29 *Ibid.*, p. 84.
30 *Ibid.*, pp. 203–204.
31 See below, p. 191.
32 Quoted by N. Webster, *Secret Societies and Subversive Movements* (London, 1955), p. 241.

however, Malkum did not adopt: far from openly attacking the influence of the ulama, he sought to harness it to the achievement of his aims. If in eighteenth-century France the clergy had been closely identified with the ancien régime, in nineteenth-century Iran the ulama were in constant conflict with the Qajar dynasty. This conflict, as a prominent factor in the situation, had to be taken into account in any plan to curtail the power of the monarchy.

Malkum gave some hints of the role he thought the ulama might fulfill. In a lecture entitled "Persian Civilisation," delivered in London in 1891, after expressing the opinion that "the Koran is, as you know, a sort of revised Bible, and there is nothing in it which is directly opposed to Christian principles," he went on to speak of the failure of missionary effort in Iran, and said that: "We found that ideas which were by no means accepted when coming from your agents in Europe, were accepted at once with the greatest delight when it was proved that they were latent in Islam."[33] The projected reforms were thus to be represented as being not only consonant with Islam, but actually enjoined by it; to give them this sanction, the cooperation of the ulama was necessary. Malkum clearly hoped for a wide use of the principle of ijtihād in this process: "L'Islam persan, repoussant le khalifat et toute orthodoxie immuable, est basé sur l'examen des docteurs vivants, principe admirable qui ouvre les portes aux interpretations les plus larges et aux idées les plus nouvelles."[34]

Not only was the cooperation of the ulama thought necessary to ease the path of reform, but their hostility was feared as a serious obstacle in the way of acceptance of innovation. Thus taqīya had a double motivation. Malkum's friend, Fatḥ 'Alī Ākhūndzāda, had suffered takfīr on account of views expressed in the fictitious *Letters of Kamāl ud-Daula,* and Malkum Khān evidently wished to protect himself from a similar fate.[35] It was moreover necessary to

33 *Contemporary Review,* LIX (1891), 239–243.

34 Papers submitted by Malkum Khān to Nāṣir ud-Dīn Shāh and communicated to the Marquess of Salisbury, dated February 13, 1888, contained in F.O. 60/497.

35 On Malkum's relations with Ākhūndzāda, see A. M. Shoitov, "Rol' Akhundova v Razvitii Persidskoi Progressivnoi Literatury," *KSIV,* IX (1953), 61–65. While passing through Tiflis in March, 1872, Malkum Khān met Ākhūndzāda and advised him to adopt more subtle methods in dealing with the religious beliefs of the Muslims which he wished to uproot, and to avoid open attack on them as fruitless (see Mirzä Fätäli Akhundov, *Fars Dilindä Yazïlmïsh Mäktublarïn Mätni,* ed. Hämid Mämmädzadä [Baku, 1963], pp. 290–291).

allay doubts about the religious orthodoxy of the Majma'-i Ādamīyat (League of Humanity), successor to the proscribed farāmūshkhāna. The following extract from *Qānūn*, dated Dhū-l-Qa'da, 1307/March–April, 1890, is clearly intended to serve this purpose. It purports to be the account of an outsider inquiring into the nature of the Majma'-i Ādamīyat. "There are trustees (*umanā*) from each guild (*ṣinf*), and from each guild they select and introduce intelligent people to the Majma'-i Ādamīyat. . . . I saw one trustee who was a very learned sayyid, the imam of a town. . . . Most of the trustees are taken from the mullās. . . . The principles of Ādamīyat are so much in accordance with Islam, and so suited to the present sufferings of Iran, that every intelligent Muslim, as soon as he perceives its truths, instinctively joins the society. . . . Some think that this World of Humanity (*'ālam-i ādamīyat*) was established by the prophets and saints (*auliyā*) of Islam."[36]

It remains to examine to what extent Malkum Khān succeeded in winning the ulama for his plans. A number of them are reputed to have joined the farāmūshkhāna, but no names have been preserved.[37] A follower of Malkum Khān writes that the mullās even set fire to his farāmūshkhāna; if not literally true, this is doubtless an indication of their hostility to him.[38] When exiled from Iran in 1280/1863–1864, he claims that "even the mullas kissed my feet"; this appears to be nothing more than a puerile *Wunschtraum*.[39] Indeed, ten years later, one of the subsidiary causes of clerical agitation against Mīrzā Ḥusayn Khān Sipahsālār was his association with Malkum Khān, who held the post of "special adviser" to the sadr-i a'ẓam.[40] Despite all precautions, his intentions were suspect.

Nonetheless, the Majma'-i Ādamīyat contained several members of the clerical classes who subsequently sat in the first Majlis (consultative assembly).[41] The most important of all Malkum's contacts with the ulama cannot, moreover, be doubted to have had an influence on the conduct of the constitutional movement. Malkum Khān continually sought to attract into the Majma'-i Ādamīyat Sayyid Ṣādiq Ṭabāṭabā'ī, an influential mujtahid of Tehran, who persisted in evading him. According to the *Tārīkh-i Bīdārī*, Sayyid Ṣādiq went one day to visit Sayyid 'Alī Darbandī in Shimīrān,

36 *Qānūn*, no. 5, p. 4.
37 *TB*, p. 120.
38 Malkum Khān, *op. cit.*, p. li.
39 Blunt, *op. cit.*, p. 84.
40 Malkum Khān, *op. cit.*, p. x.
41 Listed in Ādamīyat, *op. cit.*, p. 243.

and Malkum Khān, learning of this, pursued him to Sayyid 'Alī's house. There then ensued an encounter resulting in the total conversion of Sayyid Ṣādiq to Malkum Khān's purposes.[42] Unfortunately, nothing is known of the content of their discussion: whether Malkum again practiced taqīya, presenting his program in purely Islamic terms, or whether he exposed to Sayyid Ṣādiq its secular basis of free thinking can only be guessed. A similar query arises with respect to other members of the ulama associated with the secret societies. In the case of Sayyid Ṣādiq, the question is of particular importance, because his son Sayyid Muḥammad Ṭabāṭabā'i became one of the leading figures among the ulama supporting the constitutional movement; whatever impression Malkum produced on Sayyid Ṣādiq may well have been passed on to Sayyid Muḥammad, and thus left its imprint on the constitutional movement.[43] With evidence lacking, one is reduced to speculation. The direction this speculation might take will be indicated when discussing the events of the Constitutional Revolution.

In general, the influence of Mīrzā Malkum Khān should not be overestimated. The role of *Qānūn* (published 1889–1890) in diffusing ideas hostile to the regime was doubtless great. There were, however, other influences at work as well as that of Malkum Khān. If in his case the motivation of attempts to present reform as religiously binding or sanctioned was transparently opportunist, different, more sincere motives in other cases must not be discounted. In discussing the military reforms of 'Abbās Mīrzā it was suggested that the religious sanction accorded to reform was marked by varying degrees of sincerity and accuracy.[44] Possibly the lowest degree of sincerity was that reached by Malkum Khān, a freethinker styling himself both Muslim and Christian; but the mere fact that he chose to present reform in Islamic terms shows that the identification of practical necessity and religious duty was widely regarded as accurate. Nor was the identification expressed only by Malkum; similar ideas were put forward by, among others, Ḥājjī Abū-l-Ḥasan Mīrzā Shaykh ur-Ra'īs and Ḥājjī Zayn ul-'Ābidīn Marāghī, the author of *Siyāḥatnāma-yi Ibrāhīm Bīg*.

In the final analysis, Malkum Khān's ideological influence can-

42 *TB*, p. 120.

43 Ibrāhīm Ṣafā'ī, *Rahbarān-i Mashrūṭa IV: Sayyid 'Abdullāh Bihbihānī va Sayyid Muḥammad Ṭabāṭabā'ī* (Tehran, 1343 Sh/1964), p. 32.

44 See above, p. 77.

not be assessed with any certainty. Probably the example of the farāmūshkhāna was of greater import: the secret societies of the constitutional period were to have prolonged and intimate contact with the ulama. The personal influence of Malkum Khān was slight: even in the agitation against the regie he played virtually no part. The impact made on Iran and the ulama by his collaborator, Sayyid Jamāl ud-Dīn Asadābādī, was, if more spectacular, only slightly more profound.

SAYYID JAMĀL UD-DĪN ASADĀBĀDI

Sayyid Jamāl ud-Dīn Asadābādī forms part of the history of many Muslim countries, and despite his Iranian birth, his impact on Iran was less profound and lasting than elsewhere in the Muslim world. Both his activities and beliefs present many obscurities, none of which has yet been finally dispelled despite the many studies, of varying quality, which have been devoted to him.[45] To attempt a detailed solution of these problems is not possible in the course of this book. Nonetheless, it is necessary to indicate the main currents of his life and thought as a preliminary to assessing his role in Iranian affairs, and the nature and extent of his relations with the Iranian ulama.

In the light of documents recently published, it is no longer possible to doubt the Iranian origin of the Sayyid: he was born, in about 1839, in the village of Asadābād near Hamadan.[46] That he chose to be known as Afghani is probably accounted for by the fact that his work lay chiefly in Sunni countries and would have been hampered by knowledge of his Shi'i origin.[47] It has even been claimed that in his early youth, following the traditional path of the Shi'i theological student, he went from his native village to

45 See, however, Elie Kedourie, *Afghani and 'Abduh: An Essay on Religious Unbelief and Political Activism in Modern Islam* (London, 1966), and Nikki R. Keddie, *An Islamic Response to Imperialism: Political and Religious Writings of Sayyid Jamal ad-Din "al-Afghani"* (Berkeley and Los Angeles, 1968).

46 See list of correspondence from Jamāl ud-Dīn's relatives in *Majmū'a-yi Asnād va Madārik-i Chāp Nashuda dar bāra-yi Sayyid Jamāl ud-Dīn Mashhūr ba Afghānī*, collected and arranged by A. Mihdavī and I. Afshār (Tehran, 1342 Sh/1963), pp. 28–29. While in Afghanistan itself, he signed himself "al-Istanbulī" (*ibid.*, pp. 8–10). Clearly, he found the role of outsider as such more convenient. See too Ṣifātullāh Jamālī Asadābadī, *Asnād va Madārik dar bāra-yi Īrānī ul-Aṣl Būdan-i Sayyid Jamāl ud-Dīn* (Tehran, 1337 Sh/1958).

47 Albert Hourani, *Arabic Thought in the Liberal Age, 1798–1939* (Oxford, 1962), p. 108.

the ʿatabāt to study under the great Shiʿi divines, among them Shaykh Murtaḍā Anṣārī.[48] The influence of the Avicennan philosophical tradition, apparent in his thought and writings, tends to support this claim, for philosophical learning was more prevalent among Shiʿis than Sunnis at the time.[49] On his later visits to Iran, he conformed to Shiʿi practice in matters of ritual: while this may have been taqīya, in the sense that in concern for Islamic unity he had surmounted the Sunni-Shiʿi division, it does not exclude the probability of an early Shiʿi education.[50]

After a period spent in political activity in Afghanistan and a sojourn in India, in late 1869 he traveled by way of Egypt to Istanbul.[51] During this first brief visit to Istanbul, we see a pattern repeated almost everywhere the Sayyid alighted, including Iran: initial favor and welcome, followed, sooner or later, by suspicion and banishment. The reasons for this lay partly in his own impetuous, ambitious nature, and partly in the obscurity surrounding his real beliefs and motives. With his powerful and magnetic personality, to which many have borne witness,[52] he attracted a numerous following and may thereby have aroused the jealous hostility of the shaykh ul-Islām and other of the ulama of Istanbul.[53] It would be wrong, however, to suppose that their opposition to him was motivated solely by self-interest. A lecture he gave in Istanbul apparently reducing prophecy to the level of philosophy, by calling it an art (*ṣanʿat*), could legitimately have aroused doubts as to his orthodoxy.[54] It may in fact have been no more than a reaffirmation of the traditional belief in the identity of the conclusions reached by philosophical speculation with the revelation vouchsafed to the prophets.[55] This is, nonetheless, the first of many indications that the traditional view of Jamāl ud-Dīn's beliefs—as purely Islamic—needs qualification, if not revision.

48 See anonymous, "Faylasūf-i Sharq: Sayyid Jamāl ud-Dīn-i Asadābādī Maʿrūf ba Afghānī," *Armaghān*, XII (1310 Sh/1931–1932), 590.

49 Hourani, *op. cit.*, p. 108.

50 See *Memo by the General Superintendent of the Thagi and Dakaiti Department*, contained in F.O. 60/594.

51 Anonymous, "Faylasūf-i Sharq," p. 592; Mihdavī and Afshār, ed., *op. cit.*, pp. 11, 14, 18.

52 E.g., Blunt, *op. cit.*, p. 100; ʿAbbās Mīrzā Mulkarā, *Sharḥ-i Ḥāl*, ed. ʿAbd ul-Ḥusayn Navāʾī (Tehran, 1325 Sh/1946–1947), p. 112.

53 Murtaḍā Mudarrisī Chahārdihī, *Zindagānī va Falsafa-yi Sayyid Jamāl ud-Dīn-i Afghānī* (Tehran, 1334 Sh/1955), p. 23.

54 The context of his lecture has been described by Niyazi Berkes in his *Development of Secularism in Turkey* (Montreal, 1964), pp. 182–187.

55 Hourani, *op. cit.*, p. 123.

From Istanbul, Jamāl ud-Dīn went to Cairo, where he spent seven years (1288/1871–1294/1878), probably the most fruitful period of his life.[56] It was then that he taught a number of young Egyptians, such as Muḥammad ʿAbduh and Saʿd Zaghlūl, who were to be his most effective legacy to the Muslim world. It was in Egypt also that Jamāl ud-Dīn began his association with freemasonry. While Malkum Khān's freemasonry appears to have been superficial and unconnected with the European lodges, Jamāl ud-Dīn's commitment to freemasonry was more serious. In June, 1878, he was appointed Grand Master of the Kaukab ash-Sharq Lodge in Cairo, and evidently his masonic interests continued at least until 1884, for in that year he applied for membership of a Paris lodge.[57] Freemasonry is one of the many elements in the thought of Jamāl ud-Dīn, and to assess its relation to the others is difficult. His readiness to associate with Jews, Sikhs, Bābīs, Armenians, and others in his political activities was probably due above all to this masonic background, though doubtless expediency and necessity also played their part.[58] If freemasonry suggested to Malkum Khān the principles of his farāmūshkhāna, it is possible that the secret *majāmiʿ al-ʿurwa,* set up in Egypt and North Africa by Jamāl ud-Dīn and his pupil, Muḥammad ʿAbduh, were similarly inspired.[59] Whether, as has been suggested, the Khedive Taufīq was alarmed by the Sayyid's masonic connections,[60] or as Jamāl ud-Dīn himself is reported to have believed, the British objected to his political activities,[61] in 1879 he was exiled from Egypt and went to India.

He stayed for about four years in India, until in 1301/1883 we find him in Paris.[62] Among his manifold activities there, two are of more immediate relevance to the present discussion: the publication of the periodical *al-ʿUrwa al-Wuthqā,* and his controversy

56 Mihdavī and Afshār, ed., *op. cit.*, pp. 14, 16, 18; Chahārdihī, *op. cit.*, pp. 23–24.

57 See Mihdavī and Afshār, ed., *op. cit.*, pp. 24–25 and plates 40, 42, and 43. Chahārdihī's biography of Jamāl ud-Dīn bears a picture of him in masonic regalia on the cover.

58 Ibrāhīm Ṣafāʾī, *Rahbarān-i Mashrūṭa I: Sayyid Jamāl ud-Dīn Afghānī* (Tehran, 1342 Sh/1963), p. 32; and *Memo by the General Superintendent of the Thagi and Dakaiti Department.*

59 Mihdavī and Afshār, ed., *op. cit.*, p. 63; Rashīd Riḍā, *Tārīkh al-Ustādh al-Imām ash-Shaykh Muḥammad ʿAbduh* (Cairo, 1349 Q/1930–1931), I, 284.

60 Chahārdihī, *op. cit.*, p. 25.

61 Anonymous, "Faylasūf-i Sharq," p. 593.

62 Mihdavī and Afshār, ed., *op. cit.*, p. 30.

with Renan on Islam and science. These represent two aspects or levels of his thought and give some indication of the nature of his aims. *Al-'Urwa al-Wuthqā* was concerned above all with analyzing the internal and external situation of the Muslim world, and the remedy proposed for the troubles afflicting it was indicated by the very title of the periodical: unity, solidarity, and cooperation.[63] The Egyptian writer, Muḥammad al-Bahī, in his analysis of modern Islamic thought, has written that "all of his [Jamāl ud-Dīn's] activity was politically coloured, but the basis on which it subsisted, the source from which it sprung, remained the Quran," quoting in support of this claim Jamāl ud-Dīn's words in *al-'Urwa al-Wuthqā*: "I wish the monarch of all the Muslims to be the Quran, and the focus of their unity, the faith."[64] Against these professions must be set, however, the arguments with which he replied to Renan's polemics against Islam. Renan, in a lecture delivered at the Sorbonne on March 29, 1883, had attempted to prove the hostility of Islam to scientific research and speculation; after calling Islam "the heaviest chain ever borne by humanity," he concluded by regretting the nonexistence of artillery in the seventh century, which, in his opinion, would have had the laudable effect of checking the expansion of Islam.[65] Jamāl ud-Dīn's reply to this violent attack on Islam, published in the *Journal des Débats* on May 18, 1883, provides a remarkable contrast to the contents of *al-'Urwa al-Wuthqā*. He wrote: "Muslim society has still not freed itself from the tutelage of religion. Considering however that the Christian religion has preceded the Muslim religion by several centuries, I cannot prevent myself from hoping that Mohammedan [*sic*] society will one day succeed in breaking its bonds, and march resolutely in the path of civilisation, following the example of western society, for which the Christian faith, despite its harshness and intolerance, has never presented an unsurmountable obstacle. No, I cannot allow this hope to be denied to Islam."[66] It has been suggested that Jamāl ud-Dīn in his reply deliberately understated his case, and

63 The title, meaning "the firm link," is taken from Quran, 2:257.

64 Muḥammad al-Bahī, *al-Fikr al-Islāmi al-Ḥadīth wa Ṣilatuhu bi-l-Isti'mār al-Gharbī* (Cairo, 1379 Q/1959–1960), p. 63.

65 Ernest Renan, *L'Islamisme et la Science* (Paris, 1883), pp. 17, 23.

66 Text of his reply reprinted by A. M. Goichon, together with her translation of *ar-Radd 'alā-d-Dahrīyyīn* entitled *La Réfutation des Matérialistes* (Paris, 1942). It appears improbable that the polished French of this reply emanated from the pen of Jamāl ud-Dīn himself. There is little reason to doubt, however, that its leading ideas were his, if not the mode of expression.

that his apparent hostility to the faith sprang from his philosophic understanding of it.[67] It is difficult, however, to see what purpose of expediency would have been served on this occasion by concealment of belief in Islam.[68] The question of Jamāl ud-Dīn's beliefs is complex; but it is possible that he was seeking "the true Islam," a new interpretation of the faith.[69] It is enough to conclude here, from what has been said, that his concern was above all with the Islamic community: it was this he was defending against Renan, not the Islamic faith. Hence, too, his concern with unity, and the conflict between the West and Islam, conceived of as mutually antagonistic civilizations and communities.[70] In this context, his concept of the role of the ulama in the Islamic community may now be considered.

In *al-'Urwa al-Wuthqā*, he spoke of the need to reestablish the unity of the Muslim community. Originally this had been secured by both the caliphate and the ulama, and then, after the dispersal of political power, by the ulama alone, until they too were separated by differences of doctrine.[71] Jamāl ud-Dīn, in his call for unity, however, did not attempt to base the cohesion of the community on the caliphate or the ulama alone; rather his summons to action, based on the Quranic verse: "Allah changeth not the condition of a people until they change that which is in their hearts,"[72] was addressed to all Muslims.[73] We have seen, indeed, that he was ready to cooperate with non-Muslims—the choice of allies was purely tactical. In Iran, as Malkum Khān had similarly perceived, he saw the ulama already in opposition to the state, and issues upon which popular emotion might be aroused had traditionally been expressed in religious terms. Moreover, the ulama's concern at foreign encroachment on Iran was apparent. It was thus natural for Jamāl ud-Dīn to seek alliance with the Iranian ulama. How far he was successful in so doing, will now be examined.

67 Hourani, *op. cit.*, pp. 122–123.

68 Keddie, "Religion and Irreligion," p. 281.

69 Suggested by W. Braune, *Der islamische Orient zwischen Gegenwart und Zukunft: Eine geschichtstheologische Analyse seiner Stellung in der Weltsituation* (Berne and Munich, 1960), p. 117.

70 W. C. Smith, *Islam in Modern History* (New York, 1959), p. 55.

71 *al-'Urwa al-Wuthqā*, II, 167; Hourani, *op. cit.*, p. 119.

72 13:11.

73 Murtaḍā Mudarrisī Chahardihī, *Ārā va Mu'taqadāt-i Sayyid Jamāl ud-Dīn Afghānī* (Tehran, 1337 Sh/1958), p. 176; and Smith, *op. cit.*, p. 57.

It was the prime enemy of the ulama, the monarch, who first invited him to Iran. Nāṣir ud-Dīn Shāh had been shown a copy of *al-'Urwa al-Wuthqā* by Muḥammad Ḥasan Khān I'timād us-Salṭana and was persuaded by him to invite Sayyid Jamāl ud-Dīn to Iran, ostensibly to produce a newspaper there.[74] The invitation was accepted, and in Shavval, 1303/July–August, 1886, Jamāl ud-Dīn entered Iran by way of Bushire.[75] The transformation from welcome guest to suspect agitator took place swiftly. According to 'Abbās Mīrzā Mulkārā, in his first audience with Nāṣir ud-Dīn Shāh, he spoke openly of the need for reform, and offered his own services for the purpose: "I am like a sharp sword in your hands, do not leave me idle. Put me to any great task, or to work against any government. I am sharper than a sword."[76] Taken aback at such violence of expression, Nāṣir ud-Dīn Shāh declined to receive the Sayyid again, and instructed his host in Tehran, Ḥājj Muḥammad Iṣfahānī Amīn-i Dār uḍ-Ḍarb, to restrict his movements in the capital as much as possible.[77] Nonetheless, the Sayyid's personality exerted its usual magic in Tehran, and he talked to large numbers of the need for reform.[78] It is not clear whether during this first visit to Iran Jamāl ud-Dīn had any contact with the ulama. In Bushire he had met Mīrzā Naṣrullāh Isfahānī Malik ul-Mutakallimīn, when the latter was returning from Bombay to Isfahan, and according to the celebrated preacher's son, they thereafter maintained a constant correspondence.[79] In Tehran, however, there is no record of the ulama having visited him. Indeed it seems unlikely that they should have gone so far as to signal their respect by doing so. For his part, the Sayyid was confined to his host's residence, and though aware of the role of the ulama in Iranian society, he appears not yet to have formulated any plans requiring their participation. In early 1887 the Sayyid was persuaded to leave Iran for Russia.[80]

Nearly three years later we find him again in Iran. The circumstances surrounding his second visit are obscure. Nāṣir ud-Dīn

[74] Mulkārā, *op. cit.*, p. 111; *KhS*, p. 128.
[75] Mihdavī and Afshār, ed., *op. cit.*, p. 73.
[76] Mulkārā, *op. cit.*, p. 112.
[77] *Loc. cit.*
[78] *KhS*, p. 129.
[79] Mihdī Malikzāda, *Tārīkh-i Inqilāb-i Mashrūṭiyat-i Īrān* (Tehran, 1327 Sh/1948–1949), I, 191; see also Anonymous, "Faylasūf-i Sharq," p. 595.
[80] *KhS*, p. 129.

Shāh, during his third European trip, may have met Sayyid Jamāl ud-Dīn in St. Petersburg and Munich, and apparently a reconciliation was effected. Amīn us-Sulṭān also saw fit to invite the Sayyid to return to Iran.[81] According to Sir Henry Drummond Wolff, the British ambassador in Tehran, Nāṣir ud-Dīn Shāh was, however, "greatly annoyed" at Jamāl ud-Dīn's arrival in Tehran.[82] Again he was regarded with disfavor, both by the Shah and by his minister, and again his host's residence became a center of attraction for the malcontents of the capital.[83] It appears that on this occasion the Sayyid had more definite plans of action, in which the ulama were allotted their customary role of arousing popular feeling against the monarchy. Thus he caused a telegram to be sent from Tiflis to certain of the ulama informing them that Nāṣir ud-Dīn Shāh had accepted a Persian translation of the Bible from the hands of Wolff.[84] Moving to what he supposed to be the greater security of Shāh 'Abd ul-'Aẓīm, he continued to speak to all who visited him of the necessity of reform and an end to tyranny. At the same time he maintained correspondence with those unable or unwilling to come in person.[85]

Among the ulama, two are recorded as having visited or been in contact with Sayyid Jamāl ud-Dīn on this occasion: Sayyid Ṣādiq Ṭabāṭabā'i and Shaykh Hādī Najmābādī.[86] The *Tārīkh-i Bīdārī* mentions the former as having been regarded with suspicion because of his contacts with Jamāl ud-Dīn.[87] His association with Malkum Khān, discussed above, makes it necessary to treat his religious professions with reserve; it is significant that Shaykh Hādī also was regarded as a freethinker.[88] According to one account, Shaykh Hādī advised Jamāl ud-Dīn to teach "the concept

[81] *KhS*, pp. 139–140. The invitation may have been extended to appease the Russians after the grant of several concessions to the British. Jamāl ud-Dīn at this time enjoyed limited contacts with Russian officialdom. See Nikki R. Keddie, *Religion and Rebellion in Iran: The Tobacco Protest of 1891–1892* (London, 1966), p. 22.

[82] Cyphered telegram dated December 21, 1889, in F.O. 60/594.

[83] *KhS*, p. 144.

[84] Dispatch dated February 7, 1890 from Morier, British ambassador in St. Petersburg, in F.O. 60/594.

[85] *KhS*, p. 145; Mulkārā, *op. cit.*, p. 113.

[86] Yaḥyā Daulatābādī writes that he was in Shāh 'Abd ul-'Aẓīm at the same time as Sayyid Jamāl ud-Dīn, without claiming explicitly to have met him (*HY*, I, 90).

[87] P. 49.

[88] See Mīrzā Muḥammad Qazvīnī's note on Shaykh Hādī Najmābādī in Browne, *op. cit.*, p. 406.

of freedom" (*mafhūm-i āzādī*) by means of instruction in Quranic exegesis.[89] On the other hand, none of the ulama prominent in the agitation against the tobacco monopoly is mentioned as having met the Sayyid in Tehran. Although it is probable that some of the less prominent members of the religious classes, in particular the ṭullāb, were drawn to him, his contact with the higher levels of clerical authority was strictly limited.

It was his attempts to extend such contact that ultimately led to his expulsion. Nā'ib us-Salṭana, governor of Tehran, informed the Shah that Jamāl ud-Dīn had written to the ulama criticizing the grant of economic concessions to foreigners.[90] Orders were given for the forcible expulsion of the Sayyid from Iran.[91] This was the first time that bast at a shrine had been violently broken, and this, together with the humiliations inflicted on Sayyid Jamāl ud-Dīn, was a sign of the new ruthlessness of the state. When this ruthlessness expressed itself in the form of willingness to offend against the dignity of the ulama, the government succeeded only in increasing the power of the ulama: popular indignation was aroused in their favor. Significantly, in order to lessen the impact of the violation of bast, it was claimed that the Sayyid was not Muslim.[92]

The Sayyid's expulsion from Iran increased his bitterness toward the Qajar monarchy, and he intensified his attempts to join forces with the ulama against it. He was put over the Ottoman border into Iraq, and a promise was extracted from the governor of Baghdad not to allow him to contact the ulama at the 'atabāt.[93] Instead, he went to Basra, where he met Ḥājj Sayyid 'Alī Akbar Fālasīrī.[94] Sayyid 'Alī Akbar had similarly suffered banishment from Iran, for preaching against the tobacco concession in Shiraz.[95] From Basra, Jamāl ud-Dīn wrote to Mīrzā Ḥasan Shīrāzī Mujtahid in Samarra, condemning Nāṣir ud-Dīn Shāh and Amīn us-Sulṭān for their impiety and the concessions granted to foreigners, and urging Mīrzā Ḥasan to use his authority for preserving the national in-

89 Chahārdihī, *Zindagānī va Falsafa*, p. 65.

90 See I'timād us-Salṭana's diary entry for Jumādī ul-Ūlā 26, 1308/January 7, 1891, quoted in Mihdavī and Afshār, ed., *op. cit.*, p. 151.

91 *KhS*, p. 144.

92 Mulkārā, *op. cit.*, p. 113.

93 *TRS*, V, 1210.

94 *KhS*, p. 151.

95 See Ibrāhīm Taymūrī, *Taḥrīm-i Tanbākū yā Avvalīn Muqāvamat-i Manfī dar Īrān* (Tehran, 1328 Sh/1949), p. 68.

terests of Iran.[96] Before leaving Basra for Europe, he entrusted the letter to Sayyid 'Alī Akbar for forwarding to Mīrzā Ḥasan Shīrāzī, and wrote another of similar content to the ulama of Iran.[97]

In 1892, after a period spent in collaborating with Mīrzā Malkum Khān in propaganda against the Iranian government from London, Jamāl ud-Dīn was invited to Istanbul by Sultan 'Abd ul-Ḥamīd, and began again to correspond with the Shi'i ulama, this time in order to establish a political unity of the Muslim world under the Ottoman Sultan-Caliph.[98] Among his collaborators, typically, were Bābīs, such as Mīrzā Āqā Khān Kirmānī, Shaykh Aḥmad Rūḥī, and Afḍal ul-Mulk Kirmānī.[99] According to the last-mentioned, they succeeded in eliciting two hundred letters from the Shi'i ulama of Iraq and Iran supporting the idea of unity.[100]

In view of these activities of the Sayyid, there has been a tendency to overestimate his influence on Iran in general and the ulama in particular. His life was, moreover, as Hourani puts it, "lived very publicly,"[101] and it was natural to consider his influence as great as his character was turbulent. In the case of the tobacco monopoly, the Sayyid may have had some motive effect on the ulama; but his tirades against the impiety of the regime and the dangers of foreign economic dominance can have taught them little they did not already realize at least as well as did Jamāl ud-Dīn. E. G. Browne considers the effect of his letter to Mīrzā Ḥasan Shīrāzī decisive;[102] but, although it is true that Mīrzā Ḥasan was initially reluctant to use his potential political power, it was not, as will be indicated, Jamāl ud-Dīn who persuaded him to do so. His influence on the actual course of events during the agitation against the tobacco monopoly appears to have been nil.

Similar considerations apply to the Sayyid's advocacy of Pan-Islamism. The ideal existed independently of Jamāl ud-Dīn and, it might be added, after the campaign had been formally abandoned by 'Abd ul-Ḥamīd. It continued to be an active political

96 Arabic text in *TB*, pp. 22–24; Persian translation in Taymūrī, *op. cit.*, pp. 53–57; English translation in Browne, *op. cit.*, pp. 15–21.

97 *KhS*, p. 151. According to Chahārdihī (*op. cit.*, p. 71), Afghānī went to Samarra to present his letter in person, but was refused admittance by Mīrzā Ḥasan Shīrāzī. This is unsupported by other accounts.

98 Mīrzā Āqā Khān Kirmānī, *Hasht Bihisht* (n.p., n.d.), introduction, p. viii.

99 *Loc. cit.*

100 *Loc. cit.* See also *HY*, I, 99.

101 Hourani, *op. cit.*, p. 108.

102 Browne, *op. cit.*, p. 22.

force in Iran until 1904, finding possibly an echo in the recourse had by the ulama to the Ottoman ambassador for submitting their demands to Muẓaffar ud-Dīn Shāh the following year.

In short, it may be said that the ulama were no more than one of the groups to whom Jamāl ud-Dīn addressed himself in the pursuit of his aims. His choice was dictated by circumstances; his second sojourn in Tehran, and expulsion from Iran, coincided with a period of growing clerical discontent with the policies of the government. With this discontent, Jamāl ud-Dīn sought to identify himself and, then with characteristic ambitiousness, to direct it to an aim he himself had set—the overthrow of the Qajar dynasty.

There are few clues to the opinions held of Jamāl ud-Dīn by the ulama, but the charges against him in the *takfīrnāma* (declaration of takfīr) published by the newspaper *Akhtar* are perhaps indicative of sentiments felt not only by the writer. He recalls that the Sayyid was denounced as an infidel in Istanbul and accuses him of "donning the guise and entering the ranks of the ulama to promote certain illegitimate designs."[103] In particular he censures him for collaborating with Malkum Khān in London: "If this erring Shaykh—may God forbid!—were one of the ulama of Islam, he would on no account collaborate with these mischievous, rebellious Armenians, in order to stir up unrest in the lands of Islam."[104] Similar thoughts—though expressed hesitantly and guardedly—occurred to even so devoted a follower of the Sayyid as Ḥājj Muḥammad Iṣfahānī;[105] and although none of the ulama are recorded to have expressed similar sentiments, it is at least possible that they entertained them. Malkum Khān, as has been seen, was not regarded with favor in clerical circles. Another accusation made by the author of the takfirnāma is that the Sayyid and Malkum "even print and publish in their nonsensical rag forged letters from the ulama, the nobles and other respectable people."[106] Although, again, a specific instance of a letter from one of the ulama being forged cannot be cited, the charge is not an unlikely one. We have seen the technique used by Malkum Khān in writing the *Qānūn*, and I'timād us-Salṭana was, for his part, annoyed by the insertion

103 *Takfīrnāma* reproduced in Mihdavī and Afshār, ed., *op. cit.*, p. 144.

104 *Ibid.*, p. 146.

105 See his letter to Jamāl ud-Dīn dated Muḥarram 1, 1310/July 26, 1892, in *ibid.*, pp. 134–137.

106 *Ibid.*, p. 144.

of his name in Jamāl ud-Dīn's letter to Mīrzā Ḥasan Shīrāzī.[107] It can be tentatively concluded that Jamāl ud-Dīn's reception by the ulama was not favorable, and partly because of this he attempted to implicate them in his plans.[108] They had, however, their own plans which despite resemblance to those of Jamāl ud-Dīn were executed independently.

Writing in the *Contemporary Review* in February, 1892, Jamāl ud-Dīn claimed that "my title 'Son of the Prophet' may serve to signify to all Europeans that I am known and well accredited throughout the dominions of the Shah, recognised in my high religious dignity by the Shah himself and all his ministers and ambassadors and upholders of our holy religion, and accepted as one of the chief teachers of the people."[109] These claims were not justified and represented a dream of eminence reminiscent of Malkum Khān's statement that the ulama kissed his feet. The Sayyid's influence was chiefly outside Iran, and although through the assassination of Nāṣir ud-Dīn Shāh, his role (though remote) is of undeniable importance in Iranian history, his impact in other respects was limited. Amīn ud-Daula attributes to him a quickening of the forces of discontent,[110] and his influence on the general climate of thought is clear. The ulama, however, were the effective leaders of the nation, and the initiators of action; with these his contact was limited. It is significant that the religious orthodoxy of those associated with him must be regarded with suspicion. He sought to associate himself with the ulama, at a time of mounting discontent; yet he was never accepted by them, any more than by 'Abd ul-Ḥamīd or Nāṣir ud-Dīn Shāh. The ulama acted on their own initiative, on the basis of an authority denied to Jamāl ud-Dīn. This will be seen in the agitation against the tobacco concession.

Mīrzā Malkum Khān and Sayyid Jamāl ud-Dīn, though their approaches to the problem differed in detail, both sought reform

107 See extract from his diary dated Jumādī ul-Ukhrā 21, 1309/January 22, 1892, in *ibid.*, pp. 134–137.

108 While in Istanbul, Jamāl ud-Dīn published a pamphlet reproaching Mīrzā Ḥasan Shīrāzī for not using his authority to bring about the overthrow of Nāṣir ud-Dīn Shāh (see *HY*, I, 131).

109 "The Reign of Terror in Persia," *Contemporary Review*, LXI (1892), 238–248.

110 *KhS*, p. 130.

by an overthrow of the existing order in Iran. Although in neither case do their plans appear to have been religiously motivated, they both envisaged making use of the ulama in carrying them out, and thus sought to identify themselves with the clerical classes. As has been shown, they were, with the exception of specific cases mentioned, unsuccessful, although their influence upon other classes of the population may have been greater. As the liberals of the Constitutional Revolution were later to do, they perceived the potentialities of clerical power for agitation against the monarchy. But their role in the realization of these potentialities was slight: the ulama had, after all, nearly a century of experience in opposition to the Qajar dynasty, and their role as national leaders had often found expression. Now, in the agitation against the tobacco concession, it was again the ulama who acted as defenders of the national interests; figures such as Malkum Khān and Sayyid Jamāl ud-Dīn stood on the fringe of events.

XII

The Repeal of the Tobacco Concession and Its Consequences

The agitation against the tobacco concession represented, on the one hand, a repetition of the ulama's traditional role in opposing the state, and on the other, the prelude to the Constitutional Revolution. It has already been seen how, on numerous occasions, the ulama acted against the state in order to defend national interests. In each case, they gave expression at the same time to the demands or grievances of various persons or groups; yet in the case of the tobacco concession, virtually the whole nation was united under their leadership. The agitation was not merely a protest against a specific measure taken by the government, for although centered on the question of the tobacco monopoly, it was essentially a confrontation between the people and the state, in which the leadership exercised by the ulama showed a new determination and sense of direction. If before the agitation, the struggle of the ulama with the state had been one of the recurring themes of Qajar history, it was thereafter the dominant one until the granting of the constitution. After three-quarters of a century the issue was intensified to a point where the triumph of one side or the other seemed inevitable. The ulama's determination was paralleled by the ruthlessness of the state. The agitation took place, moreover, in a context of increasing foreign involvement in Iran, and this above all inspired it with a sense of urgency, of concern for the very survival of Iran. Thus the traditional dual role of the ulama—opposition to the state and resistance to foreign encroachment—found its greatest expression. This duality was passed on by the ulama to the constitutional movement.

The tobacco monopoly was one of a number of concessions granted to foreign economic interests at the beginning of the last decade of the nineteenth century. The preliminary negotiations were completed in London during Nāṣir ud-Dīn Shāh's third visit to Europe in 1889,[1] and in the spring of 1891, the agents of the British company to which the monopoly had been granted began to arrive in Iran.[2] All rights concerning the sale and distribution of tobacco inside Iran, and the export of all tobacco produced in Iran, were vested in the Imperial Tobacco Corporation, which in return was to pay the Iranian government £15 million a year.[3] Furthermore, the regulation of the yearly crop was to be the prerogative of the company.[4] Whether or not these conditions were known of accurately and in detail, popular discontent arose as soon as the agents of the monopoly started their activities.[5] It is of importance to note this, for the spontaneity and genuineness of popular indignation to a large extent determined the resolute and successful conduct of the agitation. Earlier, although the ulama had acted as leaders of a momentarily angry populace, they were frequently encouraged to do so by interested parties: thus in the case of the Second Perso-Russian War, ʿAbbās Mīrzā made deliberate and calculated use of clerical power, until the popular excitement no longer needed instigation. With the tobacco monopoly, the basis of the agitation was widespread discontent, not court intrigue.

Feuvrier noted the first disturbances in the capital on May 22,

1 ʿAbdullāh Mustaufī, *Tārīkh-i Idārī va Ijtimāʿī-yi Daura-yi Qājārīya ya Sharḥ-i Zindagānī-yi Man* (Tehran, 1321 Sh/1942–1943), I, 470.

2 J.-B. Feuvrier, *Trois Ans à la Cour de Perse* (Paris, 1899), p. 309.

3 *Ibid.*, pp. 307–308; Aḥmad Kasravī, *Tārīkh-i Mashrūṭa-yi Īrān* (5th imp.; Tehran, 1340 Sh/1961), p. 15. ʿAbbās Mīrzā Mulkārā (*Sharḥ-i Ḥāl*, ed. ʿAbd ul-Ḥusayn Navāʾī [Tehran, 1325 Sh/1946–1947], p. 114) gives the figure of £25 million.

4 Feuvrier, *op. cit.*, p. 308.

5 *Ibid.*, pp. 267–268.

1891,[6] and shortly afterward agitation extended to the large provincial cities. In Ramaḍān, 1308/April–May, 1891, one of the chief tobacco merchants of Fārs, Ḥājjī 'Abbās Urdūbādī, caused the bazaars of Shiraz to be closed in protest against the monopoly, and at the same time Ḥājj Sayyid 'Alī Akbar Fālasīrī mounted the minbar in the Masjid-i Vakīl to preach against the government's policy in general, and the granting of the tobacco monopoly in particular. Flourishing a sword, he called for jihad if the agents of the monopoly attempted to enter Shiraz.[7] Orders were thereupon sent from Tehran to the governor of Shiraz, Qavām ul-Mulk, for the expulsion of the Sayyid. In order to prevent the commotion an open arrest would have caused, he was ambushed one night while walking unattended outside Shiraz and, divested of his turban and cloak, dispatched immediately to Bushire and thence to Basra. When the news of the Sayyid's humiliating expulsion became known in Shiraz, the merchants of the town gathered in the shrine of Shāh Chirāgh, where they were fired upon by the troops of Qavām ul-Mulk and obliged to disperse. The following day, the agents of the monopoly entered Shiraz.[8]

It is significant that from the beginning of the agitation cooperation between the merchants and the ulama took place. This cooperation was based not only upon common interests in opposing the tobacco monopoly, but also on the position of each in Iranian society. They represented two powers largely independent of the state: that of economic enterprise and that of religious direction. The influence of the state, either in the capital or in the large provincial centers such as Tabriz, Isfahan, and Shiraz, was likely to be exercised at the expense of both merchants and ulama—excessive taxation and other forms of extortion would harm commercial interests, while 'urf jurisdiction meant a reduction of clerical power. The sanctuary offered by mosques and the residences of the ulama provided an ultimate refuge from the oppression of the state; and the closure of the bazaar, and with it the

6 *Ibid.*, p. 267.

7 Mulkārā, *op. cit.*, p. 114; Ibrāhīm Taymūrī, *Taḥrīm-i Tanbākū yā Avvalīn Muqāvamat-i Manfī dar Īrān* (Tehran, 1328 Sh/1949), pp. 68–69. Already in 1886, Sayyid 'Alī Akbar had led riots in Shiraz to protest against artificially high food prices. They were finally quelled when Ẓill us-Sulṭān ordered the removal of the Sayyid from Shiraz to Isfahan. See Ḥājjī Pīrzāda, *Safarnāma*, ed. Ḥāfiẓ Farmānfarmā'īān (Tehran, 1342 Sh/1963), I, 36–38, 89.

8 Feuvrier, *op. cit.*, p. 268; Mulkārā, *op. cit.*, pp. 114, 115–116; Taymūrī, *op. cit.*, pp. 71–72; *KhS*, pp. 149–150.

temporary paralysis of urban life, gave the ulama a powerful instrument of pressure. There was, therefore, enough reason implicit in the structure of Qajar society for an alliance between the ulama and the merchants.

This alliance became more pronounced and effective from the time of the agitation against the tobacco monopoly onward, finding its greatest expression in the events of 1905–1906. The reason for this lay primarily in what was conceived of as the growing foreign danger to Iranian independence. As the state, per se, was inimical to both traders and ulama, so too was foreign domination feared by both. This is well illustrated by the case of the tobacco monopoly. The tobacco merchants clearly resented having to sell and buy at prices arbitrarily fixed by a foreign company.[9] As for the ulama, the descent on Iran of the agents of the Imperial Tobacco Corporation seemed to be a confirmation of the fears so revealingly voiced by Ḥājjī Mullā 'Alī Kanī in his protest against the projected building of railways. According to the Qajar prince, 'Abbās Mīrzā Mulkārā, "the English came to Iran as to a conquered country. They sent their officials to every quarter. . . . Seeing themselves unhindered, they treated Iranian subjects harshly, and nowhere paid any attention to the government. Every day orders were issued to the provincial governors that they should without fail do their utmost to promote the affairs of the company's officials."[10] If foreigners were to gain such influence, it would not be long before it extended from economic and commercial affairs to the more immediate concerns of the ulama. The appearance of a large number of non-Muslim foreigners, working for the tobacco corporation, was one of the most important reasons for the agitation—their dominating presence was resented, especially by the ulama.[11] To entrust the economic affairs of the nation to foreigners endangered the existence of Iran as it was understood by the ulama: a national-religious community under their guidance. The belief that this existence was endangered was clearly expressed in

[9] Lord Salisbury, early in 1891, warned Lascelles, British ambassador in Tehran, to "guard against the suspicion that we are not labouring for the development, but only for the exploitation of Persia" (quoted in R. L. Greaves, "British Policy in Persia, 1892–1903," *BSOAS*, XXVIII [1965], 36). He appears to have had little success in so doing.

[10] Mulkārā, *op. cit.*, p. 114. On tactless behavior by the agents of the Régie, see too Nikki R. Keddie, *Religion and Rebellion in Iran: The Tobacco Protest of 1891–1892* (London, 1966), p. 50.

[11] *TM*, p. 15.

the *Maqāla-yi Millī* printed and distributed in Tehran during the agitation: it was thought that Iran might suffer the fate of India.[12]

Elsewhere in the provinces we observe the same alliance of the merchants and the ulama. In Muḥarram, 1309/August–September, 1891, protests began to be heard in Tabriz.[13] As a sign of dissatisfaction, the ulama stopped teaching in the madrasas, and the commercial life of the city was brought to a standstill by the closure of the bazaar. A telegram was sent to the Shah demanding the withdrawal of the concession, threatening armed resistance if he failed to do so.[14] The agitation in Tabriz was led by Mīrzā Āqā Javād, returned from his temporary absence and at the height of his influence. Nāṣir ud-Dīn Shāh dispatched one of his courtiers, Āqā ʿAlī Ashtīānī, to meet Mīrzā Āqā Javād and blandish him with gifts.[15] Before his arrival in Tabriz, the townspeople hung a piece of paper round the neck of a dog, and paraded it through the town, thus signifying their contempt for the communications of the Shah and his messenger.[16] Āqā ʿAlī Ashtīānī found the streets of Tabriz and Mīrzā Javād's residence full of armed men, and therefore considered it more prudent to retire after presenting the gifts than to stay and attempt any discussion.[17]

In Isfahan, the long-established clerical stronghold, the ulama, headed by the formidable Āqā Najafī, soon started agitating against the tobacco monopoly. They went so far as to prevent the sale of tobacco even before the issue of the celebrated fatvā.[18] Ẓill us-Sulṭan brought pressure to bear on Āqā Najafī to permit the sale of tobacco, but without success.[19] In Mashhad, demonstrations against the monopoly were led by Ḥājj Shaykh Muḥammad Taqī Burūjirdī and Ḥājj Ḥabīb Mujtahid Shahīdī.[20]

These expressions of discontent and anger, despite their similarity, do not appear to have formed part of a coordinated plan. Such

12 *Ibid.*, pp. 17–18; *TB*, p. 35. The fact that British policy toward Iran differed fundamentally from policy in India and was indeed for a long time subordinate to it, is immaterial in this context.

13 *KhS*, p. 152.

14 Feuvrier, *op. cit.*, p. 311; Taymūrī, *op. cit.*, p. 75; *Memorandum Respecting the Imperial Tobacco Corporation of Persia*, F.O. 539/55, p. 4.

15 Mulkārā, *op. cit.*, p. 115.

16 *KhS*, p. 152.

17 Mulkārā, *op. cit.*, p. 115.

18 *Ibid.*, p. 78.

19 *Ibid.*, p. 79.

20 *Ibid.*, p. 80.

unity, both among the ulama and, through their medium, among the people, was achieved in the first place by the fatvā prohibiting the use of tobacco, attributed to Mīrzā Ḥasan Shīrāzī Mujtahid.

We have seen already how Shaykh Murtaḍā Anṣārī established himself in the ʿatabāt as sole marjaʿ-i taqlīd. On his death in 1281/1864–1865 no immediate successor appeared. Initially, Mīrzā Ḥasan Shīrāzī and Mīrzā Habibullāh Rashtī, both pupils of Shaykh Murtaḍā, enjoyed equal authority.[21] In 1287/1870–1, on returning from the pilgrimage to Mecca, Mīrzā Ḥasan left Najaf to settle in Samarra, a town with a predominantly Sunni population and well fitted to be a new base of clerical power.[22] A number of pupils followed him there, most prominent among them Mullā Kāẓim Khurāsānī, who later became one of the chief clerical supporters of the constitution. Gradually, Mīrzā Ḥasan's authority extended until he "emerged" as the sole marjaʿ-i taqlīd and the successor to Shaykh Murtaḍā Anṣārī.[23]

Shaykh Murtaḍā had declined to make political use of his power, and initially Mīrzā Ḥasan Shīrāzī showed a similar reluctance.[24] It has been suggested that the urgings of Sayyid Jamāl ud-Dīn Asadābādī caused him to abandon his caution. His contacts with the Shiʿi ulama of Iran, however, were more direct and continuous and were probably of greater importance than one letter from the pen of Jamāl ud-Dīn. In particular, Sayyid ʿAlī Akbar Fālasīrī, no less aggrieved than Jamāl ud-Dīn at being banished from Iran in humiliating circumstances, appears to have encouraged Mīrzā Ḥasan to use his authority. After reaching Basra, where he met Jamāl ud-Dīn, he continued to Samarra and there informed Mīrzā Ḥasan Shīrāzī of the treatment to which he had been subjected, and of the agitation against the tobacco monopoly.[25] Amīn us-Sulṭān, realizing the mistake he had made in banishing Sayyid ʿAlī Akbar, and thus allowing him to make direct contact with Mīrzā Ḥasan, tried to entice him back, but in vain.[26] Another arrival at Samarra was that of Āqā Munīr ud-Dīn, whom the ulama

21 *HY*, I, 36. On Mīrzā Ḥabībullāh Rashtī, see Mīrzā Muḥammad Ḥasan Khān Iʿtimād us-Salṭana, *al-Maʾāthir va-l-Āthār* (Tehran, 1306 Q/1889), p. 144.

22 *HY*, I, 37.

23 *Ibid.*, p. 38; Muḥammad Ḥusayn Ādamīyat, *Dānishmandān va Sukhansarāyān-i Fārs* (Tehran, 1338 Sh/1959), IV, 323–325; Iʿtimād us-Salṭana, *op. cit.*, p. 135.

24 Taymūrī, *op. cit.*, p. 87.

25 Mulkārā, *op. cit.*, p. 115.

26 Taymūrī, *op. cit.*, p. 72; Mulkārā, *op. cit.*, p. 116.

of Isfahan had deputed to obtain a ruling from Mīrzā Ḥasan on the question of the tobacco concession.[27]

Mīrzā Ḥasan's intervention began with a telegram to Nāṣir ud-Dīn Shāh, on Dhū-l-Ḥijja 19, 1308/July 26, 1891, protesting against the disrespect shown to Sayyid 'Alī Akbar, and also against the granting of the tobacco monopoly.[28] Soon after the receipt of this telegram in Tehran, the Iranian chargé d'affaires in Baghdad, Maḥmūd Khān Mushīr ul-Vizāra, was sent to Samarra to point out to Mīrzā Ḥasan Shīrāzī the benefits accruing to Iran from the concession, but he was unable to deflect him from his opposition.[29] Flattering letters from Amīn us-Sulṭān and Mīrzā Zayn ul-'Ābidīn Imām Jum'a were similarly ineffective in influencing Mīrzā Ḥasan's opinion of the tobacco monopoly.[30] The Shah did not reply to his first telegram, and Mīrzā Ḥasan wrote to him again in September, 1891, setting forth in detail his objections to the tobacco concession.[31] Still unable to elicit any satisfactory response from Tehran, in Rabī' uth-Thānī, 1309/November–December, 1891, he wrote to Mīrzā Ḥasan Ashtīānī, empowering him to act on his behalf in combating the monopoly.[32]

Early in December, there appeared in Tehran a fatvā declaring the use of tobacco in any form to be tantamount to war against the Hidden Imam, i.e., ḥarām.[33] Its effect was immediate and total: throughout the country the use of tobacco was abandoned.[34] Much confusion surrounds the origin of the fatvā, doubtless in large part created by the government in the hope of lessening its effect. Popularly it was ascribed to Mīrzā Ḥasan Shīrāzī, who as sole marja'-i taqlīd might demand the obedience of all believers, and hence the totality of its effect. It was important, therefore, for the government to cast doubt on its attribution to Mīrzā Ḥasan Shīrāzī. At the same time, it is not clear whether the wording was that of Mīrzā Ḥasan Shīrāzī, or whether the fatvā had been issued by others in his name. It appears that the first rumors of Mīrzā Ḥasan Shīrāzī having issued such a fatvā arose in Isfahan toward the end

27 Taymūrī, *op. cit.*, p. 79.
28 *Ibid.*, p. 88.
29 *Ibid.*, p. 89; Feuvrier, *op. cit.*, p. 315.
30 Taymūrī, *op. cit.*, p. 92.
31 Feuvrier, *op. cit.*, p. 314.
32 Taymūrī, *op. cit.*, p. 97.
33 Mustaufī, *op. cit.*, I, 471; *TB*, p. 12.
34 Feuvrier, *op. cit.*, p. 322.

of Rabīʿ uth-Thānī, 1309/November, 1891.[35] Āqā Najafī had indeed requested the issue of a fatvā, and Āqā Munīr ud-Dīn had gone to Samarra to present the request. It is thus possible that Mīrzā Ḥasan Shīrāzī's ruling prohibiting the use of tobacco was first sent to Isfahan. In Tehran the truth or falsehood of the rumors could not be ascertained immediately, for telegraphic communications with Iraq had been interrupted. A further rumor arose that a letter, containing confirmation of the fatvā, had arrived from Samarra for Mīrzā Ḥasan Āshtīānī, and thereupon thousands of copies of the fatvā were distributed in Tehran.[36]

Amīn us-Sulṭān then set in circulation a report to the effect that the original copy of the fatvā had been forged by the chief of the tradesmen's guild (*malik ut-tujjār*) of Tehran.[37] Amīn ud-Daula in his memoirs supports this attribution, and others have also expressed doubts as to the genuineness of the fatvā.[38] The fact that copies of the fatvā were circulated in Tehran and elsewhere so soon after the alleged letter had been received by Mīrzā Ḥasan Āshtīānī points indeed to some degree of previous planning and organization. This by itself does not prove the fatvā to be a forgery. It is possible that among the powers delegated by Mīrzā Ḥasan Shīrāzī to Mīrzā Ḥasan Āshtīānī in Tehran was that of issuing in his name, at an appropriate moment, a fatvā prohibiting the use of tobacco. In any event, Mīrzā Ḥasan Shīrāzī did not reject the attribution of the fatvā to him. Amīn ud-Daula, with his usual hostility to the ulama, suggests that this was because he saw in the universal obedience paid to the ruling an illustration of his power.[39] In his earlier communications with the Shah, however, he had clearly indicated his attitude to the tobacco concession, and it was his fatvā permitting the use of tobacco that finally ended the boycott on January 26, 1892.[40]

35 Taymūrī, *op. cit.*, p. 102.

36 *Ibid.*, pp. 103–104.

37 *Ibid.*, p. 112. According to V. A. Kosogovsky (*Iz Tegeranskovo Dnevnika* [Moscow, 1960], p. 142), Malik ut-Tujjār wrote to Mīrzā Ḥasan Shīrāzī, informing him of the tobacco concession, and received in return the text of the fatvā prohibiting the use of tobacco. He then gave it to Mīrzā Ḥasan Āshtīānī, who arranged for the production of thousands of copies, to be distributed on an agreed day. Kosogovsky was not in Tehran at the time, and his account, while not unlikely, cannot be regarded as authoritative.

38 *KhS*, p. 173; *HY*, I, 108. Mustaufī (*op. cit.*, I, 470) considers the fatvā to have been a forgery, but ventures no opinion as to the identity of the forger.

39 *KhS*, p. 173.

40 Feuvrier, *op. cit.*, p. 339.

The ultimate source of opposition to the monopoly was thus in Samarra, but the determination of the ulama and people of Iran, particularly in the capital, was equally important in the agitation. In Tehran the movement against the tobacco monopoly was led by Mīrzā Ḥasan Āshtīānī who, like Mīrzā Ḥasan Shīrāzī and Mīrzā Āqā Javād, was a pupil of Shaykh Murtaḍā Anṣārī. After the death of Ḥājj Mullā ʻAlī Kanī, he had emerged as the most prominent of the ulama of the capital and presided over one of the chief sharʻ courts.[41] The disorders accompanying the boycott in the capital centered on his person. The unity of the people was due as much to his determination as to the obligatory nature of the fatvā.

Feuvrier writes of the surprise felt in Tehran, both by the court and the British embassy, at the purposeful manner in which the boycott was applied.[42] More than ever before, the ulama were in control of the people and represented an authority firmer than that of the Shah. This result had been achieved by the unity of the marjaʻ-i taqlīd and the unity of direction and could be destroyed only by breaking that unity. For this purpose too it was necessary to rely on the ulama, such was the measure of clerical ascendancy.

On December 19, 1891, the ulama of Tehran were invited to gather at the residence of Kāmrān Mīrzā Nā'ib us-Sulṭana to discuss the tobacco monopoly.[43] It was suggested to them that they should declare the use of tobacco permissible, but only Sayyid ʻAbdullāh Bihbihānī refrained from obeying the fatvā. Evidently he did not consider Mīrzā Ḥasan Shīrāzī aʻlam, and hence worthy of taqlīd.[44] At the same time he was closely allied with Amīn us-Sulṭān,[45] and material encouragements appear to have influenced his insistence on continuing to smoke.[46] Sayyid ʻAlī Akbar Tafrashī openly accused Bihbihānī of having been bribed, and the meeting dissolved in confusion and uproar.[47] As a gesture of compromise,

41 Iʻtimād us-Salṭana, *op. cit.*, p. 151; and *Biographical Notices of Persian Notables, Prepared by Lieut. Col. A. Picot,* chap. iv, contained in F.O. 60/592.

42 Feuvrier, *op. cit.*, pp. 322–323.

43 *Ibid.*, p. 324.

44 *TB*, p. 13.

45 Ibrāhīm Ṣafā'ī, *Rahbarān-i Mashrūṭa VI: Sayyid ʻAbdullāh Bihbihānī va Sayyid Muḥammad Ṭabāṭabā'ī* (Tehran, 1343 Sh/1964), p. 5.

46 According to Mulkārā (*op. cit.*, p. 116), he had received a bribe of £1,000 from Ornstein, the manager of the tobacco corporation. Later he was to be given a gold watch by the government (*Biographical Notices*, chap. iv).

47 Mustaufī, *op. cit.*, I, 470.

the monopoly of the Imperial Tobacco Corporation was restricted to the export of tobacco, but the ulama were not satisfied and persisted in the boycott.[48] Further communications from Mīrzā Ḥasan Shīrāzī confirmed the prohibition.[49]

In an act of force designed to break the boycott, but which served only to demonstrate again the power of the ulama, it was decided to threaten Mīrzā Ḥasan Ashtīānī with banishment from Tehran unless he contradicted the prohibiting fatvā. Nāṣir ud-Dīn Shāh wrote a letter to him of remarkably violent tone, presenting him with these alternatives and upbraiding him for his behavior: "Have you decided on demagogy? Or do you want to add lustre to your position by, instead of praising the government and its leaders in your circles and assemblies, speaking against it? I thought you a poor, disinterested mullā, loyal to the government. Now I see that on the contrary you are following the example of the mujtahid of Tabriz [i.e., Mīrzā Āqā Javād] and Āqā Najafī. Do you not know that none may rise against the government?"[50] This imperious assertion of tyranny contrasts strangely with Nāṣir ud-Dīn Shāh's expressions of contrite devotion to the ulama after the abolition of the monopoly. The extent of the contrast was the measure of the ulama's triumph.

This open attempt at breaking the power of the ulama, at forcing the reversal of a fatvā, caused the popular anger to assume a violent, almost uncontrollable form. Mīrzā Ḥasan Āshtīānī, refusing to declare the use of tobacco permissible, on Jumādī ul-Ūlā 3, 1309/January 4, 1892, made preparations to leave Tehran.[51] His followers became aware of his projected departure, and gathering near his home, prevented him from leaving.[52] The bazaar was closed, and about 4,000 people massed round the citadel, led by a sayyid, and dressed in shrouds as if ready for jihad.[53] Nā'ib us-Salṭana ventured out of the citadel to reason with the crowd but was hostilely received and hastened away in a carriage.[54] The pressure of the crowd besieging the citadel became so great that

48 Taymūrī, *op. cit.*, p. 126.
49 *TB*, pp. 23–26; Feuvrier, *op. cit.*, p. 328.
50 Taymūrī, *op. cit.*, p. 135.
51 Feuvrier, *op. cit.*, p. 330.
52 Mulkārā, *op. cit.*, p. 117; *KhS*, p. 159.
53 *Ibid.*, p. 161; Feuvrier, *op. cit.*, p. 332; Mustaufī *op. cit.*, I, 472.
54 Mulkārā, *op. cit.*, p. 117.

ultimately the order to fire was given, and the demonstrators withdrew. The ulama instructed them to gather again the following day.[55] By then, however, Nāṣir ud-Dīn Shāh had been convinced of the impossibility of further upholding the tobacco monopoly and sent 'Aḍud ul-Mulk to meet Mīrzā Ḥasan Āshtiānī, with the present of a ring and the promise to annul the concession.[56]

Ironically enough, Mīrzā Ḥasan now threatened to leave the capital, and the Shah begged him to stay, fearing a further assault on the citadel.[57] Being assured of the government's intention to repeal the concession, however, on Jumādī ul-Ukhrā 5, 1309/January 26, 1892, he mounted the minbar and instructed the people to return to their normal occupations.[58] It was at the same time indicative of the earnestness of the whole movement that not until Jumādī ul-Ukhrā 25, 1309/January 6, 1892, after the government's intentions had been fully established, did a telegram arrive from Mīrzā Ḥasan Shīrāzī and put an end to the boycott.[59]

Thus after a direct and violent confrontation between the government and the people of Tehran, centered on the person of Mīrzā Ḥasan Āshtiānī, Nāṣir ud-Dīn Shāh was obliged to yield to the demands of the ulama. It is remarkable that certain accounts of the episode attempt to make Nāṣir ud-Dīn Shāh himself the instigator of the agitation. Thus Dūst 'Alī Khān Mu'ayyir ul-Mamālik, in his memoirs, writes that Nāṣir ud-Dīn Shāh, soon after granting the concession, regretted having done so because of the hostile reaction of the Russians. He therefore sent 'Alā ud-Daula to meet Mīrzā Ḥasan Shīrāzī in Samarra and requested him to issue a fatvā prohibiting the use of tobacco.[60] Yaḥyā Daulatābādī, in support of a similar thesis, adduces the hostility of Kāmrān Mīrzā Nā'ib us-Salṭana to Amīn us-Sulṭān; for Amīn us-Sulṭān being deeply involved in the granting of the tobacco concession, to have it repealed would be a major blow against him.[61] The British envoy Lascelles remarked also on the role played by court intrigue in the agitation, but concluded that it was a minor

55 *Ibid.*, p. 118; Feuvrier, *op. cit.*, p. 333.
56 *Ibid.*, p. 334; Taymūrī, *op. cit.*, p. 170; *KhS*, p. 163.
57 Feuvrier, *op. cit.*, p. 172.
58 Taymūrī, *op. cit.*, p. 172.
59 *Ibid.*, p. 192; Feuvrier, *op. cit.*, p. 339; *TB*, p. 45.
60 Dūst 'Alī Khān Mu'ayyir ul-Mamālik, *Yāddāshthā'ī az Zindagānī-yi Khuṣūṣī-yi Nāṣir ud-Dīn Shāh* (Tehran, n.d.), p. 177.
61 *HY*, I, 107–108.

one.[62] It seems highly unlikely that Nāṣir ud-Dīn Shāh should have embarked on the dangerous course of arousing a religious agitation that was bound to be directed against himself and his ṣadr-i a'ẓam. Daulatābādī suggests that the threat to expel Mīrzā Ḥasan Āshtīānī was a final maneuver, designed to convince the British embassy of the Shah's good intentions in supporting the tobacco concession, before finally appearing obliged to repeal it.[63] Despite Nāṣir ud-Dīn Shāh's lack of political acumen, he must have been aware of the danger involved in attempting the expulsion of a popular mujtahid, and unwilling to face that danger unless the attempt were serious. Moreover, the violent tone of his letter to Mīrzā Ḥasan Āshtīānī appears completely genuine. Mu'ayyir ul-Mamālik's account is probably motivated by a desire to free Nāṣir ud-Dīn Shāh from the odium attaching to an unpopular measure; that of Daulatābādī by a wish to minimize the initiative taken by the ulama.[64]

The resemblance of many features of the agitation to earlier events is striking. In the same way as Āqā Sayyid Muḥammad had in 1826 firmly and continuously insisted on jihad against Russia, Mīrzā Ḥasan showed great persistence in prohibiting the use of tobacco. After the murder of Griboyedov, the government had attempted to expel Ḥājjī Mīrzā Masīḥ from Tehran, and met with an angry response from the people of the capital; now the threat to banish Mīrzā Ḥasan Āshtīānī aroused similar fury. As before, the immediate object of the agitation was provided by the activities of foreigners, and it was at the same time directed against the state. The agitation against the tobacco monopoly, however, differed both in extent and quality from earlier displays of clerical power. The discontent that found expression was greater, and its direction firmer and more unified. The role of the ulama as de facto leaders of the nation against the state and its defenders against foreign encroachment was restated with new clarity.

Possibly, too, the agitation, for the first time, enabled foreign observers to realize the extent of clerical power in Iran. On December 24, 1891, Lascelles wrote to Salisbury, "it is evident that if the mollahs succeed in asserting their power and introduce a

62 Letter to Lord Salisbury, quoted by R. L. Greaves, "British Policy in Persia, 1892–1903," p. 39.

63 *HY*, I, 109.

64 As will be seen, his account of the constitutional movement has a similar tendency, though perhaps with greater justification.

fanatical and anti-European reign, we should have to give up all hope of seeing the regeneration of Persia by means of commercial enterprise."[65] At the same time, Lascelles wondered whether the agitation, apart from being an assertion of clerical power, was not at the same time "an expression of public opinion hitherto unknown in Persia."[66] Such considerations were to form the basis for later contacts between British diplomacy and certain of the ulama.

It is interesting to note two misconceptions of the nature of the agitation frequent in European, even diplomatic, accounts. First, the fatvā prohibiting the use of tobacco is meant to have declared it "unclean," presumably because of having passed through the hands of Christians and other non-Muslims.[67] As we have seen, however, the fatvā made no such declaration, nor do Persian accounts make any mention of it. The origin of the misconception is difficult to find; probably the general tendency to ascribe purely obscurantist, "fanatical" motives to the ulama was responsible. More important was the confusion in Enropean minds surrounding the function, whereabouts, and person of Mīrzā Ḥasan Shīrāzī. He is frequently referred to as "the High Priest of Kerbala."[68] Even Feuvrier, the Shah's French physician, imagined that he resided in Karbala, not Samarra.[69] Jamāl ud-Dīn Asadābādī, for his own reasons, saw fit to confirm the prevailing misconception and wrote that "the chief priest of Karbala" was "practically a Persian Pope."[70] The Tsar, for one, however, knew something of Mīrzā Ḥasan Shīrāzī's functions and whereabouts, and shortly after the repeal of the tobacco concession wrote to him, promising his assistance in favorably influencing the internal affairs of Iran.[71] British contact with the ulama of the 'atabāt for political purposes began somewhat later.

[65] Quoted by R. L. Greaves, *Persia and the Defence of India, 1884–1892* (London, 1959), p. 183.

[66] Quoted by Greaves, "British Policy in Persia, 1892–1903," p. 39.

[67] See, for example, Greaves, *Persia and the Defence of India*, p. 184; *Memorandum Respecting the Imperial Tobacco Corporation of Persia*, p. 7; A. H. S. Landor, *Across Coveted Lands* (London, 1902), I, 150; T. P. Brockway, "Britain and the Persian Bubble, 1888–1892," *Journal of Modern History*, XIII (1941), 43.

[68] See, for example, *Memorandum Respecting the Imperial Tobacco Corporation of Persia*, p. 8; T. E. Gordon, *Persia Revisited* (London, 1896), p. 26.

[69] Feuvrier, *op. cit.*, p. 314.

[70] Jamāl ud-Dīn Afghānī, "The Reign of Terror in Persia," *Contemporary Review*, LXI (1892), 246.

[71] Taymūrī, *op. cit.*, p. 204.

The immediate consequence within Iran of the successful conclusion was a noticeable increase in clerical power. Shortly after the ending of the boycott, Nāṣir ud-Dīn Shāh felt himself obliged to summon the ulama of Tehran, and thank them for "strengthening the foundations of the state," and promised thereafter to consult them on all important matters.[72] He also wrote flatteringly to Mīrzā Ḥasan Shīrāzī,[73] and when the death of the great mujtahid on Sha'ban 8, 1312/February 4, 1895, was accompanied by universal mourning, he felt it incumbent upon him to attend the commemorative ceremony in the Masjid-i Shāh.[74] Inwardly, however, he resented having had to yield to the ulama and complained bitterly of their influence to Amīn ud-Daula.[75]

Amīn us-Sulṭān's position was seriously weakened by the repeal of the tobacco concession, and in order to reinforce it he abandoned his close association with British policy and became instead a symbol of Russian ascendancy in Iran.[76] No less essential for his survival was a rapprochement with the clerical power that had just asserted itself so strikingly. His main collaborator among the ulama was, according to Amīn ud-Daula, none other than Mīrzā Ḥasan Āshtīānī who had led the agitation in Tehran against the tobacco monopoly.[77] It must be remembered that Amīn ud-Daula was hostile to both Amīn us-Sulṭān and Mīrzā Ḥasan Āshtīānī, and both appear to have played a part in frustrating his plans of reform when he was appointed ṣadr-i a'ẓam in Rajab, 1315/November-December, 1897. It is possible therefore that he makes the tactical alliance between the two men begin earlier that it in fact did. Amīn us-Sulṭān, far from allying himself with Mīrzā Ḥasan Āshtīānī, may have sought to avenge himself on him. Thus he incited Sayyid 'Alī Akbar Tafrashī to circulate rumors that Mīrzā Ḥasan Āshtīānī was receiving bribes from Ẓill us-Sulṭān.[78] It is not, however, impossible that an alliance, at least temporary, was formed between the two men. According to one account, Mīrzā Ḥasan Āshtīānī visited Mīrzā Ḥasan Shīrāzī in Samarra before the latter's death in an attempt to regain his "lost pres-

72 *Ibid.*, p. 195.
73 *Ibid.*, p. 201.
74 Mustaufī, *op. cit.*, I, 508; *HY*, I, 133.
75 *KhS*, p. 164.
76 Feuvrier, *op. cit.*, p. 343.
77 *KhS*, p. 253.
78 *HY*, I, 120–121.

tige";[79] this loss may well have been caused as much by connections with Amīn us-Sulṭān as by the rumors put about by Sayyid 'Ali Akbar Tafrashī. Such a reconciliation would have been similar to that partially effected between the ulama and Mīrzā Ḥusayn Khān Sipahsālār after the repeal of the Reuter Concession. In any event, Mīrzā Ḥasan's son, Mīrzā Muṣṭafā, later established a close relationship with Amīn us-Sulṭān.[80] In general, also, many of the more venal ulama appear to have become assimilated into the structure of corruption and oppression. Titles and allowances were lavished upon them, and their recommendation became essential for the success of any petition or request presented to the government.[81] The wealth and ambition of many of the earlier ulama—such as Sayyid Muḥammad Bāqir Shaftī—has already been noted. Their ambition was exercised primarily in opposition to the state, and their wealth constituted a firm basis for their independence of action. Now it seemed that the ulama were to become partners of the state in oppression.

The reasons for this are not far to seek. The increase in clerical influence brought about by the repeal of the tobacco concession whetted the appetites of many of the ulama. They sought to monopolize this source of influence, and their attempts to do so led to rivalry among them, in turn offering the state the possibility of intervention. An alliance between a minister and one of the prominent ulama might prove mutually beneficial. Thus the rivalry between Amīn us-Sulṭān and 'Ayn ud-Daula was later to be reflected in that between 'Abdullāh Bihbihānī and Shaykh Faḍlullāh Nūrī. On the other hand, the unity of the marja'-i taqlīd was unable to survive the death of Mīrzā Ḥasan Shīrāzī. Precisely because the power concentrated in the hands of the sole marja'-i taqlīd had been clearly demonstrated, many rival claimants arose, none of whom was able to assert his supremacy. In Tehran both Shaykh Faḍlullāh Nūrī and Mīrzā Ḥasan Āshtīānī claimed a'-lamīyat, but met with no positive response.[82] This virtual cessation of direction of the ulama further encouraged the state to make use of the rivalry existing among the leading mujtahids, who sought assistance in asserting their claims. Thus the appearance of an alliance arose.

79 *Ibid.*, p. 132.
80 *KhS*, p. 238.
81 *Ibid.*, p. 236; Mustaufī, *op. cit.*, I, 496–497.
82 *HY*, I, 133.

The alliance was, however, temporary, and no basic common interests existed. The attachment of certain of the ulama to rival representatives of secular power was to play its part in the events leading to the Constitutional Revolution, but this part was a minor one. When Amīn us-Sulṭān returned to office after his dismissal in late 1896, no basis remained for cooperation with the state.

A similar ambiguity—continuing rivalry between the state and the ulama and apparent alliance—can be observed in events in the provinces in the last years of Nāṣir ud-Dīn Shāh. In Khurasan, a group of ṭullāb, under the direction of Sayyid Zayn ul-'Ābidīn Sabzavārī, formed themselves into an armed band for the execution of clerical directives.[83] In Hamadan disturbances directed partly against the Jews but also against the government, broke out under the leadership of a certain Mullā 'Abdullāh; an army had to be sent to reduce the town to obedience.[84] Meanwhile in Isfahan, the traditional center of clerical resistance to the state, Āqā Najafī came to an understanding with Ẓill us-Sulṭān similar to that reached by Amīn us-Sulṭān and the ulama of Tehran. Reece, the British consul in Isfahan, reported on October 13, 1893: "As far as my information goes, the Zil os Sultan and Agha Nedjefy have formed a sort of partnership and have affected a corner in wheat. . . . The discontent has shown itself in the placing of placards on the walls of the bazaar and caravanserai doors, abusing Agha Nedjefy and calling him a wheat merchant. Amongst the people he is spoken of in most unmeasured terms, especially by those who a few weeks ago held him in the highest respect. It is a matter of common talk that he has now entirely become the servant of the prince."[85] Two weeks later, bread riots occurred, and Āqā Najafī, to free himself of blame for the artificial shortage, attempted to divert popular anger to Ẓill us-Sulṭān.[86] In 1898 the governor of Tabriz was in similar circumstances to use the same tactics against the ulama, though less successfully.[87] We see then that there was no firm basis for cooperation between the state and

[83] *KhS*, p. 167.

[84] Ḥabīb Levi, *Tārīkh-i Yahūd-i Īrān* (Tehran, 1339 Sh/1960–1961), III, 757.

[85] Report to Lascelles, contained in F.O. 60/543. See also Mihdī Malikzāda, *Tārīkh-i Inqilāb-i Mashrūṭīyat-i Īrān* (Tehran, 1327 Sh/1948–1949), I, 166.

[86] See Reece's reports dated October 28 and 30, 1893, in F.O. 60/543.

[87] See report of C. G. Wood, British consul in Tabriz, dated September 19, 1898, contained in F.O. 60/598.

the ulama, even when they had a common aim. At the same time, the ulama must have lost an amount of the respect they had previously enjoyed. Although this loss was not serious enough to deprive them of their essential function of leading and expressing popular discontent, it nonetheless earned them suspicion during the constitutional movement, as will be shown.

When in 1896 the bullet fired by Mīrzā Riḍā Kirmānī put an end to the reign of Nāṣir ud-Dīn Shāh, Iran was in a condition of anarchy, corruption, and poverty. The discontent bred thereby was to increase continuously in the reign of his successor, and with it the predominant political role of the ulama. The ascendancy gained by the ulama through the repeal of the tobacco concession was not immediately exploited by them for any serious attempt at weakening the Qajar dynasty. Indeed there appeared to be even cooperation between ulama and state. This cooperation had, however, no firm basis, and when Russian economic influence came to threaten the independence of Iran, the example of the agitation against the tobacco concession was not forgotten. Appeals in religious terms, expressed by religious leaders, brought about the movement against the Qajar monarchy known as the Constitutional Revolution. The events of January, 1892, foreshadowed this mass agitation.

XIII

The Clerical Opposition to Amīn ud-Daula and Amīn us-Sulṭān (1896-1903)

On Dhū-l-Ḥijja 25, 1313/June 8, 1896, Muẓaffar ud-Dīn Shāh entered his capital, and soon after, with the expenses of his coronation defrayed by a loan from the Imperial Bank, was able to mount the throne.[1] This financial weakness, the result of the extravagance of Nāṣir ud-Dīn Shāh and the mismanagement of Amīn us-Sulṭān, was to prove the chief source of unrest in the reign of Muẓaffar ud-Dīn Shāh. For impecunity, together with continuing extravagance, led to the necessity of foreign loans, and these in turn to the entrenchment of Russian economic influence. Resentment felt at the growth of this influence brought together again the ulama and the merchants in opposition to the government. The movement that was to develop into the Constitutional Revolution had its origin in the traditional dual role of the ulama—resistance to foreign encroachment and to the power of the state. Events, now to be discussed, caused this role to be fulfilled with a greater determination and seriousness, ultimately leading to an unprecedented clash between the power of the ulama and that of the state.

[1] *KhS*, p. 222.

The first year of the new reign brought little development. Amīn us-Sulṭān retained his position as ṣadr-i a'ẓam, and when he was displaced on Jumādī ul-Ukhrā 17, 1314/November 24, 1896, by 'Abd ul-Ḥusayn Mīrzā Farmānfarmā,[2] his successor followed similar policies with respect to the ulama. According to Amīn ud-Daula, meetings of the cabinet were attended by representatives of the ulama, and their fatvās determined the appointment and dismissal of provincial governors and other officials.[3]

In the middle of 1897, Amīn ud-Daula resigned his appointment as vazīr to the governor of Azerbayjan, and coming to Tehran was prevailed upon to head the cabinet, being formally appointed ṣadr-i a'ẓam toward the end of the year.[4] With his appointment open conflict between ulama and state recommenced. This was inevitable, for like earlier reformers, notably Amīr Kabīr and Mīrzā Ḥusayn Khān Sipahsālār, Amīn ud-Daula opposed, as a matter of principle, the intervention of the clerical classes in matters of state. The fact that they found occasion to do so he attributed to the corruption and injustice of the administration, and hence if the administration were to be reformed, they would no longer have any legitimate concern with political affairs.[5] In fact, one of the secondary results of the introduction of a constitutional form of government would be to wipe out their influence, and therefore—Amīn ud-Daula concluded—they represented the greatest obstacle to reform.[6] A contemporary summarizes his policy as separation of political and religious power.[7] Such a policy was bound to meet clerical opposition.

Shortly after Amīn ud-Daula became chief minister, the ulama brought pressure to bear on him to dismiss the governors of Khurasan and Arabistan for their disrespect to the ulama and failure to obey clerical directives. The governor of Arabistan, 'Alā ud-Daula, eventually fled of his own accord, but Amīn ud-Daula refused to dismiss Ghulām Riḍā Īnānlū Āṣaf ud-Daula, governor of Khurasan.[8] Indeed he rejected any intervention of the ulama in the affairs of state, whether in the capital or provinces.

2 *Ibid.*, p. 228.
3 *Ibid.*, p. 331.
4 *Ibid.*, p. 235.
5 See his remarks to Nāṣir ud-Dīn Shāh after the repeal of the tobacco concession (*KhS*, p. 164).
6 *Ibid.*, p. 272.
7 *HY*, I, 207.
8 *KhS*, pp. 235–236, 243.

Probably the most important achievement of his short term of office was the encouragement given to education, and the establishment of primary schools of European type in Tehran, under the direction of the Anjuman-i Maʻārif (Council on Education). While governor of Azerbayjan, he had invited back to Tabriz Mīrzā Ḥasan Rushdīya, the founder of a school (called Rushdīya) which taught the alphabet according to new methods. Mīrzā Ḥasan had been pronounced an infidel by the ulama, and his school destroyed by a mob of ṭullāb, but now under the protection of Amīn ud-Daula he was able to reestablish it in security.[9]

Now that Amīn ud-Daula was ṣadr-i aʻẓam, he brought the declared infidel to Tehran to establish a school modeled on the Tabriz Rushdīya.[10] Among the ulama, it was particularly Mīrzā Ḥasan Āshtīānī who opposed the new type of school, declaring that it would bring about a weakening of religious faith.[11] The reasons for the opposition of the ulama to the new schools are many. Mīrzā Ḥasan Āshtīānī doubtless regarded the question as another means of arousing hostility to Amīn ud-Daula, in retaliation for his disregard of the ulama's requests and pleadings. It is also possible that the new type of school was popularly confused with the missionary schools of Tehran and Tabriz, and hence conceived of as hostile to the faith. Above all, the opposition of many of the ulama to the Rushdīya should be interpreted as a defense of their traditional privileges and functions. In the same way as the extension of ʻurf jurisdiction restricted their judicial power, the new kind of school represented an intrusion into another traditional domain of the ulama, one where their monopoly had been almost complete: that of education. The open enmity of the ulama was largely countered through the establishment of the Islām school by Sayyid Muḥammad Ṭabāṭā'ī, himself one of the leading ulama of the capital.[12]

Amīn us-Sulṭān, by no means resigned to a compulsory retirement in Qum, now allied himself with certain of the discontented ulama to bring about Amīn ud-Daula's fall from power.[13]

9 See M. Mujtahidī, *Rijāl-i Ādharbāyjān dar ʻAṣr-i Mashrūṭīyat* (Tehran, 1327 Sh/1948–1949), pp. 77–80; Mihdī Malikzāda, *Tārīkh-i Inqilāb-i Mashrūṭīyat-i Īrān* (Tehran, 1327 Sh/1948–1949), I, 150.

10 Malikzāda, *op. cit.*, I, 151; *TM*, p. 21.

11 Malikzāda, *op. cit.*, I, 154.

12 Ibrāhīm Ṣafā'ī, *Rahbarān-i Mashrūṭa IV: Sayyid ʻAbdullāh Bihbihānī va Sayyid Muḥammad Ṭabāṭabā'ī* (Tehran, 1343 Sh/1964), p. 34.

13 *TB*, p. 125.

'Abdullāh Bihbihānī, despite his previous and subsequent contacts with Amīn us-Sulṭān, appears to have taken no prominent part in the agitation. The leading role was taken by Mīrzā Ḥasan Āshtīānī, assisted by his son, Mīrzā Muṣṭafā.[14] Amīn us-Sulṭān deputed his brother, Shaykh Ismā'īl Amīn ul-Mulk, to distribute money among the ulama of the capital and thus fortify their hostility to Amīn ud-Daula.[15] A number of them gathered in the Madrasa-yi Marvī, threatening to leave for the 'atabāt, unless further endowments were granted to the madrasa.[16] Although Amīn ud-Daula refused their demands, they refrained from emigrating. Similarly, Mīrzā Ḥasan Ashtīānī one day remarked that it was becoming impossible for him to remain in Tehran, and that he was contemplating emigration to the 'atabāt. Clearly he was hoping for a repetition of the violent incidents surrounding the attempt at banishing him during the agitation against the tobacco concession, or at least that Amīn ud-Daula would fear such a repetition. On this occasion, he paid no attention to the threats of emigration.[17] Nonetheless, sensing the mounting pressure against him, on Muḥarram 15, 1316/ June 4, 1898, he resigned from office, and soon after, Amīn us-Sulṭān resumed his normal sway.[18]

Although Amīn us-Sulṭān had thus regained power partly through clerical pressure, he was himself destined to be the target of far more serious agitation. 'Abd ul-Ḥusayn Mīrzā Farmānfarmā, at the beginning of Amīn us-Sulṭān's second ministry, gave financial encouragement to the ulama of Tehran to bring about his dismissal,[19] but the reasons for their opposition lay rather in his policies toward Russia. During the ministry of Amīn ud-Daula, Muẓaffar ud-Dīn Shāh, encouraged by his personal physician, Ḥakīm ul-Mulk, had begun to plan a trip to Europe, ostensibly for medical reasons. In order to cover the expenses of the projected journey, Amīn ud-Daula had attempted to negotiate a loan, first from governments with no direct interests in Iran, and then from

[14] *KhS*, p. 253. Ibrāhīm Ṣafā'ī (*Rahbarān-i Mashrūṭa III: Mīrzā 'Alī Khān Amīn ud-Daula* [Tehran, 1342 Sh/1963], p. 22) states that Mīrzā Ḥasan went so far as to declare Amīn ud-Daula an infidel, giving as reference this same page of the *Khāṭirāt*. It contains, however, no mention of takfīr.

[15] *KhS*, p. 237.

[16] *HY*, I, 207–208.

[17] *KhS*, p. 254.

[18] *Ibid.*, p. 273.

[19] *TB*, p. 128.

Britain, but without success.[20] Amīn us-Sulṭān, on the other hand, in 1317/1900 negotiated a loan of 2½ million rubles from the Russian government, with interest at 5 percent, to be repaid within seventy-five years. Among the conditions attached to the loan was one to the effect that Iran should not contract debts to any other government until it was repaid.[21] The threat of foreign financial domination thus came closer to Iran, and this, together with the extravagant spending of the borrowed money on the European trip of 1900, aroused the combined hostility of the ulama and the merchants, much as the tobacco concession had done previously.

Perhaps even more than the Russian loan, the activities of a certain Naus aroused resentment at Amīn us-Sulṭān's policies. Shortly before his dismissal, Amīn ud-Daula had brought to Iran a number of Belgians, among them Naus, to reorganize the customs on European lines. Naus held the post of Director-General of Customs and was responsible to the ṣadr-i a'ẓam. In 1900, when Amīn us-Sulṭān accompanied the Shah to Europe, Naus was appointed Minister of Customs, with full powers and responsibilities.[22] He had meanwhile become, like Amīn us-Sulṭān, closely associated with Russian policy,[23] and was to be a living symbol of foreign economic domination until the early days of the constitutional movement.

During Muẓaffar ud-Dīn Shāh's first absence in Europe, protests were raised against both Amīn us-Sulṭān and Naus. In these protests we see again an alliance between the merchants and the ulama.[24] The merchants considered the new customs tariffs harmful to their interests, and accused the Belgians moreover of discriminating in favor of Armenian and other non-Muslim merchants.[25] As for the ulama, their opposition to the assumption of a ministry by a non-Muslim foreigner was inevitable. Foreign dominance was a danger feared by both, and their cooperation in opposing it natural.

If later the ulama were the chief opponents of Amīn us-Sulṭān, initially they were only one among the elements opposed to him.

20 *Khs*, p. 260.
21 *TM*, pp. 24–25.
22 *Ibid.*, p. 29.
23 *KhS*, p. 276.
24 *TM*, p. 29.
25 *Loc. cit.* According to *TB* (p. 187), Naus used his influence to secure the employment of his Jewish coreligionaries in government offices.

His hostility to the Anjuman-i Ma'ārif and the Rushdīya school, founded under the aegis of Amīn ud-Daula, had caused the latter to become a center of agitation against him.[26] Pamphlets attacking his policies were distributed, until a number of those responsible were discovered and arrested.[27] Such pamphlets, however, were not the product of the Rushdīya group alone: after its dissolution, other pamphlets appeared attacking Amīn us-Sulṭān, which Naus attributed to the "Pan-Islamists," though not specifically to the ulama.[28]

We see already how wide was the basis of opposition to the government, and how closely intertwined were the ulama and the other opponents of the regime in agitating against it. Hardinge, the British ambassador, reported on September 6, 1901, that the events leading to the arrest of the Rushdīya group had been inspired by opponents of Amīn us-Sulṭān and also by Pan-Islamists. According to one of his informants, the meeting place for the two elements was a masonic lodge in Tehran, which "numbers among its members certain persons who take advantage of it for purposes utterly alien to the principles of freemasonry, and seek to use it as a bond of union between the aristocratical miscontents of the Court and Opposition parties, and Mahommedan fanatics and revolutionists whose views and objectives are entirely different."[29] The confusion surrounding the aims of the secret societies and the ulama in the Constitutional Revolution thus resulted in part from the continuation of earlier coalitions. The complexity of the matter is further increased by the nature of Pan-Islamism, which, though self-evidently religious in inspiration, did not claim the loyalty of all the ulama, nor provide the ultimate basis for their policy toward the state.

During the second ministry of Amīn us-Sulṭān, however, the opposition of the ulama to the state was expressed partly in Pan-Islamic terms; the period from 1900 to 1903 was that of the greatest political effectiveness of Pan-Islam in Iran. Sayyid Jamāl ud-Dīn Asadābādī had died on Shavvāl 5, 1314/March 9, 1897, and the original group working under his direction in Istanbul to attract Shi'i support for unity under the Ottoman sultan-caliph had been

26 *TM*, pp. 25–26.
27 *Ibid.*, p. 26.
28 Hardinge's dispatch dated August 18, 1901, in F.O. 60/637.
29 Report dated September 6, 1901, in F.O. 60/637.

dissolved even earlier.[30] Sultan 'Abd ul-Ḥamīd continued his efforts to gain support among the Shi'i ulama, both at the 'atabāt and in Iran. In Tehran the Ottoman ambassador, Shams ud-Dīn Bey, managed to establish close and friendly relations with the ulama of the capital, and in addition a certain Shaykh Muḥammad Abū Ṭālib Zanjānī acted as intermediary between the Ottomans and the Iranian ulama.[31] Meanwhile, contact was more easily established with the 'atabāt, which lay in Ottoman territory. The prestige and authority that had been won for Mīrzā Ḥasan Shīrāzī by the repeal of the tobacco concession had doubtless also impressed the Ottoman government, and although the unity of the marja'-i taqlīd was not preserved, something of the same prestige was kept by the 'atabāt as a whole. Particular respect was shown to Shaykh Muḥammad Fāḍil Sharabīānī, one of the most prominent mujtahids to emerge after the death of Mīrzā Ḥasan Shīrāzī: the Sultan gave instructions that the Shaykh might daily send, free of charge, a telegram of up to forty words to Istanbul.[32]

There appears to have been no serious attempt at doctrinal rapprochement between Sunnī and Shi'i. Hostility had abated to a point where Shi'i travelers and pilgrims in Ottoman territory were no longer obliged to practice taqīya,[33] but further steps toward unity in matters of faith and practice were not taken. Practical cooperation required no such unity, and it was above all for unity in political action that Pan-Islamists such as Abū-l-Ḥasan Mīrzā Shaykh ur-Ra'īs called. In his tract, *Ittiḥād-i Islām*, probably the best reformist treatment in Persian of Islamic problems in the nineteenth century, he proposes union of Iran and the Ottoman Empire under the Sultan, recalling that in the early days of Islam, 'Umar and 'Alī, around whom so many later controversies were centered, worked together for the progress of the faith.[34] Similar

30 See *HY*, I, 99.

31 See Sir Arthur Hardinge, *A Diplomatist in the East* (London, 1928), pp. 273–274. Shaykh Muḥammad, in July, 1903, expressed disappointment at the results of his work (see *Further Correspondence Respecting the Affairs of Persia and Arabia, July–September 1903*, p. 158 in F.O. 416/14).

32 Muḥammad 'Alī Tabrīzī Khiābānī, *Rayḥānat ul-Adab* (Tehran, 1326 Sh/1947–1948), II, 302–303.

33 Mīrzā Muḥammad Ḥasan Khān I'timād us-Salṭana, *al Ma'āthir va-l-Āthār* (Tehran, 1306 Q/1889), p. 107; and Mīrzā Ḥusayn Farāhānī, *Safarnāma*, ed. Ḥāfiẓ Farmānfarmā'īān (Tehran, 1342 Sh/1963), p. 242.

34 Mīrzā Abū-l-Qāsim Shaykh ur-Ra'īs, *Ittiḥād-i Islām* (Bombay, 1312 Q/1894–1895), pp. 55–56.

cooperation was again necessary to save Islam, the very survival of which seemed to be in question.[35] Naturally, that aspect of Islam thus endangered was its outward one, the existence of the community; hence the appeal of Pan-Islam was primarily political, though ultimately no meaningful separation of political and religious spheres in Islam is possible.

This feeling of danger threatening Islam, noted above in connection with the Reuter and tobacco concessions, together with the situation of the 'atabāt in Ottoman territory, secured Pan-Islam a measure of acceptance in Iran. Hardinge wrote in September, 1901, that although few of the mujtahids were in sympathy, "it is gaining strength daily . . . among the students both of the theological and secular schools, the former . . . being attracted by its religious, the latter by its democratic aspect."[36] The reserve of most mujtahids with respect to Pan-Islam is significant: better acquainted with Shi'i doctrine than the ṭullāb, their understanding of the obstacles to cooperation probably helped to prevent their participation. Although some mujtahids worked for Pan-Islam, its political life in Iran was short. When in 1904, the Shi'i ulama of the 'atabāt began corresponding with the Shi'is of the Caucasus and Central Asia, Russia brought pressure to bear on the Ottoman government, and the ulama were obliged to cease their correspondence, both with the Russian Empire and Iran, under pain of banishment to Medina.[37] This practically ended the political significance of Pan-Islamism in Iran.[38] The cooperation with it of the Shi'i ulama was largely tactical, and their preoccupation was with the problems of Iran. Pan-Islam does not appear as a motive in the Constitutional Revolution. Its effectiveness was virtually limited to the period of the agitation against Amīn us-Sulṭān.

The first journey to Europe had been accomplished without any serious disturbances taking place in Iran, and the opposition centered on the Rushdīya temporarily dispersed. Amīn us-Sulṭān's policy, however, tended as before to the establishment of Russian

[35] *Ibid.*, pp. 51–52.

[36] Report contained in F.O. 60/637.

[37] See reports dated May 27 and June 10, 1904, of British vice-consul in Karbala, in *Further Correspondence Respecting the Affairs of Persia and Arabia*, Part XIX, pp. 14, 102, in F.O. 416/19.

[38] It is true that in 1914 the ulama of the 'atabāt issued a fatvā demanding the entry of Iran into the war on the side of the Ottoman Empire and the Central Powers, but political considerations other than Pan-Islam influenced their action. See L. I. Miroshnikov, *Iran in World War I* (Moscow, 1964), p. 40.

ascendancy. One of the results of this growing Russian influence was a recrudescence of antagonism to the Bahā'īs. One of the chief centers of Bahā'ī activity, Ashkhabad, lay, since the conquest of Transcaspia, in Russian territory, and Bahā'īs were widely held to be agents of Russian policy in Iran.[39] At the same time, tentative attempts were made by Bahā'īs to establish friendly contact with Muẓaffar ud-Dīn Shāh, and to present themselves as allies of the state against the ulama.[40] The charge of Bahā'ism, true or false, was frequently used against personal enemies, especially by the ulama; now that Bahā'ism appeared to be identified with both foreign encroachment and with the treacherous regime that permitted this encroachment, a violent reaction was bound to follow. This too would be expressed and directed by the ulama.

Amīn us-Sulṭān was contemplating the request of another loan to pay for a further royal excursion to the pleasure grounds of Europe.[41] In February, 1902, rumors of the proposed loan began to circulate in Tehran, and the ulama to protest against it as a further surrender of Iran to foreign interests. A letter was sent by them to the Shah, accusing him, among other offenses, of being "about to sell the government and faith of Persia to Christians, by your own whim and caprice," and reproaching him for entrusting the government to Amīn us-Sulṭān, "the son of a Georgian."[42] Bribery was applied in order to lessen clerical hostility to the proposed loan, but without notable success.[43] Among the conditions reputedly attached to the grant of the loan was the establishment of a Russian-controlled fisheries monopoly in Gilan, and this aroused the immediate opposition of Ḥājjī Muḥammad Rafī' Sharī'atmadār, the chief mujtahid of Gilan. In early April, 1902, he came from Rasht to Tehran to coordinate opposition to the loan with

[39] *HY*, I, 315.

[40] This thesis was put forward by 'Abbās Efendi in his *Risāla-yi Siyāsīya*. See H. Roehmer, *Die Babi-Behai* (Potsdam, 1912), p. 158, according to whom there even existed a secret pact between Muẓaffar ud-Dīn Shāh and the Bahā'īs (*ibid.*, p. 155). See also H. Dreyfus, "Les Béhaïs et le Mouvement Actuel en Perse," *RMM*, I (1906), 198–206.

[41] *TM*, p. 29.

[42] Hardinge's dispatch of February 4, 1902, in F.O. 60/650. Amīn us-Sulṭān's mother was a Georgian, although he was sometimes thought to be of Armenian origin (see *TM*, p. 26).

[43] Hardinge's dispatch of same date. Malikzāda (*op. cit.*, I, 157) claims that on the contrary the bribery was successful. Clerical opposition to Amīn ud-Sulṭān steadily increased, however.

the ulama of the capital.[44] Furthermore, a concession was to be granted to a Russian company to construct a road from the border at Julfā to Tabriz, and the ulama of Tabriz raised their voices in protest.[45] In April, Muẓaffar ud-Dīn Shāh and Amīn us-Sulṭān left for Europe, and such was the hostility of the ulama that they refused to bid the Shah farewell. Indeed threats were voiced that "the Shah, on his return from Europe, would not be permitted to re-enter his domains unless he signed a pledge to grant no further concessions to Russia."[46] Evidently the loan agreement had already been signed, but not publicly announced, and the ulama sent a circular to foreign legations, requesting their intervention to prevent the Russian loan from being granted.[47]

Among the ulama present in Tehran during the absence of the Shah in Europe was Āqā Najafī, who appears to have led this stage of the ulama's opposition to the government.[48] He was in contact with Sharabīānī in Najaf,[49] and together with other of the ulama is reputed to have supported Pan-Islamic proposals for the recognition of Sultan 'Abd ul-Ḥamīd as supreme head of the Muslim world.[50] In the following events leading to the fall of Amīn us-Sulṭān, the influence of the 'atabāt became more apparent, and the Ottoman government, in accordance with its policy of promoting Pan-Islam, allowed this influence to continue unchecked until the application of pressure by the Russian government in 1904.

44 Hardinge's dispatch of April 2, 1902, in F.O. 60/650. On Sharī'atmadār, see Muḥammad Mihdī Kāẓimī, *Aḥsan al-Wadī'a* (Baghdad, 1347 Q/1928–1929), I, 75.

45 *TM*, p. 27. Mīrzā Āqā Javād had similarly opposed the construction of a road by the Russians from Rasht to Tabriz (see T. E. Gordon, *Persia Revisited* [London, 1896], p. 26).

46 Hardinge's dispatch of May 19, 1902, in F.O. 60/650. Clearly, the agitation against Mīrzā Ḥusayn Khān in similar circumstances had not been forgotten.

47 *Ibid.*

48 Dispatch of May 5, 1902, in F.O. 60/650.

49 See *Further Correspondence Respecting the Affairs of Persia and Arabia, July–September 1903*, p. 364, in F.O. 416/14.

50 Dispatch of May 5; E. G. Browne, *The Persian Revolution of 1905–1909* (Cambridge, 1910), pp. 107–108. Allegedly Āqā Najafī received a telegram from Sultan 'Abd ul-Ḥamīd himself, promising his support whenever needed (*Further Correspondence, July–September 1903*, p. 379). It seems probable that the ulama esteemed 'Abd ul-Ḥamīd little higher than they did Nāṣir ud-Dīn Shāh. Once a certain Arab reproached Mīrzā Ḥasan Āshtīānī for having excessive patience in enduring the rule of Nāṣir ud-Dīn Shāh. He replied, "You idiot! And who is your leader modelling himself on? On Abu Bakr, 'Uthmān, 'Umar? Why do you submit to him?" (see V. A. Kosogovsky, *Iz Tegeranskovo Dnevnika* [Moscow, 1960], pp. 48–49).

Coordination of policy between the ulama of Iran and those at the ʻatabāt was at least as effective as it had been during the agitation against the tobacco concession.

The ulama had failed to prevent the Russian loan, but on the Shah's return from Europe, their agitation against Amīn us-Sulṭān and his policies was intensified. In Tehran Āqā Sayyid ʻAlī Akbar Tafrashī, Sayyid Muḥammad Ṭabāṭabā'ī, and Mīrzā Abū-l-Qāsim Ṭabāṭabā'ī joined forces to work for his overthrow.[51] Later Shaykh Faḍlullāh Nūrī also joined the clerical coalition against Amīn us-Sulṭān.[52] The first serious disturbances, however, occurred not in Tehran but in the provinces.

In June, 1902, demands were sent from the mujtahids of Najaf to the Iranian government for the publication of an exact account of how the Russian loan had been spent; for the prohibition of the sale of alcohol; and for the suppression of the Bahā'īs.[53] The first item was passed over in silence, but the other two accepted. There then followed a persecution of the Bahā'īs, primarily in Isfahan, a fact that points to a probable arrangement made between Sharabīānī and Āqā Najafī. The government doubtless considered the persecution a suitable means of distracting popular attention from the more important question of the Russian loans.[54] This purpose may well have been attained, at least temporarily, for it was not until the following year that clerically inspired disturbances broke out again, this time in Tabriz.

In Rabīʻ uth-Thānī, 1321/June, 1903, a certain Mullā Mīrzā ʻAlī Akbar was passing by a wineshop in Tabriz when a drunkard emerged and offered him a glass of wine. On the pretext that the ulama had been insulted thereby, he went to the house of Ḥājjī Mīrzā Ḥasan Mujtahid, son and successor of Mīrzā Āqā Javād,

51 *KhS*, p. 281, and *TB*, p. 130. The latter mentions the imām jumʻa of Tehran as being among the conspirators against Amīn us-Sulṭān. It is true that his son, Mīrzā Abū-l-Qāsim, was an opponent of Amīn us-Sulṭān, but he did not inherit the title of imām jumʻa until the death of Mīrzā Zayn ul-ʻĀbidīn on Dhū-l-Qaʻda 16, 1321/February 3, 1904, i.e., about four months after the dismissal of Amīn us-Sulṭān. See Dūst ʻAlī Khān Muʻayyir ul-Mamālik, "Sayyid Zayn ul-ʻĀbidīn Imām Jumʻa," *Yaghmā*, XII (1338 Sh/1959–1960), 567.

52 *TM*, p. 31. According to *TB* (p. 130), Amīn us-Sulṭān earned his hostility by refusing to pay off various debts he had incurred.

53 *HY*, I, 315, where he considers these demands British-inspired. The British role in events is discussed below.

54 *Ibid.*, I, 316–319. The persecution coincided significantly with the conclusion of a new Perso-Russian customs agreement, giving Russian trade a privileged position in Iran. See Browne, *op. cit.*, p. 106, and *TM*, p. 35.

and with him went to the Masjid-i Shāhzāda, gathering a number of the ulama on the way. The merchants of Tabriz, angered at the conduct of the Belgian customs officer in the town, Priem, joined the protest meeting. The protest was directed against certain symbols of foreign influence in the town: schools, hotels, wineshops. Muḥammad 'Alī Mīrzā, governor of Azerbayjan, was obliged to yield to the combined protests of the merchants and the ulama, and the ṭullāb were permitted to destroy the objectionable buildings. Priem himself was obliged to flee from the town.[55] When the disorders had subsided, he was able to return, and Ḥājjī Mīrzā Ḥasan was expelled in his turn, to receive a triumphal welcome from the ulama and people of Tehran.[56]

The incident is interesting as an illustration of the ulama's diligence in making use of, even searching for, pretexts for gathering in protest against the government. So widespread and deep was the discontent that, the pretext having been found, support gathered almost instantaneously around the ulama. During the ministry of 'Ayn ud-Daula, the amazing readiness of the government to supply the ulama with such pretexts was matched only by their alacrity in seizing them. Thus the traditional role of the ulama—the development, expression, and direction of popular protest—was fulfilled with remarkable ease and effectiveness.

It is probable that the mujtahids of the 'atabāt, notably Sharabīānī, were connected with these disturbances as well as those in Isfahan, although they explicitly denied any responsibility, claiming even to have ordered the cessation of agitation in Tabriz.[57] The impression made on both Muẓaffar ud-Dīn Shāh and Amīn us-Sulṭān was great. Hardinge wrote on June 4, 1903, that "the Shah and the Grand Vizier are a good deal afraid of the priesthood, and this fear may go a long way to prevent their contracting, for purely selfish and personal reasons, a third loan from Russia. . . ."[58]

55 *Ibid.*, p. 30; *Further Correspondence, July–September 1903*, p. 33.

56 *Ibid.*, p. 217; *TM*, p. 30.

57 See report of Stevens, consul in Tabriz, dated June 25, 1903, in *Further Correspondence, July–September 1903*, pp. 159–160, according to whom Russo-Belgian economic interests in the city were so dominant that they had almost gained control of the city's bakeries; Hardinge's dispatch of July 9 (*ibid.*, p. 161); and letter of Newmarch, Political Agent in Baghdad, to Hardinge, dated July 29 (*ibid.*, p. 111). According to Browne (*op. cit.*, p. 107), Ḥājjī Mīrzā Ḥasan produced letters, purporting to be from the 'atabāt, demanding the closure of schools, hotels, etc.

58 See *Further Correspondence, July–September 1903*, p. 37.

Mushāvir ul-Mulk, the Iranian consul in Baghdad, visited the chief mujtahids of Najaf (Fāḍil Sharabīānī, Fāḍil Mamaqānī,[59] Mīrzā Ḥusayn Khalīlī, and Mullā Kāẓim Khurāsānī), in order to assure them that the reports they had heard about the growth of Russian influence in Iran were unfounded. Sharabīānī is reputed to have replied that if satisfaction were not given to the demands of the ulama, "we will remove the present dog [Muẓaffar ud-Dīn Shāh] and put another dog in his place."[60]

It is thus clear that the ulama were by now fully conscious of their power in the situation created by Amīn us-Sulṭān's involvement with the Russians, and having long since abandoned the restraint shown by Shaykh Murtaḍā Anṣārī and Mīrzā Ḥasan Shīrāzī, were prepared to work for the overthrow of the monarchy. Previously, their power had been exercised for specific purposes against specific targets, although the basic contradiction between religious and secular power had always existed. Now it was to be used against the monarchy itself. In this sense also, the Constitutional Revolution is the culmination of a process: the doctrinally-based enmity of the ulama to the monarchy was intensified in practice as the danger of foreign dominance increased. The policies of Amīn us-Sulṭān helped to increase that danger, and with it the depth and seriousness of clerical opposition to the state.

In Jumādī ul-Ukhrā, 1321/September–October, 1903, rumors arose in Tehran that Amīn us-Sulṭān had been declared an infidel by the ulama of Najaf.[61] The origin of this takfīr, like that of the fatvā prohibiting the use of tobacco, has been disputed, and no final verdict appears possible. The mujtahids of Najaf denied the attribution to them of the takfīrnāma circulated in Tehran,[62] and various suggestions have been made that it was forged. Thus Daulatābādī claims that the British attempted to obtain the takfīr

59 About a year later, Fāḍil Mamaqānī went on pilgrimage to Mashhad. His progress through Iran was marked by disorder. He declared ḥarām the tolls levied on the Bushihr-Qum highway and refused to pay them; he ostentatiously avoided Tehran, because of the presence in it of Muẓaffar ud-Shāh (see Hardinge, *A Diplomatist in the East*, p. 321).

60 Hardinge's dispatch of July 21, 1903, in *Further Correspondence, July–September 1903*, p. 176.

61 *TM*, p. 32. *TB* (p. 129) erroneously places the takfīr after Muẓaffar ud-Dīn Shāh's return from his first European journey.

62 See Hardinge's dispatch of December 30, 1903, in *Further Correspondence Respecting the Affairs of Persia and Arabia*, Part XVI, in F.O. 416/16. Amīn ud-Daula (*KhS*, p. 281) supports the attribution.

of Amīn us-Sulṭān from the mujtahids of Najaf, and having failed to do so, proceeded to forge a takfīrnāma in their name.[63] Naturally a certain community of interest existed between the ulama and the British, and restricted contacts, now to be discussed, took place; but these were marked by extreme caution on both sides, and diplomatic correspondence of the period gives no indication of pressure on the ulama to obtain takfīr. It is possible that other elements hostile to Amīn us-Sulṭān were responsible for the takfīrnāma: its text was not published until after his dismissal, by Sayyid Muḥammad 'Alī, brother of Mu'bid ul-Islām Kāshānī, owner of the newspaper *Ḥabl ul-Matīn*,[64] and copies of it were circulated in Tehran and the provinces.[65] Whether or not the takfīr emanated from Najaf, the effect of the rumors, occurring as they did in an atmosphere of mounting clerical hostility to the government, was doubtless great, and yielding to the agitation, Muẓaffar ud-Dīn Shāh dismissed Amīn us-Sulṭān from office toward the end of Jumādī ul-Ukhrā, 1321/early September, 1903.[66]

Allusion has been made to contacts between the ulama, particularly those of the 'atabāt, and British diplomats. Certain modern Iranian historians, of whom Maḥmūd Maḥmūd is an example, see in the Constitutional Revolution above all a product of British policy, designed to defeat Russian designs and reestablish British ascendancy in Iran, and they assign to the ulama a prime role in the execution of this plan.[67] Clearly, such considerations are important in determining the real role of the ulama in the Constitutional

63 *HY*, I, 323. Maḥmūd Maḥmūd (*TRS*, VI, 1687, 1695, VII, 1912), although considering the takfīrnāma genuine, also attributes it to British policy. He adduces in support of this Hardinge's visit to the 'atabāt, and a passage in a book called *The Middle Eastern Question or Some Political Problems of Indian Defence*, by V. Chirol (London, 1903). Hardinge first saw the takfīrnāma while in Bandar 'Abbās at the end of 1903, i.e., after the dismissal of Amīn us-Sulṭān (at least according to his own account in *A Diplomatist in the East*, p. 307); while the passage in question in Chirol's book (p. 109) appears to be nothing more than a prediction inspired by the course of events, and not a proposal for action. The Russians similarly attributed the takfīr to British machinations (see *Novoye Vremya* for September 7, 1903, quoted by Ibrāhīm Taymūrī, *'Aṣr-i Bīkhabarī yā Tārīkh-i Imtiyāzāt dar Īrān* [Tehran, 1336 Sh/1957], p. 76).

64 The *Ḥabl ul-Matīn* was published in Calcutta, and originally presented Pan-Islamist views (see E. G. Browne, *The Press and Poetry of Modern Persia* [Cambridge, 1914], p. 73; Muḥammad Ṣadr Hāshimī, *Tārīkh-i Jarā'id va Majallāt-i Īrān* [Isfahan, 1327–1329 Sh/1948–1950], II, 200).

65 Browne, *op. cit.*, p. 73; *TM*, p. 33 n. 1.

66 *TM*, p. 32.

67 *TRS*, VIII, 2166–2173.

Revolution. It is therefore instructive to examine in some detail, on the basis of diplomatic correspondence, the extent and motivation of contacts between the Shi'i ulama and the British in the period July to December, 1903.

The initiator of these contacts was the British ambassador in Tehran, Sir Arthur Hardinge. The agitation against the tobacco concession had often been ascribed to Russian intrigue among the ulama, and Hardinge, seeing the extent of clerical opposition to Amīn us-Sulṭān, recommended a similar tactical alliance with the ulama. "The Russians, of course, used them at the time of the Régie in a much more unscrupulous manner than would be consonant with our traditions or diplomacy, but I think we can profit by their example without resorting to such extreme methods as theirs."[68] Writing to Newmarch, political agent in Baghdad, after discussing the fear of the Shah and Amīn us-Sulṭān of contracting a further loan from Russia, he points out that it "would increase their dependence on that power and react unfavourably on our interests. For this reason, I should deprecate any discouragement of agitation among the Ulema at the Attabat against Persian financial relations with Russia. His Majesty's Representatives can obviously not give such a movement their official countenance, but I do not think it a bad thing that the Persian Government should suspect that it has our sympathy, and might, in certain eventualities, receive from us more active support. . . . For the present there is no question of a further Russian loan, but if the Shah goes to Europe next year, he may be tempted to apply again to the Russians, and it is desirable that the clergy should be prepared with a strong protest beforehand. I have often wished that we had a reliable secret agent at Kerbala and Najaf for working [*sic*] the principal Mujtehids, and giving us information here as to the state of feeling among them as to Persian politics. . . . I see the Russians have just appointed a Consular Agent there. . . ."[69] There was then an obvious community of interest between the ulama and the British, and a desire on the part of the latter to give this practical effect.

In Tehran, Hardinge himself attempted to establish contact with the ulama, frequently meeting them at the residence of the Ottoman ambassador, and on occasion they too visited him at the

[68] Instructions sent to Kimball, consul in Shiraz, on July 17, 1903, in *Further Correspondence, July–September 1903*, p. 178.

[69] Letter dated June 4, 1903, *ibid.*, p. 37.

British embassy.[70] He realized, however, the political importance of the mujtahids at the 'atabāt, and most of his efforts were directed at establishing with them a relationship of cooperation.[71]

Not only did the 'atabāt at this time have a particular relevance to the affairs of Iran, but also there existed a convenient means of developing British influence there. This was the "Oudh bequest." The Shi'i ruler of Oudh and Lucknow, Sultan Ghāzī ud-Dīn Ḥaydar, had established a vaqf of a hundred lakhs of rupees, the proceeds of which were to be divided among two mujtahids, one in Najaf and one in Karbala, for distribution among the deserving.[72] In 1856 his dynasty was extinguished by the British, and the kingdom of Oudh and Lucknow incorporated into British India.[73] Thereafter, the administration of the endowment was in British hands: the political agent in Baghdad was responsible for forwarding the money to the mujtahids of Najaf and Karbala. For a time, Shaykh Murtaḍā Anṣārī appears to have been responsible for the distribution of the money in Najaf.[74] In 1318/1900–1901, Colonel Newmarch became British political agent in Baghdad, and the manner of distribution of the bequest was changed: it was entrusted now to ten mujtahids in both Najaf and Karbala, instead of only to one in each.[75]

Of this bequest, Hardinge intended to make discreet political use. "One powerful lever, which helped to promote good relations between the Persian ecclesiastics and myself was the so-called Oude bequest. . . . It amounted in my time in Persia to a very consider-

70 Hardinge, *op. cit.*, p. 273; his dispatch of July 21, 1903, *Further Correspondence, July–September 1903*, p. 170.

71 Strangely enough, Hardinge was remarkably ignorant of Islam, despite his eagerness for contacts with the ulama. Thus he thought ijtihād to mean "God's divine revelation" (*A Diplomatist in the East*, p. 309); and the number of daily prayers prescribed by Islam to be seven (*ibid.*, p. 261).

72 *TRS*, VI, 1742.

73 J. N. Hollister, *The Shia of India* (London, 1953), p. 163.

74 *TRS*, VII, 1742. According to Daulatābādī (*HY*, I, 25–26), the Oudh bequest was divided equally among Najaf, Karbala, and Kāẓimayn, under the direction of Shaykh Murtaḍā. It was, however, sent only to Najaf and Karbala (see Hardinge's dispatch of December 23, 1905, in F.O. 371/102), and it is possible that Daulatābādī is here confusing the bequest with the *sahm-i imām* (money destined for the 'atabāt; literally, "the share of the Imam") sent from India, which may well have been entrusted directly to Shaykh Murtaḍā as sole marja'-i taqlīd.

75 *TRS*, VI, 1743, according to whom Newmarch reinterpreted the word *mujtahidān* in the *vaqfnāma* as the Persian plural, rather than the Arabic dual!

able sum. I was therefore being constantly asked by my numerous clerical friends to appoint deserving youths, connected by hereditary or other family ties with the Shiah clergy, to what might be called scholarships or fellowships at the Sacred Thresholds. . . . The impartial care which was brought to bear upon all applications to me and to Col. Newmarch on reference to him for these minor ecclesiastical appointments, afforded opportunities for influencing the leading Persian Ulema which I strove to utilize for the purpose of maintaining my own contact with the chiefs of that powerful class."[76] This attempt to exploit the Oudh bequest appears to have been marked by the inconclusiveness which characterized all of Hardinge's dealings with the ulama. Of the important mujtahids of the 'atabāt, only Mullā Kāẓim Khurāsānī consented to receive any of the money.[77] Sharabīānī, on the other hand, with whom Hardinge did establish contact, was not a recipient.[78] It appears that the tact shown by Newmarch in administering the bequest was inadequate, and that far from establishing cordial relations with the ulama, he succeeded only in offending them.[79]

While it is not possible to gauge with any certainty the influence on the ulama of the Oudh bequest and its administration, Hardinge's contacts with Sharabīānī may be assessed more satisfactorily. In July, 1903, he sought the permission of the British government to communicate with Sharabīānī, on the pretext of "assisting the Persian Government to suppress the religious riots in Northern Persia." Early in the same month, permission was cabled to him, but the India Office in particular counseled restraint: Hardinge should be careful "in no way to associate himself with those who, by encouraging outbreaks of religious fanaticism, disturb the authority of the Government to which he is accredited."[80] Newmarch was instructed to deliver Hardinge's message to Sharabīānī, but on August 4, 1903, Lansdowne expressly forbade Hardinge to enter into regular correspondence with Sharabīānī, saying that "the message already delivered to Agha Shara-

[76] Hardinge, *A Diplomatist in the East,* pp. 323–324. See also dispatch of December 23, 1905, and Nikki R. Keddie, "Religion and Irreligion in Early Iranian Nationalism," *Comparative Studies in Society and History,* IV (1962), 290 n. 30.

[77] *TRS,* VI, 1744.

[78] Telegram of Newmarch to Hardinge, dated June 19, 1903, *Further Correspondence, July–September 1903,* p. 362.

[79] Letter of 'Abd ul-'Alī Harātī to Hardinge, in *ibid.,* p. 180.

[80] Lansdowne's instructions to Hardinge dated July 9, 1903, in *ibid.,* p. 20.

biani goes quite far enough."[81] Certain contacts continued, however, and Sharabīānī cautiously intimated his willingness to open correspondence with Hardinge, on condition that the initiative came from the latter.[82] It was decided to deliver a message to Sharabīānī in Najaf, through the Persian dragoman of the consulate in Baghdad, to the effect that England supported Iranian independence and respected Islam, and hence would "never favour measures which could weaken or injure Persia."[83] The dragoman, Muḥammad Muḥsin Khān, saw Sharabīānī in Kufa, and told him that "what I think is necessary for him is to make friendship with the British high officials, and to sincerely attach himself to them by means of correspondence in all secret and public affairs."[84] Despite these overtures, nothing came of the relations between Sharabīānī and Hardinge. When in late 1903, Hardinge visited Iraq, with the purpose of pursuing his contacts with the 'atabāt, he was unable to visit Karbala because of an outbreak of cholera, and in Najaf contented himself with sending his compliments to Sharabīānī.[85]

The following year, Sharabīānī died, and in 1905, Hardinge was recalled. The policy he had initiated terminated inconclusively and was at all times marked by great reserve and caution. In the Constitutional Revolution again certain contacts between the ulama and the British took place, but it is not possible to consider these the outcome of a consistent and conscious policy. Amīn us-Sulṭān's successor, 'Ayn ud-Daula, pursued policies similar to those that had led to clerical opposition to "the son of a Georgian," and that they should arouse similar opposition was inevitable. That the opposition and the agitation it engendered took the form of a demand for a constitution, points indeed to an alliance of the ulama with other forces and interests, although not with British diplomacy. It is necessary now to examine how these were linked in the Constitutional Revolution with a demonstration of the traditional role of the ulama.

81 Telegram of August 4, 1903, in *ibid.*, p. 136.
82 Newmarch to Lansdowne, July 29, 1903, in *ibid.*, p. 111.
83 Newmarch to Hardinge, August 29, 1903, in *ibid.*, p. 323.
84 *Ibid.*, pp. 334–337.
85 Hardinge, *A Diplomatist in the East*, pp. 317–320.

XIV

The Ulama and the Early Constitutional Movement

The events of the Constitutional Revolution have been recounted in detail in a number of Persian works, and no effort will be made here to present a comprehensive account of the happenings leading to the granting of the constitution in Jumādī ul-Ukhrā, 1324/August, 1906. A summary will be undertaken, however, indicating the part played by the ulama in the early stages of the constitutional movement, as a basis for assessing their motives.

From the appointment of 'Ayn ud-Daula as ṣadr-i a'ẓam in Rajab, 1321/September-October, 1903, until the first mass emigration of ulama from Tehran, we see a series of incidents opposing the state and the ulama, and preparing the way for the confrontation culminating in the demand for a constitution. Pretexts were sought and found for the excitement of popular religious emotions against the state, and the fulfillment of this task was made easier by the determination of 'Ayn ud-Daula to suppress manifestations of clerical power. The oppression exerted by the state brought the ulama and the people, notably the merchants, closer together, and its disregard of the traditional respect accorded to the ulama served only to further this alliance.

The reverence accorded to the religious classes was often unconnected with the issues opposing them to the government, and their function as the symbol and embodiment of national aspirations ensured them almost unconditional support. This emerges clearly from the incidents, in 'Ayn ud-Daula's first month of office, involving the Muhammadīya and Ṣadr madrasas in Tehran. The ṭullāb attached to the two madrasas started to fight each other, ostensibly on account of the rich auqāf settled on the former. Interested parties ensured that the struggle should be prolonged. The imām jum'a of Tehran, Mīrzā Abū-l-Qāsim, took advantage of the situation to pursue his own feud with Sayyid 'Abdullāh Bihbihānī, who, he felt, had once insulted his father, Mīrzā Zayn ul-'Ābidīn.[1] Bihbihānī had given refuge to one of the ṭullāb involved, thus arousing the hostility of those on the opposing side who were then encouraged by Mīrzā Abū-l-Qāsim to harass Bihbihānī. Since 'Ayn ud-Daula knew Bihbihānī to be a supporter of his rival and predecessor, Amīn us-Sulṭān, he did not intervene until forced to do so by supporters of Bihbihānī among the Tehran ulama, notably Sayyid 'Alī Akbar Tafrashī.[2] A number of the ṭullāb were arrested by 'Alā ud-Daula, governor of Tehran, and after being beaten, were banished to Ardabīl.[3]

This act, however, far from settling the disturbances, gave them a new direction, one hostile to the government. 'Ayn ud-Daula appears to have seen in the affair a means of chastising clerical presumptions, while the ulama of Tehran, with the exception of the imām jum'a, were alarmed at the violent treatment accorded to the ṭullāb, seeing it as an indirect threat to themselves.[4] Bihbihānī himself wrote to 'Ayn ud-Daula, pleading for the release of the ṭullāb.[5] The popular reaction was at least as great, and the people of Zanjān obtained the freedom of the ṭullāb even before they reached Ardabīl.[6] It is interesting to note that despite the complexity of intrigue and personal rivalry, the issue resolved itself as a further confrontation between the power of the ulama and that

1 *TM*, p. 34. For the cause of Mīrzā Abū-l-Qāsim's grievance, see *TB*, p. 278.

2 Thus Nāẓim ul-Islām Kirmānī (*TB*, p. 133). Daulatābādī, however, represents Tafrashī, together with Shaykh Faḍlullāh Nūrī and the imām jum'a, as one of the clerical associates of 'Ayn ud-Daula (*HY*, II, 3).

3 *TM*, p. 34.

4 *TB*, p. 138.

5 *TM*, p. 35.

6 *TB*, p. 138.

of the state. This complexity lessened in the period up to the Constitutional Revolution, and as it did so, the conflict between state and ulama became clearer and more pronounced.

Subsequent events were moreover to strengthen the alliance that had been largely responsible for the downfall of Amīn us-Sulṭān—that of the ulama and the merchants. It was this alliance that made the Constitutional Revolution as much nationalist in inspiration as constitutionalist. Not only was an end demanded to the unfettered tyranny of the monarchy and its agents, but also to the ever-increasing penetration of the nation's economic life by foreign interests, a process directly furthered by the tyranny. The existence of the religio-national community was felt to be in danger, and as before the ulama led and expressed the reaction to that danger.

The influence of the rivalry between Amīn us-Sulṭān and 'Ayn ud-Daula was, however, still to be seen in the actions of the ulama. For it was Muḥammad Taqī Khān, one of Amīn us-Sulṭān's agents, who in Muḥarram, 1323/March–April, 1905, supplied the ulama with a photograph of Naus, the Belgian Minister of Customs, in the dress of a mullā.[7] This photograph, taken at a fancy-dress ball some years previously, became a new pretext for agitation against Naus: the dignity of the ulama had been insulted.[8] At the same time, there was little need for such a pretext; the new customs tariff, which favored Russian trade in Iran, had begun to be applied, and shortly afterward Naus was given further powers. He was appointed Minister of Posts and Telegraphs and given responsibility for the issuance of passports.[9] According to well-established tradition, the grievances thus aroused were absorbed into a protest expressed in religious terms, and this protest centered on the objectionable photograph of Naus.

The protest was ineffectual, and shortly before Muẓaffar ud-Dīn Shāh left on his third journey to Europe in Rabī' uth-Thānī, 1323/

[7] *Loc. cit.* According to 'Abdullāh Mustaufī (*Tārīkh-i Idārī va Ijtimā'ī-yi Daura-yi Qājārīya ya Sharḥ-i Zindagānī-yi Man* [Tehran, 1321 Sh/1942–1943], II, 90), the photograph was given to Bihbihānī by Mīrzā Javād Khān Sa'd ud-Daula, former chargé d'affaires in Brussels and an acquaintance of Naus. Yet another account claims that Naus himself gave the photograph to Amīn us-Sulṭān as a souvenir, and that it then fell into the hands of Mīrzā Muṣṭafā Āshtīānī (Ibrāhīm Ṣafā'ī, *Rahbarān-i Mashrūṭa VI: Sayyid 'Abdullāh Bihbihānī va Sayyid Muḥammad Ṭabāṭabā'ī* [Tehran, 1343 Sh/1964], p. 9). The photograph is reproduced by Kasravī in *TM*, p. 36.

[8] *HY*, II, 4.

[9] *TM*, pp. 35, 48.

June–July, 1905, the merchants of Tehran closed the bazaars and took refuge in the shrine of Shāh 'Abd ul-Aẓīm in protest against Belgo-Russian economic influence. The Crown Prince, Muḥammad 'Alī Mīrzā, who was entrusted with the government of the capital during his father's absence in Europe, was able to restrict the scope of the disturbances with the aid of Sayyid 'Abdullāh Bihbihānī.[10] This use of Bihbihānī's influence makes it clear that tacit cooperation now existed between the ulama and the merchants in their opposition to the government.

Events in the provinces largely reflected those in the capital and provided the ulama with further pretexts for their agitation against the government. Violent and disrespectful treatment of the ulama supplied more evidence of the impiety of the government. In Shiraz there was a straightforward conflict between the governor, Shu'ā' us-Salṭana, and the people of the town, led by the ulama.[11] In Kirman it was rivalries among the ulama themselves, that ended, like the fights between ṭullāb in Tehran, by becoming yet another source of grievance against the government. Kirman had been a center of Shaykhism since the days of Shaykh Aḥmad Aḥsā'ī, and the life of the town, like that of Tabriz, was repeatedly interrupted by clashes between the Shaykhīs and their opponents. The wealth of Ḥājji Muḥammad Khān, leader of the Shaykhīs and successor to Ḥājjī Muḥammad Karīm Khān, was probably at least as important a cause of the hostility to the Shaykhīs as any doctrinal objections. In early 1905 the hostility was aggravated by the arrival from Mashhad of a certain Shaykh Barīnī, who started to preach against the Shaykhīs. The agitation was reinforced by Mīrzā Muḥammad Riḍā, one of the ulama of Kirman recently returned from the 'atabāt, who declared the Shaykhis "unclean" (*najis*), and their dominance of Muslims (i.e., non-Shaykhīs) unlawful.[12] On the basis of this pronouncement, he tried to remove the Masjid-i Bāzār-i Shāh and its auqāf from the control of the Shaykhīs and to transfer it to his cousin, Shaykh Muḥammad Ṣādiq.[13] The governor of Kirman, Rukn ud-Daula, sent some of his troops to protect the disputed mosque, and in the ensuing disturbances a number of Mīrzā Muḥammad Riḍā's fol-

10 *Ibid.*, p. 51. According to Nāẓim ul-Islām Kirmānī (*TB*, p. 223), Muḥammad 'Alī promised Bihbihānī to obtain the dismissal of Naus.

11 *TM*, p. 52.

12 *TB*, p. 240.

13 *TB*, p. 242; *TM*, p. 52.

lowers were killed. Others who went to attack Ḥājji Muḥammad Khān's house met a similar fate.[14] The ulama communicated with their colleagues in Tehran, and their protests obtained the dismissal of Rukn ud-Daula.[15] The new governor, Ẓafar us-Salṭana, proved equally unable to suppress the fervor of the ulama, which had by now directed itself against the Jewish community of Kirman. In despair, he retired into his andarūn, abandoning control of the town to the two brothers of Rukn ud-Daula who had stayed behind. They gave orders that certain of the ulama be seized and bastinadoed at the citadel; among them was Shaykh Muḥammad Riḍā who was banished to Rafsinjān, a town about 110 kilometers distant from Kirman, whence he proceeded to Mashhad.[16] Again, news of these events penetrated to Tehran, and as a result of the representations of the ulama Ẓafar us-Salṭana was replaced by 'Abd ul-Ḥusayn Mīrzā Farmānfarmā, who initially permitted Mīrzā Muḥammad Riḍā to return to Kirman, but then exiled him to Mashhad for a further two months before 'Ayn ud-Daula instructed him to permit his final return.[17] This disrespect shown to the ulama of Kirman supplied the clerical opponents of the government with material for their Ramaḍān sermons. The occasion for the disturbances was less important than the outcome—a clash between ulama and state. Yet another example of the impiety and tyranny of the state was furnished, and the popular indignation inspired by disrespectful treatment of the ulama increased.

Although in all these incidents, an element of planning, and of cooperation, both among the ulama themselves, and between the ulama and the merchants is discernible, conscious preparation for the overthrow of 'Ayn ud-Daula and for the achievement of more far-reaching aims appears to have begun only with the alliance between Sayyid 'Abdullāh Bihbihānī and Sayyid Muḥammad Ṭabāṭabā'ī, founded on Ramaḍān 25, 1323/November 23, 1905.[18]

[14] *TB*, p. 242.

[15] *Ibid.*, p. 243. Muẓaffar ud-Dīn Shāh himself was credited with Shaykhī tendencies, and it is possible that the disturbances in Kirman were, to a certain extent, a further expression of discontent with the government. His Shaykhī inclinations had first aroused the attention of the ulama during the agitation against Mīrzā Ḥusayn Khān Sipahsālār (see Maḥmūd Farhād Mu'tamad, *Mushīr ud-Daula Sipahsālār-i A'ẓam* [Tehran, 1326 Sh/1947–1948], pp. 189–191, and Murtaḍā Mudarrisī Chahārdihī, *Shaykh Aḥmad Aḥsā'ī* [Tehran, 1334 Sh/1955], p. 19). He appears, however, to have been either unwilling or unable to protect the Shaykhīs.

[16] *TM*, p. 53.

[17] *TB*, p. 251.

[18] *TM*, p. 49; Ṣafā'ī, *op. cit.*, p. 11.

The motives of the two men, and the nature of the plans they agreed upon, will be discussed below; here it is enough to note the importance of the event. The historian Kasravī considers it to mark the beginning of the Constitutional Revolution. The leadership of the movement, at least outwardly, was to be provided by these two men, in particular the latter, and the large popular following their prestige commanded was a force considerable enough to arouse fear in the government and readiness to submit to the ulama's demands. Around them centered the later agitation during the emigrations to Shāh 'Abd ul-'Aẓīm and Qum, and also the attempts of 'Ayn ud-Daula to suppress the constitutional movement.

The first visible product of their alliance was the destruction of the new building of the Russian Bank in Tehran. A plot of land, occupied by the ruins of a madrasa (Madrasa-yi Chāl) which had been turned into a coal depot, and by a disused graveyard, had been selected by the officials of the Russian Bank for the erection of a new headquarters.[19] The land being vaqf, the agreement of the ulama was necessary for its disposal. Certain parts had already been sold (as conducive to the improvement of the vaqf: *tabdīl ba aḥsan*), but Ṭabāṭabā'ī refused to give his consent to the plans of the Russian Bank. Shaykh Faḍlullāh Nūrī, on the other hand, agreed to the sale of the land in question for a sum of 750 tomans.[20] The opposition to 'Ayn ud-Daula, centered on Bihbihānī and Ṭabāṭabā'ī, saw in the affair a means of striking a blow both against him and against his principal clerical supporter. Their plans were put into execution by Mīrzā Muṣṭafā Āshtiānī, who had under his control the Madrasa-yi Khāzin ul-Mulk, situated opposite the disputed site. Toward the end of Ramaḍān, a suitable pretext offered itself for an attack on the half-finished structure of the Russian Bank. In the course of the building, a number of corpses that had secretly been buried in the disused graveyard during the cholera epidemic of the previous year, were discovered by the workers, and disposed of down a well.[21] Arousing anger at this lighthearted treatment of the dead, Mīrzā Muṣṭafā was able to persuade a mob (among them his own ṭullāb) to attack and destroy the half-completed building.[22] Here again, we observe the

19 *TM*, p. 55.
20 *Loc. cit.*; *TB*, p. 265.
21 *TM*, p. 56; *HY*, II, 8.
22 *TM*, p. 56.

use of a well-chosen, expressive pretext to arouse agitation against the government: religious feelings were shown to be affronted, and the government to be associated with the foreigners who behaved thus insultingly.

If the ulama were thus diligent in their search for pretexts, 'Ayn ud-Daula for his part seems to have been almost eager to supply them. The beating given to some of the merchants of Tehran on Shavvāl 14, 1323/December 12, 1905, started the chain of events that culminated in the issue of the decree granting the constitution. Various circumstances, notably the disruption of the Russian economy by war with Japan, had caused a rise in the price of sugar, and using this as pretext, 'Ayn ud-Daula decided to punish the merchants of Tehran for their protests against his policies, and at the same time to intimidate the ulama allied to them. A number of merchants, not all concerned with the sale of sugar, were summoned by 'Alā ud-Daula, governor of Tehran, and bastinadoed in his presence.[23] Far from intimidating the ulama, however, 'Ayn ud-Daula provided them with the final pretext for conducting open agitation. As the news of the bastinadoing became known, the people of Tehran, led by the ulama, gathered in the Masjid-i Shāh to protest. Mīrzā Abū-l-Qāsim Imām Jum'a attended the meeting, but only in order to carry out the wishes of 'Ayn ud-Daula. He insisted on Sayyid Jamāl ud-Dīn Vā'iẓ mounting the minbar to address the crowd. Then, interrupting the sayyid's speech at a certain point, the imām jum'a gave a signal to his followers scattered among the crowd, who began to create panic, and finally the meeting dissolved in chaos.[24] This use of force by 'Ayn ud-Daula against the ulama was to characterize his policy throughout the agitation. His attempted use of bribery to bring about dissension among the ulama largely failed, and no way remained to oppose the ulama's demands except that of force. By thus provoking the mass emigration of the ulama from Tehran, he succeeded only in giving the movement greater momentum. Their withdrawal from the capital was a symbolic demonstration of the illegitimacy of the government, clear enough to be acted upon and understood by the people of Tehran.

After the dispersal of the first meeting in the Masjid-i Shāh, the ulama decided, at the suggestion of Sayyid Ṭabāṭabā'ī, to leave

23 *TB*, p. 275; *TM*, p. 58.
24 *Ibid.*, pp. 60–62.

Tehran for the security offered by Shāh 'Abd ul-'Aẓīm.[25] Here they formulated their demands to be submitted to Muẓaffar ud-Dīn Shāh. The precise nature of these demands is crucial for the whole question of the participation of the ulama in the constitutional movement, yet cannot be determined with certainty. Up to now, we have seen little more than a clerical movement against the government, comparable with many earlier ones; no demand for a representative form of government had been voiced. Among the demands presented to the Shah, in the name of the ulama, was, however, one for the foundation of a "house of justice" (*'adālatkhāna*).[26] It is not clear that this demand emanated in fact from the ulama. The secret societies working for the establishment of a constitutional regime had decided to establish contact with the ulama in Shāh 'Abd ul-'Aẓīm, and the brother of Yaḥyā Daulatābādī was dispatched to receive from them the list of their demands.[27] According to Daulatābādī, the list did not contain any mention of the 'adālatkhāna, and he took it upon himself to add this item before forwarding it to Shams ud-Dīn Bey, the Ottoman ambassador, for presentation to Muẓaffar ud-Dīn Shāh.[28] The account given by Nāẓim ul-Islām Kirmānī, himself active in the secret societies, confirms Daulatābādī's claim, adding that the ulama had intended to include the demand for an 'adālatkhāna in their petition, but forgot to do so.[29] Such forgetfulness appears highly improbable. It is on the other hand possible that the ulama, or their leaders, while intending to demand a constitution, did not yet think the time ripe, and that the secret societies wished to force them to move more quickly than they thought wise. The attitude of the ulama to the concept of constitutional government will be discussed below.

Doubts about the real nature of the ulama's intentions were evidently widespread and resulted in pressure being exerted on them from various directions. 'Ayn ud-Daula sent emissaries to Shāh 'Abd ul-'Aẓīm to attempt to divide the leadership of the

25 *TM*, p. 63.
26 *Ibid.*, p. 67.
27 *HY*, II, 17, 22.
28 *Ibid.*, II, 22–23.
29 *TB*, pp. 297–298. Kasravī (*TM*, p. 67) does not discuss the attribution of the demand to the ulama. It does not seem possible to pronounce either way on the accuracy of Daulatābādī's claim. His motives in assigning to himself so central a role in the constitutional movement might well be questioned; and Nāẓim ul-Islām Kirmānī's account offers an unsatisfactory explanation of the matter.

ulama.[30] On Dhū-l-Qa'da 14, 1323/January 12, 1906, four of their number were delegated to discuss their demands with 'Ayn ud-Daula in Tehran; whether their prolonged stay in his residence was voluntary or compulsory is not clear.[31] At the same time, many of the ṭullāb at Shāh 'Abd ul-'Aẓīm attempted to dissuade Bihbihānī and Ṭabāṭabā'ī from returning to Tehran.[32] After Muẓaffar ud-Dīn Shāh had accepted in principle the demand for an 'adālatkhāna, on Dhū-l-Qa'da 16/January 14, they decided, however, to return and were met in the capital with popular rejoicing.[33]

The rejoicing was premature for many reasons. 'Alā ud-Daula had indeed been dismissed from the governorship of Tehran, and the demand for an 'adālatkhāna had been accepted. But the nature of the 'adālatkhāna, by what method and at what time it was to be established—there were matters left unsolved by the Shah's decree.[34] Moreover, 'Ayn ud-Daula was by no means prepared to accept the finality of the ulama's triumph. His hostility, obstinacy, and repeated use of violence indeed helped the agitation toward a clearer formulation of the demand for a constitution. At the same time, doubts surrounding the intentions of the ulama were reflected in pressure brought to bear by other quarters.

In particular, doubts were entertained about Bihbihānī. On returning to Tehran, he found his authority almost complete, and his rival, Shaykh Faḍlullāh Nūrī, shorn of all his prestige, despite his great learning.[35] Some feared that he would now consider his own aim—primacy among the ulama—attained, and abandon the demand for an 'adālatkhāna.[36] As signs of 'Ayn ud-Daula's reluctance to implement the decree multiplied, doubts as to the determination of the ulama increased, and pamphlets indicting their weakness in the face of 'Ayn ud-Daula's procrastination began to appear, emanating probably from the secret societies.[37] Ṭabāṭabā'ī even found it necessary to mount the minbar and swear on the

[30] *TM*, p. 64.
[31] *TB*, p. 299.
[32] *Ibid.*, p. 305.
[33] *TM*, p. 73.
[34] Text given in *TM*, pp. 71–72.
[35] *TB*, p. 428.
[36] *HY*, II, 34–35.
[37] *TB*, pp. 320, 324–326. Muḥammad Ḥasan Adīb Haravī, in *Tārīkh-i Paydāyish-i Mashrūṭīyat-i Īrān* (Mashhad, 1331 Sh/1952), p. 128, reproduces the contents of one such pamphlet. See also Mihdī Malikzāda, *Tārīkh-i Inqilāb-i Mashrūṭīyat-i Īrān* (Tehran, 1327 Sh/1948–1949), II, 69.

Quran that he and his associates had not been bribed by 'Ayn ud-Daula to withdraw their demands.[38]

Whether as a result of the pressure exerted by the secret societies, or because of the basic determination of the ulama themselves, open enmity between the ulama and 'Ayn ud-Daula was resumed. He promised solemnly to Ṭabāṭabā'ī that he would, as soon as possible, establish the 'adālatkhāna, but when Ṭabāṭabā'ī saw no sign of the promise being fulfilled, he began to demand openly the establishment of a majlis,[39] a consultative assembly. The constant preaching of the ulama left their continuing opposition to 'Ayn ud-Daula in no doubt.

Events in the provinces again offered a parallel to those in the capital and added to the grievances of the ulama. In Shiraz, Shu'ā' us-Salṭana gave orders for certain of the people who had taken refuge in the shrine of Shāh Chirāgh to be shot in front of the sacred edifice. The ulama of Shiraz, sending a telegram to Tehran, were at last able to obtain his dismissal.[40] In Mashhad, a similar act of violence was committed in the shrine of Imam Riḍā. The governor of the town, Āṣaf ud-Daula, together with one of the chief merchants, Ḥājjī Muḥammad Ḥasan, had been hoarding grain, and as a result the price of bread rose, but not to a level high enough to induce them to sell their stocks. The people, led by the ulama, gathered in front of the house of Ḥājjī Muḥammad Ḥasan to protest, but on being met by rifle fire, took refuge in the shrine. They were pursued by the troops, who fired on the gathering in the courtyard of the shrine. It was rumored that the dome of the shrine itself was also hit by bullets, either accidentally or intentionally. This insult to the holiest shrine of Shi'ism within the borders of Iran, unparalleled since the outrages committed by the Afsharid pretendant, Nādir Mīrzā, further intensified popular hatred of the impious government, and was exploited in this sense by Ṭabāṭabā'ī.[41]

Similar tyrannical acts in the capital were directed primarily against the ulama and their supporters and were of a nature to add to the feelings of religious hostility against the government. One of the followers of Bihbihānī, Mihdī Gāvkush, was murdered on

38 *TB*, p. 345. That some bribes were distributed with effect is, however, probable. See *General Report on Persia for the Year 1906*, p. 4, in F.O. 416/30.

39 *TB*, pp. 327, 374.

40 *Ibid.*, pp. 331–332; *TM*, p. 83.

41 *TM*, p. 84; *TB*, pp. 333–336.

the orders of ʿAyn ud-Daula and his pregnant wife beaten by the soldiers.[42] The final outrage which was to cause the second emigration of the ulama from Tehran significantly concerned a sayyid: again the offense committed by the state was against an object of religious veneration. On Jumādī ul-Ūlā 18, 1324/July 10, 1906, orders were given for the arrest of one of the ulama prominent in preaching against the government, Shaykh Muḥammad Vāʿiẓ. Before the Shaykh could be taken to prison, ṭullāb belonging to the Ḥājjī Abū-l-Ḥasan madrasa attacked the soldiers escorting him and were able to set him free. Aḥmad Khān, commander of the soldiers, gave orders for the ṭullāb to be fired upon and, reproached for so doing by a certain Sayyid ʿAbd ul-Ḥamīd, shot the sayyid dead at point-blank range.[43] When the corpse was recovered, it was taken with mourning and anger to lie in the Masjid-i Shāh.[44] Here it was to be used as a rallying point for the anger of the people.

As before, the ulama of the capital gathered in the mosque to express their outraged feelings, and this time announced that they would not leave until an ʿadālatkhāna had been established, demanding also the dismissal of ʿAyn ud-Daula.[45] Meanwhile, troops were sent to prevent anyone from joining the meeting, and when a procession mourning the death of Sayyid ʿAbd ul-Ḥamīd came out of the mosque, it was met with a volley of gunfire. The ulama then presented the government with three choices: either to accept their demands, to remove them from the mosque by force, or to permit them to leave the city in peace.[46] The last of these three was accepted, and on Jumādī ul-Ūlā 23, July 15, about a thousand of the ulama set out for Qum.[47]

The merchants of Tehran made a similar use of bast in the grounds of the British embassy in Tehran. The association this implied between British policy and the constitutional movement makes the origin of the stratagem a matter of some importance. Shortly before the shooting of Sayyid ʿAbd ul-Ḥamīd and the emigration of the ulama to Qum, Sayyid ʿAbdullāh Bihbihānī contacted the British chargé d'affaires, Grant Duff, at the summer quarters of the embassy in Qulhak. He "applied for assistance . . .

42 *TM*, p. 95; *HY*, II, 66.
43 *TM*, p. 95.
44 *Loc. cit.*
45 *Loc. cit.*
46 *Ibid.*, p. 106.
47 *Ibid.*, p. 107; *HY*, II, 70.

but was informed by His Majesty's chargé d'affaires that he could in no way support a movement directed against the Persian Government."[48] On Jumādī ul-Ūlā 27, 1324/July 19, 1906, four days after the beginning of the exodus to Qum, about thirty representatives of the clerical and mercantile classes sought refuge in the grounds of the British embassy.[49] The exact nature of the "assistance" requested by Bihbihānī is unknown, but it seems likely that the merchants seeking bast in the embassy knew of his contacts with the British, even if not acting under explicit instructions from him. On the other hand, Grant Duff claims to have warned 'Ayn ud-Daula of the merchants' intentions in advance.[50] During the first emigration, the mediation of the Ottoman ambassador had been sought, and now that Ottoman attacks on Azerbayjan had made further contact impossible,[51] a similar role may have been allotted to Grant Duff by the ulama. For it was Grant Duff who submitted the demands of the merchants to the Shah. The nature of these makes clear the extent of cooperation between the ulama and the merchants. They demanded that the ulama be permitted to return to Tehran, that 'Ayn ud-Daula be dismissed, and that a majlis be established.[52] 'Ayn ud-Daula attempted as before to resist the demands as long as possible, but on Jumādī ul-Ukhrā 7, 1324/July 29, 1906, he saw himself obliged to resign, and a week later, the decree was issued for the calling of a majlis.[53] 'Aḍud ul-Mulk was sent to Qum, and formally invited the ulama back to Tehran on behalf of the government. On Jumādī ul-Ukhrā 27/August 18, they reentered the capital in triumph.[54]

Thus the grant of a constitution had been obtained. Whatever the attitude of the ulama was to the constitution as such, their predominant role in the events leading to the issue of the decree cannot be denied. Throughout, religious motives determined the course of the agitation, and these motives were directed and ex-

48 *General Report on Persia for the Year 1906*, p. 5.

49 *TM*, p. 110.

50 *General Report on Persia for the Year 1906*, p. 5. According to Daulatābādī (*HY*, II, 71), the merchants were acting under Bihbihānī's instructions; while Kasravī (*TM*, p. 110) attributes their seeking refuge in the British embassy to the influence of minor agitators.

51 *TM*, p. 85. Bihbihānī's earlier contacts with the Ottoman embassy had given cause for regret (see *TB*, pp. 349–350; *HY*, II, 58).

52 *TM*, p. 58.

53 *Ibid.*, p. 119; *HY*, II, 78.

54 *TM*, pp. 118, 120.

pressed by the ulama. In this sense, the movement was no more than a repetition of the ulama's traditional role of leading opposition to the state. The state was seen to be surrendering the control of the nation's economic life to foreigners, and added to its burden of guilt by treating the ṭullāb and the ulama with disrespect, murdering sayyids, and violating shrines. Ṭabāṭabā'ī in one of his sermons compared the tyranny of the Qajars with that of the Umayyads who had martyred the Imam Ḥusayn,[55] and by many the comparison was taken literally. It was thought that the Qajars were directly descended from the Umayyads, and even that the dagger which had been used to behead the Imam Ḥusayn was in the possession of 'Alā ud-Daula.[56] So firm was the conviction, that the blockade imposed on the Masjid-i Shāh had to be relaxed for fear of suggesting another point of comparison with the Umayyads—that of denying food and drink to the descendants of the Prophet.[57] It was therefore natural for a call to jihad against the Qajars to be made, and though this was resisted by the ulama,[58] the religious nature of the agitation ensured that the ulama should play a leading role.

This role is complicated, however, by the existence of the secret societies. Some of their members, like Malkum Khān earlier, realized that only the ulama had the power to set the masses in motion and bring about change. The question therefore arises whether the ulama, despite their seeming prominence, were in reality serving, consciously or unconsciously, as the tools of reformist groups with purposes different from their own. Moreover, while in the light of Qajar history and Shi'ī doctrine it was natural for the ulama to lead a movement against the state, their support of the demand for a constitution requires more explanation. The matters involved in this question are extremely complex in their ramifications, and it cannot be claimed that the suggestions presented here furnish an exhaustive answer. An examination of the aims and purposes of the ulama and the secret societies in the constitutional movement will suggest, however, the form an answer might take.

Precise ideas concerning the meaning of the word *mashrūṭa* (constitutional government) seem to have been held by very few,

55 *TB*, p. 378.
56 *Ibid.*, p. 415.
57 *Loc. cit.*
58 *TM*, p. 88.

and this confusion was in large measure common to the ulama and the secret societies. Indeed, it was precisely this confusion that made their cooperation possible. In another sense, too, it may have been deliberate. We have seen that first the demand was for a "house of justice," later defined as a place "where the complaints of the people should receive attention," and the word "majlis" did not occur until later in the speeches of the ulama.[59] Possibly there was then a deliberate progression toward the demand for constitutional government.[60] If for some the apparent confusion was the result of a stratagem, it appears in general to have been real enough.[61]

Questions were often asked about the relation between the reforms demanded and Islamic law. Often the answer was provided by an identification of the two: "*mashrū'īyat* and *mashrūṭīyat* are the same: government according to the law of Islam, justice and equality, or according to science and civilisation."[62] This equation had already been suggested by Malkum Khān, and it was possibly intended as a means of enlisting the support of those of orthodox religious outlook for the constitutional movement. Similar ideas were put forward by Zayn ul-'Ābidīn Marāgha'ī in his *Siyāḥatnāma-yi Ibrāhīm Bīg*[63] and Ḥājjī Abū-l-Ḥasan Mīrzā Shaykh ur-Ra'īs in his *Ittiḥād-i Islām*.[64] Whether or not such an equation appears accurate to latter-day observers is a question of little importance; it might be remarked in passing that many in Iran, as elsewhere in the Islamic world, noted the vigor of Western life and, comparing it with the unfolding of human energy brought about by Islam, tended to assume an identical source for the two phenomena. It is enough to note the currency of such ideas as a probable factor determining the support given to the constitutional movement by the ulama. Furthermore, it appeared initially that the purpose of the 'adālatkhāna was to secure the application of Islamic law.[65] The duality of shar' and 'urf had left much of that

59 See *TB*, p. 374.

60 This theory is upheld by Kasravī, *TM*, p. 72.

61 The word *mashrūṭa* appears to have been equated with republicanism. As late as Jumādī ul-Ūlā 14, 1324/July 6, 1906, Ṭabāṭabā'ī found it expedient to reject any imputation of desiring a *mashrūṭa* (see *TB*, pp. 374 ff.).

62 *Ibid.*, p. 214.

63 Pp. 77 ff.

64 Pp. 12 ff.

65 See the text of the farmān dated Dhū-l-Qa'da, 1323/ December, 1905–January, 1906, given in *TM*, pp. 71–72.

law in abeyance, and it is possible that the ulama saw in the constitution a means of applying the sharīʿat in its entirety. The identification of the reforms, however, with a governmental system prescribed by the sharīʿat led to a clash between those whose ultimate loyalties lay with the one or the other, between the "liberal" reformers and the ulama. The expectations of the ulama were not fulfilled.

Generalizations about the ideology of the secret societies are not possible. They appealed in part to the ulama and drew heavily on religious inspiration.[66] Thus the Imam Ḥusayn was held to have founded the first secret society in Islam for the attainment of freedom and justice.[67] At the same time, these societies contained those who saw cooperation with the ulama as a temporary expedient, to be abandoned after the attainment of a constitution.[68]

The complexities of the problem are further increased by the fact that many of the ulama prominent in the agitation belonged also to the secret societies. ʿAbdullāh Bihbihānī appears to have acted, at least initially, out of personal enmity to ʿAyn ud-Daula, and was not personally involved with any of the groups in Tehran.[69] Sayyid Muḥammad Ṭabāṭabāʾī, Mīrzā Naṣrullāh Malik ul-Mutakallimīn, and Sayyid Jamāl ud-Dīn Vāʿiẓ, however, were all associated with various societies, and it is significant that their religious orthodoxy is open to doubt.[70] Ṭabāṭabāʾī had enjoyed a traditional religious education, studying under Mīrzā Ḥasan Shīrāzī among others, yet as mentioned above, he had through his father, Sayyid Ṣādiq, masonic or pseudo-masonic connections.[71] According to Malikzāda, it was through these that his association with the constitutional movement began.[72] Malik ul-Mutakallimīn is mentioned by Browne as being an Azalī, though no supporting evidence is offered, and his son's history of the constitution bears no hint of this.[73] Sayyid Jamāl ud-Dīn was coauthor of the anti-

66 See A. K. S. Lambton, "Secret Societies and the Persian Revolution of 1905–1906," *St. Anthony's Papers*, IV (1958), 49.

67 *TB*, p. 206.

68 *HY*, II, 47.

69 See *General Report on Persia for the Year 1906*, p. 29.

70 See *TB*, p. 217; and Malikzāda, *op. cit.*, II, 10.

71 Originally Nāṣir ud-Dīn Shāh had brought him to Tehran as a counterweight to the authority of Mīrzā Ḥasan Āshtīānī after the repeal of the tobacco concession (see Ṣafāʾī, *op. cit.*, p. 33).

72 Malikzāda, *op. cit.*, II, 19.

73 E. G. Browne, *Materials for the Study of the Babi Religion* (Cambridge, 1918), p. xviii.

clerical *Ru'yā-yi Ṣādiqa* (*The True Dream*) with Malik ul-Mutakallimīn,[74] and his son, Sayyid Muḥammad 'Alī Jamālzāda, has defined him as a freethinker.[75]

The members of this group—the ulama engaged in the work of the secret societies—cannot be said to belong wholly to the ulama, nor to stand totally apart from it. The nature of their beliefs cannot be assessed with any certainty, but it may be suggested that, while belonging to the ulama by upbringing, education, and position, in outlook they differed considerably from the religious classes. Their mastery of traditional forms of expression enabled them to create at least the semblance of a unity of purpose.

To conclude, the agitation leading to the granting of the constitution was largely inspired and directed by the ulama. They might legitimately have expected from its realization a systematic application of Islamic law, and hence an expansion or at least perpetuation of their function, but little if any thought was in fact given to their role in a constitutional system of government. While the secret societies in part consisted of ulama and were based in part on Islamic ideology, they contained also men opposed to clerical influence, who did not intend to apply the sharī'at. Contradictions concealed by the confusion of thought and the common struggle against 'Ayn ud-Daula began later to become apparent, and the role of the ulama, as discussed in the present work, to come to an end.

With the emergence of at least the semblance of a Western-type political life, the role of the ulama as sole leaders and spokesmen of popular discontent was over. Although the connection of the ulama with certain classes of the urban population remains strong, and recently references have again been heard to "the Yazīd of the age," political and social grievances are no longer voiced in predominantly religious terms, through the medium of the ulama. It is paradoxical that it was the immediate Western impact, and the danger it presented to Iran, that accentuated the importance of the ulama's role throughout the nineteenth century; and yet its ideological influence led to the beginning of an erection of barriers between the secular and the religious, and hence to a decline of the social and political role of the ulama. The

74 Muḥammad 'Alī Jamālzāda, "Tarjuma-yi Ḥāl-i Sayyid Jamāl ud-Dīn Vā'iẓ," *Yaghmā*, III (1329 Sh/1950–1951), 120.

75 Nikki R. Keddie, "Religion and Irreligion in Early Iranian Nationalism," *Comparative Studies in Society and History*, IV (1962), 291 n. 31.

ulama, by their participation in the constitutional movement, helped in the fulfillment of this paradox. The obtaining of the constitution was a climax to a century of friction and conflict between the state and the ulama, and at the same time tended to reduce the influence of the clerical classes on politics and society. It may thus be fittingly regarded as the final episode in the exercise of their dominant role in Qajar Iran.

XV

Conclusion

The Constitutional Revolution appears as the culmination of a long period of conflict between the state and the ulama. This conflict was perhaps inevitable, given the functions assigned by Shī'ī Islam to the ulama and its refusal to provide the state with any theoretical justification, to allot it a place in the system of belief. The resultant tension between clerical and secular authority received growing expression throughout the century. Whether this constituted an irreversible process or not, events almost continually reinforced the basic alienation and turned theoretical contradiction into open conflict.

The rise of Qajar rule had coincided with a reassertion of Shī'i theological technique, and this reassertion placed heavy emphasis on the functions and duties of the ulama. The condition of Iran under the first Qajar monarch, Āghā Muḥammad Khān Qajar, was still too unsettled to permit any widespread manifestation of clerical influence, but the relative order and security provided by Qajar administration established the environment in which the ulama were to fulfill their role.

By the end of the reign of Fatḥ 'Alī Shāh, many of the themes repeated in relations between the state and the ulama later in the Qajar period had already found expression. The monarch, motivated both by personal piety and considerations of policy, sought an accommodation with clerical power. The tyranny of the state he ruled, however, was ultimately irreconcilable with his protestations of devotion to the ulama, and on many occasions the contradiction became apparent. Fatḥ 'Alī Shāh's concern to restrict its scope was able to achieve no more than a temporary truce. Russian aggression against Iran, taking place during his reign, evoked a powerful response from the ulama, and their function as national leaders—possibly self-appointed, but also popularly approved—in the face of both internal tyranny and foreign encroachment became established.

Muḥammad Shāh, with his attachment to Sufism, made no attempt to secure any kind of a working relationship with the ulama, and as a result their hostility to the state, partially restrained by the policies of his predecessor, became more explicit.

It was in the long reign of Nāṣir ud-Dīn Shāh that this hostility, with all its ramifications, began to cast a constant shadow over the affairs of Iran. The piety of the monarch was effusive, but not of a kind likely to impress the ulama. Moreover, tentative attempts at reform which would strengthen the state, undertaken by Amīr Kabīr, Mīrzā Ḥusayn Khān Sipahsālār, and others, threatened the ulama with a reduction of their powers and prerogatives. The question of reform was also linked with that of foreign influence, and the predominant hostility of the ulama's reaction inevitable.

As Nāṣir ud-Dīn Shāh abandoned all serious attempts at reform, the growing corruption and extravagance of the court led to the necessity for foreign loans, and thus invited the establishment of foreign economic influence in Iran. This was bound to be resisted by the ulama as much as Russian expansionism in the Caucasus earlier in the century. At the same time, thoughts of reform were taken up by other elements in opposition to the state, and with these the ulama found themselves in uneasy and temporary alliance.

The outcome of this alliance was the movement of 1905–1906 culminating in the establishment of a consultative assembly. In these events, the ulama not only gave the greatest display of their political power, but also effectively ended their previous role as principal leaders and organizers of resistance to the state.

The role fulfilled by the ulama throughout the period from 1785 to 1905 was fairly constant, both in inspiration and mode of expression. In conclusion, a qualitative judgment on the nature of that role and its effectiveness may be hazarded. In the attainment of immediate political aims, the ulama were frequently successful. Yet while specific causes might give rise to much determination and courage, ability to foresee consequences and even concern for secondary results were all too often lacking. This is seen clearly in the agitation leading to the Perso-Russian War of 1826–1828, which ended disastrously for Iran with military humiliation and territorial losses. Similarly, the campaign led by the ulama in 1891 against the tobacco monopoly resulted in the repeal of the obnoxious concession, but also ended in Iran's taking up the burden of foreign debt in order to pay compensation. We have spoken of the ulama as leaders of political opposition, and this indeed they were. Throughout the period of our concern (and still more later) they allied themselves, however, with various groups and interests, and when their alliance was with "liberal" reformers in the early stages of the constitutional movement, they failed to perceive the nature of what was being demanded and its implications for Iran and themselves.

Above all, they failed to provide any real answer to the manifold problems—political, social, economic—facing Iran in the second half of the nineteenth century, as a result of its own stagnation and the impact of the West. Ijtihād was on the whole used narrowly, in a strictly legalistic sense; its genuine potentialities, much vaunted by a few reformers, were seldom activated with honesty or perceptiveness. The Prophet is reputed to have said: "The ulama of my community are as the Prophets of the Children of Israel." The ulama of Qajar Iran failed to exert the comprehensive and assured leadership thus demanded of them.

Yet perhaps it would be altogether wrong to expect so high an achievement from the ulama. Their traditional preoccupations and the scholastic nature of the learning that was the basis of their entire function hardly permitted accurate comprehension of problems deriving from the Western impact. In addition, their essential lack of hierarchic organization would have been an obstacle to any active reshaping of the political structure. Most important, while the Qajar dynasty possessed no legitimizing authority, the ulama enjoyed only that conferred by the process of taqlīd, one for which no adequate machinery was ever established. Intervention in political affairs to gain permanent control thereof never appears to have been even a distant aim of the ulama. The continued occultation of the Imam meant, inescapably, the absence of all legitimizing authority from worldly affairs, so that the political attitudes of the ulama could, in the final analysis, be only quietism or opposition. Any wish to reshape definitively the norms of political life and the bases of the state was foreign to the ulama in Qajar Iran.[1] Thus it was that the forces of renewal passed them by.

[1] These considerations may help to account for the absence, in more recent times, of any extensive movement in Iran calling for the establishment of an Islamic state, comparable to the Muslim Brethren in the Arab world and the Jamā'at-i Islāmī in Pakistan.

Glossary

ākhūnd (آخوند) a lesser member of the religious classes, performing everyday religious functions such as leading prayer in the smaller mosques, etc.; synonymous with *mullā*.

aᶜlam (اعلم) one who is most learned (elative of *ᶜālim*).

aᶜlamīyat (اعلميت) the quality of being most learned.

ᶜālim (عالم) one learned in the religious law and its sources (pl., *ulamā*).

andarūn (اندرون) the interior of an Iranian home; the part occupied by the womenfolk and children (cf. Arabic *ḥarīm*).

ᶜaql (عقل) reason, or the fruit of its exertion, contrasted with *naql*, authoritative tradition.

ᶜatabāt (عتبات) the "thresholds": the Shiᶜi Holy Places in Iraq, at Karbalā, Kāẓimayn, Najaf, and Samarra.

auqāf (اوقاف) the plural of *vaqf*.

— *bāshī* (باشی) a suffix meaning "chief."

bast (بست) the sanctuary from secular authority provided by mosques, residences of the ulama, and other places.

bidᶜat (بدعت) reprehensible innovation in matters of faith.

dārūgha (داروغه) the headman of a city district.

dhimmat (ذمت) the protection contractually accorded by a Muslim state to a non-Muslim community inhabiting its territory.

dīvānbīgī (دیوانبیگی) chief official of secular jurisdiction.

dīvānkhāna (دیوانخانه) the highest organ of secular jurisdiction.

faqīh (فقیه) a jurisprudent.

farmān (فرمان) a royal decree.

fatvā (فتوی) a legal ruling; an expression of opinion, by one of the ulama, on a point of religious law or on a legal case.

fiqh (فقه) jurisprudence.

furūᶜ (فروع) the branches of the religious law, deduced from its principles (*uṣūl*).

ghaybat (غیبت) the occultation of the Twelfth Imam.

ghaybat-i kubrā (غیبت کبری) the "Greater Occultation," the period marked by the absence of human intermediaries between the Imam and the faithful, beginning with the death of the last *vakīl* (agent) in 940, and still continuing.

hadith (*ḥadīth* — حدیث) the traditions concerning the sayings and deeds of the Prophet; for the Shiᶜis, also those relating to the Imams.

ḥarām (حرام) that which is prohibited by the law of Islam.

idhān (اذان) the call to prayer.

ijāza (اجازه) a certificate of competent knowledge and good character sought by aspirants to the rank of *mujtahid*.

ijmāᶜ (اجماع) for Shiᶜis, the consensus of opinion of the ulama, both the living and the dead.

ijtihād (اجتهاد) independent exertion in deciding matters relating to religious law; or, the competence and ability so to exert oneself.

ᶜilm (علم) knowledge; more particularly, that of the religious law and its sources.

imam (*imām* — امام) the leader of congregational prayer.

Imam (*imām* — امام) for Ithnāᶜasharī Shiᶜis, one of the succession of twelve divinely appointed guides of the community.

imām jumʿa (امام جمعه) one designated by the monarch to lead congregational prayer and pronounce the Friday sermon in each major city.

imamzāda (امامزاده) a relative or descendant of any of the Twelve Imams; or, the shrine where such a person is buried.

ʿirfān (عرفان) mystically attained knowledge; gnosis.

ithnāʿasharī (اثنی عشری) "Twelver"; a believer in the cycle of Twelve Imams which culminated in the occultation of the last in the series.

jihad (*jihād* — جهاد) personal striving for the cause of religion, particularly in religiously sanctioned warfare.

kadkhudā (کدخدا) a village headman.

karāmāt (کرامات) miraculous deeds performed by men of exceptional piety as a sign of God's favor.

kharvār (خروار) a unit of weight equivalent to approximately 300 kilograms.

khums (خمس) a fifth of all profit earned in trade, to be levied as a charitable tax.

khuṭba (خطبه) the sermon pronounced before congregational prayer at midday on Fridays.

lashkarnavīs (لشکر نویس) the clerk of the army.

lūṭī (لوطی) a member of the originally chivalrous brotherhoods that, in the nineteenth century, turned increasingly to brigandage.

madhhab (مذهب) a school of law.

madrasa (*madrasa* — مدرسه) a college of religious learning.

Mahdi (*mahdī* — مهدی) for the Ithnāʿasharī Shiʿis, the Twelfth Imam, reappearing at the end of the Greater Occultation to establish the true faith throughout the world and inaugurate a brief reign of justice before the coming of the apocalypse.

maktab (مکتب) an elementary, primarily Quranic, school.

marjaʿ-i taqlīd (مرجع تقلید) a *mujtahid* whose practices and pronouncements furnish a binding example for those unable to exert independent judgment in matters relating to the religious law (pl., *marājiʿ-i taqlīd*).

maʿrifat (معرفت) mystic knowledge; a synonym of *ʿirfān*.

masjid (مسجد) mosque.

miḥrāb (محراب) the niche in a mosque indicating the direction of the Kaᶜba.

minbar (منبر) the pulpit in a mosque.

mīrghaḍab (میرغضب) the executioner of bodily penalties.

muftī (مفتی) one whose opinion is sought on a point of religious law; who pronounces a *fatvā*.

mujtahid (مجتهد) one who may act according to his own judgment in matters relating to religious law; who practices *ijtihād*.

mullā (ملا) a lesser member of the religious classes; synonymous with *ākhūnd*.

muqallid (مقلد) one who is unable to exercise independent judgment in matters relating to religious law and is obliged to follow an exemplary model; who practices *taqlīd*.

murshid (مرشد) a spiritual guide on the Sufi path.

mustaufī (مستوفی) a treasurer or accountant.

mutavallī (متولی) the administrator of an endowment.

pīshnamāz (پیشنماز) a leader of congregational prayer; synonymous with imam.

qadi (*qāḍī* — قاضی) a judge.

qirān (قران) an alternative name for the rial (originally *ṣāḥib-qirān*, "Lord of the Conjunction," after a coin struck by Fatḥ ᶜAlī Shāh who bore this title).

qiyās (قیاس) the use of analogical reasoning in deducing the specific ordinances of the law from its principles.

quṭb (قطب) literally, "pole"; the head of a Sufi order.

rauḍakhvānī (روضه خوانی) the recitation of verse concerning the martyrdom of the Imams, particularly that of the Imam Ḥusayn at Karbala (from the work of Ḥusayn Vāᶜiẓ Kāshifī [d. 1504–1505] entitled *Rauḍat ush-Shuhadā* [*Garden of the Martyrs*]).

risāla (رساله) a treatise.

ṣadr-i aᶜẓam (صدر اعظم) the chief minister; or, before the establishment of separate ministries, the chancellor.

sahm-i imām (سهم امام) monies sent to the ulama at the *ᶜatabāt*, both for their support and for charitable distribution at their discretion (literally, the "share of the Imam").

sayyid (سید) a descendant of the Prophet.

*shar*ᶜ (شرع) religious jurisdiction.

*sharī*ᶜ*at* (شريعت) the law of Islam.

shaykh ul-islām (شيخ الاسلام) the dignitary presiding over *shar*ᶜ courts in each major city.

ṣinf (صنف) a tradesmen's guild.

sunnat (سنت) the exemplary practice of the Prophet; and, for Ithnāᶜasharī Shiᶜis, that of the Imams.

takfīr (تكفير) the formal denunciation by the ulama of an individual as an infidel.

takya (تكيه) a Sufi gathering place; or, a building for the performance of religious dramas.

taqīya (تقيه) the prudential dissimulation of belief, especially in time of danger.

taqlīd (تقليد) the process of following the practices and pronouncements of a scholar more learned than oneself in matters relating to the religious law, with faith in his correctness and without independent investigation of his reasons.

ṭarīqat (طريقت) the Sufi path to mystic knowledge.

*ta*ᶜ*zīya* (تعزيه) the commemoration in dramatic performances of the martyrdom of the Imams, particularly that of the Imam Ḥusayn at Karbala.

ṭullāb (طلاب) the student at a madrasa (employed both as a singular and a plural noun, although an exclusively plural form in Arabic).

toman (*tūmān* — تومان) a unit of currency, equivalent to ten rials.

ulama (ᶜ*ulamā* — علما) those learned in the religious law (pl. of ᶜ*ālim*).

ᶜ*urf* (عرف) secular jurisdiction; customary law.

uṣūl (اصول) the principles or sources of the religious law.

vājib (واجب) enjoined by the law of Islam.

vaqf (وقف) an inalienable endowment, established for religious or charitable purposes, or to ensure security of tenure within a family (pl., *auqāf*).

vazīr (وزير) a minister.

vilāyat (ولایت) the loyalty and devotion of the Shiʿi faithful to the Hidden Imam.

zakāt (زکات) the "purifying tax" levied on the property of Muslims for purposes enumerated in Quran, chap. IX v. 60, often translated erroneously as alms.

Bibliography

Great Britain. VOLUMES OF DIPLOMATIC AND CONSULAR CORRESPONDENCE AND OTHER DOCUMENTS PRESERVED IN THE PUBLIC RECORDS OFFICE. London: F.O. 60/27, 96, 153, 154, 483, 497, 498, 543, 557, 592, 594, 598, 637, 650; F.O. 371/102; F.O. 416/14, 16, 19, 30; F.O. 539/55.

WORKS IN PERSIAN, ARABIC, AND TURKISH

Ādamīyat, Firīdūn. *Amīr Kabīr va Īrān.* Tehran, 1334 Sh/1955.

——. *Fikr-i Āzādī va Muqaddima-yi Nihḍat-i Mashrūṭīyat-i Īrān.* Tehran, 1340 Sh/1961.

Ādamīyat, Muḥammad Ḥusayn. *Dānishmandān va Sukhansarāyān-i Fārs.* Tehran, 1338 Sh/1959. 4 vols.

'Aḍud ud-Daula, Aḥmad Mīrzā. *Tārīkh-i 'Aḍudī.* Ed. Ḥusayn Kūhī Kirmānī. Tehran, 1327 Sh/1948.

al-Aḥsā'ī, 'Abdullāh b. Aḥmad. *Sharḥ-i Ḥālāt-i Shaykh Aḥmad ul-Aḥsā'ī.* Bombay, 1310 Q/1892–1893.

Akhundov, Mirzä Fätäli (Mīrzā Fatḥ 'Alī Ākhūndzāda). *Fars Dilindä Yazïlmïsh Mäktublarïn Mätni.* Ed. Hämid Mämmädzadä. Baku, 1963.

Amīn ud-Daula, Mīrzā 'Alī Khān. *Khāṭirāt-i Siyāsī.* Ed. Ḥāfiẓ Farmānfarmā'īān. Tehran, 1341 Sh/1962.

Anonymous. "Fāji'a-yi Qatl-i Muḥammad-i Akhbārī," *Iṭṭilā'āt-i Māhāna,* IV (1330 Sh/1951), 30–33.

———. "Faylasūf-i Sharq: Sayyid Jamāl ud-Dīn-i Asadābādī Ma'rūf ba Afghānī," *Armaghān*, XII (1310 Sh/1931–1932), 586–601.

Arif, M., and H. Hüsaynov. *Mükhtäsär Azärbayjan Ädäbiyatï Tarikhi*. Baku, 1944. 2 vols.

Asadābādī, Ṣifātullāh Jamālī. *Asnād va Madārik dar bāra-yi Īrānī ul-Aṣl Būdan-i Sayyid Jamāl ud-Dīn*. Tehran, 1337 Sh/1958.

al-'Azzāwī, 'Abbās. *Tārīkh al-'Irāq bayn Iḥtilālayn*. Baghdad, 1373 Q/1953–1954. 8 vols.

al-Bahī, Muḥammad. *al-Fikr al-Islāmī al-Ḥadīth wa Ṣilatuhu bi-l-Isti'mār al-Gharbī*. Cairo, 1379 Q/1959–1960.

Bīdābādī, Muḥammad 'Alī Mu'allim. *Makārim ul-Āthār dar Aḥvāl-i Rijāl-i Daura-yi Qājār*. Isfahan, 1337 Sh/1958. Vol. I (only volume issued).

Burūjirdī, Ḥusayn Ṭabāṭabā'ī *Tauḍīḥ ul-Masā'il*. Tehran, n.d.

Chahārdihī, Murtaḍā Mudarrisī. *Ārā va Mu'taqadāt-i Sayyid Jamāl ud-Dīn-i Afghānī*. Tehran, 1337 Sh/1958.

———. *Shaykh Aḥmad-i Aḥsā'ī*. Tehran, 1334 Sh/1955.

———. *Zindagānī va Falsafa-yi Sayyid Jamāl ud-Dīn-i Afghānī*. Tehran, 1334 Sh/1955.

Daulatābādī, Yaḥyā. *Tārīkh-i Mu'āṣir yā Ḥayāt-i Yaḥyā*. Tehran, n.d. 4 vols.

Dunbulī, 'Abd ur-Razzāq. *Ma'āthir-i Sulṭānīya*. Tabriz, 1242 Q/1826.

Farāhānī, Mīrzā Ḥusayn. *Safarnāma*. Ed. Ḥāfiẓ Farmānfarmā'īān. Tehran, 1342 Sh/1963.

Ḥaqā'iqnagār, Mīrzā Ja'far Khān. *Ḥaqā'iq-i Akhbār-i Nāṣirī*. Tehran, 1284 Q/1867–1868.

Haravī, Muḥammad Ḥasan Adīb. *Tārīkh-i Paydāyish-i Mashrūṭīyat-i Īrān*. Mashhad, 1331 Sh/1952.

al-Ḥasanī, 'Abd ar-Razzāq. *al-Bābīyūn wa-l-Bahā'īyūn fī Ḥāḍirihim wa Māḍīhim*. Sidon, 1376 Q/1956–1957.

Hāshimī, Muḥammad Ṣadr. *Tārīkh-i Jarā'id va Majallāt-i Īrān*. Isfahan, 1327–1329 Sh/1948–1950. 4 vols.

Hazhīr, 'Abd ul-Ḥusayn. "Dar Rāh-i Valī-'Ahdī-yi 'Abbās Mīrzā," *Mihr*, I (1313 Sh/1934–1935), 707–709.

Hidāyat, Riḍā Qulī Khān. *Majma' ul-Fuṣaḥā*. Tehran, 1288 Q/1871-1872. 6 vols.

———. *Rauḍat uṣ-Ṣafā-yi Nāṣirī*. Tehran, 1339 Sh/1960–1961. 10 vols.

al-Ḥurr al-'Āmulī, Muḥammad Ḥasan. *Wasā'il ash-Shī'a ilā Taḥṣīl Masā'il ash-Sharī'a*. Tehran, 1372–1378 Q/1952–1958. 8 vols.

Ḥusaynī, Muḥammad Ṣādiq. *Makhzan ul-Inshā*. Tabriz, 1274 Q/1857.

Iqbāl, 'Abbās. "Ba'd az Ṣad Sāl," *Yādgār*, V (1327 Sh/1948–1949), 5–8.

———. "Ghurāmāt-i Mu'āhada-yi Turkumānchāy," *Yādgār*, I (1324 Sh/1945–1946), 21–35.

———. "Ḥujjat ul-Islām Ḥājj Sayyid Muḥammad Bāqir Shaftī," *Yādgār*, V (1327 Sh/1948–1949), 25–39.

———. *Mīrzā Taqī Khān Amīr Kabīr*. Tehran, 1340 Sh/1961.

———. "Sharḥ-i Ḥāl-i Marḥūm Ḥājj Mullā 'Alī Kanī," *Yādgār*, IV (1326 Sh/1947–1948), 72–78.

Iṣfahānī, 'Imād ud-Dīn Ḥusayn. *Tārīkh-i Jughrāfīyā'ī-yi Karbalā-yı Mu'allā*. Tehran, 1326 Sh/1947.

Iṣfahānī, Muḥammad Mihdī. *Nisf-i Jahān fī Ta'rīf ul-Iṣfahān*. Tehran, 1340 Sh/1961.

Istakhrī, Iḥsānullāh. "Taṣavvuf-i Dhahabīya," *MM*, I (1335 Sh/1956), 8–14.

I'timād us-Salṭana, Mīrzā Muḥammad Ḥasan Khān. *al-Ma'āthir va-l-Āthār*. Tehran, 1306 Q/1889.

———. *Mir'āt ul-Buldān-i Nāṣirī*. Tehran, 1294–1297 Q/1877–1880. 4 vols.

———. *Rūznāma-yi Khāṭirāt-i I'timād us-Salṭana*. Ed. Īraj Afshār. Tehran, 1345 Sh/1967.

———. *Tārīkh-i Muntaẓam-i Nāṣirī*. Tehran, 1300 Q/1883. 3 vols.

———. *Vaqāyi'-i Rūzāna-yi Darbār*. Tehran, n.d.

Jahāngīr Mīrzā. *Tārīkh-i Nau*. Ed. 'Abbās Iqbāl. Tehran, 1327 Sh/1948.

Jalāl ud-Dīn Mīrzā. *Nāma-yi Khusruvān*. Bombay, n.d. 4 parts.

Jamālzāda, Muḥammad 'Alī. "Tarjuma-yi Ḥāl-i Sayyid Jamāl ud-Dīn Vā'iẓ," *Yaghmā*, III (1329 Sh/1950–1951), 118–123; 163–170; 394–401.

Karal, Enver Ziya. *Osmanlı Tarihi*. Ankara, 1947–1956. 7 vols.

Karīmī, Bahman. *Mīrzā Abū-l-Qāsim Qā'im Maqām*. Tehran, n.d.

Kashmīrī, Muḥammad 'Alī. *Nujūm us-Samā*. Lucknow, 1303 Q/1885–1886.

Kasravī, Aḥmad. *Bahā'īgarī*. Tehran, n.d.

———. *Tārīkh-i Mashrūṭa-yi Īrān*. 5th imp. Tehran, 1340 Sh/1961.

———. *Zindagānī-yi Man*. Tehran, 1323 Sh/1944.

Kayvān, Ḥājj Shaykh 'Abbās 'Alī. *Kayvānnāma*. Tehran, 1340 Sh/1961.

Kāẓimī, Muḥammad Mihdī. *Aḥsan al-Wadī'a*. Baghdad, 1347 Q/1928–1929. 2 vols.

Khiābānī, Muḥammad 'Alī Tabrīzī. *Rayḥānat ul-Adab*. Tehran, 1326 Sh/1947–1948. 10 (?) vols.

Khurāsānī, Majd ul-'Alī. "Raf'-i Ishtibāh-i Nabdhī az Ḥālāt-i Ḥājj Mullā Aḥmad Narāqī," *Armaghān*, VII (1304 Sh/1925–1926), 604–609.

Khvānsārī, Muḥammad Bāqir. *Rauḍāt al-Jannāt fi Aḥwāl al-'Ulamā' wa-s-Sādāt*. Tehran, 1304 Q/1887.

Kirmānī, Mīrzā Āqā Khān. *Hasht Bihisht*. N.p., n.d.

Kirmānī, Muḥammad Hāshim. "Ṭā'ifa-yi Shaykhīya," *MM*, II (1337 Sh/1958), 238–254; 348–361.

———. "Tārīkh-i Madhāhib-i Kirmān," *MM*, I (1335 Sh/1956), 97–104; 122–133.

Kirmānī, Nāẓim ul-Islām. *Tārīkh-i Bīdārī-yi Īrānīān*. New ed. Tehran, 1332 Sh/1953.

Kirmānī, Shaykh Abū-l-Qāsim. *Fihrist-i Kutub-i Marḥūm Shaykh Aḥmad-i Aḥsā'ī va Sharḥ-i Ḥāl-i Sā'ir-i Mashāyikh-i 'Iẓām*. Kirman, 1337 Sh/1958–1959.

al-Kulaynī, Muḥammad b. Ya'qūb. *al-Kāfī fī 'Ilm ad-Dīn*. Tehran, 1379 Q/1959–1960. 10 vols.

——. *al-Uṣūl min al-Jāmi' al-Kāfī*. Lucknow, 1302 Q/1884–1885.

Levi, Ḥabīb. *Tārīkh-i Yahūd-i Īrān*. Tehran, 1339 Sh/1960–1961. 3 vols.

Lisān ul-Mulk, Mīrzā Muḥammad Taqī Sipihr. *Nāsikh ut-Tavārīkh*. Tehran, n.d.

Maḥmūd, Maḥmūd. *Tārīkh-i Ravābiṭ-i Siyāsī-yi Īrān va Inglīs dar Qarn-i Nūzdahum-i Mīlādī*. Tehran, 1328 Sh/1949–1950. 8 vols.

Majlisī, Muḥammad Bāqir. *Biḥār al-Anwār*. Tehran, 1327 Sh—/1948— (continuing).

——. *Kitāb-i Su'āl va Javāb*. Isfahan, 1247 Q/1831–1832.

Makkī, Ḥusayn. *Zindagānī-yi Mīrzā Taqī Khān Amīr Kabīr*. Tehran, 1327 Sh/1948–1949.

Malikzāda, Mihdī. *Tārīkh-i Inqilāb-i Mashrūṭīyat-i Īrān*. Tehran, 1327 Sh/1948–1949. 6 vols.

Malkum Khān, Mīrzā. *Majmū'a-yi Āthār*. Ed. with introduction by Muḥammad Muḥīṭ Ṭabāṭabā'ī. Tehran, 1327 Sh/1948–1949. Vol. I (only volume issued).

Marāgha'ī, Zayn ul-'Ābidīn. *Siyāḥatnāma-yi Ibrāhīm Bīg*. Calcutta, 1910.

Ma'ṣūm 'Alī Shāh (Nā'ib uṣ-Ṣadr). *Ṭarā'iq ul-Ḥaqā'iq*. Tehran, 1318 Q/1900–1901. 3 vols.

Mihdavī, Aṣghar and Īraj Āfshār. *Majmū'a-yi Asnād va Madārik-i Chāp Nashuda dar bāra-yi Sayyid Jamāl ud-Dīn Mashhūr ba Afghānī*. Tehran, 1342 Sh/1963.

Minorsky, Vladimir. *Tārīkh-i Tabrīz*. Trans. 'Abd ul-'Alī Kārang. Tabriz, 1337 Sh/1959.

Mu'ayyir ul-Mamālik, Dūst 'Alī Khān. "Sayyid Zayn ul-'Ābidīn Imām Jum'a," *Yaghmā*, XII (1338 Sh/1959–1960), 565–576.

——. *Yāddāshthā'ī az Zindagānī-yi Khuṣūṣī-yi Nāṣir ud-Dīn Shāh*. Tehran, n.d.

Mujtahidī, Mihdī. *Rijāl-i Ādharbāyjān dar 'Aṣr-i Mashrūṭīyat*. Tehran, 1327 Sh/1948–1949.

Mukhbir us-Salṭana, Mihdī Qulī Khān Hidāyat. *Khāṭirāt va Khaṭarāt*. Tehran, 1329 Sh/1950.

Mulkārā, 'Abbās Mīrzā. *Sharḥ-i Ḥāl*. Ed. 'Abd ul-Ḥusayn Navā'ī. Tehran, 1325 Sh/1946–1947.

Mustaufī, 'Abdullāh. *Tārīkh-i Idārī va Ijtimā'ī-yi Daura-yi Qājārīya yā Sharḥ-i Zindagānī-yi Man*. Tehran, 1321 Sh/1942–1943. 2 vols.

Mu'tamad, Maḥmūd Farhād. "Musāfarat-i Nāṣir ud-Dīn Shāh ba Urupā va Barkinārī-yi Mīrzā Ḥusayn Khān Sipahsālār," *Yādgār*, II (1325 Sh/1946–1947), 44–50.

——. *Mushīr ud-Daula Sipahsālār-i A'ẓam*. Tehran, 1326 Sh/1947–1948.

——. "Qarārdād-i Reuter," *Yaghmā*, II (1328 Sh/1949–1950), 208–213.

——. *Tārīkh-i Ravābiṭ-i Īrān va 'Uthmānī*. Tehran, n.d. Vol. I (all to appear).

Mu'tamad ud-Daula, Farhād Mīrzā. *Hidāyat us-Sabīl*. Tehran, 1294 Q/1877.

Nādir Mīrzā. *Tārīkh va Jughrāfī-yi Dār us-Salṭana-yi Tabrīz*. Tehran, 1323 Q/1905.

Nafīsī, Sa'īd. "Jalb-i Muhājirīn-i Urupā'ī dar Sāl-i 1242," *Sharq*, I (1310 Sh/1931–1932), 57–64; 125–127; 190–192; 261–264; 326–327; 507–512.

——. *Tārīkh-i Ijtimā'ī va Siyāsī-yi Īrān dar Daura-yi Mu'āṣir*. Tehran, 1340–1344 Sh/1961–1965. 2 vols.

Najmī, Nāṣir. *Īrān dar Miān-i Ṭūfān yā Sharḥ-i Zindagī-yi 'Abbās Mīrzā dar Janghā-yi Īrān va Rūs*. Tehran, 1337 Sh/1958–1959.

Nakhchivānī, Ḥājj Ḥusayn. *Chihil Maqāla*. Tabriz, 1343 Sh/1964.

Nāṣir ud-Dīn Shāh. *Dīvān-i Kāmil-i Ash'ār*. Tehran, 1339 Sh/1960.

Navā'ī, 'Abd ul-Ḥusayn. "Ḥājj Muḥammad Karīm Khān Kirmānī," *Yādgār*, V (1328 Sh/1949–1950), 62–73; 106–118.

Ni'ma, 'Abdullāh. *Falāsifat ash-Shī'a*. Beirut, n.d.

Pīrzāda, Ḥājjī. *Safarnāma*. Ed. Ḥāfiẓ Farmānfarmā'iān. Tehran, 1342–1343 Sh/1963–1964. 2 vols.

Qā'ānī. *Dīvān*. Ed. Muḥammad Ja'far Maḥjūb. Tehran, 1336 Sh/1957.

Qahramānī, Sharaf ud-Dīn Mīrzā. "Yak Silsila Asnād-i Tārīkhī yā 'Ilāl-i Vāqi'ī-yi Jang-i Duvvum-i Rūs-Īrān," *Sharq*, I (1310 Sh/1931–1932), 253–257; 318–331; 439–440; 564–567; 625–632; 669–672.

Qā'im Maqām, Abū-l-Qāsim. *Munsha'āt*. Ed. Jahāngīr Qā'im Maqāmī. Tehran, 1337 Sh/1958–1959.

Qā'im Maqām, Bāqir. *Qā'im Maqam dar Jahān-i Adab va Siyāsat*. Tehran, 1320 Sh/1941–1942.

Qā'im Maqāmī, Jahāngīr. *Tārīkh-i Taḥavvulāt-i Siyāsī-yi Niẓām-i Īrān*. Tehran, n.d.

——. "Tauṭi'a-yi Ḥusayn 'Alī Mīrzā Farmānfarmā-yi Fārs," *Yaghmā*, V (1328 Sh/1949–1950), 35–40.

Qūzānlū, Jamīl. *Jang-i Īrān va Rūs*. Tehran, 1314 Sh/1935–1936.

——. *Tārīkh-i Niẓāmī-yi Īrān*. Tehran, 1315 Sh/1936–1937. 2 vols.

Riḍā, Rashīd. *Tārīkh al-Ustādh al-Imām ash-Shaykh Muḥammad 'Abduh*. Cairo, 1349 Q/1930–1931. 2 vols.

Riyāḍī, Muḥammad Amīn. "Dau Nāma-yi Muhimm-i Siyāsī va Tārīkhī az 'Abbās Mīrzā Nā'ib us-Salṭana," *Yādgār*, IV (1327 Sh/1948–1949), 15–23.

Ṣafā'ī, Ibrāhīm. *Rahbarān-i Mashrūṭa* — I: *Sayyid Jamāl ud-Dīn Afghānī*; II: *Mīrzā Malkum Khān*; III: *Mīrzā 'Alī Khān Amīn ud-Daula*; IV:

Sayyid 'Abdullāh Bihbihānī va Sayyid Muḥammad Ṭabāṭabā'ī. Tehran, 1342–1343 Sh/1963–1965.

Ṣafī 'Alī Shāh. *Dīvān*. Ed. Taqī Tafaḍḍulī. Tehran, 1336 Sh/1957–1958.

Sanglajī, Ḥujjat ul-Islām Muḥammad. *Qaḍā dar Islām*. Tehran, 1338 Sh/1959–1960.

Sāsānī, Khān Malik. *Siyāsatgarān-i Daura-yi Qājār*. Tehran, 1338 Sh/1959.

Shamīm, 'Alī Aṣghar. *Īrān dar Daura-yi Salṭanat-i Qājār*. 2d ed. Tehran, 1342 Sh/1963.

Shaykh ur-Ra'īs, Mīrzā Abū-l-Qāsim. *Ittiḥād ul-Islām*. Bombay, 1312 Q/1894–1895.

Shīrāzī, Furṣat. *Āthār-i 'Ajam*. Tehran, 1314 Q/1896–1897.

Shīrvānī, Zayn ul-'Ābidīn. *Bustān us-Siyāḥa*. Tehran, 1315 Q/1897–1898.

Tājbakhsh, Aḥmad. *Tārīkh-i Ravābiṭ-i Īrān va Rūsīya dar Nīma-yi Avval-i Qarn-i Nūzdahum*. Tabriz, 1337 Sh/1958–1959.

Ṭāliqānī, Āyatullāh Sayyid Maḥmūd. *Jihād va Shihādat*. Tehran, 1385 Q/1965.

Taymūrī, Ibrāhīm. *'Aṣr-i Bīkhabarī yā Tārīkh-i Imtiyāzāt dar Īrān*. Tehran, 1336 Sh/1957.

———. *Taḥrīm-i Tanbākū yā Avvalīn Muqāvamat-i Manfī dar Īrān*. Tehran, 1328 Sh/1949.

Ṭihrānī, Āqā Buzurg. *Ṭabaqāt A'lām ash-Shī'a*. Najaf, 1373 Q/1953–1954.

Tunukābunī, Muḥammad b. Sulaymān. *Qiṣaṣ ul-'Ulamā'*. Tehran, 1304 Q/1887.

Valā'ī, Mihdī. "Sharḥ-i Ḥāl-i Navvāb-i Taulīat-i 'Uẓmā-yi Āstān-i Quds-i Raḍavī," *Nāma-yi Āstān-i Quds*, V (1344 Sh/1965–1966), 86–95.

Vazīrī, Aḥmad 'Alī Khān. *Tārīkh-i Kirmān*. Ed. Ḥāfiẓ Farmānfarmā'īān. Tehran, 1340 Sh/1962.

al-Wā'ilī, Ibrāhīm. *ash-Shi'r as-Siyāsī al-'Irāqī fī-l-Qarn at-Tāsi'-'ashar*. Baghdad, 1381 Q/1961–1962.

Zarīnkūb, 'Abd ul-Ḥusayn. "Yāddāshtī dar bāra-yi Ta'zīya-yi Māh-i Muḥarram," *Sukhan*, IX (1337 Sh/1958–1959), 310–314.

Ẓill us-Sulṭān, Mas'ūd Mīrzā. *Tārīkh-i Sargudhasht-i Mas'ūdī*. Tehran, 1325 Q/1907.

WORKS IN OTHER LANGUAGES

Afghānī, Jamāl ud-Dīn. "The Reign of Terror in Persia," *Contemporary Review*, LXI (1892), 238–248.

———. *La Réfutation des Matérialistes*. Trans. A.-M. Goichon. Paris, 1942.

Afschar, Mahmud. *La Politique Européenne en Perse*. Berlin, 1921.

Arasteh, A. Reza. *Man and Society in Iran*. Leiden, 1964.

Atrpyet (pseud.). *Imamat': Strana Poklonnikov Imamov*. Alexandropol, 1909.

Avery, P. W., *Modern Iran*. London, 1965.

Baddeley, J. N. *The Russian Conquest of the Caucasus*. London, 1908.

Bassett, J. *Persia, the Land of the Imams*. London, 1887.

Bausani, Alessandro. *Persia Religiosa*. Milan, 1959.

Benjamin, S. G. W. *Persia and the Persians*. London, 1887.

Binder, Leonard. "The Proofs of Islam: Religion and Politics in Iran," *Arabic and Islamic Studies in Honour of Hamilton A. R. Gibb*. Leiden, 1966, pp. 120–138.

Bleibtreu, J. *Persien: Das Land der Sonne und des Löwen*. Freiburg, 1894.

Blunt, W. S. *Secret History of the English Occupation of Egypt*. London, 1907.

Bode, C. A. de. *Travels in Luristan and Arabistan*. London, 1845. 2 vols.

Braune, W. *Der islamische Orient zwischen Vergangenheit und Zukunft: eine geschichtstheologische Analyse seiner Stellung in der Weltsituation*. Berne and Munich, 1958.

Brockway, T. P. "Britain and the Persian Bubble, 1888–92," *Journal of Modern History*, XIII (1941), 36–47.

Browne, E. G. *A Literary History of Persia*. Vol. IV. Cambridge, 1924.

———. *Materials for the Study of the Babi Religion*. Cambridge, 1918.

———. *The Persian Revolution of 1905–1909*. Cambridge, 1910.

———. *The Press and Poetry of Modern Persia*. Cambridge, 1914.

———. *A Year amongst the Persians*. New ed. London, 1950.

Browne, E. G., ed. *Tārīkh-i-Jadīd or New History of Mīrzā 'Alī Muḥammad the Bāb*. Cambridge, 1893.

———. *A Traveller's Narrative Written To Illustrate the Episode of the Bab*. Cambridge, 1891. 2 vols.

Brugsch, H. *Reise der königlichen preussischen Gesandtschaft nach Persien*. Leipzig, 1862. 2 vols.

Brydges, Sir Harford Jones. *Account of the Transactions of His Majesty's Mission to the Court of Persia in the Years 1807–1811*. London, 1834.

———. *The Dynasty of the Kajars*. London, 1833.

Burnes, A. *Travels into Bukhara*. London, 1834. 2 vols.

Chirol, V. *The Middle Eastern Question or Some Political Problems of Indian Defence*. London, 1903.

Chunara, A. J. *Noorum Mubin, or the Sacred Cord of God: A Glorious History of Ismaili Imams*. Bombay, 1951. (In Gujarati).

Conolly, A. *Journey to the North of India, Overland from England, through Russia, Persia, and Affghaunistaun*. London, 1834. 2 vols.

Corbin, H. "L'Ecole Shaykhie en Théologie Shî'ite," *Annuaire de l'Ecole Pratique des Hautes Etudes, Section des Sciences Religieuses*. 1960–1961, pp. 1–60.

———. *Histoire de la Philosophie Islamique*. Paris, 1963.

———. "Pour une Morphologie de la Spiritualité Shî'ite," *Eranos-Jahrbuch* (Zurich), XXIX (1960), 57–107.
———. *Terre Celeste et Corps de Résurrection.* Paris, 1960.
Costello, D. P. "Griboyedov in Persia in 1820: Two Diplomatic Notes," *Oxford Slavonic Papers,* V (1954), 81–92.
———. "The Murder of Griboyedov," *Oxford Slavonic Papers,* VIII (1957), 64–78.
———. "A Note on 'The Diplomatic Activity of A. S. Griboyedov' by S. V. Shostakovich," *Slavonic and East European Review,* LX (1961–1962), 235–244.
Curzon, G. *Persia and the Persian Question.* London, 1892. 2 vols.
Denis, A. "Affaire du Kerbela," *Revue de l'Orient,* I (1843), 138–143.
Dieulafoy, J. *La Perse, la Chaldée et la Susiane.* Paris, 1887.
Donaldson, D. M. *The Shi'ite Religion.* London, 1933.
Dreyfus, H. "Les Béhais et le Mouvement Actuel en Perse," *RMM,* I (1906), 198–206.
Drouville, G. *Voyage en Perse.* Paris, 1825. 2 vols.
Dunlop, H. *Perzië: Vorheeren en Thans.* Haarlem, 1912.
Eastwick, E. B. *Journal of a Diplomate's Three Years' Residence in Persia.* London, 1864.
Feuvrier, J.-B. *Trois Ans à la Cour de Perse.* Paris, 1899.
Forster, G. *A Journey from Bengal to England.* London, 1798.
Francklin, W. *Observations Made on a Tour from Bengal to Persia in the Years 1786–1787.* London, 1790.
Frank, C. "Über den schiitischen Mudschtahid," *Islamica,* II (1926), 171–192.
Fraser, J. B. *An Historical and Descriptive Account of Persia from the Earliest Ages to the Present Time.* Edinburgh, 1834.
———. *Narrative of a Journey into Khorassan.* London, 1825.
———. *Travels in Koordistan, Mesopotamia, etc.* London, 1840. 2 vols.
———. *A Winter's Journey from Constantinople to Tehran.* London, 1838. 2 vols.
Gardane, A. M. de. *Journal d'un Voyage dans la Turquie d'Asie et la Perse.* Paris, 1809. 2 vols.
Gibb, H. A. R. "Government and Islam under the Early 'Abbāsids: The Political Collapse of Islam," *L'Elaboration de l'Islam.* Paris, 1961, pp. 110–127.
Gobineau, A. de. *Correspondance entre le Comte de Gobineau et le Comte de Prokosch-Osten.* Paris, 1933.
———. *Dépêches Diplomatiques.* Ed. A. D. Hytier. Geneva, 1959.
———. *Les Religions et les Philosophies dans l'Asie Centrale.* Paris, 1865.
———. *Trois Ans en Asie.* Paris, 1859.
Gordon, T. E. *Persia Revisited.* London, 1896.

Gramlich, R. *Die schiitischen Derwischorden Persiens, erster Teil: die Affiliationen. AKM,* XXXVI, 1. Wiesbaden, 1965.

Greaves, R. L. "British Policy in Persia, 1892–1903," *BSOAS,* XXVIII (1965), 34–60; 284–307.

——. *Persia and the Defence of India, 1884–1892.* London, 1959.

Greenfield, J. "Die geistlichen Schariagerichte in Persien," *Zeitschrift für vergleichende Rechtswissenschaft,* XLVIII (1934), 157–167.

Guillou, A. "Les Dynasties Musulmanes de la Perse," *Revista del Instituto de Estudios Islámicos en Madrid,* VII–VIII (1959–1960), 126–149.

Hardinge, A. *A Diplomatist in the East.* London, 1928.

Heyd, U. "The Ottoman 'Ulemā and Westernization in the Time of Selīm III and Maḥmūd II," *Scripta Hierosolymitana,* IX (1961), 63–96.

Hollister, J. N. *The Shia of India.* London, 1953.

Holmes, W. R. *Sketches on the Shore of the Caspian.* London, 1845.

Hourani, A. *Arabic Thought in the Liberal Age, 1798–1939.* Oxford, 1962.

Ivanov, M. S. *Babidskiye Vosstaniya v Irane.* Moscow and Leningrad, 1939.

——. *Iranskaya Revolyutsiya 1905–1911 Godov.* Moscow, 1957.

——. *Ocherk Istorii Irana.* Moscow, 1952.

Ivanow, W. *Ismaili Literature: A Bibliographical Survey.* Tehran, 1963.

Jaubert, P. A. *Voyage en Arménie et en Perse.* Paris, 1821.

Keddie, N. R. "Religion and Irreligion in Early Iranian Nationalism," *Comparative Studies in Society and History,* IV (1962), 265–295.

——. *Religion and Rebellion in Iran: The Tobacco Protest of 1891–1892.* London, 1966.

Kosogovsky, V. A. *Iz Tegeranskovo Dnevnika.* Moscow, 1960.

Kotzebue, M. von. *Narrative of a Journey into Persia in the Suite of the Imperial Russian Embassy in the Year 1817.* London, 1819.

Lambton, A. K. S. *Landlord and Peasant in Persia.* London, 1953.

——. "Persian Society under the Qajars," *JRCAS,* XLVIII (1961), 123–138.

——. "Quis Custodiet Custodes: Some Reflections on the Persian Theory of Government," *SI,* V–VI (1955–1956).

——. "A Reconsideration of the Position of the *Marja' Al-Taqlīd* and the Religious Institution," *SI,* XX (1964), 115–135.

——. "Secret Societies and the Persian Revolution of 1905–1906," *St. Anthony's Papers,* IV (1958) 43–60.

——. "The Tobacco Régie: Prelude to Revolution," *SI,* XXII (1965), 119–157.

Landor, A. H. S. *Across Coveted Lands.* London, 1902.

Lockhart, L. *Nadir Shah.* London, 1938.

——. *The Fall of the Safavi Dynasty and the Afghan Occupation of Persia.* Cambridge, 1958.

McNeill, J. *Memoir of the Right Hon. Sir John McNeill.* London, 1910.

Malcolm, Sir J. *A History of Persia.* London, 1815. 2 vols.

——. *Sketches of Persia.* London, 1845.

Malcolm, N. *Five Years in a Persian Town.* London, 1905.

Malcom (Malkum Khān). "Persian Civilisation," *Contemporary Review,* LIX (1891), 238–244.

Martyn, H. *Controversial Tracts on Christianity and Mohammedanism.* Cambridge, 1824.

Migeod, H.-G. "Die Lutis: ein Ferment des städtischen Lebens in Persien," *Journal of the Economic and Social History of the Orient,* II (1959), 82–91.

Morier, J. *A Journey through Persia, Armenia, and Asia Minor to Constantinople.* London, 1812.

——. *A Second Journey through Persia, Armenia, and Asia Minor to Constantinople.* London, 1818.

Muhammad, Khan Bahadur Agha Mirza. "Some New Notes on Babism," *JRAS,* n.v. (July, 1927), 443–470.

Olivier, G. A. *Voyage dans l'Empire Othoman, l'Egypte et la Perse.* Paris, 1802. 3 vols.

Ouseley, Sir W. *Travels in Various Countries of the East.* London, 1821. 3 vols.

Pakravan, E. *Abbas Mirza, Prince Réformateur.* Tehran, 1958. 2 vols.

——. *Agha Mohammad Ghadjar.* Tehran, 1953.

Perkins, J. *A Residence of Eight Years in Persia among the Nestorian Christians with Notices of the Muhammadans.* Andover, 1843.

Polak, J. E. *Persien: das Land und seine Bewohner.* Leipzig, 1865. 2 vols.

Rawlinson, H. *England and Russia in the East.* London, 1875.

Renan, E. *L'Islamisme et la Science.* Paris, 1883.

Roehmer, H. *Die Babi-Behai.* Potsdam, 1912.

"S". "De l'état administratif et politique de la Perse," *Revue de l'Orient,* IV (1844), 98–116.

Savory, R. M. "The Principal Offices of the Safavid State during the Reign of Ismā'īl I," *BSOAS,* XXIII (1960), 91–105.

Scarcia, G. "A Proposito del Problema della Sovranità presso gli Imamiti," *Annali del Istituto Universitario Orientale di Napoli,* VII (1957), 95–126.

——. "Intorno alle Controversie tra Aḫbārī e Uṣūlī presso gli Imāmiti di Persia," *RSO,* XXXIII (1958), 211–250.

——. "Kerman 1905: La 'Guerra' tra Šeiḫī e Bālāsarī," *Annali del Istituto Universitario Orientale di Napoli,* XIII (1963), 186–203.

Schlechta-Wssehrd, O. von. "Der letzte persisch-russische Krieg (1826–1828)," *ZDMG,* XX (1866), 288–325.

Sepsis, A. "Quelques Mots sur l'État Religieux Actuel de la Perse," *Revue de l'Orient,* III (1844), 96–105.

Shehabi, Mahmood. "Shi'a," *Islam: The Straight Path.* Ed. K. W. Morgan, New York, 1958, pp. 198–220.

Sheil, Lady. *Glimpses of Life and Manners in Persia.* London, 1856.

Shoitov, A. M. "Rol' Akhundova v Razvitii Persidskoi Progressivnoi Literatury," *KSIV*, IX (1953), 58–65.

Strothman, R. "Shi'a," *Handwörterbuch des Islam*, Leiden, 1941.

Stuart, W. K. *Journal of a Residence in Northern Persia and the Adjacent Provinces of Turkey.* London, 1854.

Sykes, P. M. *Ten Thousand Miles in Persia.* London, 1902.

Tancoigne, M. *Narrative of a Journey into Persia.* London, 1820.

Tornau, A. von. "Aus der neuesten Geschichte Persiens: Die Jahre 1833–1835," *ZDMG*, II (1848), 401–425.

Ussher, J. *A Journey from London to Persepolis.* London, 1865.

Vambéry, H. *Meine Wanderungen und Erlebnisse in Persien.* Pest, 1867.

Waring, E. S. *A Tour to Sheeraz, by the Route of Kazroon and Feerozabad.* London, 1807.

Watson, R. G. *A History of Persia from the Beginning of the Nineteenth Century to the Year 1858.* London, 1866.

Wilbraham, R. *Travels in the Transcaucasian Provinces of Russia.* London, 1839.

Wills, C. J. *Persia as It Is.* London, 1886.

Wolff, J. *Missionary Journal.* London, 1829. 3 vols.

———. *Researches and Missionary Labours among the Jews, Mohammadans and Other Sects.* London, 1835.

Index

PERSONS

The listing of Persian and other Near Eastern names is a complex task, difficult to reduce to logical and consistent principles. In using this index, the following points should be borne in mind. Titles such as Khān, Khānum, Mīrzā (in the sense of prince), Bey, Efendi, and Pasha, which follow the name, are treated as a subordinate part of the designation by which an individual was known and are not therefore the key word under which he is listed. Thus, the name Hulāgū Khān is listed as such, not as "Khan, Hulāgū." Shah (without the diacritic) precedes certain names, but—with diacritic—follows others. In either case, the monarch in question is listed under his name, not under Shah. By contrast, Sufis, of whose name Shāh is a part, are listed under that word. Those of the Twelve Imams whose names occur in the text are to be found listed under their names, not under the title Imam. Mujtahid has been treated as the significant part of the designation of those ulama in conjunction with whose name it commonly occurs. Titles preceding the name, such as Mīrzā (in the sense of scribe or government official), Shaykh, Mullā, Ākhūnd, and Sayyid are not treated as key words: thus Shaykh Riḍā is listed as "Riḍā, Shaykh," not "Shaykh Riḍā." Finally, there are several compound names of which the second half is ʻAlī (e.g., Faḍl ʻAlī): these are to be found listed under the first element of the compound.

PLACES